Universal Basic Income in Historical Perspective

Peter Sloman
Daniel Zamora Vargas • Pedro Ramos Pinto
Editors

Universal Basic Income in Historical Perspective

palgrave
macmillan

Editors
Peter Sloman
Department of Politics and International Studies
University of Cambridge
Cambridge, UK

Daniel Zamora Vargas
Institut de sociologie
Université Libre de Bruxelles
Brussels, Belgium

Pedro Ramos Pinto
Faculty of History
University of Cambridge
Cambridge, UK

ISBN 978-3-030-75705-2 ISBN 978-3-030-75706-9 (eBook)
https://doi.org/10.1007/978-3-030-75706-9

This Palgrave Macmillan imprint is published by the registered company Springer Nature Switzerland AG.
The registered company address is: Gewerbestrasse 11, 6330 Cham, Switzerland

Acknowledgements

This volume has its origins in a workshop on 'The Intellectual History of Universal Basic Income' which took place in Cambridge on 14 January 2019. We are very grateful to the Cambridge History Faculty's G.M. Trevelyan Fund, the Department of Politics and International Studies, and the Wiener-Anspach Foundation for providing financial support for the workshop, and to the many colleagues and other scholars who contributed to the event as speakers, panel chairs, and delegates. We would also like to thank Maeve Sinnott at Palgrave Macmillan for taking on the project and Lucy Kidwell and Raghupathy Kalyanaraman for taking it through to publication. Finally, we are grateful to Charles Lockwood for his invaluable assistance in preparing the manuscript, to Emily Stacey for her work on the index, and to our contributors for helping to bring this volume to completion in the difficult and unforeseen circumstances of a global pandemic.

Contents

Notes on Contributors

Alyssa Battistoni is Assistant Professor of Political Theory at Barnard College. She is the co-author of *A Planet to Win: Why We Need a Green New Deal* (New York, NY, 2019).

E. Fouksman is a lecturer at the Centre for Public Policy Research, King's College London, UK, and a research associate at the Society, Work and Politics Institute (SWOP), the University of the Witwatersrand, and the African Studies Centre at the University of Oxford. Fouksman's research interests focus on the normative fixation with work and working (with an empirical focus on the long-term unemployed in southern Africa), and the impediment this pose to the politics of both universal income guarantees and shorter working hours.

Louise Haagh is Professor of Politics at the University of York, UK, and a former co-chair of the Basic Income Earth Network. She has written extensively on basic income, human development, and democratization, and her books include *Basic Income, Welfare Systems, and Human Development Freedom* (2017) and *The Case for Universal Basic Income* (2019).

Anton Jäger is a postdoctoral researcher at the University of Cambridge, UK, and Université Libre de Bruxelles, Belgium, working on the history of populism in the United States. His book *Welfare Without the Welfare State: an Intellectual History of Basic Income*, co-authored with Daniel Zamora Vargas, is forthcoming with The University of Chicago Press.

Samuel Moyn is Henry R. Luce Professor of Jurisprudence at Yale Law School and Professor of History at Yale University, USA. He has written several books in the fields of European intellectual history and human rights history, including *The Last Utopia* (2010), *Christian Human Rights* (2015), and *Not Enough* (2018).

Pedro Ramos Pinto is Associate Professor of International Economic History at the University of Cambridge, UK, and a fellow of Trinity Hall. He has written widely on social movements, welfare reform, and the history of inequality, and is the author of *Lisbon Rising: Urban Social Movements in the Portuguese Revolution, 1974–1975* (2013).

Marc-Antoine Sabaté is teaches political theory at the Université Libre de Bruxelles, Belgium, where he obtained a PhD in political science in October 2020. He was a Wiener-Anspach Post-Doctoral Fellow and a visiting scholar at the University of Cambridge's History Faculty, UK, in 2020–21. His research focuses on the history and theory of universal basic income and the future of the welfare state in the age of ecological crisis.

Andrew V. Sanchez is a Fulbright Scholar at the Center for Contemporary History, Berlin, and a PhD candidate at the University of Oxford, UK. His research addresses technological productivity, work, and basic income in the post-war period.

Peter Sloman is Associate Professor of British Politics at the University of Cambridge, UK, and a fellow of Churchill College. He is the author of two books: *The Liberal Party and the Economy, 1929–1964* (2015) and *Transfer State: The Idea of a Guaranteed Income and the Politics of Redistribution in Modern Britain* (2019).

Philippe Van Parijs is Professeur Ordinaire at the Université Catholique de Louvain, Belgium, and has written extensively in political philosophy, with a particular focus on basic income. His books include *Real Freedom for All* (1995), *What's Wrong with a Free Lunch?* (2001), *Linguistic Justice for Europe and for the World* (2011), and *Basic Income* (2017, with Yannick Vanderborght).

Walter Van Trier has written widely on the history of basic income, most notably in his book *Every Man a King* (1995) which was based on his PhD thesis at Katholieke Universiteit (KU) Leuven. He is a former chair of the Scientific Committee of the European Research Network on Transitions in Youth, and is now affiliated with the Faculty of Economics and Business Administration at Ghent University, Belgium.

Daniel Zamora Vargas is Assistant Professor of Sociology at the Université Libre de Bruxelles, Belgium. His recent work includes, with Mitchell Dean, *The Last Man Takes LSD: Foucault and the End of Revolution* (2021), and with Anton Jäger, *Welfare Without the Welfare State: An Intellectual History of Basic Income* (The University of Chicago Press, forthcoming).

List of Figures

CHAPTER 1

Introduction

Peter Sloman, Daniel Zamora Vargas, and Pedro Ramos Pinto

The idea of a universal basic income (UBI) is one of the most powerful and resonant policy proposals in contemporary public debate. Google Trends data shows that global internet searches for the term rose more than twenty-fold between 2015 and 2019, and then doubled again in March and April 2020 in the face of the COVID-19 pandemic. A series of UBI pilots—most notably in India (2011–2012), Kenya (since 2016), Finland (2017–2018), and Stockton, California (2019–2021)—have helped to raise the profile of the idea and build a sense of momentum around it. Even Pope Francis has suggested that 'it is time to explore concepts like the universal basic income', which would 'acknowledge and

P. Sloman (✉)
Department of Politics and International Studies, University of Cambridge, Cambridge, UK
e-mail: pjs93@cam.ac.uk

D. Zamora Vargas
Institut de sociologie, Université Libre de Bruxelles, Brussels, Belgium
e-mail: daniel.zamora.vargas@ulb.ac.be

P. Ramos Pinto
Faculty of History, University of Cambridge, Cambridge, UK
e-mail: pr211@cam.ac.uk

P. Sloman et al. (eds.), *Universal Basic Income in Historical Perspective*, https://doi.org/10.1007/978-3-030-75706-9_1

dignify' all forms of work and 'concretely achieve the ideal, at once so human and so Christian, of no worker without rights'.[1]

The economic shock caused by the COVID-19 pandemic has reinforced a global wave of interest in UBI which emerged during the 2010s and shows no sign of receding.[2] In the global south, UBI proposals have gained traction as part of a wider effort to break away from the paternalism of traditional development strategies and 'just give money to the poor'—creating what the anthropologist James Ferguson has called a 'new politics of distribution'.[3] In Western Europe and North America, basic income shows signs of becoming a totemic demand for some left-wing activists, partly through the influence of bestselling books setting out a vision of a 'post-work world' and partly as a reaction against the coerciveness and complexity of existing welfare policies.[4] Mainstream economists and social policy specialists have also begun to grapple seriously with the question of what UBI might look like in practice. Yet the intellectual roots of the idea remain under-explored, and the relationship between UBI and traditional forms of leftist politics continues to provoke vigorous debate. For some, UBI offers a way of reasserting a progressive vision of the welfare state as an embodiment of universal rights and a symbol of inclusive social citizenship.[5] For others, the popularity of basic income schemes shows how traditional socialist arguments for collective provision and trade union power have been supplanted by a thin approach to

[1] Pope Francis, *Let us Dream: The Path to a Better Future* (New York, NY: Simon and Schuster, 2020), p. 131; Pope Francis, 2020 Easter message, delivered at the Vatican, 12 April 2020, and available online at https://www.catholicnewsagency.com/news/full-text-pope-francis-easter-sunday-urbi-et-orbi-blessing-43012.

[2] Peter Sloman, 'Universal Basic Income in British Politics, 1918–2018: From a "Vagabond's Wage" to a Global Debate', *Journal of Social Policy*, 47, no. 3 (2018): 625–642.

[3] Joseph Hanlon, Armando Barrientos, and David Hulme, *Just Give Money to the Poor: The Development Revolution from the Global South* (Sterling, VA: Kumarian Press, 2010); James Ferguson, *Give a Man a Fish: Reflections on the New Politics of Distribution* (Durham, NC: Duke University Press, 2015).

[4] Nick Srnicek and Alex Williams, *Inventing the Future: Postcapitalism and a World Without Work* (London: Verso 2015); Rutgar Bregman, *Utopia for Realists: And How We Can Get There* (London: Bloomsbury, 2017); Annie Lowrey, *Give People Money: How a Universal Basic Income Would End Poverty, Revolutionize Work, and Remake the World* (New York, NY: Crown, 2018).

[5] Louise Haagh, *The Case for Universal Basic Income* (Cambridge: Polity, 2019).

redistribution through cash transfers, which reflects neoliberal influences and reinforces the logic of the market.[6]

In an attempt to rectify the ahistorical nature of much of the discourse around UBI, we convened a one-day workshop at the University of Cambridge in January 2019 on 'the intellectual history of basic income'. The call for papers attracted submissions from a number of historians and social scientists who were working on the topic, with a particularly strong focus on the origins and reception of UBI proposals in Europe and North America. Alongside these historical contributions, we also invited four leading members of the Basic Income Earth Network (BIEN)—Louise Haagh, Philippe Van Parijs, Eduardo Suplicy, and Malcolm Torry—to reflect on how the UBI debate has developed over the years. This book draws together seven of the papers presented at the workshop, together with three other chapters which we have commissioned from established scholars, and an edited transcript of an interview which Daniel Zamora Vargas has conducted with Philippe Van Parijs.

Pedro Ramos Pinto began the workshop by asking a provocative question: what might be the use of a history of UBI? When bringing an idea into the public arena, inserting it in a genealogy—whether it be the tradition of Tom Paine or of Milton Friedman—is a way of seeking legitimation. It anchors the unusual in the familiar and helps the argument gain the ear and trust of an audience. But it is also a distortion, since ideas are always a product of their world, and so change with it. Modern historians are instinctively suspicious of grand developmental narratives which see the past as a series of rehearsals on the way to the present. In different ways, all of the contributions to this book seek to lift the historical analysis of basic income out of the realm of genealogy by situating UBI proposals in their time and place and studying them through the lens of established scholarly literatures.

The Problem with Genealogies

The prevailing narrative of the history of basic income mainly reflects the efforts of UBI supporters to establish a historical lineage for their proposals. Most UBI campaigners have been drawn to the idea for political or philosophical reasons; for instance, Philippe Van Parijs developed his

[6] Daniel Zamora, 'The Case Against a Basic Income', *Jacobin*, Dec. 2017, available online at https://www.jacobinmag.com/2017/12/universal-basic-income-inequality-work.

proposal for an 'allocation universelle' in 1982–1983 as a way of trying to answer the problem of persistent unemployment outside the classic Keynesian framework. Van Parijs' frame of reference was distinctly contemporary, reflecting economic debates over inflation and deindustrialization (including the critique of Keynesian macroeconomics by figures such as Milton Friedman) and sociological concerns about the future of work highlighted by André Gorz. It was only as the European, and later global, UBI network matured—particularly after the creation of Basic Income European Network (BIEN) in 1986—that scholars began to investigate the history of the idea, connecting figures as disparate in time and place as Thomas Paine, Bertrand Russell, Mabel and Dennis Milner, and Milton Friedman.

In some cases, the fruits of this research have been based on rigorous archival work: for instance, Walter Van Trier's book *Every One a King* (1995) provides a richly textured analysis of basic income proposals in inter-war Britain and their relationship with other strands of radical economic thought, such as Major C. H. Douglas' Social Credit movement.[7] More often, however, the effort to tell the history of UBI as a '500-year-old idea' has meant reading contemporary definitions back into the past to construct a genealogy.[8] In popular works such as Rutger Bregman's best-seller *Utopia for Realists*, the history of basic income has been written in the service of the present.

Bregman, for instance, claims that 'Thomas More dreamed about [UBI] in his book *Utopia* in 1516'.[9] Guy Standing, one of the most important proponents of the idea, has pushed the genealogy further back in his paperback introduction to UBI, suggesting that the Athenian reformer Ephialtes—who introduced payments to citizens for carrying out jury service—was 'the true originator of the basic income'.[10] Though this 'enlightened system of deliberative democracy, facilitated by the basic income', did not survive the oligarchic coup of 411 BC, basic income returned during the Middle Ages with 'the epochal Charter of the Forest

[7] Walter Van Trier, *Every One A King: An Investigation into the Meaning and Significance of the Debate on Basic Incomes with Special Reference to Three Episodes from the British Inter-War Experience* (Leuven: Katholieke Universiteit Leuven, 1995).

[8] This phrase has been used very widely: see, for instance, Gideon Haigh, 'Basic Income for All: A 500-Year-Old Idea Whose Time Has Come?', *The Guardian*, November 10, 2016.

[9] Bregman, *Utopia for Realists*, p. 33.

[10] Guy Standing, *Basic Income: And How We Can Make It Happen* (London: Penguin, 2017), p. 10.

in 1217', which 'asserted the rights of the common man to subsistence'.[11] Standing's genealogy then runs through Thomas More, Thomas Paine, Edward Bellamy, Bertrand Russell, and Erich Fromm to the 1960s US guaranteed income debate and the formation of BIEN, before culminating with Silicon Valley entrepreneurs such as Sam Altman. In a similar vein, John Cunliffe and Guido Erreygers argue that basic income has had 'an intellectually rich albeit neglected past under various titles', which can be traced through 'apparently isolated and episodic occurrences in quite different contexts over some two hundred years'. From time to time, without any 'easily identifiable transmissions of intellectual or political influence', the 'deceptively simple ideas of a universal capital grant or lifetime income' have been '(re)invented or (re)discovered'.[12]

Attempts to construct a genealogy of UBI in this way are classic examples of what Quentin Skinner has called the 'mythology of doctrines'. As Skinner pointed out in his famous 1969 essay on 'Meaning and Understanding in the History of Ideas', attempting 'to trace the morphology of some given doctrine "through all the provinces of history in which it appears"' runs the risk of reifying an 'ideal type' of the idea and launching into an 'endless debate … about whether a given idea may be said to have "really emerged" at a given time, and whether it is "really there" in the work of some given writer'.[13]

> As the historian duly sets out in quest of the idea he has characterized, he is very readily led to speak as if the fully developed form of the doctrine was always in some sense immanent in history, even if various thinkers failed to 'hit upon' it, even if it 'dropped from sight' at various times, even if an entire era failed … to 'rise to a consciousness' of it.[14]

This reification is doubly problematic in the case of UBI, because both the term itself and its prevailing definition—as a universal and unconditional payment to every individual—have only been widely used since the 1980s. Most proposals for universal payments have appeared under other labels and in very different political contexts. For instance, Thomas Spence's

[11] Ibid., p. 10.

[12] John Cunliffe and Guido Erreygers, eds., *The Origins of Universal Grants* (New York, NY: Palgrave, 2004), xiii.

[13] Quentin Skinner, 'Meaning and Understanding in the History of Ideas', *History and Theory*, 8, no. 1 (1969): 3–53, at 10, 11.

[14] Ibid., 10.

1803 proposal to give each person 'an equal share of the rents of the parish where they have settlement' was deeply rooted in a radical critique of the Enclosure Acts, in his practical experience of the Elizabethan settlement laws, and in a historical narrative which complained of the dispossession of 'free-born Englishmen'. Assimilating Spence's ideas to a canon of UBI proposals based on a contemporary definition is likely to distort their original meaning.

Since the very meaning of basic income is unstable, its history cannot be written as a single story, let alone a triumphant narrative of 'an idea whose time has come'. As Walter Van Trier has argued, 'The meaning of any particular basic incomes proposal depends crucially and in a very strong sense on its substantive features' and on the particular 'frames of reference' within which it is set.[15] When we talk about basic income, we are really talking about a family of ideas, linked by a common set of characteristics. The changing content and impact of these proposals can only be properly understood by setting them in their social, political, and intellectual contexts.

How Should We Write the History of UBI?

What, then, might a better history of basic income look like? We would identify four broad objectives.

Firstly, histories of UBI should be sensitive to the *language and context* of different schemes and to the ways in which their reference points have changed over time. This historical concern to recognize the 'otherness' of the past leads many of the contributors to this volume to emphasize the distinctiveness of 'modern' UBI proposals. Attitudes to redistribution, for instance, have been powerfully reshaped by what Martin Ravallion has called the 'Second Poverty Enlightenment'—the explosion of research and interest in poverty relief after the Second World War, which has intersected with global discourses around human rights and 'basic needs', as Samuel Moyn shows in Chap. 9.[16] The notion that the state should set a 'poverty line' below which citizens cannot fall has become a political commonplace over the last century, at the same time as the technology of

[15] Van Trier, *Every One A King*, pp. 417, 427.

[16] Martin Ravallion, *The Economics of Poverty: History, Measurement, and Policy* (Oxford: Oxford University Press, 2016).

redistribution has been transformed by the growth of centralized bureaucracies, population registers, and automated payments systems.

Alongside this temporal shift, conceptions of what a basic income should look like have also varied widely between national contexts, according to the structure of welfare states, the problems they create, and the social expectations they set. For example, proponents of a guaranteed income in the 1960s United States were primarily attracted to the idea of an unconditional safety net which would replace the complex patchwork of state and federal welfare programmes, and tended to blur the distinction between a universal system of cash payments and selective programmes such as Milton Friedman's Negative Income Tax (NIT). By contrast, the UK has had a long tradition of centralized means-tested support which grew out of the old 'Poor Law' and persisted into the post-war period, as José Harris has shown.[17] British campaigners have thus tended to see UBI as a way of extending the principle of 'flat-rate universalism' which William Beveridge articulated in his report on *Social Insurance and Allied Services* (1942), and of removing the stigma and complexity which they associate with the means-tested benefit system. Likewise, as E. Fouksman shows in Chap. 10, campaigners in South Africa and Namibia have presented basic income as a response to the economic and social legacies of apartheid, including high levels of black unemployment and the continuing divide between contributory (social insurance) and means-tested (social assistance) benefits.

Secondly, a history of UBI must recognize that ideas are never free-floating; rather, they are nurtured and disseminated by ***individuals and institutions***, which carry them into public debate. Many basic income proposals have been championed by individual 'policy entrepreneurs', who (in John Kingdon's words) 'invest their resources—time, energy, reputation, and sometimes money'—in the pursuit of policy change, and 'attempt to "soften up" both policy communities ... and larger publics, getting them used to new ideas and building acceptance for their proposals'.[18] Dennis Milner, Juliet Rhys-Williams, and Hermione Parker in the UK are classic examples, as Peter Sloman shows in Chap. 2. Over time, basic

[17] José Harris, 'From Poor Law to Welfare State? A European Perspective', in *The Political Economy of British Historical Experience, 1688–1914*, eds. Donald Winch and Patrick K. O'Brien (Oxford: Oxford University Press, 2002), pp. 409–37.

[18] John Kingdon, *Agendas, Alternatives and Public Policies* (second edition, New York, NY: Longman, 1995), pp. 122, 128.

income campaigning has increasingly become institutionalized, both on a national scale (for instance, through the Citizen's Basic Income Trust in the UK and the BIG Coalition in Namibia) and through BIEN. Other organizations have taken up UBI alongside other goals or demands, as in the case of the National Welfare Rights Organization (NWRO) in the United States, which Alyssa Battistoni discusses in Chap. 5, and the Dutch Council Against the Work Ethic, which Anton Jäger analyses in Chap. 6.

Close study of individuals and formal institutions forces us to grapple with wider intellectual and political influences on social policy debate, which have given UBI proposals their form and meaning. Both the NWRO and the Dutch Council Against the Work Ethic, for instance, can only be properly understood by situating them in the context of larger social movements: the US civil rights movement (particularly in its late 1960s guise, radicalized by frustration with the limits of Lyndon Johnson's War on Poverty) and the transnational New Left which emerged out of the 1968 student protests and anti-Vietnam War campaigning. Such movements, in turn, are shaped by deeper patterns in political economy and political culture, as Louise Haagh argues in Chap. 11.

Among academics and policy-makers, discussions of UBI have similarly been structured by intellectual agendas and disciplinary assumptions. As Daniel Zamora Vargas shows in Chap. 3, many post-war US economists were drawn to guaranteed income proposals as a liberal solution to poverty which respected the superior allocative efficiency of the price system—reflecting the preference for fiscal transfers over collective provision which Alice O'Connor has traced in her study of *Poverty Knowledge*.[19] By contrast, political philosophers such as Philippe Van Parijs have mainly been attracted to the principle of unconditional income support as a way of achieving 'real freedom for all'. The growth of interest in UBI within the Anglo-American academy during 1980s and 1990s arguably owed less to real-world developments in social policy than to the post-Rawlsian revival of debates on distributive justice, and particularly to Van Parijs' attempt to justify 'why surfers should be fed' in his dialogue with Rawls.[20] André Gorz's efforts to rethink socialism for a post-industrial age had a similarly galvanizing effect on sociologists and left-wing intellectuals in

[19] Alice O'Connor, *Poverty Knowledge: Social Science, Social Policy, and the Poor in Twentieth-Century US History* (Princeton, NJ: Princeton University Press, 2001).

[20] Juliana Uhuru Bidadanure, 'The Political Theory of Universal Basic Income', *Annual Review of Political Science*, 22 (2019): 481–501.

continental Europe.[21] As Walter Van Trier points out in Chap. 8, Gorz framed his analysis in relation to a Marxist analysis of political change in a way that Van Parijs did not: a reflection, perhaps, of the slightly different intellectual contexts in which they were writing.

Thirdly, we need to understand the *reception* of basic income in public debate, both in order to explain the repeated waves of interest in the idea over the last century and to see why UBI proposals have so rarely been implemented. There is already a growing literature on the politics of UBI by scholars such as Jurgen de Wispelaere, which has highlighted problems that proponents frequently face: deep concerns about the cost of universal payments, shallow and inconsistent support from political actors, and the difficulty of constructing a durable coalition around particular proposals.[22] Clearly governing institutions matter: for instance, Finland's high-profile 2017–2018 basic income experiment was launched as a result of coalition negotiations after an election held under proportional representation.[23] The structure of existing welfare states—and the existing distribution of income—also has major implications for the likely pattern of winners and losers from a UBI system.[24]

As Brian Steensland has pointed out in his study of the US guaranteed income debate, *The Failed Welfare Revolution* (2008), however, the politics of social reform cannot be understood wholly in rationalist terms. Steensland argues that 'guaranteed income plans failed' in the 1960s and early 1970s 'because they challenged the cultural logic of American welfare policy, which is based on sorting the poor into different programs according to assessments of their "deservingness"'.[25] Similar cultural

[21] Adrian Little, *The Political Thought of André Gorz* (London: Routledge, 1996).

[22] See especially Jurgen de Wispelaere and José Antonio Noguera, 'On the Political Feasibility of Universal Basic Income: An Analytic Framework', in *Basic Income Guarantee and Politics: International Experiences and Perspectives on the Viability of Income Guarantee*, ed. Richard K. Caputo (New York/Basingstoke: Palgrave Macmillan, 2012), pp. 17–38, and Jurgen de Wispelaere, 'The Struggle for Strategy: On the Politics of the Basic Income Proposal', *Politics*, 36, no. 2 (2016): 131–41.

[23] Antti Halmetoja, Jurgen de Wispelaere and Johanna Perkiö, 'A Policy Comet in Moominland? Basic Income in the Finnish Welfare State', *Social Policy & Society*, 18, no. 2 (2019): 319–30, at 321.

[24] This is, of course, the founding insight of both standard political economy models of redistribution (such as the Meltzer-Richard model) and the literature on the difficulties of welfare state reform associated with scholars such as Paul Pierson.

[25] Brian Steensland, *The Failed Welfare Revolution: America's Struggle over Guaranteed Income Policy* (Princeton, NJ: Princeton University Press, 2008), x.

factors figure prominently in several of the chapters included here. Anton Jäger and Marc-Antoine Sabaté both highlight the commitment of the twentieth-century European left to a producerist vision of society oriented towards 'inclusion' through paid work, which has continued to shape policy in France and the Netherlands until very recently, in spite of the rise of the 'second left' and the impact of deindustrialization. Likewise, E. Fouksman draws on her own anthropological research to show that many poorer Namibians and South Africans retain a strong normative attachment to paid work and are wary of direct income transfers. Fouksman's analysis echoes Luke Martinelli and Nick Pearce's warning to British basic income advocates that 'many of those who might stand to benefit from BI in material terms might oppose it on normative grounds of fairness or reciprocity, particularly if it were extended to "undeserving" groups'.[26] Recent experience suggests that this distinction between the 'deserving' and 'undeserving' poor remains a powerful weapon for conservative politicians, and a major obstacle to UBI in many contexts.

Finally, a *global* history of basic income must uncover the *networks* that have brought UBI supporters together and placed the idea at the heart of a wide-ranging transnational movement. Early basic income proposals tended to be episodic and disconnected, partly because the terminology around the idea was so fluid and its advocates struggled to gain acceptance in mainstream social policy circles. As Walter Van Trier has pointed out, many proponents of UBI have thought they were coming up with a completely new idea, and then stumbled across earlier cases; Philippe Van Parijs (who was probably one of the last to 'discover' UBI in this way) explains the origins of his interest in the idea in his interview with Daniel Zamora Vargas.[27] From the 1960s onwards, however, debates over the US War on Poverty, deindustrialization, and 'third-world' development spilled across national borders, and the conference which Van Parijs organized at Louvain-la-Neuve in September 1986 brought together UBI enthusiasts from across Europe to form BIEN.[28] Although BIEN is formally a research organization—which 'fosters evidence-based research and plural debate about Basic Income' and 'remains neutral among competing arguments

[26] Luke Martinelli and Nick Pearce, 'Basic Income in the UK: Assessing Prospects for Reform in an Age of Austerity', *Social Policy & Society*, 18, no. 2 (2019): 265–75, at 270.

[27] Van Trier, *Every One A King*, p. 20.

[28] Anne G. Miller, ed., *Basic Income. Proceedings of the First International Conference on Basic Income, Louvain-La-Neuve, Belgium*, 4–6 September 1986 (Antwerp, 1986).

for and against' UBI—many of its members are actively involved in campaigning. More recently, groups such as UBI Europe have adopted a more overtly activist posture.

The fact that basic income lies at the heart of a global movement today does not mean that the idea has an 'immanent' and 'internal' logic that has always had the potential to 'universalize' itself. As Samuel Moyn has noted, concepts do not spread one by one, but are always 'bound up with larger political and cultural processes' and 'selected out of larger actual and possible sets of alternative concepts'.[29] The emergence of the modern UBI movement reflects both the agency of basic income advocates and the trend towards the globalization of policy discourse. Jamie Peck and Nik Theodore, for instance, have drawn attention to the rise of 'fast policy':

> a condition of deepening transnational interconnectedness, in which local policy experiments exist *in relation to* near and far relatives, to traveling models and technocratic designs, and to a host of financial, technical, social, and symbolic networks that invariably loop through centres of power and persuasion.[30]

Basic income provides a striking case of how a policy idea can migrate between contexts and mutate in the process. Indeed, the circulation and 'hybridization' of UBI ideas across space is critical to understanding UBI's global 'success' in the last few years. UBI is often presented as the future of social policy in the global south, and perhaps in the global north as well. Where once the International Labour Organization's 1944 Philadelphia declaration promised to universalize the western industrial welfare model, the global south now shows the north how to create a welfare society that is not based on productivism. The embrace of UBI by the development community is linked to the rise of 'conditional cash transfers' (CCTs) such as Brazil's *Bolsa Família* programme—a family allowance conditional on the educational participation of children—and means-tested social grants, which are now in widespread use across the global south. As Fouksman argues in this volume, it is important to distinguish CCTs from UBI, and the mechanisms and legitimating rationales for the former can in fact militate against a truly unconditional and universal system.

[29] Samuel Moyn, 'On the Nonglobalization of Ideas', in *Global Intellectual History*, eds. Samuel Moyn and Andrew Sartori (New York, NY: Columbia University Press, 2015), p. 201.

[30] Jamie Peck and Nik Theodore, *Fast Policy: Experimental Statecraft at the Thresholds of Neoliberalism* (Minneapolis, MN: University of Minnesota Press, 2015), xxxi.

Nonetheless, it could be argued that one of the major impetuses for the current attention devoted to UBI has been its grafting on to the seemingly positive experience of other cash transfer schemes.

As such—and regardless of the position one takes on the desirability of UBI—James Ferguson's call to historicize development and social policy discourses, in order to understand how cash transfer programmes have arisen as a solution to the problems of global poverty and inequality, seems to us to be crucial. Direct allocations by the state are not themselves a new invention, but have a long history in colonial and post-colonial contexts.[31] The rise of cash transfers must also be set against the backdrop of an even longer history of in-kind provision, typified by systems of collective feeding in both ancient and recent empires. In India, for instance, British administrators organized 'gratuitous relief' for the purposes of emergency relief following the late nineteenth-century famine codes, and later developed a public distribution system for food during the Second World War, which the Indian government expanded after independence and which remains a major form of social transfer in the world's largest democracy.[32] Likewise, it is important to explore how ideas about cash transfers intersect with other ideas with long genealogies, including the Islamic practice of *zakat*, a tax on wealth—which is sometimes voluntary, sometimes not, and in some instances state-administered.

To the extent that the debate about basic income is also a debate about what is a basic or sufficient command of resources, then, it is intrinsically linked to a larger history of the politics of defining, measuring, and fighting over vital and social minima. These minima have taken a wide variety of forms—including wages, calories, bushels of grain—and have been integral to the conceptualization of standards of living and debates over rights.[33] As Frederick Cooper reminds us, the debate about social minima

[31] James Midgley, 'Colonialism and Welfare: A Post-Colonial Commentary', *Journal of Progressive Human Services*, 9 (1998): 31–50; Frederick Cooper, *Decolonization and African Society: The Labor Question in French and British Africa* (Cambridge: Cambridge University Press, 1996).

[32] Jean Drèze, 'Famine Prevention in India', in *The Political Economy of Hunger, Vol. 2: Famine Prevention*, eds. Jean Drèze and Amartya Sen (Oxford: Oxford University Press, 1990); Jos Mooij, 'Food Policy and Politics: The Political Economy of the Public Distribution System in India', *Journal of Peasant Studies*, 25 (1998): 77–101.

[33] Nick Cullather, 'The Foreign Policy of the Calorie', *American Historical Review*, 112 (2007): 337–64; Vincent Bonnecase, 'When Numbers Represented Poverty: The Changing Meaning of the Food Ration in French Colonial Africa', *Journal of African History*, 59

has a long history within colonial empires, from anti-slavery to ILO-sanctioned projects of colonial reformism in the middle of the twentieth century.[34] The terms and shape of basic income debates can only be properly understood in the light of these legacies, as Grace Davie has shown with regard to the Basic Income Grant (BIG) campaigns in South Africa.[35]

In short, the history of UBI needs to be set within the broader history of global social policy, and of development agendas and ambitions. This history is complex, and on a global level much of it remains to be written. What is clear is that the circulation of ideas about UBI cannot be divorced from the structural asymmetries of the modern world, including the legacy of the colonial past, the influence of western institutions and ideas, and the dependency relationships created by global capitalism. The imbalances of power between and within nations that define social policy agendas, making some interventions possible and others unfeasible, must be a central part of the story.

Competing Narratives, Contested Meanings

As previously noted, most of the chapters collected in this volume were first presented as papers at a workshop in Cambridge in January 2019. All of them emerge out of ongoing (and independent) research agendas, in many cases by doctoral students and early career academics, and with research questions which range well beyond the history of basic income. Our contributors are also drawn from a variety of disciplines, and include two sociologists (Daniel Zamora Vargas and Walter Van Trier), two applied political theorists (Alyssa Battistoni and Louise Haagh), and a social anthropologist (E. Fouksman) as well as political and intellectual historians. Though we have sought to include a wide range of perspectives, we have made no attempt to steer the contributors in particular directions or to achieve comprehensive coverage. This book thus makes no pretence to offer a total history of UBI. Rather, we believe the chapters make an important set of focussed contributions to our understanding of basic

(2018): 463–81; Poornima Paidipaty, 'Testing Measures: Decolonization and Economic Power in 1960s India', *History of Political Economy*, 52 (2020): 473–97.

[34] Frederick Cooper, 'Afterword: Social Rights and Human Rights in the Time of Decolonization', *Humanity: An International Journal of Human Rights, Humanitarianism, and Development*, 3 (2012): 473–92, at 481.

[35] Grace Davie, *Poverty Knowledge in South Africa: A Social History of Human Science, 1855–2005* (Cambridge: Cambridge University Press, 2015).

income debates in the twentieth and early twenty-first centuries, in line with the broad objectives set out in the previous section.

Taken together, the chapters collected here can be seen to contest existing narratives around basic income in three main ways. Firstly, several of the contributors show that the modern UBI movement, formed in the 1980s and institutionalized through BIEN, built on arguments and proposals which had circulated in Europe and the United States since the middle decades of the twentieth century. Peter Sloman points out in Chap. 2 that the costed basic income schemes which Hermione Parker and Malcolm Torry have produced in the UK show close structural affinities with the proposals for 'a new social contract' which Juliet Rhys-Williams drew up during the Second World War, and that figures such as James Meade and Sir Brandon Rhys-Williams provided a direct link between these two eras. In Chaps. 3, 4, and 5, Daniel Zamora Vargas, Andrew Sanchez, and Alyssa Battistoni, respectively, explore how economic ideas, futurist visions of 'cybernation', and feminist and environmentalist campaigning in the post-war United States produced very different conceptions of the nature and purpose of a guaranteed income. Likewise, Anton Jäger shows in Chap. 6 that concerns about automation and the future of work circulated widely in Europe as well as North America from the 1960s onwards, and helped shape the New Left's anti-productivism and anti-statism. These early attempts to rethink the prevailing models of work and welfare provide crucial contexts for understanding how the UBI movement took off when unemployment surged in the 1980s.

Secondly, the contributors point out that the political meaning of UBI can vary markedly according to the content of proposals and the political agendas of its advocates. One perspective which has featured prominently in recent literature sees UBI as part of a larger field of essentially liberal and technocratic cash transfer programmes, which reflects the neoclassical orientation of mainstream Anglo-American economists and seeks to alleviate poverty without interfering directly in labour and product markets. Peter Sloman has made this point in relatively neutral terms in his recent study of UK guaranteed income proposals, *Transfer State* (2019); Daniel Zamora Vargas and Anton Jäger have pushed the same line of argument further and given it a critical form in two articles, arguing that UBI proposals are 'firmly rooted in a neoliberal understanding of social justice' which left-wingers should reject.[36] Zamora Vargas fleshes out this interpretation in Chap. 3 by putting Milton Friedman at the heart of his analysis of the US guaranteed income debate, and Marc-Antoine Sabaté's analysis of the growing interest in UBI in France in Chap. 7 expresses similar caution about its implications. Likewise, in Chap. 9 Samuel Moyn sets the popularity of basic income against the backdrop of the global 'basic needs' agenda which has emerged since the 1970s, and argues that the prevailing focus on poverty relief has served to marginalize more radical calls for greater equality.

As Alyssa Battistoni points out in Chap. 5, however, this is far from being the only way in which UBI and similar proposals can be read. Battistoni shows that US guaranteed income proposals drew support from thinkers and campaigners well beyond the ranks of the economics profession, tapping into welfare rights activism, ecological concerns about over-consumption, and the feminist politics of the Wages for Housework movement. The social work students who founded the US Ad Hoc Committee for a Guaranteed Income in 1966—which Andrew Sanchez discusses in Chap. 4—also backed the idea for very different reasons to market economists. There are thus good reasons to be careful about seeing the growing popularity of cash transfers as intrinsically 'neoliberal'. On the other hand, as Louise Haagh notes in Chap. 11, there is no necessary correspondence between the origins of an idea and its effects. The fact that many UBI proponents identify with the political left has not prevented market liberals from appropriating their arguments, and is no guarantee that basic income will not be used to shore up support for financialized capitalism.

Thirdly, and relatedly, this awareness of the mutability of basic income has implications for debates about development policy in the global south. Over the last decade, scholars such as Ferguson have held up UBI campaigns and pilot schemes as examples of a 'new politics of distribution' which bypasses the wage-labour relationship and subverts the paternalism of traditional development strategies.[37] As Fouksman points out in Chap.

[36] Daniel Zamora and Anton Jäger, 'Historicizing Basic Income: Response to Daniel Zeglen', *Lateral*, 8, no. 1 (spring 2019), available online at https://csalateral.org/forum/universal-basic-income/historicizing-basic-income-zamora-jager/; see also Daniel Zamora and Anton Jäger, 'One Question: Universal Basic Income', *State of Nature* blog, 30 July 2018, available online at https://stateofnatureblog.com/one-question-universal-basic-income/.

[37] Ferguson, *Give a Man a Fish*.

10, however, the vast majority of social grants programmes in southern Africa are restricted to certain categories of claimants (for instance, the unemployed and disabled) or subject to means-testing, and so pose a much less radical challenge to traditional social norms than a full-fledged UBI. Likewise, the political goals of grassroots civil rights movements tend to be very different to the technocratic focus on poverty relief, work incentives, and human capital development which continues to prevail within leading global institutions such as the World Bank and IMF.[38] We must be careful not to allow superficial similarities between social welfare proposals to blur profound differences in meaning.

We are well aware that these findings only scratch the surface of a large and complex topic. More work is needed in a host of areas: most obviously, on the regions which we have not looked at here (particularly Latin America, Asia, and the Pacific), on the connections between UBI and other global social policy initiatives (such as the ILO's social protection floors), and on BIEN's role in the development of a transnational 'instrument constituency'.[39] Nevertheless, we hope that the research collected in this volume will enrich our understanding of where UBI proposals have come from, and help to integrate the basic income debate with other research fields. After all, the contextual sensitivity which historical research requires is relevant not only to the past but also to the present and future. Social programmes have enormous power to change people's lives, for good or ill. Careful analysis of how a particular form of basic income might function in a particular society is thus essential to informed debate and successful policy-making.

[38] Peck and Theodore, *Fast Policy*, 85–129.

[39] For the social protection floors, see Bob Deacon, *Global Social Policy in the Making: The Foundations of the Social Protection Floor* (Bristol: Bristol University Press, 2013); for the concept of an instrument constituency, see Daniel Béland and Michael Howlett, 'How Solutions Chase Problems: Instrument Constituencies in the Policy Process', *Governance*, 29, no. 3 (2016): 393–409.

PART I

Poverty in the Midst of Plenty: The Rise of Basic Income in Britain and the United States

CHAPTER 2

Basic Income as Technocratic Liberalism: Framing a Policy Idea in Twentieth-Century Britain

Peter Sloman

The global basic income movement which has emerged over the last forty years is largely a product of deindustrialization. During the 1970s and 1980s, the decline of manufacturing employment in North America and Western Europe dovetailed with the rise of environmentalism, second-wave feminism, and other forms of New Left politics to undermine the 'Fordist' industrial model and open up political space for new approaches to work and welfare. The formation of the Basic Income Research Group (BIRG)—now the Citizen's Basic Income Trust (CBIT)—in London in 1984 and the Basic Income European Network (BIEN)—now the Basic Income Earth Network—in Louvain-la-Neuve in 1986 testify to the importance of this post-industrial moment. It was also in this period that 'basic income' became established as the principal term for the idea, supplanting older labels such as 'social dividends'.

P. Sloman (✉)
Department of Politics and International Studies, University of Cambridge, Cambridge, UK
e-mail: pjs93@cam.ac.uk

P. Sloman et al. (eds.), *Universal Basic Income in Historical Perspective*, https://doi.org/10.1007/978-3-030-75706-9_2

In the face of the mass unemployment created by the early 1980s recession, British basic income campaigners such as Hermione Parker frequently presented universal basic income (UBI) as a 'revolutionary concept' which represented 'a real attempt to come to terms with social, demographic and technological change' by adapting the welfare state to a post-industrial context.[1] Yet basic income was not a new idea. Proposals for universal payments can be traced back to Thomas Paine and Thomas Spence at the turn of the nineteenth century, and circulated widely in British social policy debates from the First World War onwards as a result of campaigns by Dennis Milner and Juliet Rhys-Williams.[2] The founders of the Basic Income Research Group were thus building on more than half a century of policy debate and activism.

This chapter explores the emergence of basic income as a policy option in mid-twentieth-century Britain and examines how these early debates have shaped subsequent basic income proposals. In particular, it argues that Dennis Milner's 'state bonus' scheme and Juliet Rhys-Williams' campaign for a 'new social contract' framed UBI as a tax-benefit reform, designed to establish a minimum income floor and simplify the financial relationship between the individual and the state. This focus on the tax-benefit interface was reflected in academic work—for instance, in the writings of economists such as James Meade and Tony Atkinson—and served to crowd out alternative conceptions of UBI in British policy-making circles during the post-war period. As a result, basic income came to be understood as a form of technocratic market liberalism, which promised to alleviate poverty without the need for trade union activity, public ownership, or central planning. Although New Left activists such as the Claimants' Unions developed a more radical case for UBI during the 1970s and 1980s, most Labour politicians and trade unionists continued to treat the idea with deep suspicion, as a diversion from the real struggle for control of economic power.[3] It is only in the last few years that this antipathy has finally broken down.

[1] Hermione Parker, 'The "BIG" way to full employment', June 18, 1983, Rhys-Williams papers, B 8/6, British Library of Political and Economic Science, London (hereafter BLPES).

[2] The inter-war history of basic income has been meticulously reconstructed by Walter Van Trier: Walter Van Trier, *Every One A King: An Investigation into the Meaning and Significance of the Debate on Basic Incomes with Special Reference to Three Episodes from the British Inter-War Experience* (Leuven: Katholieke Universiteit Leuven, 1995).

[3] Rory O'Kelly, 'Why Social Dividends Are Not the Answer', *Policy Studies* 5, no. 2 (1984): 24–30. For a recent restatement of this view, see Jon Cruddas and Tom Kibasi, 'A Universal Basic Mistake', *Prospect* no. 224 (July 2016): 50–52.

Three Approaches to Basic Income, c. 1797–1945

The concept of a universal basic income is now widely understood to mean 'a regular cash income paid to all, on an individual basis, without means test or work requirement'.[4] This definition marks basic income off from means-tested guaranteed income schemes (such as Milton Friedman's Negative Income Tax (NIT)) and 'workfare' schemes which make benefits conditional on availability for work or other contribution requirements. By focussing attention on the structure and administration of the benefit—rather than, for instance, its rate or how it is paid for—the definition has enabled BIEN and other campaigners to tap into support from a range of political traditions and build a broad 'instrument constituency' around the idea.[5] In practice, however, the political meaning of basic income is so dependent on its level, its financing, and the way it is framed that it is far from clear that we should regard it as a single instrument. As David Purdy has argued, UBI is really 'a field of debate, rather than a settled programme'.[6]

An analysis of early British proposals suggests that UBI can be conceptualized and justified in at least three different ways. Firstly, a basic income can be understood as *a share of the return on assets which are owned by the community*—as in Thomas Paine's *Agrarian Justice* (1797) and Thomas Spence's *The Constitution of Spensonia* (1803), which rooted the case for universal payments in radical narratives of dispossession and restitution. Paine called for a stiff inheritance tax to build up a fund which would pay out a universal endowment of £15 at the age of twenty-one plus a pension of £10 per annum for the over-fifties, as 'compensation ... for the loss of his or her inheritance, by the introduction of the system of landed property'; Spence argued the land was 'the common estate of the inhabitants' and that each citizen was entitled to an equal share of the rents from it.[7]

[4] Philippe Van Parijs and Yannick Vanderborght, *Basic Income: A Radical Proposal for a Free Society and a Sane Economy* (Cambridge, MA: Harvard University Press, 2017), 1.

[5] Daniel Béland et al., 'Instrument Constituencies and Transnational Policy Diffusion: The Case of Conditional Cash Transfers', *Review of International Political Economy* 25, no. 4 (2018): 463–82.

[6] David Purdy, 'Citizenship, Basic Income and the State', *New Left Review* no. 208 (1994): 30–48, at 31.

[7] Thomas Paine, *Agrarian Justice* (1797), reprinted in *The Writings of Thomas Paine*, ed. Moncure Daniel Conway, 4 vols. (New York: G. P. Putnam's Sons, 1894), 3:322–44, at 331; Thomas Spence, *The Constitution of Spensonia* (1803), reprinted in *The Political Works of Thomas Spence*, ed. H. T. Dickinson (Newcastle: Avero (Eighteenth-Century) Publications Ltd., 1982), 104–18.

In a similar vein, inter-war market socialists such as James Meade and Oskar Lange suggested that the state should nationalize profitable industries in order to obtain an independent revenue stream, which could be paid out 'as a social dividend ... on any desired principle of equality'.[8] Alaska's Permanent Dividend Fund, set up in the late 1970s to invest the US state's oil revenues, is perhaps the best-known application of this principle. Whether public ownership of this kind is regarded as natural (i.e., a reflection of underlying social rights to common assets) or strategic (as part of an effort to establish public control over key resources), a dividend based on rent or profit is likely to vary according to economic performance. It is not easy to see how a basic income of this sort could provide recipients with a stable regular income.

Secondly, a basic income can be seen as *a way of distributing all or part of the output of society as a whole*, in line with Marx's famous distributive principle—'from each according to his ability, to each according to his needs'—and the most ambitious strands of socialist egalitarianism. The inter-war Labour intellectual G. D. H. Cole, for instance, proposed in *Principles of Economic Planning* (1935) that in a socialist society

> Incomes will be distributed partly as rewards for work, and partly as direct payments from the State to every citizen as 'social dividends'—a recognition of each citizen's claim as a consumer to share the common heritage of productive power.[9]

Cole argued that the social dividend should be sufficient not only to cover 'bare physical necessities' but also to ensure a certain amount of purchasing power beyond this, and suggested that it should rise to at least two-thirds of national income, turning wages into a kind of 'pocket money' for most people.[10] This reflected a belief in the collective character of the *whole* production process, which also led him to propose conditionality requirements. As Ben Jackson has pointed out, Cole worried that a strictly universal payment would encourage free-riding, and so insisted that the social dividend should be conditional on 'a proven readiness to play

[8] J. E. Meade, 'Outline of Economic Policy for a Labour Government', in *The Collected Papers of James Meade*, eds. Susan Howson and Donald Moggridge, vol. 1 (London: Unwin Hyman, 1988), 33–78, at 53; Oskar Lange, 'On the Economic Theory of Socialism: Part I', *Review of Economic Studies*, 4, no. 1 (1936): 53–71, at 61.

[9] G. D. H. Cole, *Principles of Economic Planning* (London: Macmillan, 1935), 235.

[10] Cole, *Principles*, 235–36.

[one's] part in the common tasks and duties of the whole community'—which for able-bodied adults meant a willingness to work.[11] Likewise, Bertrand Russell argued in *Roads to Freedom* (1918) that the state should abolish the wage system and pay everyone a 'small income, sufficient for necessities'. This 'vagabond's wage' would be supplemented by a larger payment for those willing to engage in useful work, and perhaps an additional premium for those in 'specially disagreeable' occupations.[12]

Thirdly, UBI can be seen as *a social security policy designed to provide citizens with all or part of the means of subsistence*. This interest in providing a 'national minimum' can be detected in Cole and Russell's work, but it emerges most clearly in two other British proposals: Dennis and Mabel Milner's *Scheme for a State Bonus* (1918) and Juliet Rhys-Williams' pamphlet *Something to Look Forward To* (1943). Writing at the end of the First World War, the Milners proposed to extend the wartime system of separation allowances which the British government had created to support servicemen's families to cover the entire community. The 'state bonus' scheme would provide a

> small allowance ... sufficient to maintain life and liberty if all else failed ... based on the primal needs of individuals (which are nearly the same for all), namely food, shelter, and a minimum of recreation, say, for instance, what could be bought before the War for 5/- a week.[13]

The Milners thought this 'state bonus' could be paid for by levying a 20 per cent tax on all other income. Twenty-five years later, Juliet Rhys-Williams followed the Milners' lead, proposing to replace income tax allowances and social security benefits with a system of universal cash payments. Rhys-Williams set the rates of her cash allowances according to her estimates of subsistence needs—21/- for a man, 19/- for a woman, and 10/- for each child—and presented her plan for a 'new social contract' as an alternative to Sir William Beveridge's National Insurance proposals.[14]

[11] Ben Jackson, *Equality and the British Left: A Study in Progressive Political Thought, 1900–1964* (Manchester: Manchester University Press, 2007), 64; Cole, *Principles*, 252.

[12] Bertrand Russell, *Roads to Freedom* (London: George Allen & Unwin, 1918), 119.

[13] E. Mabel and Dennis Milner, *Scheme for a State Bonus: A Rational Method of Solving the Social Problem* (Darlington: North of England Newspaper Company, 1918), 7.

[14] Juliet Rhys-Williams, *Something to Look Forward To* (London: MacDonald and Co., 1943).

This threefold typology is not exhaustive. We might also conceptualize basic income as a kind of helicopter money, financed by aid agencies (in the developing world) or credit creation (as suggested by monetary reformers such as C. H. Douglas), or link it to new revenue streams such as pollution taxes. Nevertheless, each of these three ways of financing UBI places it in a particular frame of reference which shapes its political meaning. Paying basic income out of public assets links it to radical-liberal discourses about 'the commons' and raises questions about the nature and extent of public ownership. Defining basic income as a share of national income links it to socialist visions of equality and philosophical debates about distributive justice, and highlights the possibility of superseding the wage system through central planning. Treating basic income as a subsistence income floor sets it firmly in the context of tax and benefit policy and suggests that it should be evaluated by comparison with other anti-poverty strategies.

Juliet Rhys-Williams and the 'New Social Contract'

During the first half of the twentieth century, proposals for universal cash payments in Britain were eclectic and amorphous in character, as this typology shows. If anything, inter-war interest in 'social dividends' tended to be clustered in the more radical and utopian parts of the British left, among libertarian socialists such as Russell and left-wing economists such as Cole. The Fabian banker George Wansbrough wrote to John Maynard Keynes in 1939 to suggest a basic income 'on a scale equivalent to present unemployment insurance benefits', and Keynes agreed that it was 'an important and excellent' idea, which—though not easy to justify politically at the outbreak of the Second World War—'should certainly have a place in any Utopian political programme'.[15] Apart from the cost, the main problem was that the idea of unconditional benefits ran up against the trade unions' focus on achieving higher wages through collective bargaining, as Dennis Milner found when he tried to press his 'state bonus' on Labour in the 1920s. 'We have already upon our agenda nationalisation, workers' control, the raising of all wages, the raising of unemployment insurance, to say nothing of the scores of minor measures',

[15] George Wansbrough to John Maynard Keynes, December 11, 1939, and Keynes to Wansbrough, December 14, 1939, in John Maynard Keynes papers, HP/1, King's College, Cambridge.

a Labour Party committee concluded in 1921, and 'it is more in accord with our principles to establish high wages and high unemployment benefit, than to offer merely the means to live'.[16]

In the course of the 1940s, however, interest in basic income migrated from the radical fringe towards the centre of the British political spectrum as a result of Juliet Rhys-Williams' proposals for tax-benefit integration. Rhys-Williams was a Liberal Party (and later Conservative Party) activist whose political outlook reflected an idiosyncratic mixture of Tory imperialism, maternalist feminism, and a concern about unemployment and work incentives which had emerged from her experiences in South Wales during the 1930s.[17] Her earliest proposals, in *Something to Look Forward To*, envisaged a subsistence-level system of cash allowances financed by a flat-rate income tax (which she estimated at 45 per cent) and backed up by work requirements.[18] This 'new social contract' would provide mothers and housewives with an independent source of income and allow the unemployed to take casual work without losing their benefits. In later versions of the scheme, however, Rhys-Williams abandoned the work requirements and reduced the allowance below subsistence level in order to make the tax rate required more palatable. For instance, she gave evidence to the Royal Commission on the Taxation of Profits and Income (1951–1955) on a plan for a weekly cash payment of 10/- per person, paid for by a flat tax of 20 per cent on earned income up to £600 a year, which would only partly replace National Insurance benefits.[19]

Rhys-Williams' approach to basic income reflected the influence of three overlapping currents in British economic and social thought. The first was the tradition of quantitative social research established by Seebohm Rowntree and Charles Booth at the turn of the twentieth century, which defined poverty in income terms and focussed on raising

[16] Labour Party, *Report of the Twenty-First Annual Conference. Brighton, 1921* (London: Labour Party, 1921), 60–62, at 61.

[17] Peter Sloman, 'Beveridge's Rival: Juliet Rhys-Williams and the Campaign for Basic Income, 1942–55', *Contemporary British History* 30, no. 2 (2016): 203–23.

[18] Rhys-Williams' maternalist approach was reflected in the differential structure of her proposed work requirements, which involved full-time paid work for adult men and part-time work for single women and young widows without dependent children.

[19] *Minutes of Evidence Taken Before the Royal Commission on the Taxation of Profits and Income* (London: Her Majesty's Stationery Office, 1953), 3–9.

households above an absolute or relative 'poverty line'.[20] As José Harris has pointed out, the British welfare state has long been unusually materialistic in its approach to poverty relief, reflecting the distinctive form of Anglo-American 'poverty knowledge'—'emphasizing income over services, targeting individuals rather than empowering communities, and favouring interventions that worked outside the market over attempts to achieve market reform'—which Alice O'Connor has identified in the post-war United States.[21] Rowntree's 'poverty line', which informed Beveridge and Rhys-Williams' benefit rates, was based on an empirical investigation of subsistence needs; from the 1960s onwards this was largely supplanted by the use of the National Assistance or Supplementary Benefit scales (as in Brian Abel-Smith and Peter Townsend's landmark study of *The Poor and the Poorest* [1965]) and then by more sophisticated measures of relative poverty, such as the Blair government's child poverty threshold (set at 60 per cent of median equivalized household income). However the poverty line was calculated, the very notion that poverty was a matter of inadequate resources suggested that a guaranteed income might be the simplest way to eliminate it.

Secondly, Rhys-Williams linked basic income to the liberal case for consumer choice, and presented it as an alternative to the subsidies and benefits in kind which proliferated in Britain and elsewhere during the 1940s. Her preference for cash transfers chimed with the critique of collective provision which had emerged among mainstream neoclassical economists in the wake of the socialist calculation debate, and was most clearly voiced by Milton Friedman and George Stigler in the United States and James Meade and Alan Peacock in Britain.[22] Where earlier welfare economists such as A. C. Pigou had feared that a basic income would reduce work incentives, post-war economists were more concerned by the allocative

[20] Ian Gazeley, *Poverty in Britain, 1900–1965* (Basingstoke: Macmillan, 2003); J. H. Veit-Wilson, 'Paradigms of Poverty: A Rehabilitation of B.S. Rowntree', *Journal of Social Policy* 15, no. 1 (1986): 69–99.

[21] José Harris, 'From Poor Law to Welfare State? A European Perspective', in *The Political Economy of British Historical Experience, 1688–1914*, eds. Donald Winch and Patrick K. O'Brien (Oxford: Oxford University Press, 2002), 409–37, at 437; Alice O'Connor, *Poverty Knowledge: Social Science, Social Policy, and the Poor in Twentieth-Century U.S. History* (Princeton: Princeton University Press, 2001), 214.

[22] Milton Friedman and George J. Stigler, *Roofs or Ceilings? The Current Housing Problem* (Irvington-on-Hudson: Foundation for Economic Education, 1946); Peter Sloman, *Transfer State: The Idea of a Guaranteed Income and the Politics of Redistribution in Modern Britain* (Oxford: Oxford University Press, 2019), 29–60.

inefficiency of food subsidies and other forms of state provision: as Meade put it in *Planning and the Price Mechanism* (1948), the 'method of control by the quantitative allocation of resources ... is bound to be clumsy, inefficient and wasteful as compared with a properly functioning price system'.[23] In a Cold War context, this defence of market pricing was overlaid by a politically charged assault on the Attlee government's 'paternalism' (as symbolized by Douglas Jay's incautious claim that 'the gentleman in Whitehall knows best') and the suggestion that consumer choice was a form of democratic freedom, which allowed citizens to give expression to their own preferences and values.[24]

Thirdly, Rhys-Williams presented basic income as a solution to the practical problems which emerged from the growth of income tax and the overlap between tax collection and the welfare system. The tax threshold was reduced during the Second World War to help curtail private consumption, as Keynes had recommended in *How to Pay for the War* (1940), and the number of income tax payers rose from 3.8 million in 1938–1939 to 14.5 million a decade later (and 21.4 million by 1978–1979).[25] The Inland Revenue introduced PAYE in 1944 as a way of deducting tax at source from weekly wage-earners, but many policy-makers were concerned by the way tax deductions interacted with National Insurance and means-tested benefit entitlements. Rhys-Williams' proposal for a flat-rate income tax and universal cash allowances held out a promise of simplification which would become increasingly attractive over time as a way of reducing administrative costs and removing perverse incentives.

Basic Income in Post-War Social Policy

Juliet Rhys-Williams' campaign culminated in her appearance before the Royal Commission on the Taxation of Profits and Income, set up by the Attlee government in 1951, which was asked to consider the effectiveness of 'the present system of personal allowances, reliefs and rates of tax as a

[23] A. C. Pigou, *The Economics of Welfare*, 4th ed. (London: Macmillan, 1932), part IV, chap. 10; J. E. Meade, *Planning and the Price Mechanism: The Liberal-Socialist Solution* (London: George Allen & Unwin, 1948), 7.

[24] Richard Toye, 'The "Gentleman in Whitehall" Reconsidered: Douglas Jay's Views on Economic Planning and Consumer Choice, 1937–1947', *Labour History Review* 67, no. 2 (2002): 187–204.

[25] Tom Clark and Andrew Dilnot, *Long-Term Trends in British Taxation and Spending* (London: Institute for Fiscal Studies, 2002), 5.

means of distributing the tax burden fairly among the individual members of the community' and took evidence on 'whether it would be advantageous to link income tax with social security payments and contributions'.[26] To Rhys-Williams' chagrin, however, the Royal Commission insisted that the potential social advantages of basic income were beyond its terms of reference, and concluded that 'the proposal for general cash payments without regard to means, need or circumstance' was 'contrary to the generally accepted principle that, apart from family allowances, cash payments by the State should be confined to those who suffer an involuntary loss of earnings'.[27]

Despite this dismissive verdict, Rhys-Williams' energetic campaigning helped establish her scheme as the paradigmatic form of basic income in British politics. James Meade discussed her 'exceedingly stimulating proposal' in *Planning and the Price Mechanism*, and a host of other economists and social policy experts also engaged with her ideas. For instance, Alan Peacock and his LSE colleague Nancy Seear (later a senior Liberal peer) helped work up a version of the scheme for the Liberal Party and gave evidence to the Royal Commission, whilst Roy Harrod endorsed the Rhys-Williams scheme in a 1949 article, Barbara Wootton urged the Labour Party to take it seriously, and the sociologist Michael Young wrote to Rhys-Williams to ask for further details.[28] After Rhys-Williams' death in 1964, her son Brandon picked up where she left off, using his position as Conservative MP for South Kensington (1968–1988) to canvass support for the idea. Sir Brandon Rhys-Williams argued that the replacement of tax allowances with cash transfers should be seen 'as a Business Efficiency Exercise' which would produce 'great administrative savings'. In common with Friedman and other neoliberal thinkers, such as Arthur Seldon of the Institute of Economic Affairs, he also hoped that an expanded system of

[26] Cmd. 9105, *Royal Commission on the Taxation of Profits and Income. Second Report* (London: Her Majesty's Stationery Office, 1954), 2, 9.

[27] Cmd. 9105, *Royal Commission ... Second Report*, 17.

[28] *Minutes of Evidence*, 39–46, 49–59; Alan Peacock, *Anxious to Do Good: Learning to be an Economist the Hard Way* (Exeter: Imprint Academic, 2010), 45–85; Roy Harrod, 'The Outlook for 1949', *World Review* (Jan. 1949): 15–19; Barbara Wootton, 'The Labour Party and Social Services', *Political Quarterly* 24, no. 1 (1953), 55–67, at 64–65; and Michael Young to Juliet Rhys-Williams, April 25, May 12 and May 18, 1952, Rhys-Williams papers, J 2/6.

cash transfers would make it easier to open up public services such as health and education to the private sector.[29]

Tax-benefit integration attracted wide interest across the political spectrum in the wake of the 1960s 'rediscovery of poverty', as both Labour and Conservative governments came under pressure from the Child Poverty Action Group (CPAG) to provide more help for low-paid working families with children. As I have shown elsewhere, much of this attention focussed on Friedman's NIT, which seemed to be cheaper than UBI and derived glamour from the New Jersey/Pennsylvania Income Maintenance Experiment (1968–1972) and the prospect of computerization.[30] Even so, Rhys-Williams' scheme continued to shape British policy debates at two levels. Firstly, it provided a starting point for economic analysis of how a universal 'social dividend' might work and how far it would eliminate poverty, most notably in Tony Atkinson's first book, *Poverty in Britain and the Reform of Social Security* (1969).[31] Atkinson modelled the impact of replacing the social security system with a basic income set at the Supplementary Benefit level, paid for by a flat-rate tax of 50 per cent on all other income, and found that this would benefit single people earning up to about £1000 a year and families with children earning up to about £2000 a year, plus the very rich, at the expense of those in between.[32] Although he found the idea of a social dividend logical and attractive, Atkinson feared that the tax rate involved could reduce work incentives and encourage tax evasion, and so came down in favour of a piecemeal approach—for instance, combining National Insurance with

[29] Sir Brandon Rhys-Williams, 'Notes on Reform of Redistribution of Income as a Business-Efficiency Exercise', 13 May 1969, Conservative Party Archive, CRD 3/7/26/11, Bodleian Library, Oxford; see also Sir Brandon Rhys-Williams, *The New Social Contract* (London: Conservative Political Centre, 1968).

[30] Sloman, *Transfer State*, 95–124.

[31] Tony Atkinson to C. V. Brown, 1 Oct. 1969, Atkinson papers, 03/01, BLPES. Atkinson recalled later in life that he was 'first prompted to look at basic income schemes by James Meade', who introduced him to Juliet Rhys-Williams' work and put him in touch with Sir Brandon Rhys-Williams: A. B. Atkinson, *Public Economics in Action: The Basic Income/Flat Tax Proposal* (Oxford: Oxford University Press, 1995), x. Atkinson also analysed a Political and Economic Planning pamphlet by Chuck Brown and Diane Dawson, which itself drew on Juliet Rhys-Williams' work: C. V. Brown and D. A. Dawson, *Personal Taxation, Incentives and Tax Reform* (London: Political and Economic Planning, 1969).

[32] A. B. Atkinson, *Poverty in Britain and the Reform of Social Security* (Cambridge: Cambridge University Press, 1969), 169–84.

minimum wage legislation and CPAG's plan for a universal child benefit.[33] Atkinson's friend and mentor James Meade also returned to Rhys-Williams' ideas, for instance in his 1972 Sidney Ball Lecture on 'Poverty in the Welfare State' and in the investigation into 'The Structure and Reform of Direct Taxation' (1975–1978) which he chaired for the Institute for Fiscal Studies (IFS).[34] Meade was still instinctively attracted to a 'social dividend' approach, but his colleagues on the IFS committee—including Atkinson—seem to have persuaded him that a 'New Beveridge scheme' based on improved social insurance benefits was a more realistic option.[35]

Alongside this emerging academic interest in UBI, Rhys-Williams' scheme also influenced moves towards tax-benefit integration within government, particularly once it became clear (in 1969–1970) that a means-tested NIT could not be delivered through the PAYE system.[36] The Heath government's special adviser Arthur Cockfield, who had written a 'hatchet job' on the Rhys-Williams proposals as an Inland Revenue official in the early 1950s, dug out her plan in 1971 and used it as the basis for a 'Tax Credit Scheme' in which refundable weekly tax credits would be netted off against income tax liability.[37] Cockfield was adamant that his goal was tax simplification, not poverty relief; the credits would only be large enough to replace tax allowances, not social security benefits, and he proposed to restrict the scheme to employees and those entitled to National Insurance benefits (who, with their families, made up 90 per cent of the population) in order to avoid giving 'the vagrants, the drifters, the drop-outs, [and] the petty criminals ... a weekly handout'.[38] Nevertheless, the scheme would have replaced family allowances and the means-tested Family Income Supplement, and the Heath government took it up in a 1972 Green Paper as a way of re-establishing its 'One Nation' credentials.[39]

[33] Atkinson, *Poverty in Britain*, 185–95.

[34] James Meade, 'Poverty in the Welfare State', *Oxford Economic Papers* 24, no. 3 (1972): 289–326; J. E. Meade, *The Structure and Reform of Direct Taxation. Report of a Committee chaired by Professor J. E. Meade* (London: George Allen & Unwin, 1978), 269–307.

[35] See correspondence on Social Security and Income Maintenance chapter in Meade papers, 6/9, BLPES.

[36] Sloman, *Transfer State*, 119–21, 125–43.

[37] Peacock, *Anxious to Do Good*, 78; F. A. Cockfield, 'A Negative Income Tax', August 2, 1971, T227/3335, The National Archives, Kew.

[38] Cockfield, 'A Negative Income Tax'.

[39] Cmnd. 5116, *Proposal for a Tax-Credit System* (London: Her Majesty's Stationery Office, 1972).

Plans for legislation were dropped after Labour won the February 1974 election, but Cockfield's scheme 'lived on in a strange half-life' during the late 1970s, as Florence Sutcliffe-Braithwaite has noted, and came to function as a concrete example of what tax-benefit integration might achieve.[40] Some Tory MPs continued to hanker after the idea during the Thatcher years.[41] As in the 1950s and 1960s, these discussions of integration tended to foreground the administrative logic rather than the principle of universalism, and so blurred the relationship between tax credits, UBI, and NIT schemes.

Enter the Radicals

With the onset of deindustrialization, however, basic income began to attract support from beyond the ranks of the liberal economists and welfare experts who had taken an interest in the idea during the early post-war decades. The Claimants' Unions movement, which began in Birmingham in 1968–1969 and grew rapidly as unemployment mounted in the early 1970s, called for a 'Guaranteed Minimum Income' to liberate unemployed workers and other claimants from the complexity of the Supplementary Benefit system. The US welfare rights movement seems to have been an important inspiration, and the idea of a guaranteed income may have picked up from American sources.[42] For claimants' activists—perhaps especially the unmarried and deserted mothers who featured prominently in many unions—the principle of *unconditionality* was particularly important: as Bill Jordan put it, claimants were 'opposed in principle to the Social Security system, its means tests, its humiliating claims procedure and its authoritarian powers' and sought the dignity of 'a real living income ... that would not have to be crawled and grovelled for at the feet of a bureaucratic overlord'.[43] Some members also took the idea of UBI into the Women's Liberation Movement, where they sought to tap into the controversy stirred up by Selma James' 'Wages for Housework'

[40] Florence Sutcliffe-Braithwaite, 'Neoliberalism and Morality in the Making of Thatcherite Social Policy', *Historical Journal* 55, no. 2 (2012): 497–520, at 507.

[41] Minutes of first meeting of Tax and Social Security Policy Group, November 24, 1982, and report, March 31, 1983, Conservative Party Archive, CRD 4/4/200.

[42] Hilary Rose, 'Up Against the Welfare State: The Claimant Unions', *Socialist Register* 10 (1973): 179–203.

[43] Bill Jordan, *Paupers: The Making of the New Claiming Class* (London: Routledge & Kegan Paul, 1973), 73.

campaign and to present it as a way of securing 'legal and financial independence for all women'.[44]

Alongside the Claimants' Unions, basic income was also taken up by some of the environmentalist groups that emerged in the wake of the 1973 oil crisis. Tony Whittaker and Teddy Goldsmith's PEOPLE—the earliest forerunner of the Green Party—included a 'National Income Scheme' in *A Manifesto for Survival* (1974), and the idea became a central plank of Ecology Party policy during the 1970s and 1980s, on the grounds that 'basic material security for all' was a 'necessary precondition' for a shift to a zero-growth economy.[45] This vision of a post-industrial economic model based on job-sharing, small-scale cooperatives, and greater self-sufficiency gained a wider audience through the 'Turning Point' network which James Robertson and Alison Pritchard set up in 1975, and became increasingly resonant during the 1980s as mass unemployment prompted a wide-ranging debate over 'the future of work'.[46] Management theorist Charles Handy, for instance, argued that 'the employment society' had 'overstretched itself', and policy-makers needed 'to look beyond employment to a society which is less job-fixated in its values, its structures and its systems'.[47] Handy suggested that a basic income could help ease the transition to 'new patterns of work', including a shorter working week, greater self-employment, and a more equal distribution of unpaid care and domestic work.[48]

It was in this context that BIRG was established in 1984, sparked by a discussion of basic income schemes at a conference held by the National Council for Voluntary Organisations (NCVO).[49] The head of the NCVO's

[44] Toru Yamamori, 'A Feminist Way to Basic Income: Claimants Unions and Women's Liberation Movements in 1970s Britain', *Basic Income Studies* 9, no. 1–2 (2014): 1–24.

[45] PEOPLE, *A Manifesto for Survival* (Coventry: PEOPLE, 1974); Ecology Party, *Manifesto for a Sustainable Society* (Stroud: BIJA Press, 1978), 18.

[46] For instance, the Turning Point network held a day conference on 'The Redistribution of Work' in London in November 1980, with talks by Charles Handy, Sheila Rothwell, and James Robertson, and Annie Miller spoke about 'A Guaranteed Income' at a Turning Point meeting in November 1984: see Turning Point, *The Redistribution of Work* (Ironbridge: Turning Point, 1981), and *Turning Point Newsletter*, August 1984, available online at http://www.jamesrobertson.com/turningpoint.htm.

[47] Charles Handy, *The Future of Work: A Guide to a Changing Society* (Oxford: Basil Blackwell, 1984), xi.

[48] Handy, *The Future of Work*, ix.

[49] Annie Miller, interview with the author, April 17, 2018. Miller recalled that the NCVO conference on 'Income Maintenance Systems' took place in autumn 1983, and that the idea of forming a research group took shape in the pub afterwards; the group adopted the title of BIRG in July 1984.

Policy Analysis Unit, Peter Ashby, saw UBI as a way of tackling 'growing defeatism' about mass unemployment, and secured NCVO support for a three-year research project to 'establish whether a Basic Income scheme would be feasible and whether the costs to be borne by taxation would be capable of commanding a broad consensus'.[50] The founding members of BIRG came from a diverse array of backgrounds: for instance, Bill Jordan was a sociologist who had worked closely with the Claimants' Unions, whilst the Scottish economist Annie Miller had reacted against the National Insurance system on feminist grounds, and the physicist Keith Roberts had drawn up a 'national dividend scheme' whilst working at the UK nuclear research laboratory at Culham.[51] Ashby also used his contacts to draw in a wide range of sympathizers from across the voluntary sector, such as Evelyn McEwen of Age Concern (who subsequently became the group's chair) and Cathy Ashton of Business in the Community (later a Labour peer and European Commissioner). The group's main driving force, however, was Hermione Parker, a St Andrews PPE graduate who was working as a research assistant to Sir Brandon Rhys-Williams and had already helped him update his mother's basic income scheme for a Select Committee inquiry in 1982–1983.[52] Most of the group's members leaned to the left, but Parker's political instincts were conservative and market-oriented. She dismissed proposals for a living wage as 'inflationary non-sense', and hoped that UBI could restore full employment by helping to create 'a more flexible labour market' in which 'wage bargaining would concentrate on questions of profitability, competition and equity' instead of larger conceptions of social justice.[53]

BIRG defined basic income as a universal, unconditional cash benefit and strongly criticized selective income support schemes, such as the IFS's proposals for *The Reform of Social Security* (1984) and the means-tested Income Support and Family Credit systems created by the Thatcher government's 1986 Social Security Act.[54] The group also built links with other European basic income enthusiasts, such as Philippe Van Parijs, and

[50] Peter Ashby, *Social Security After Beveridge – What Next?* (London: National Council for Voluntary Organisations, 1984), 1; *BIRG Bulletin* no. 2 (1984): 1.

[51] Miller, interview; Keith Roberts, *Automation, Unemployment and the Distribution of Income* (Maastricht: European Centre for Work and Society, 1982).

[52] Malcolm Torry, interview with the author, March 30, 2017; 'Mimi' (Hermione Parker) to Sir Brandon Rhys-Williams, 'BIG scheme', August 3, 1982, Rhys-Williams papers, B 8/6.

[53] Parker, 'The "BIG" way to Full Employment'.

[54] 'Note of meeting of the Basic Income Group, Friday 13 July [1984] at 11.30am at NCVO', Annie Miller papers (private collection); 'Why Basic Incomes and Not a Negative Income Tax', *BIRG Bulletin* no. 2 (1984): 3.

played a leading role in the development of BIEN.[55] The main focus of the research programme, however, was on establishing 'whether it is possible to fund acceptable levels of basic income at acceptable rates of tax', since without 'detailed costings' UBI faced a 'credibility gap'.[56] Parker persuaded Tony Atkinson and Holly Sutherland to run her scheme through their TAXMOD microsimulation model at the LSE in order to assess the cost and distributional effects of different proposals.[57] It quickly became apparent that replacing the whole benefit system with UBI would either require a tax rate of about 70 per cent or impose unacceptable losses on lower-income households. As early as December 1984, Parker concluded that 'a full-blown social dividend or basic income scheme is not a viable option', and that any feasible UBI would have to be combined with a means-tested Housing Benefit and extra payments for the elderly and disabled.[58] BIRG revised its constitution in 1987–1988 to make it clear that basic income would not necessarily be 'sufficient to meet basic living costs', and Parker worked up a detailed scheme for 'partial basic incomes' of £26 a week, which she set out in her book *Instead of the Dole* (1989).[59]

Parker's focus on making UBI realistic and affordable allowed her to present it as a mainstream supply-side measure, which could help support the government's efforts to promote the expansion of service-sector jobs. Liberal Democrat leader Paddy Ashdown took basic income up in the late 1980s, and James Meade reiterated his support for the idea as a way of managing the distributional effects of labour-market deregulation.[60]

[55] Anne G. Miller, ed., *Basic Income: Proceedings of the First International Conference on Basic Income, Louvain-la-Neuve, Belgium, 4–6 September 1986* (Antwerp: Basic Income European Network, 1986).

[56] Hermione Parker, 'Costing Basic Incomes', December 4, 1984, Rhys-Williams papers, B 8/8.

[57] Tony Atkinson and Holly Sutherland, 'Notes on Social Dividend Schemes', February 1983, and Tony Atkinson, 'Note on Tax/Benefit Models', March 1, 1985, Atkinson papers, 04/37. Atkinson was happy to provide advice for BIRG but declined to become a member: Tony Atkinson to Peter Ashby, November 14, 1984, Atkinson papers, 04/37.

[58] Parker, 'Costing Basic Incomes'.

[59] Tony Walter, 'What Are Basic Incomes?', *BIRG Bulletin* no. 8 (1988): 3–5; Hermione Parker, *Instead of the Dole: An Enquiry into Integration of the Tax and Benefit Systems* (Abingdon: Routledge, 1989).

[60] Paddy Ashdown, *Citizen's Britain: A Radical Agenda for the 1990s* (London: Fourth Estate, 1989); J. E. Meade, *Fifteen Propositions Concerning the Building of an Equitable, Full-Employment, Non-Inflationary, Free-Enterprise Economy* (London: Employment Policy Institute, 1993).

Meade also returned to the idea of an asset-based social dividend, which he had previously floated in the 1930s and again in *Efficiency, Equality and the Ownership of Property* (1964), and suggested that it could help give citizens a share in profits at a time when automation and other structural changes were reducing the wage share. As Martin O'Neill and Stuart White have noted, however, Alaska's oil-based dividend fund attracted surprisingly little interest from British campaigners.[61] The *Financial Times* columnist Samuel Brittan called for 'a people's stake in North Sea oil' in 1978, but his plan was based on issuing free shares—a distinctly individualist approach to 'property-owning democracy'.[62]

Though Hermione Parker's campaign seemed to be gaining traction during the early 1990s, when BIRG changed its name to the Citizen's Income Trust and used a grant from the Joseph Rowntree Charitable Trust to set up an office at the LSE, it ultimately fizzled out for two main reasons. Firstly, both Labour and the Liberal Democrats—stung by the Conservatives' 'tax bombshell' campaign in the 1992 general election—concluded that a major expansion of universal benefits was prohibitively expensive.[63] Means-tested benefits for working families, such as the tax credits system which Gordon Brown introduced after 1997, offered a much cheaper way of reducing child poverty and could be phased in incrementally. Secondly, many politicians worried that giving citizens 'something for nothing' would be politically toxic and risked encouraging welfare dependency. Tony Atkinson, who served on the Commission on Social Justice set up by Labour leader John Smith in 1992–1994, felt that 'a major objection to basic income lies in its lack of conditionality', and developed a proposal for a 'participation income' in an attempt to address these concerns. As Atkinson pointed out, making cash payments conditional on an adult's willingness to work or make some form of 'social contribution' (such as 'approved forms of voluntary work' or 'caring for

[61] Martin O'Neill and Stuart White, 'James Meade, Public Ownership, and the Idea of a Citizens' Trust', *International Journal of Public Policy* 15, no. 1–2 (2019): 21–37.

[62] Samuel Brittan and Barry Riley, 'A people's stake in North Sea Oil', *Lloyds Bank Review*, April 1978: 1–18.

[63] Ruth Lister, interview with the author, July 18, 2018; Commission on Social Justice, *Social Justice: Strategies for National Renewal* (London: Vintage, 1994); Liberal Democrats, *Opportunity and Independence for All* (London: Liberal Democrats, 1994); Patrick Wintour, 'Tax and Benefits Plan Survives but "Utopian" Scheme Scrapped', *The Guardian*, September 22, 1994.

young, elderly or disabled dependents') 'would in fact be in line with the original proposal of Lady Rhys Williams' for a 'new social contract' between the citizen and the state.[64]

Parker's attention drifted away from the Citizen's Income Trust during the 1990s, as she threw herself into the work of the Family Budget Unit (1987–2011), reviving the empirical approach to minimum income standards which Rowntree had pioneered a century earlier. By the turn of the millennium, basic income had largely fallen off the mainstream policy agenda, and discussions of UBI were increasingly philosophical in nature—reflecting the influence of Philippe Van Parijs' conception of 'real freedom for all' in academic debates on distributive justice, together with engagement from political theorists such as Brian Barry and Stuart White.[65] These arguments over social rights have helped to set the case for basic income in a broader intellectual context. Even so, the pursuit of costed and realistic UBI schemes has continued to be a hallmark of the British debate. In particular, Malcolm Torry (who served as director of the Citizen's Income Trust, now the Citizen's Basic Income Trust, from 2001 to 2020) has taken up where Parker left off by using Holly Sutherland's EUROMOD tax-benefit model to simulate the effects of different proposals. Torry has used a trial and error approach to try to devise a scheme which is revenue-neutral, requires no more than a 3p increase in income tax rates, and avoids creating losses for low-income households at the point of implementation. Recently, Torry has calculated that the government could introduce a basic income of about £65 a week by eliminating the personal allowance, adding 3p to income tax rates, and charging the 12 per cent rate of employee's National Insurance contributions on all earnings. If existing social security benefits were left in place (but means-tested benefits were reduced to take account of the UBI), this would cut relative poverty by about one-third and lower the Gini coefficient for disposable income from 0.31 to 0.28.[66]

[64] A. B. Atkinson, 'Beveridge, the National Minimum and its Future in a European Context', in *Incomes and the Welfare State: Essays on Britain and Europe* (Cambridge: Cambridge University Press, 1995), 290–304, at 300, 301.

[65] Philippe Van Parijs, *Real Freedom for All: What (If Anything) Can Justify Capitalism?* (Oxford: Oxford University Press, 1995); Brian Barry, 'Real Freedom and Basic Income', *Journal of Political Philosophy* 4, no. 3 (1996): 242–76; Stuart White, *The Civic Minimum: On the Rights and Obligations of Economic Citizenship* (Oxford: Oxford University Press, 2003).

[66] Malcolm Torry, 'Static Microsimulation Research on Citizen's Basic Income for the UK: A Personal Summary and Further Reflections' (EUROMOD Working Paper EM13/19, University of Essex, Colchester, 2019).

Conclusion

The history of basic income campaigning in Britain has been a fragmented one, littered with gaps, connections not drawn, and long lulls in activity, and the historian must take care not to impose a misleading sense of coherence on it. It is not clear whether Juliet Rhys-Williams ever encountered Dennis Milner's work, or whether subsequent campaigners were fully aware of the 1940s debate. Nevertheless, as Tony Atkinson and Holly Sutherland have noted, it is hardly a stretch to trace a direct line of descent from Juliet Rhys-Williams, through her son Brandon, to Hermione Parker and BIRG.[67] At a deeper level, there have also been intellectual continuities in the way UBI has been conceptualized in the UK. In some ways it is surprising that the term 'basic income' only came into widespread use during the 1980s, because the parameters (and dysfunctions) of the tax and benefit systems had already structured discussions of the concept in Britain for more than thirty years. 'Social dividend' was always quite an odd label for a payment which was designed to be regular, predictable, and financed by income tax revenues.

British activists' focus on developing feasible schemes has helped establish UBI as a credible policy option, but it has also left it vulnerable to criticism. In particular, the notion that a 'fully-fledged' basic income should be high enough to meet subsistence needs has allowed critics to point to a 'basic income trilemma'. As Luke Martinelli has put it, UBI schemes are either 'inadequate, giving rise to unacceptable income losses among the poor; ... unaffordable, necessitating excessive and unsustainable tax increases; or ... compromise the very principles underlying BI'.[68] The Inland Revenue made the same point when it examined Rhys-Williams' proposals in 1951:

> If the scheme is satisfactory as social insurance the rate of tax required is so high as to be disincentive. If the rate of tax is kept down on incentive grounds, the benefits which can be given are too small to be effective as

[67] A. B. Atkinson and Holly Sutherland, 'Analysis of a Partial Basic Income Scheme', in A. B. Atkinson, *Poverty & Social Security* (Hemel Hempstead: Harvester Wheatsheaf, 1989), 327–35, at 327.

[68] Luke Martinelli, 'A Basic Income Trilemma: Affordability, Adequacy, and the Advantages of Radically Simplified Welfare', *Journal of Social Policy* 49, no. 3 (2020): 461–82, at 480.

> social security. No amount of arithmetical skill in constructing a scheme can provide any escape from this dilemma.[69]

This vulnerability has been exacerbated by the prominence given to static distributional analysis and 'head-count' measures of poverty which are based on a snapshot of family incomes at a given point in time. Universal benefits are always likely to be an expensive way of lifting poor households above a 'poverty line'. As a result, it has been difficult to sell basic income to policy-makers as a pragmatic and cost-effective response to labour-market change, as the trajectory of UK welfare policy since the 1980s has shown.

It may be significant, then, that the latest wave of support for basic income in Britain has been accompanied by signs of a shift in framing. The Royal Society for Arts, in particular, has emphasized the need to adopt a dynamic perspective which takes into account the ways in which UBI would empower individuals to make meaningful choices about work, training, creativity, and care responsibilities over time.[70] This offers a way out of the 'basic income trilemma' by providing a coherent rationale for a relatively modest weekly payment on the lines suggested by Parker and Torry. Even if it would not lift people out of poverty by itself, it would give them a stable source of income to fall back on, strengthening their ability to resist exploitation by employers and making it easier to move in and out of full-time work at different points in the life cycle. Reducing the 'cognitive load' of economic insecurity could also contribute to wider social policy goals by improving educational performance and health outcomes.[71]

Alongside this reframing, basic income has also shown signs of becoming increasingly politicized. At a time of mounting concern about automation, precarious work, and the growth of the 'gig economy', left-wing commentators and trade unionists have become more receptive to UBI as a way of liberating workers from the complexity of Universal Credit, and especially its system of work requirements and benefit sanctions. The

[69] *Minutes of Evidence*, 62.

[70] Anthony Painter, Jake Thorold and Jamie Cooke, *Pathways to Universal Basic Income: The Case for a Universal Basic Opportunity Fund* (London: Royal Society of Arts, 2018).

[71] Lisa A. Gennetian and Eldar Shafir, 'The Persistence of Poverty in the Context of Instability: A Behavioral Perspective', *Journal of Policy Analysis and Management*, 34, no. 4 (2015): 904–36.

growth of interest in basic income among Green Party, Scottish National Party, and even Labour Party politicians—particularly those with links to anti-austerity groups—is particularly striking. Such a politicization of UBI is not without its risks, since it is likely to make it harder to win support from the kind of liberals and conservatives who have traditionally shown an interest in tax-benefit integration in Britain. Even so, it could be a price worth paying for lifting the basic income debate out of a narrowly technocratic frame of reference and turning it into a central part of a new social policy paradigm.

CHAPTER 3

Basic Income in the United States, 1940–1972: How the 'fiscal revolution' Reshaped Social Policy

Daniel Zamora Vargas

During the summer of 1963, Wilbur H. Ferry, co-founder of the Center for the Study of Democratic Institutions—one of the most influential liberal think-tanks of the period—met up with some of his closest friends and fellow political activists in the Princeton office of Robert Oppenheimer.[1] Their idea was to discuss the writing of a political statement that would challenge how Americans were to think the future of work, social policy, or human rights in the 'age of abundance'. Packed in the room with Oppenheimer and Ferry, figures ranged from the economist and futurologist Robert Theobald to the leaders of the *Students for Democratic Society* (SDS) Todd Gitlin and Tom Hayden, who had just released the 'Port Huron Statement' a year before. What they would later publish as the

[1] James A. Ward, *Ferrytale. The Career of W.H. 'Ping' Ferry* (Stanford, CA: Stanford University Press, 2001), 93.

D. Zamora Vargas (✉)
Institut de sociologie, Université Libre de Bruxelles, Brussels, Belgium
e-mail: daniel.zamora.vargas@ulb.ac.be

P. Sloman et al. (eds.), *Universal Basic Income in Historical Perspective*, https://doi.org/10.1007/978-3-030-75706-9_3

'Manifesto for a Triple Revolution' emerged in part from the concern the group shared about the possible 'disappearance of work' and the specific challenge it constituted for liberals. For them, the entirety of the post-war 'industrial productive system' seemed 'no longer viable'. The left, as they saw it, needed to 'form a new consensus' centred around the realization that 'the traditional link between jobs and incomes [was] being broken'. An 'unqualified right to an income', inspired by Milton Friedman's Negative Income Tax, had now to 'take the place of the patchwork of welfare measures' in order to ensure 'that no citizen or resident of the United States actually starves'.[2] The idea of establishing (in Friedman's words) 'a floor below which no man's income ... could fall' would constitute one of the most distinctive innovations in the field of social policy.[3] To Ferry and his colleagues, 'new circumstances' demanded 'radically new strategies'.

With no less than thirty-four signatories—including Nobel Prize winners Linus Pauling and Gunnar Myrdal, socialist Norman Thomas, writer and social critic Dwight Macdonald, and major figures of the New Left such as Michael Harrington and James Boggs—the statement was sent to President Lyndon B. Johnson and immediately made it to the front page of *The New York Times*. Consecutively, proposals for a guaranteed income were the object of more than 500 editorials in the country, becoming a nationally publicized topic of discussion in the following years. In fact, the debate opened by the memorandum far exceeded Ferry's wildest expectations, with guaranteed income schemes receiving substantial popular support, including from the civil rights leader Martin Luther King Jr. By 1968, large-scale guaranteed income experiments were launched in several cities and the following year, Richard Nixon, who had initially presented himself as a firm opponent of the idea, tried to implement a version of it through his Family Assistance Plan (FAP). However, FAP never made it past the legislative brokering in the Senate.

Ferry attributed the phenomenal media attention which his memorandum received to the 'sheerest luck', since 'nothing [was] happening in D.C.' that weekend.[4] Retrospectively, his interpretation is, of course, unconvincing. It is however surprising that, apart from a few exceptions focused on the institutional career of the proposal, the history of basic income in the United States—and more specifically the intellectual setting

[2] Ad Hoc Committee on the Triple Revolution, *The Triple Revolution* (Santa Barbara: Ad Hoc Committee on the Triple Revolution, 1964).

[3] Friedman quoted in Austin C. Wehrwein, 'Economist Says Negative Tax Should Replace All Poverty Aid', in *The New York Times*, December 16, 1965, 41.

[4] Ward, *Ferrytale*, 94.

and conditions under which it captured the public imagination—has not yet been the object of much scholarly attention.[5] This chapter will explore what the political success of guaranteed income proposals in the 1960s tells us about wider debates over the place of the price mechanism and the role of the state in social policy. Far from dividing the economics profession into clear political camps, we will argue that these discussions were articulated along new lines, slowly promoting a 'fiscal revolution' in US public policy. This allowed the state to work increasingly through 'market friendly' cash transfers rather than collective provision and categorial relief, and to rely on the 'sovereign consumer' as the most efficient agent to allocate goods while preserving redistributive aims.

Milton Friedman's Negative Income Tax

The earliest version of what could be seen as a basic income in the United States is probably Milton Friedman's Negative Income Tax (NIT). While the proposal reached a large audience with Friedman's 1962 bestseller *Capitalism and Freedom*, he had articulated the idea well before.[6] The earliest known discussion was probably held when he was the principal economist at the Treasury Department's Division of Tax Research between 1941 and 1943, under Henry Morgenthau's administration.[7] While he had been concerned with the idea of guaranteeing a 'minimum standard

[5] See in particular Daniel P. Moynihan, *The Politics of a Guaranteed Income* (New York: Vintage, 1973); Leslie Lenkowsky, *Politics, Economics and Welfare Reform: Failure of Negative Income Tax in Britain and the United States* (New York: Rowman & Littlefield, 1986); Dennis J. Ventry, 'The Negative Income Tax: An Intellectual History', *Tax Notes*, 27 (1997); Alice O'Connor, *Poverty Knowledge* (Princeton, NJ: Princeton University Press, 2001); Romain D. Huret, *La fin de la pauvreté? Les experts sociaux et la Guerre contre la pauvreté aux États-Unis (1945–1974)* (Paris: Ed. de l'EHESS, 2008); Brian Steensland, *The Failed Welfare Revolution* (Princeton, NJ: University Press, 2008).

[6] For Friedman's thoughts on the origin of his idea see Milton Friedman, Letter to Christopher Green, January 20 1966, Box 201, File 201.6 and 7, Negative Income Tax 1966–80; Milton Friedman, Letter to Martin Bronfenbrenner, March 30 1964, Box 21, File 21.35; Milton Friedman, Letter to Mr. Melvin Rosen, March 4 1969, Box 201, File 201-9, Negative Income Tax 1965–1992. All at Milton Friedman papers, Hoover Institution.

[7] See: Milton Friedman, Letter to Dennis Ventry Jr., December 3, 1996, Milton Friedman papers, Hoover Institution, Box 201, File 201.7, Negative Income Tax 1966–2004; Christopher Green, *Negative Taxes and the Poverty* (Washington, DC: The Brookings Institution, 1967), 57; Robert J. Lampman, 'The decision to undertake the New Jersey experiment', in *The New Jersey Income-Maintenance Experiment*, Volume 1, eds. David Kershaw, Jerilyn Fair, (New York: Academic Press, 1977), xiii and Moynihan, *The Politics of a Guaranteed Income*, 50.

of living' since 1939, Friedman probably came up with the general idea through the very rich interwar English economic debates about welfare economics.[8] The idea, as he noted himself, 'was very much in the air' at that time.[9] Among the proposals he encountered as a young economist were the 'social dividend' put forward by Oskar Lange and then by Abba P. Lerner in the mid-1930s, the 'national dividend' promoted by the Social Credit theory of C. H. Douglas, and the utopian schemes advanced by Edward Bellamy in *Looking Backward*, which Friedman included in his courses at the University of Wisconsin between 1940 and 1941.[10]

Friedman's own NIT proposal, however, included several innovations that would later define our contemporary understanding of basic income and that were specifically shaped by his early work in federal agencies. There was his use of the fiscal system to shape social policy, his focus on cash rather than collective provision and, perhaps more importantly, the fact that his proposal was completely detached from any normative or contractual requirement towards work (either past or future). These specific features, articulated into a single and simple proposal, would constitute a distinctive innovation in the field of American social policy. The simplicity of it was extremely attractive: the moment someone falls under a certain level of income, they begin receiving the negative tax. This crucial innovation emerged essentially during the discussions Friedman had with the small team at the Treasury including Walter Heller, Louis Shere, and William Vickrey about the development of a federal withholding tax.[11] The

[8] See especially Milton Friedman, 'An objective method of determining a "Minimum Standard of Living"', 1939, Milton Friedman papers, Hoover Institution, Box 37, file 37.8.

[9] See Milton Friedman email to Eduardo Suplicy, April 11, 2000. Available online at https://usbig.net/newsletters/june.html, accessed December 10, 2020.

[10] See in particular Oskar Lange, 'On the Economic Theory of Socialism: Part I', *Review of Economic Studies*, 4, no. 1 (1936): 53–71. Later, both Stigler and Friedman published accounts of 'The Economics of Control' (1944) where Abba Lerner explains in detail the idea of a 'social dividend' he had taken from Lange but also about how it could be implemented through a 'negative tax'. Stigler is even thanked at the beginning of the book for 'reading the manuscript and correcting a number of errors'. See George J. Stigler, 'Reviewed Work: The Economics of Control: Principles of Welfare', *Political Science Quarterly*, 60, no. 1 (1945): 113–15; Milton Friedman, 'Lerner on the Economics of Control', *Journal of Political Economy*, 55, no. 5 (1947): 405–16. For Friedman's early use of these ideas, see Milton Friedman, *Lecture Notes at the University of Wisconsin*, October 1940, Box 75, file 5, Milton Friedman papers, Hoover Institution.

[11] Angus Burgin, *The Great Persuasion. Reinventing Free Markets since the Depression* (Cambridge, MA: Harvard University Press, 2012), 164.

idea arose, Friedman recalls, 'as part of the thinking about an appropriate structure of income tax which would take care of averaging fluctuating income over time'.[12] Indeed, for persons whose income rose and fell from one year to another, the system could make them pay more taxes than those receiving the same amount but whose income was steady. This problem was particularly acute for low-income workers, constantly moving from a zero-tax bracket to another. In order to compensate this inequality in treatment, Friedman conceived a 'negative income tax' in which during a bad year the taxpayer would receive rather than pay money to the Treasury.

Friedman's use of the tax system to this purpose wasn't however a contingent choice. It was during the war period that the US federal government shifted to mass taxation. If, by 1945 two-thirds of Americans were paying taxes, before the war taxpayers constituted only between 4 and 8 per cent of the working population.[13] As observed by Gary Gerstle, to finance the war, the government had to extract revenue from a large percentage of the population, helping to 'fundamentally alter the landscape of possibility for federal government activity'.[14] As such, as argued by Dennis Ventry, 'before World War II, the idea of negative income taxation was inconceivable'.[15] It was the war effort, overall, that brought more than fifty million new taxpayers onto the payrolls, making it seem that, when thinking about the distribution of income, it would be more efficient to use negative rates of taxation rather than complex welfare schemes. For the first time, fiscal policy was regarded as a proper tool for social policy. But when Heller, Vickrey, and Friedman discussed the scheme during the early 1940s, they rapidly considered it 'too innovative and experimental' and put it aside.[16]

Equality and the Price System

However, among economists, the Negative Income Tax would become a powerful idea. It promised to tackle poverty while preserving the price system, which had emerged as the crucial tool for an efficient allocation of

[12] Friedman, Letter to Mr. Melvin Rosen. This is also mentioned by Moynihan, *The Politics of a Guaranteed Income*, 50.

[13] Gary Gerstle, *Liberty and Coercion: The Paradox of American Government from the Founding to the Present* (Princeton, NJ: Princeton University Press, 2015), 270.

[14] Ibid., 272.

[15] Ventry, 'The Negative Income Tax: An Intellectual History', 2.

[16] Huret, *La fin de la pauvreté?*, 109.

resources in the aftermath of the socialist calculation debate of the 1920s.[17] It was in that context that cash transfers began to gain traction as a more suitable alternative to collective provision and heavy-handed state interventions within the market. While admitting 'strong egalitarian leanings' until the late 1940s, Friedman always consistently defended the centrality of the price system when it came to the allocation of goods.[18] 'Even with a completely competitive order', he argued at the 1947 Mont Pelerin Society in a panel about 'Taxation, Poverty and Income Distribution', there would always be a 'problem of poverty', and 'no democratic society is going to tolerate people starving to death, if there is food with which to feed them'.[19] This scepticism about laissez-faire was not unusual for him at that time. The same year, in a letter to the economist Robert de Fremery, he argued that 'almost no matter how you would define a free market, it will imply inequalities at the bottom of the scale which you, like I, would find socially intolerable'.[20] In fact, this line of thinking will be characteristic of the neoliberal project from the very beginning. As argued by Niklas Olsen, during the 1930s and 1940s many of the members of the neoliberal network were 'deeply suspicious of nineteenth-century capitalism' and associated unregulated markets with both widespread poverty and monopolies.[21] Friedman himself had been deeply influenced by Henry Simons' 1934 *Positive Program for Laissez-Faire* who advocated a more extensive role for the state in organizing and preserving the economic life. In other words, as the members of the conference put it, it meant to imagine 'the possibility of establishing minimum standards by means not inimical to initiative and the functioning of the market'.[22] His 'progressive negative

[17] On the socialist calculation debate and collective decision making see, among others, Peter Boettke, ed., *Socialism and the Market: The Socialist Calculation Debate Revisited* (London: Routledge, 2000); Beatrice Cherrier and Jean-Baptiste Fleury, 'Economists' Interest in Collective Decision after World War II: A History', *Public Choice*, 172, no. 1/2 (July 2017): 23–44.

[18] Milton Friedman, Letter to Martin Bronfenbrenner, July 18 1947, Box 21, File 21.35.

[19] Thanks to Peter Sloman for indicating to me the existence of this presentation. See 'Taxation, Poverty and Income Distribution. Tuesday April 8th, 8.30 p.m.', Mont Pèlerin Society records, Hoover Institution Archives, Stanford University, 5.12 Meeting File—Mont Pèlerin, Minutes, 1947.

[20] Milton Friedman, Letter to Robert de Fremery, December 18, 1947, Milton Friedman papers, Hoover Institution, Box 25, File 25.15

[21] Niklas Olsen, *The Sovereign Consumer: A New Intellectual History of Neoliberalism* (Cham, Switzerland: Palgrave Macmillan Springer, 2019), 128–9.

[22] Friedman, 'Taxation, Poverty and Income Distribution'.

taxation' could then work as 'a substitute, not as an addition, to present social policy'. 'The major fault of the collectivist philosophy', Friedman usually argued, 'is not in its objectives' but rather 'in the means'. 'Failures to recognize the difficulty of the economic problem of efficiency', he continued, 'led to readiness to discard the price system without an adequate substitute and to a belief that it would be easy to do much better by a central plan'.[23] The idea, while being received with scepticism by some, was then seen, to quote Karl Popper, as 'an attractive alternative to socialism', a way to deal with the poverty generated by capitalism while preserving its fundamental mechanism.[24]

More important, perhaps, was the series of lectures Friedman gave at Wabash College in 1956, where he argued that the entire architecture of the Welfare State was, in fact, designed to aggravate things for the poor. It was not designed for them, but for privileged and unionized workers, who couldn't be described as 'poor' by any standard. In Friedman's view, minimum wage laws were creating unemployment, Social Security was transferring money from the poor to the rich and public housing was an essentially a 'paternalistic' programme aggravating the problem it was designed to solve. All the New Deal policies were directed in his view 'against the symptoms', but 'the real problem' was 'poverty'.[25] His argument turned the common sense about poverty on its head. If we used to think that poverty was symptom of low wages, bad housing and irregular work, Friedman had managed to argue that it was in fact the other way around. As he wrote in an exchange with the Keynesian economist Don Patinkin, 'the social costs that are ordinarily attributed to poor housing are really the social costs of poverty'. 'What they justify', he followed, 'is a program of establishing a minimum income and seeking to eliminate at least certain kinds of poverty'.[26] Friedman's conjecture was simple: rather than working through the categorical order of the New Deal, he advocated 'a program directed at helping the poor … as people not as members of particular occupational groups or age groups or wage-rate groups or labor organizations or

[23] Milton Friedman, 'Neoliberalism and Its Prospects', *Farmand* (1951): 89–93.

[24] Friedman, 'Taxation, Poverty and Income Distribution'.

[25] Milton Friedman, 'The Distribution of Income and the Welfare Activities of Government", Lecture, Wabash College, (1956), 7. Available online at https://miltonfriedman.hoover.org/friedman_images/Collections/2016c21/MFlecture_06_1956_5.pdf (accessed 10 Dec. 2020).

[26] Milton Friedman, Letter to Don Patinkin, November 8 1948, Box 31, File 31.24.

industries'.[27] Whether you had 'egalitarian' aims or not, the point was to rely on 'the price system for distribution of goods' and, if confronted by undesirable outcomes, to 'achieve changes in the distribution of income by general measures superimposed on the price system'.[28] Within such a framework, readers are more than able to apprehend the interest of a NIT. As argued by Friedman, such a programme was not only 'directed specifically at the problem of poverty' but 'while operating through the market' would 'not distort the market or impede its functioning'.[29] The economic planning that had gained traction during war time rapidly became something to avoid among economists, in favour of a conception of equality organized instead through 'market friendly' cash transfers. The new line of 'poverty' under which a citizen was to receive the NIT, then, operated *under* the market rather than *against* the market.

During that period, while remaining marginal, the idea fizzled among fiscal economists in small circles clustered around state administrations and economics seminars. It was finally made public for the first time in 1946 when Milton Friedman, George Stigler and Walter Heller were all teaching at the University of Minnesota. Stigler had published his famous paper on 'The economics of minimum wage legislation', and Heller advocated the scheme in his courses.[30] While it did not immediately reach the broader public, during the following years it rapidly attracted an increasing number of economists as an interesting alternative to welfare programmes and state regulations. For example, during the 1950s, several economic textbooks mentioned the previous scheme proposed by Juliet Rhys-Williams, and public finance textbooks by economists such as Earl Rolf and James Buchanan talked about the 'amalgamation of direct taxation with social insurance' to provide a guaranteed income.[31] But what is perhaps the most articulated version of the idea was given by the econo-

[27] Milton Friedman, 'The Distribution of Income', 7.

[28] Milton Friedman, Letter to Martin Bronfenbrenner, July 18 1947, Box 21, File 21.35.

[29] Friedman, 'The Distribution of Income', 7.

[30] George J. Stigler, 'The Economics of Minimum Wage Legislation', *The American Economic Review* 36, no. 3 (June 1946): 358–365; Walter Heller, *New Dimensions of Political Economy* (Cambridge, MA: Harvard University Press, 1966), 115.

[31] William D. Grampp and Emanuel T. Weiler, *Economic Policy: Readings in Political Economy* (Homewood, IL: Richard D. Irwin, 1953), 284–292; H. S. Booker, 'Lady Rhys Williams' Proposal for the Amalgation of Direct Taxation with Social Insurance', *Economic Journal*, 56, no. 222 (June 1946): 230–243; Earl Rolph and George Break, *Public Finance*, (New York: Ronald Press, 1961), 404; James Buchanan, *The Public Finances: An Introductory Textbook* (Homewood, IL: Richard D. Irwin, 1965), 157–58.

mist Robert R. Schultz in 1952.[32] In his dissertation, Shultz argued that the post-war welfare state and its 'categorical relief' had become an 'oppressive administration', 'often highly inequitable and inadequate for the relief of poverty' and a 'waste' of money affecting 'morale and incentive' among beneficiaries.[33] This situation created the need to call for a complete re-examination of these institutions and possibly a fresh approach to a solution for the problem of poverty.[34] To 'replace' New Deal programmes, Shultz advocated for what he called 'continuous taxation'. The idea was similar to the one of Friedman, but instead of receiving the negative income *after* taxes, 'every person' would receive *up front* 'a minimum subsistence income' and only then pay taxes 'above this subsidy', making it similar to our contemporary notion of basic income. But depending on where the 'break-even point' was set, both systems could lead to the exact same outcome in terms of income distribution. The difference is important from a symbolic and political point of view but not from the standpoint of economics. As Friedman himself later argued, 'a basic or citizen's income is not an alternative to a negative income tax. It is simply another way to introduce a negative income tax if it is accompanied with a positive income tax with no exemption.'[35]

Guaranteed Incomes Against the New Deal Order

While the idea became relatively popular among economists and policy makers during the 1950s, it took another decade to slowly overcome the dominant vision shaped by the New Deal. The income-centred approach was indeed philosophically at odds with the assumptions on which Keynesian programmes were founded. Public services, labour market regulation, and full employment policies were widely preferred to simple cash transfers. New Deal policies were organized around the idea that the inherent failures of the market stipulated the need for an interventionist state capable of reducing market dependency, shrinking income gaps, regulating the labour market, and increasing economic growth in order to reach full employment. Of course, these policies included cash transfers like

[32] Robert Rudolph Schutz, 'Transfer Payments and Income Inequality', (PhD diss., University of California, Berkeley, 1952).

[33] Ibid., 11.

[34] Ibid., 5.

[35] See Friedman email to Eduardo Suplicy.

unemployment benefits and pension schemes. But those transfers were embedded in a broader reorganization of the labour market. Unemployment benefits being then, not only cash or 'anti-poverty' transfers, but also a tool to decasualize labour. Until the early 1960s, as argued by Alice O'Connor, 'poverty, as such, was not yet seen as a distinctive social problem, much less as the target of a concerted government attack'.[36] In that configuration, the logical remedy for an affliction such as 'poverty' was the extension of welfare programmes and economic growth eventually eradicating it sooner or later. The question then was essentially treatable through classical Keynesian policies and within the existing institutions. A representative example of this perspective could be found in Wilbur J. Cohen, himself a central figure in the creation and expansion of the American welfare state and Welfare Secretary under Kennedy and Johnson. What was needed, he argued in 1957 at a conference at the University of Wisconsin, was 'more schools, more roads, more hospitals beds, and more housing. We want more teachers, more doctors, nurses, social workers.'[37] The state, using ambitious service-based programmes, had to guarantee a 'minimum level of living' that would in turn increase the national product.[38]

The view was quite common in the administration at the time. Even at the height of the poverty debate, Johnson, who grew up in poverty in a small farmhouse in Texas and had been an active New Dealer, always expressed strong opposition to a reorientation around cash transfers. This president, who had been deeply influenced by the legacy of the People's Party and whose grandfather had run on the Populist ticket, described himself as 'a Roosevelt New Dealer'; Walter Heller recalled that he imagined his programme on poverty to involve 'bulldozers', 'tractors' and 'heavy machinery', a service rather than cash-centred programme.[39] 'Our chief weapon', he declared in his 1964 State of the Union, 'will be better schools, and better health, and better homes, and better training, and better job opportunities to help more Americans, especially young Americans, escape from squalor and misery and unemployed rolls'. 'Very often' he added, 'a lack of jobs and money is not the cause of poverty, but the symptom. The cause may lie deeper—in our failure to give our fellow citizens a fair chance

[36] O'Connor, *Poverty Knowledge*, 139.

[37] Edward D. Berkowitz, *Mr. Social Security: The Life of Wilbur J. Cohen* (Lawrence, KS: University Press of Kansas, 1995), 110.

[38] Berkowitz, *Mr. Social Security*, 146.

[39] Robert A. Caro, *The Years of Lyndon Johnson. Volume 4, The Passage of Power* (New York: Vintage Books, 2012), 540; Huret, *La fin de la pauvreté?*, 119.

to develop their own capacities, in a lack of education and training, in a lack of medical care and housing, in a lack of decent communities in which to live and bring up their children.'[40] In this framework, it was clear that the post-war welfare architecture was not yet perceived as a problem. Its legacy, as argued by Leslie Lenkowsky, 'seemed above politics'.[41]

However, while this vision remained dominant until the mid-1960s, the climate had begun to change by the late-1950s. The 'slowdown' of poverty reduction and the unexpected increase of the recipients of the Aid to Dependent Children (ADC) programme slowly raised doubts about classical post-war remedies.[42] An increasing number of younger social scientists, generally trained in economics rather than social work like Robert Lampman, progressively collected data giving a grimmer view of the efficiency of the existing institutions.[43] Indeed, while it was largely expected that the assistance programme would naturally disappear with economic growth and the expansion of social security, the data gathered by these new social scientists was rather bleak. Lampman in particular was extremely pessimistic about post-war hopes of an upcoming 'people's capitalism' in 'a classless homogenized state of affluence'.[44] Focusing very early on the study of income distribution, he thought that the conclusions of Simon Kuznets concerning the decrease of inequality were misleading,[45] In 1958, his claims began to draw more attention after the public success of *The Affluent Society*, in which John K. Galbraith argued that poverty had become 'insular', composed essentially of isolated 'islands' in rural areas and urban ghettos.[46] Struck by what they felt was an overoptimistic view, several economists began to collect more systematic data to measure the extent of poverty in an 'affluent' America. The next year, Lampman showed that the 'exit from poverty' had considerably slowed during the late-1950s, putting in question the efficiency of existing welfare

[40] Lyndon B. Johnson, *Annual Message to the Congress on the State of the Union*, January 8, 1964.

[41] Lenkowsky, *Politics, Economics and Welfare Reform*, 16.

[42] Moynihan, *The Politics of Guaranteed Income*, 81–86.

[43] Robert Lampman, 'The Effectiveness of Some Institutions in Changing the Distribution of Income', *American Economic Review* 47, no. 2 (1957): 519–528.

[44] Robert Lampman, 'One-Fifth of a Nation', *Challenge* 12, no. 7 (April 1964): 11.

[45] Robert Lampman, 'Recent changes in Income Inequality Reconsidered', *American Economic Review*, 44, no. 3 (June 1954): 251–268.

[46] John K. Galbraith, *The Affluent Society* (New York: Houghton Mifflin Company, 1958).

programmes.[47] That same year, Michael Harrington published his first piece on the topic in *Commentary*, and began to change the general perceptions of poverty in America. While Lampman estimated that nearly 20 per cent of the population was living in poverty (at a $2,000 poverty line), Harrington put the figure as high as a third (using a $3,000 poverty line).[48] The claim was stunning, given that more than twenty years had passed since Roosevelt highlighted the scandal of 'one-third' of the nation being 'ill-housed, ill-clad, ill-nourished' in his Second Inaugural Address.[49]

These numbers were a tremendous blow for the post-war aims of social policy. Poverty in such a magnitude would essentially mean that, for the poor, almost nothing had changed since the New Deal and that, if 'new strategies' weren't deployed, this 'hidden' America would 'irrevocably stay away from abundance'.[50] For Lampman and many experts of his generation, 'a redefinition of the contours of New Deal liberalism' was 'essential to better tackle relative poverty'.[51] The shift would be completed with the publication of Michael Harrington's *The Other America* in March 1962 and with the book review by Dwight McDonald in *The New Yorker* in January 1963.[52] The review in particular would be widely read, including by President Kennedy himself.[53] The ensuing debate popularized across political divisions the idea that 'poverty' was now a 'specific' condition, detached from the questions of inequality and of the labour market. Using a very different tone to the dry statistical work of Lampman, Harrington had captured the public imagination. He claimed that millions of poor families were in fact 'scarcely been affected by the reforms of the past quarter-century'.[54] When Friedman and Harrington debated on poverty issues in December 1964 at Cornell University, the extent of their agreement on the failures of the New Deal and the need for 'more innovation and experimentation' stunned part of the audience. 'The world is full of

[47] U.S. Congress, Joint Economic Committee, 'The Low-Income Population and Economic Growth' by Robert Lampman, study paper 12 (1959).

[48] Michael Harrington, 'Our Fifty Million Poor', *Commentary* 28, no. 1 (July 1959): 25–27.

[49] Franklin Delano Roosevelt, 'One Third of a Nation. Ill-housed, ill-clad, ill-nourished', *Second Inaugural Address*, January 20, 1937.

[50] Huret, *La fin de la pauvreté?*, 82.

[51] Ibid., 89.

[52] Dwight McDonald, 'The Invisible Poor', *The New Yorker*, January 19, 1963, 130–139.

[53] Carl M. Brauer, 'Kennedy, Johnson, and the War on Poverty', *Journal of American History* 69, no. 1 (1982): 98–119.

[54] Harrington, 'Our Fifty Million Poor', 25–27.

surprises', wrote the *Cornell Daily* the next day: 'the perspicacious observer at last Thursday's lecture by Milton Friedman may have detected a strong area of agreement between the conservative, laissez-faire Friedman and the left-wing author of *Poverty in America*, Michael Harrington'. 'Although these men approach the problem of poverty from diametrically opposite points of view' the student newspaper added, 'they both agree that American welfare measures have benefited the middle classes and lower middle classes more than the abject poor'.[55]

But then, of course, if 'the other America' formed 'a distinct system', different from the post-war categorical order, it might need a specific policy.[56] As argued by Leslie Lenkowsky, in that new framework, 'traditional welfare policies seemed unlikely to be productive and, some thought, caused social and political problems of their own'.[57] In a certain sense, what Milton Friedman began to advocate in the mid-forties became widespread among reformers and policy makers by the early 1960s. The 'other America' was then composed, as Harrington wrote, of those 'who are beyond the welfare state'.[58] 'These people', Lampman thought, remained 'remarkably untouched by the New Deal welfare state measures'.[59] What was needed, argued Robert Theobald, another signatory of the Triple Revolution statement, was instead 'the principle of an economic floor', an 'economic basic security' that could guarantee to lift them out of poverty.[60] Therefore, the shift towards cash, promoted by figures both from the right and the left, while diverging strongly in their analysis of the *causes* of poverty, would slowly make guaranteed income schemes a central policy aim. The specificity of poverty as a problem had made welfare state expansion obsolete as a remedy.

Therefore, when Friedman republished his idea in his 1962 bestseller *Capitalism and Freedom* the response was very different: it attracted widespread intellectual attention. The idea he though ahead of its time in the early 1940s was now discussed in Washington. Indeed, the circle close to the president, especially the Council of Economic Advisers, was now composed of economists like Walter Heller, Robert Lampman, James Tobin,

[55] Steven B. Wolinetz, 'Friedman, Harrington and Poverty', *Cornell Daily Sun*, December 16, 1964.

[56] Michael Harrington, *The Other America* (Baltimore: Penguin, 1962), 168–69.

[57] Lenkowsky, *Politics, Economics and Welfare Reform*, 52.

[58] Harrington, *The Other America*, 169.

[59] Robert Lampman, 'One-Fifth of a Nation', *Challenge* 12, no. 7 (April 1964): 11–13.

[60] Robert Theobald, *Free Men and Free Markets* (New York: C. N. Potter, 1963), 115.

or Joseph A. Pechman who were all essentially 'fiscal Keynesians', and promoted a fiscal understanding of social policy, depicting Social Security just as another (and generally less efficient) form of taxation. Walter Heller in particular, who would become the most influential chairman in the history of CEA, was emblematic of this abstract vision of the state promoted by young advisers often trained in top economic departments. His commitment was to the 'new economics' launched by Paul Samuelson and Robert Solow, which aimed at integrating Keynesianism into a neoclassical framework, and tended to downplay the political and cultural dimension of social policy and reduce market imperfections to technical problems of asymmetric information. As James Tobin would later argue, this approach tended to treat problems as 'technical rather than ideological', separating, as Jacqueline Best has noted, 'economic questions from the complications of politics and ideas'.[61] This was a vision disconnected from the transactional deals traditionally associated with social policy, made of categorial expansions generally motivated by electoral agreements. Heller, as Nicholas Lemann pointed out, lived rather in 'a clean, precise world of numbers and orderly concepts', viewing society (like his father) as an engineer.[62] He was more attracted to the beauty of taxation incentives than to the muddiness and uncertainty of the public spending that interested Galbraith. As Binyamin Appelbaum noted, 'Heller's ideas marked a tactical break with the traditional Keynesian emphasis on increased government spending'; rather than borrowing money to spend it on public plans, Heller claimed that the state could simply 'borrow money from the private sector and then give it back to the private sector to spend it'.[63]

This would lead the Kennedy administration to pass two costly tax cuts in 1962 and 1964 in order to boost the economy. This emphasis on tax cuts reflected a strong preference for private initiative and 'sovereign consumers' with a fear of inflation when it comes to state regulation of the labour market and wages. 'Why cut taxes rather than go the Galbraith way?' Heller asked Kennedy, rhetorically, in a 1962 memo.[64] The main

[61] James Tobin, *The New Economics One Decade Older* (Princeton, NJ: Princeton University Press, 1974), 5; Jacqueline Best, 'Hollowing out Keynesian Norms: How the Search for a Technical Fix Undermined the Bretton Woods Regime', *Review of International Studies* 30, no. 3 (July 2004), 386.

[62] Lemann, *The Promised Land*, 130.

[63] Binyamin Appelbaum, *The Economists' Hour* (New York: Little, Brown, 2019), ebook.

[64] Walter Heller, *Brief Book on Economic Matters*, 20 December 1962, 3. John F. Kennedy Presidential Library, Boston, MA, folder identifier JFKPOF-063a-009-p014, https://www.jfklibrary.org/asset-viewer/archives/JFKPOF/063a/JFKPOF-063a-009.

argument of the Wisconsin economist was rooted in a neoclassical theory according to which the expansion of public spending in that context would 'lead to waste, bottlenecks, profiteering, and scandal' and would increase the opposition to the 'expansion of government' and 'over-centralization, to a "power grab" and a "take-over" of the cities, the educational system, the housing market'.[65] Finally, and this was perhaps the most important aspect to this shift, 'tax-cuts induced deficits' Heller argued that 'are also more acceptable to the world financial community than expenditure-induced deficits'.[66] This modernized Keynesianism offered a way to break with the balanced budgets and under-production which Kennedy faced when taking office while at the same time recognizing—as Heller noted—'the importance of working through the market system'.[67] The central tenet of this strand of Keynesianism was then, as Aaron Major argued, 'that when the economy falls into recession the government needs to prop up demand by substituting public spending for private investment and by bolstering the purchasing power of the poor and middle class'.[68] In other words, classical Keynesians would address unemployment through public work programmes, while modernized Keynesians focused on boosting private investment through tax cuts.

This 'fiscal community'—as Wilbur J. Cohen bitterly observed—'analyzed' social security as 'an ordinary tax, and as a tax it constituted a dubious form of social policy'.[69] What Cohen termed the 'Harvard-Yale-MIT-Brookings economists' would later become the main proponents of Friedman's NIT within the Democratic administration, reframing social policy and poverty alleviation in terms of efficient 'transfers'.[70] This 'fiscal revolution' (as the future chairman of the CEA under Nixon, Herbert Stein, called it, because of its technocratic character) would be characterized by Aaron Major as a clear 'transition period between post-war Keynesianism and contemporary neoliberalism'.[71] Therefore, while the

[65] Ibid.

[66] Ibid., 4.

[67] Cathie J. Martin, *Shifting the Burden: The Struggle over Growth and Corporate Taxation* (Chicago, IL: University of Chicago Press, 1991), 52.

[68] Aaron Major, *Architects of Austerity* (Stanford, CA: Stanford University Press, 2014), 129.

[69] Berkowitz, *Mr. Social Security*, 292.

[70] Ibid.

[71] Major, *Architects of Austerity*, 131.

1960s saw Keynesianism triumph among economists, it constituted 'a major departure from the basic policy paradigm of the 1950s'.[72] If Kennedy was, as Jacqueline Best argued, 'the first Keynesian president', 'he was decidedly of a neoclassical bent', shaping policies significantly different from the ideas of the Cambridge economist decades before.[73] 'Economics', wrote Heller to Friedman in 1961, 'makes strange bedfellows'. On the topic of tax cuts, he continued, 'I find Ken Galbraith fighting against me and you fighting with me'—'thank heaven, one can't identify economic positions by labels alone'.[74] This marked a significant evolution in field of economics, that would slowly, as Stein noted, make 'the distinction between Keynesians and non-Keynesians' less significant. 'Within this general consensus', he added, 'differences' existed of course, but they were essentially 'of emphasis and of degree'.[75] 'In one sense', Friedman famously claimed, 'we are all Keynesians now; in another, nobody is any longer a Keynesian'.[76]

'Black Poverty' and the Triumph of the Income Strategy

The mid-1960s witnessed an unprecedented proliferation of guaranteed income proposals, sent off from all sides of the political spectrum. It took a while for this enthusiasm to reach government itself, however. Kennedy and Johnson, in particular, had repeatedly refused consideration of the income strategy. If Sargent Shriver, the head of the newly created Office of Economic Opportunity (OEO), had been promoting the idea of negative income tax and included it in his 1965 'antipoverty budget' Johnson, as Lampman recalls, 'wanted no part of it from the outset'.[77] Things only began to change with the mixed results of the Community Action Program as urban unrest in inner cities increased after the 1965 Watts riots and budget restraints imposed by the escalation of the Vietnam War limited

[72] Major, *Architects of Austerity*, 130.

[73] Best, 'Hollowing out Keynesian Norms', 394.

[74] Walter Heller, Letter to Milton Friedman, March 28, 1961, Milton Friedman papers, Hoover Institute archives, Box 28, File 28–5.

[75] Herbert Stein, *The Fiscal Revolution in America* (Washington, DC: American Enterprise Institute Press, 1990), 381–382.

[76] Milton Friedman, 'Letter: Friedman & Keynes', *Time*, February 4, 1966.

[77] See in particular Robert J. Lampman, Oral Interviews, 5/24/83/, by Michael L. Gillette, LBJ Library Oral Histories, LBJ Presidential Library, accessed June 11, 2020, 41.

further the options of the president. The conjunction of the increasing criticisms towards the efficiency of the government action, the continuous increase of welfare rolls, the rising dissatisfaction with the growth of bureaucracy and, perhaps more importantly, the 'culturalization' of poverty—especially 'black poverty'—granted guaranteed income the momentum its proponents craved.

One of the most conspicuous factors driving the proposal's popularity was an increasingly culturalist reading of post-war black poverty. In his 1962 bestseller Harrington himself did not hesitate to qualify 'Negro poverty' as 'unique in every way', growing out of a 'subculture' that could easily, if no targeted measured were introduced, 'reproduce itself for years to come'.[78] Therefore, as for poverty in general, Harrington's understanding of 'black poverty' made him also quite sceptical about solutions such as welfare state expansion. He rather thought that within the New Deal order 'the Negroes were being asked to help to build a welfare state that would discriminate against them in a double sense, that would not really benefit them because they are so poor as to be beyond the reach of the new benefits, and that would continue and reinforce the racist pattern of all American society'.[79]

The definite blow to the integrationist perspective came however with the publication of Daniel Moynihan's 1965 report *The Negro Family: The Case for National Action*. Moynihan's conclusion was unexpectedly radical, suggesting, as Touré Reed notes, that the welfare crisis was now divorced from unemployment and economic factors.[80] This 'new kind of problem', Moynihan argued, could not be alleviated by a mere expansion of public service provision or full employment but only through the 'establishment of a stable Negro family structure'.[81] As he claimed:

> at this point, the present tangle of pathology is capable of perpetuating itself without assistance from the white world. ... In a word, a national effort

[78] Harrington, *The Other America*, 67.

[79] Ibid., 84.

[80] Touré F. Reed, 'Why Moynihan Was Not So Misunderstood at the Time, *Nonsite* 17 (September 2014).

[81] Daniel P. Moynihan, 'The Negro Family: The Case for National Action', in *The Moynihan Report and the Politics of Controversy: A Trans-Action Social Science and Public Policy Report*, eds. Lee Rainwater and William L. Yancey (Cambridge, MA: MIT Press, 1967), 47. See also Melinda Cooper, *Family Values: Between Neoliberalism and the New Social Conservatism* (New York: MIT Press, 2018).

> towards the problems of Negro Americans must be directed towards the question of family structure. (...) After that, how this group of Americans chooses to run its affairs, take advantage of its opportunities, or fail to do so, is none of the nation's business.[82]

Moynihan ventured further than mere culturalization, however. His lament did not only seek to blame the black family structure pathology as such, but also castigated the existing welfare system. The incentive structure built in the AFDC programme, he claimed, literally tore up Afro-American families. Ironically, such culturalist analyses also explained Moynihan's perfunctory interest in guaranteed income schemes, including his later conceptualization of Nixon's Family Assistance Plan (FAP). Indeed, the income framework provided not only innovative ways to think about welfare, but also a way to restore 'some sense of individual responsibility for outcomes' within Afro-American families. As he noted, 'where a services strategy tended to locate in government blame for services that do not succeed, an income strategy would tend to implicate the individuals, who would make their own choices in the market'.[83]

In the same vein, a 1965 article by economist James Tobin—at the time member of the Council of Economic Advisers—entitled 'On improving the economic status of the Negro' praised the idea of a negative income tax as the solution to the 'specific character' of black poverty.[84] Deeply influenced by Moynihan's writings, Tobin claimed that 'public assistance encourage[d] the disintegration of the family, the key to so many of the economic and social problems of the American Negro'.[85] The existing structures of social assistance, he argued, created a situation where 'he, or likely she, is essentially forced to be both idle and on a dole'.[86] The post-war framework, he added, 'no longer operates'.[87] Poverty could no longer be solved by public jobs or better schools, or 'by minimum wage laws, trade unions wage pressures, or other devices which seek to compel employers to pay [workers] more than their work is worth'.[88] From that

[82] Ibid.

[83] Moynihan, *The Politics of a Guaranteed Income*, 108.

[84] James Tobin, 'On Improving the Economic Status of the Negro, *Daedalus* 94, no. 4 (Fall 1965): 880.

[85] Ibid., 890.

[86] Ibid.

[87] Tobin, 'On Improving the Economic Status of the Negro', 880.

[88] Ibid., 889.

perspective, 'the biggest issue the nation face[d] in the war of poverty', he thought, was to establish a 'system of income supplementation and maintenance' that would integrate 'public assistance with a vastly simplified and reformed system of income taxation' in order to preserve 'incentives to work', 'encourage' black parents to 'maintain stable families', and provide a decent income.[89] The racialization of the poverty question only seemed to favour the cash-based approach. Tobin's proposals gathered traction within the maelstrom of the Johnsonian 'war on poverty', and reinforced the conviction of Sargent Shriver, the head of the OEO, to push the income strategy within the administration (Fig. 3.1).[90]

This shift was particularly marked within the Civil Rights Movement itself, which 'was no longer pushing integration' in the field of social policy.[91] Within this framework, guaranteed incomes became an attractive alternative for organizations like the National Welfare Rights Organization (NWRO), which was slowly breaking with the coalition politics of the former generation. Founded in 1966 in the wake of the famous 'Cloward-Piven' strategy, the NWRO would step forward as the most vocal supporter of the cash strategy. Political scientists Richard Cloward and Frances Fox Piven first formulated the tactic in a piece published in *The Nation* called 'A Strategy to End Poverty' that would become a catalyst for grassroots welfare organizations across the country. The two professors at the Columbia University School of Social Work first aimed at dramatically increasing the number of poor on welfare rolls—since many people were eligible but did not claim their benefits. The outcome would be a bureaucratic and budgetary nightmare that could force the Democratic Party to reform public welfare. 'The ultimate objective' they argued, was 'to wipe out poverty by establishing a guaranteed annual income'.[92] The idea prompted the unification of welfare rights activists from all the country, gathering in Chicago in

[89] Tobin, 'Raising the Incomes of the Poor', 97.

[90] The idea was strongly promoted within the OEO since 1965, but was strongly blocked by Johnson and, perhaps more importantly, by Wilbur Cohen and Wilbur Mills, who were the key figures in the field of social policy. See Walter Williams, 'The Struggle for a Negative Income Tax: A Review Article', *Journal of Human Resources* 10, no. 4 (October 1975): 427–444; Robert Lampman, 'The Negative Income Tax Experiment', extracts from the Archives Oral History Project, University of Wisconsin-Madison, *Focus* 23, no. 2 (2004): 4–7.

[91] Lemann, *The Promised Land*, 197.

[92] Frances Fox Piven and Richard A. Cloward, 'The Weight of the Poor: A Strategy to End Poverty', *The Nation*, May 2, 1966: https://www.thenation.com/article/archive/weight-poor-strategy-end-poverty/

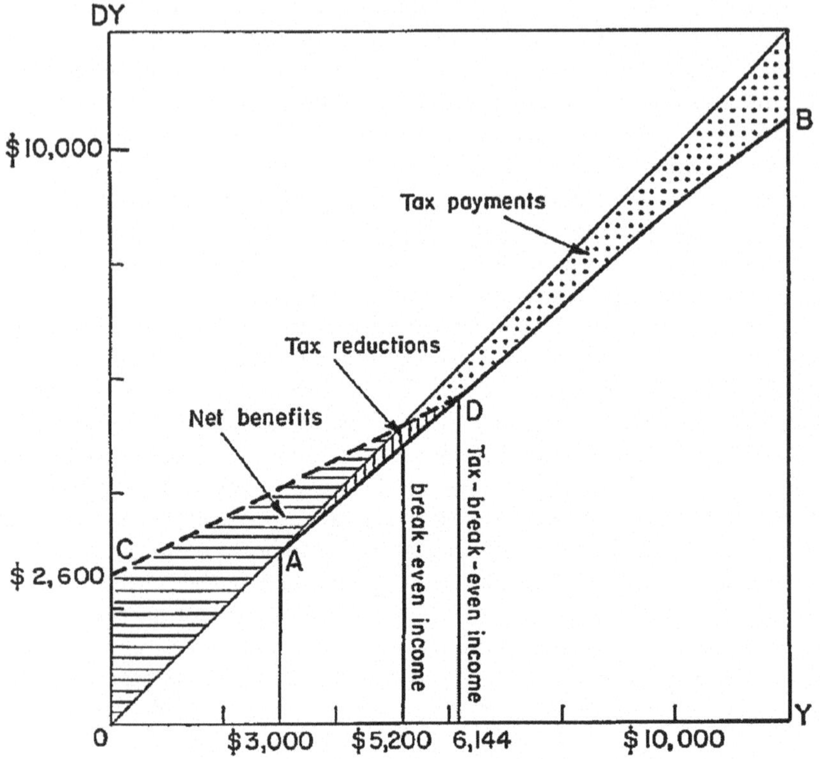

Fig. 3.1 James Tobin, Joseph A. Pechman, Peter M. Mieszkowski's 1967 plan for a guaranteed income. In: James Tobin, Joseph A. Penchman, Peter M. Mieszkowski, 'Is a Negative Income Tax Practical?', *Yale Law Journal* 77 (November 1967): 7

August 1966 to create the NWRO. Among the most famous figures in the newly created movement were George Wiley, a former associate director of the Congress of Racial Equality (CORE), and Johnnie Tillmon, who in 1963 had founded Aid to Needy Children (ANC), one of the first grass-roots welfare mothers' organizations. The NWRO included in its goals the establishment of a 'system that guarantees enough money for all Americans to live dignified lives above the level of poverty', making guaranteed income programmes the object of mass activism.[93]

[93] Premilla Nadasen, *Welfare Warriors* (London: Routledge, 2004).

The argument's attractiveness mainly stemmed from the degree of autonomy guaranteed income schemes would grant to recipients. This would allow women to invest themselves in the community, for instance, rather than in a jobless labour market. To a certain extent, Moynihan's argument about the family structure had actually gained the support of welfare activists. This question would notably be the object of a small conflict between Beulah Sanders and George Wiley, respectively vice president and president of the NWRO, on one side and Martha Griffiths, a feminist Democrat Congresswoman, on the other, during a 1968 Congressional hearing. For Griffiths there was something deeply upsetting in sorting people on welfare rolls without granting them a prospect in the labour market. Keeping 'a group of people who are on welfare ... forever', she argued, might be 'all right for the country, but it is not all right for the people on welfare. Those people have a right to participate in the economy of this country. They have just as much right to have a job as anybody else has.' The vast majority of women drawing on welfare, she added, 'wanted to work if they had a place where to put their children'.[94] Sanders and Wiley, on the other hand, proposed an argument strikingly close to Moynihan before them. 'If you are going to give us jobs', Sanders argued, 'give our men the jobs, let us stay home and take care of our children'.[95] What Sanders desired, as she would later frame it, was 'mother power'. 'The important thing' Wiley added, 'is that the men, that the people who are able to be heads of households or ought to be legitimate heads of households be the ones that get those jobs'.[96] Following this line of argument, a guaranteed income became the natural solution to poverty and joblessness crisis. 'If the department can pay a tremendous amount of money for people to live in slum houses', Sanders argued, 'they can pay that money for people to live in a decent apartment'. 'The main problem for poor people', Wiley added, 'is money'.[97] Rather than subsidizing inefficient public housing or public works, welfare activists began to push for autonomy through cash.

Within the administration, the income shift came during the late 1960s. 'The antipoverty program enacted in 1964', Moynihan argued, 'came to

[94] *Hearings Before the Subcommittee on Fiscal Policy of the Joint Economic Committee Congress of the United States*, Second Session, Volume 1: Proceedings (Washington, DC: U.S. Government Printing Office, 1968), 77.

[95] Ibid., 67.

[96] Ibid., 77.

[97] Ibid., 81.

embody many of the ambiguities and uncertainties of an ambitious services strategy directed to the problems of poverty. A good deal of money was being expended [and] it was going, in large degree, to purchase services, which could not be shown to benefit the poor.'[98] In this context, he added, 'an assertion came forth, labelled conservative but in historical terms almost classically liberal, that government administration did not work, while the market did'.[99] This approach would allow for the realization of what neoliberal economist Arthur Kemp and Chicago economist Yale Brozen called 'welfare without the welfare state'.[100] If 'welfare statists' always sought the expansion of the federal government to tackle poverty, the task was now 'much more difficult' and consisted in moving 'away from the welfare state without [a] decrease in welfare'.[101] Only then did the idea of an income strategy gain appeal in Washington, offering a way of tackling poverty but without expanding the federal government in a political climate which was turning increasingly anti-statist and anti-bureaucratic. The final turn would come with the publication of two reports related to welfare matters. First, a research report published by the Department of Health, Education, and Welfare (HEW) directly attacked the government's strategy on poverty. The report claimed that 60 per cent of Americans living under the poverty line did not benefit from existing programmes, casting doubt on the effectiveness of the Great Society strategy.[102] Second, the report of the highly anticipated Kerner Commission on civil disorders, established by President Johnson to investigate the causes of the 1967 urban riots. The report was received with an exceptional amount of public scrutiny and notably recommended a guaranteed income as 'long-range goal' to fix a broken welfare system and provide a 'basic floor ... for all Americans'.[103] The proposal would have the advantage of providing for both 'employed persons working at substandard hours or

[98] Moynihan, *The Politics of a Guaranteed Income*, 54.

[99] Ibid., 54.

[100] Arthur Kemp, 'Welfare Without the Welfare State, *Il Politico* 31, no. 4 (December 1966): 716–730; Yale Brozen, 'Welfare Without the Welfare State', *The Freemen* 16, no. 2 (March 1966): 40–52.

[101] Kemp, 'Welfare Without The Welfare State', 729.

[102] Otto Eckstein and Robert Harris, *Program Analysis: Income and Benefit Programs* (Washington, DC: Office of the Assistant Secretary for Program Evaluation, 1966).

[103] *Report of the National Advisory Commission on Civic Disorders* (Washington, DC: US Government Printing Office, 1968), 254.

wages' and for those who 'cannot work', like 'mothers who decide to remain with their children'.[104]

By then, the legislative career of the guaranteed income appeared unstoppable. In January 1967 President Johnson finally established a Commission on Income Maintenance Programs. While he warned that the scheme was being pushed 'by some of the sturdiest defenders of free enterprise' and that it was 'almost surely beyond our means at this time', he added that 'we must examine any plan, however unconventional, which could promise a major advance'.[105] That same year, the Office of Economic Opportunity, driven by a Sargent Shriver initiative, launched the first of several large-scale experiments in boroughs of New Jersey.[106] Finally, in 1968 more than a thousand economists, sharing a wide array of political affiliations and from some of the nation's most prestigious institutions, signed an open letter to the president supporting a guaranteed income.[107] At that point, the question was not *whether* the idea was going to be adopted, but rather *when*. Even Republicans were now considering the implementation of such a measure. And after Hubert Humphrey's defeat in the 1968 presidential election, Nixon felt a sense of urgency to solve the 'welfare mess' with radical measures such as NIT, especially in the face of continuous social and urban unrest.[108]

The idea's most notable propagandist within the Nixon administration was Moynihan. The policymaker had left the Johnson administration in 1965—never reaching the ear of the president—only to be hired by Nixon

[104] Ibid., 256.

[105] 'Assuring a Decent Living Standard', *Newark Evening News,* May 1, 1967.

[106] Between 1967 and 1978, five experiments were held in US and Canadian cities: the New Jersey Graduated Work Incentive experiment (1968–1972), the Rural Income Maintenance Experiment (1970–1972), the Seattle/Denver Income Maintenance Experiments (1970–1976), the Gary Indiana Experiment (1971–1974), and the Manitoba Basic Annual Income Experiment (1975–1978). See Karl Widerquist, 'A Failure to Communicate: What (If Anything) Can we Learn from the Negative Income Tax Experiments?', *The Journal of Socio-Economics* 34, no. 1 (February 2005), 49–81.

[107] The statement was circulated in May of 1968 to 275 universities and research organizations. It received signatures from, Paul Samuelson, Harold Watts, James Tobin, John K. Galbraith, and Robert Lampman, but also included Abba P. Lerner, Kenneth Arrow, T. C. Koopmans, and Joseph Stiglitz. See 'A Statement by Economists on Income Guarantees and Supplements', 27 May 1968 in *Income Maintenance Programs: Hearings before the Subcommittee on the Fiscal Policy of the Joint Economic Committee Congress of the United States Ninetieth Congress*, Volume II, Appendix Materials, Appendix 17, 676.

[108] Moynihan, *The Politics of a Guaranteed Income*, 86.

as a chief adviser on urban affairs. When he pushed for the Family Assistance Plan (FAP), a version of guaranteed income supposedly aimed at eliminating the 'disincentives to family formation that were built into the AFDC', Moynihan argued that the plan would eliminate a lot of social workers-jobs.[109] While Nixon had opposed the general principle during the election campaign, the idea of his administration embracing an '"income strategy" against poverty to replace Johnson's "service strategy"' convinced him to go ahead with the idea in April 1969.[110] As noted by Lemann, this was an attractive framework for conservatives too, as it did not require 'promoting integration or expanding the federal bureaucracy' and would 'cost only [$]2 billion a year and cut back on the size of government'.[111] Moreover, Moynihan was convinced that the service strategy had transformed the 'black middle class' into 'providers of social services to the black lower class', allowing them to blackmail government into inflationary social demands.[112] The mode in which this middle class had benefitted from the jobs created by the Office of Economic Opportunity, and the power it had gained over the federal government, grew into an even more vexing problem. Choosing the income strategy, Moynihan argued in a memo to Nixon, would 'deprive "the militant middle class" of the ability to make an ongoing threat to the larger society, much as the desperate bank robber threatens to drop the vial of nitroglycerin'.[113] Indirectly, transferring money became a way of disempowering the newly created class of welfare workers and bureaucrats, breaking its grip on the poor and, by extension, on the federal government.

Following this cash-centred perspective, Nixon began by abolishing taxes for those living under the poverty line in 1969. He then moved rapidly towards the FAP. While the plan was approved in 1970 in a Democrat-controlled House, it would face a backlash in a Senate worried about its effects on work incentives. The proposal's 'centrist' inflection dissatisfied most of its natural constituency. Liberals tended to argue that the benefits were too low, whilst conservatives reacted against the idea of an income floor that was perceived as a free ride for idleness.[114] In 1972, after a round of heavy revisions, the Nixon plan was definitively defeated in the Senate

[109] Cooper, *Family Values*, 43.
[110] Ibid., 212.
[111] Ibid., 210.
[112] Daniel Moynihan, Memo to the president, quoted in Lemann, *The Promised Land*, 215.
[113] Lemann, *The Promised Land*, 215.
[114] Brian Steensland, *The Failed Welfare Revolution*, 176–177.

again and the president lost interest in the reform. The following year, however, Nixon was able to introduce two more modest plans which would become his lasting legacy in social policy. The first of these was the Supplemental Security Income (SSI) that would provide a federal guaranteed income to the blind, aged, and disabled. Second, and perhaps more important, was the Earned Income Tax Credit (EITC)—partially designed after Friedman's NIT, but restricted to those who worked. These policies, as noted by Brain Steensland, 'partially attained some of the goals of GAI proposals' by expanding the income strategy, yet without eroding the symbolic boundaries between the 'deserving' and 'undeserving' poor that would remain a crucial aspect of welfare policy in the United States.[115] There thus was victory in defeat; as Lemann notes, in the field of welfare 'the specific program failed politically', yet its 'general principle succeeded'. 'The Nixon administration', he added, 'in effect did implement the income strategy by greatly increasing the payment levels of welfare, food stamps, social security, and disability pensions, while allowing government social welfare employment to level off'.[116] The shift towards cashification proved premonitory for later administrations. Even during the two Reagan terms, income support programmes like AFDC, unemployment benefits or food stamps were generally spared from hard cuts, unlike the public housing policy. The overall shift was then, as Paul Pierson noted, 'from subsidizing "bricks and mortar" to subsidizing people'.[117]

Conclusion

When a twenty-seven-year-old Milton Friedman, concerned about the poverty generated by the play of free markets, began to think of innovative techniques to eradicate it, he could not have anticipated the immense success of his proposal. The idea, shaped in a period of intense economic debates, captured one of the fundamental shifts in the field of economics during that period: the rising centrality of the sovereign consumer as an economic agent. This evolution formed the starting point of what the British economist John Kay called 'Redistributive Market Liberalism'—an approach to social policy in which 'the state must have a dominant role in

[115] Ibid., 176–177.

[116] Lemann, *The Promised Land*, 215.

[117] Paul Pierson, *Dismantling the Welfare State? Reagan, Thatcher and the Politics of Retrenchment*, (Cambridge: Cambridge University Press, 1994), 90

matters of income distribution, but should discharge this responsibility with as little interference as possible in the workings of the free market'.[118] A 'capitalism with human face' as Samuel Brittan envisioned it, could then reconcile the pursuit of self-interest with egalitarian concerns.[119]

Of course, on many topics, the idea's main proponents like Friedman, Tobin, Galbraith, Lampman, or Harrington had very dissimilar views. But while their own readings of the poverty problem differed radically on internal lines, a guaranteed income appeared to them as a fruitful solution to their strong criticism of the welfare state, of full employment as a policy aim and their scepticism towards the state as a collective decision maker. The Negative Income Tax, which Milton Friedman had shaped in the 1940s, appeared then as an innovative idea, capable of transcending classical oppositions between left and right, and offering an alternative to both the patronizing views of classical liberalism and the work-centred welfare policies of the 'old left'. It was the very foundation of *how* modern economics thought about redistribution that changed. And while, after the mid-1970s, the US welfare debate took on a much more conservative bent, on the other side of the Atlantic—in countries such as France, Belgium, and the Netherlands—the career of basic income and its cousins was only just beginning.

[118] John Kay, 'Redistributive Market Liberalism', *New Statesman*, February 5, 1997.
[119] Samuel Brittan, *Capitalism With a Human Face* (Cheltenham: Edward Elgar, 1995).

CHAPTER 4

American Cybernation: Technological Upheaval and Guaranteed Income Advocacy in the 1960s United States

Andrew V. Sanchez

Introduction

During the boom years of postwar economic expansion in the United States, consistent increases in productivity materially improved the lives of millions of Americans.[1] But by the early 1960s, stubbornly high unemployment, emerging concerns about nascent computing technologies, and the effects of automated manufacturing prompted a new interrogation of the liberal-capitalist project by a range of futurists, economists, and activists, who came to be known as 'cybernation theorists'. In 1964, a report

[1] See Dale Jorgenson, 'Productivity and Postwar U.S. Economic Growth', *Journal of Economic Perspectives* 2, no. 4 (1988): 23–42.

A. V. Sanchez (✉)
Center for Contemporary History, Berlin, Germany

University of Oxford, Oxford, UK
e-mail: andrew.sanchez@ccc.ox.ac.uk

P. Sloman et al. (eds.), *Universal Basic Income in Historical Perspective*, https://doi.org/10.1007/978-3-030-75706-9_4

authored by several cybernation experts from the 'Ad Hoc Committee on the Triple Revolution' was delivered to President Lyndon Johnson that proposed a government-funded income guarantee to accommodate the economic and social changes brought about by a highly automated economy. The committee comprised a variety of intellectuals from the New Left, including Robert Theobald, Tom Hayden, and Wilbur Ferry, and their predictions elicited news coverage, praise, and criticism from across the ideological spectrum. The committee's report was the most publicized document in a much wider field of cybernation research which explored the scientific background and social implications of predicted technological change. This chapter is devoted to unpacking and contextualizing the rich intellectual history surrounding cybernation and its relationship to guaranteed income proposals in the United States.

American interest in basic income proposals during the 1960s had varied origins. On the right, the pioneering work of Milton Friedman laid the theoretical foundations for Richard Nixon's Family Assistance Plan and prompted new thinking about efficient taxation among conservative politicians and policymakers.[2] On the left, however, deep concerns about the intersection of automation and cybernetic technology—what Donald Michael first called 'cybernation' in 1962—gave rise to a new set of social and economic critiques that reconsidered the role of wage labour and challenged the very underpinnings of postwar American capitalism.[3] As early as 1949, the famed MIT professor and inventor of cybernetics, Norbert Wiener, first opined on the potential implications of cybernetic technologies on economic and social structures.[4] While Wiener's work and that of other cyberneticists during the late 1940s and 1950s prognosticated about the potentially destabilizing effects of widespread automation, the cybernation theorists of the 1960s sounded a far louder alarm. As distinct from earlier discussion about cybernetics, writings about cybernation emphasized that economic dislocations from technological change were concerns of the present that necessitated a new system of state welfare provision. For the futurist Robert Theobald, a cybernated age had

[2] Brian Steensland, *The Failed Welfare Revolution: America's Struggle over Guaranteed Income Policy* (Princeton, NJ: Princeton University Press, 2008).

[3] Donald Michael, *Cybernation: The Silent Conquest* (Santa Barbara, CA: Center for the Study of Democratic Institutions, 1962).

[4] Norbert Wiener, *The Human Use of Human Beings: Cybernetics and Society* (Boston, MA: Houghton Mifflin, 1950).

already arrived and fundamental changes, like a guaranteed annual income, were necessary to stabilize a rapidly evolving economy.

The 1960s-era discussions of cybernation were also distinct from cybernetic discourse in their specific concerns about the ethical ramifications of economic abundance. Cybernation theorists were deeply concerned about the destabilizing effects of a massive increase in productivity, but they also saw cybernation as the key to transcending a world of scarcity and achieving an economy of abundance. Without the harsh trade-offs dictated by conditions of scarcity, the terms of economic organization in an abundant economy could be rewritten according to ethical and moral principles around inclusion, equity, and fairness. These visions frequently imagined a post-work world, and they emphasized the importance of leisure, mental well-being, and aspects of human existence which are not readily expressed in terms of economic utility. As this chapter will demonstrate, the work of cybernation theorists helped advance ideas around abundance and a post-work world by tethering improvements in productivity to a guaranteed annual income.

The impending economic rupture predicted by the cybernation theorists never did materialize, but the publicity generated by documents like the 'Triple Revolution Report' and the works of Robert Theobald influenced the trajectory of public and academic discourse about technology, economic growth, and equitable social outcomes. Recent work on the role of economic and political forecasting by sociologist Jenny Andersson has argued that historical visions of the future had little immediate impact in their time, but helped develop 'artifacts and devices' for policy analysis and cultural understanding which have reappeared in subsequent decades.[5] The present study both challenges and extends Andersson's argument. On the one hand, the predictions of futurists like Robert Theobald did not lead to the enactment of novel redistributive social programmes, but concerns about cybernation and the role of technology economic life took on a new meaning during the 1960s. Although cybernation fell out of favour during the 1970s, the themes of technological unemployment, income guarantees, and economic fairness raised by the cybernation theorists have remained a potent force in later decades. At the time of writing in the second decade of the twenty-first century, it is clear that although the timeline of cybernation theorists was wrong, their predictions about the

[5] Jenny Andersson, *The Future of the World: Futurology, Futurists, and the Struggle for the Post Cold War Imagination* (Oxford: Oxford University Press, 2018), 11.

role of technology and equitable economic distribution proved prescient and are echoed in numerous contemporary writings on the topic.

This section will examine the concept of economic abundance and something I will call 'technological eschatology' which predicted an imminent economic and social transformation through the adoption of cybernation technologies. Beliefs about the nature of abundance and the potential for technological transformation came under increasing scrutiny throughout the 1960s in light of changing economic trends and government reports which undermined the credibility of the cybernation theorists. By examining how thinkers, such as Robert Theobald, Donald Michael, and others leveraged predictions about technological change to justify their support for an income guarantee, this section will demonstrate both the potential power and ultimate limitations of arguments grounded in an imminent technological eschatology. The section will conclude by analysing how discussion around cybernation differed from earlier concerns raised by cybernetic theorists.

The impact of productivity improvements on equitable economic progress formed the basis of Donald Michael's inquiry into cybernation in the early 1960s. Michael first coined the term 'cybernation' in a 1962 report as a portmanteau of 'cybernetics' and 'automation' to describe an automated system controlled by a self-regulating machine.[6] As technological innovation seemed poised to revolutionize the nature of production, Michael began to reconsider the role of the labourer in a cybernated economy. In a cybernated age, the Marxist conception of the machine as a tool for enslavement took on a pernicious new dimension. The machine not only could subordinate the human; now it could replace the human labourer altogether. In his report, entitled *Cybernation: The Silent Conquest*, Michael wrote in no uncertain terms about the effects of fully functioning cybernated systems:

> It is no fantasy, then, to be concerned with the implications of the thinking machine. There is every reason to believe that within the next two decades machines will be available outside of the laboratory that will do a credible job of original thinking, certainly as good as thinking as that expected of most middle-level people who are supposed to 'use their minds' [...] the capabilities and potentialities of these devices are unlimited. They contain extraordinary implications for the emancipation and enslavement of mankind.[7]

[6] Michael, *Cybernation*.
[7] Ibid., 8.

Although Michael's predictions were hardly mainstream, they became increasingly influential throughout the decade as social-scientific research began to migrate into a broader field of debate.

While Michael's work initially garnered attention among leftist social scientists and futurists, broader concerns about cybernation first gained national prominence through the 'Report on the Triple Revolution' which was sent to President Lyndon Johnson and the Department of Labor in March 1964. The report anticipated a so-called triple revolution in which cybernation, weaponry, and human rights would fundamentally transform the American social and economic order. The document was authored by the 'Ad Hoc Committee for the Triple Revolution' which had been organized by Wilbur H. Ferry, and the committee's membership read like a laundry list of the most important thinkers in the New Left. Among the more prominent cosignatories of the report were Michael Harrington, author of *The Other America*, Tom Hayden, a central figure in *Students for Democratic Society* (SDS), as well as several notable economists such as Gunnar Myrdal, Robert Heilbroner, and Robert Theobald. As noted by historian James Miller, the influence of the New Left—as represented by Harrington, Hayden, and others—is clear in the text of the report, but the work of economist-futurist Robert Theobald left the most significant mark on the report's conclusions.[8] The report's opening section on cybernation, which would generate the most controversy and press coverage, was effectively a summary of Theobald's thought from his earlier works, *Free Men and Free Markets* and the *Challenge of Abundance*.[9] The cybernated age had arrived:

> A new era of production has begun. Its principles of organization are as different from those of the industrial era as those of the industrial era were different from the agricultural. The cybernation revolution has been brought about by the combination of the computer and the automated self-regulating machine. This results in a system of almost unlimited productive capacity which requires progressively less human labor. Cybernation is already reorganizing the economic and social system to meet its own needs.[10]

[8] James Miller, *Democracy Is in the Streets: From Port Huron to the Siege of Chicago* (Cambridge, MA: Harvard University Press, 1994), 190.

[9] Robert Theobald, *The Challenge of Abundance* (New York, NY: New American Library, 1962).

[10] The Ad Hoc Committee on the Triple Revolution, *The Triple Revolution* (Santa Barbara, CA: Center for the Study of Democratic Institutions, 1964).

The report's predictions received significant coverage in a variety of national publications, including a front-page article in the *New York Times* entitled 'Guaranteed Income Asked for All, Employed or Not'.[11] It is important to note that the *New York Times* headline and the accompanying article focused almost exclusively on the cybernation prong of the Triple Revolution. The emphasis on cybernation, and in particular, the call for an income guarantee in the *Times* article, helped set the terms for debate about guaranteed income by clearly linking the ideas cybernation and income supplementation in popular press coverage.

Although the possibility of enacting an income guarantee was remote in 1964, the report helped bring attention to new forms of government aid, just as the Johnson administration was laying the foundation for its War on Poverty. Although Johnson remained opposed to any form of state-sponsored cash transfer, his commitment to eradicating poverty through government intervention reflected a widespread belief that government should play an active role in influencing social and economic trends. The recommendations of the Ad Hoc Committee on the Triple Revolution appeared in a political moment when American citizens actively looked to government to shape their political and financial realities.[12] At a time when government willingness to undertake wide-reaching policy initiatives was especially high, the 'Report on the Triple Revolution' marked a significant, albeit unrealized, step towards using federal policies to ensure equitable socio-economic outcomes.

The 'Report on the Triple Revolution' also shed light on the role of cybernation by reconsidering the role of scarcity and abundance in the American economy: 'An adequate distribution of the potential abundance of goods and services will be achieved only when it is understood that the major economic problem is not how to increase production but how to distribute the abundance. That is the great potential of cybernation.'[13] The concept of abundance, which appeared only fleetingly in the 'Report on the Triple Revolution', was a central pillar of the guaranteed income arguments advanced by many in the cybernation camp. Robert Theobald had extensively theorized the idea through extending John Kenneth

[11] 'Guaranteed Income Asked for All, Employed or Not', *The New York Times*, March 23, 1964.

[12] Mike Alberti and Kevin Brown, 'Guaranteed Income's Moment in the Sun', *Remapping Debate*, April 24, 2013, http://www.remappingdebate.org/node/1867.

[13] The Ad Hoc Committee on the Triple Revolution, 'The Triple Revolution'.

Galbraith's conception of affluence from his famous 1958 work, *The Affluent Society*.[14] Three years after Galbraith's work first appeared, Theobald authored *The Challenge of Abundance* in which he credited Galbraith with refocusing discussion on economic growth as a way to satisfy public rather than private needs.

Although Theobald's interest in abundance derived from the immediate effects of cybernation technology, economic abundance was hardly a novel concept. In the United States, the work of Simon Patten in the nineteenth century had already explored the relationship between economies governed by abundance rather than scarcity: 'The habits and appetites of men were formed in the environment of the distant past. Human nature became so adjusted to this environment that it clings to the old and distrusts the new. The feelings and pleasure inherited from a long line of ancestors cannot change as readily as our productive power has done.'[15] Already in the late nineteenth century, Patten anticipated a time in which human invention would be sufficient to satisfy basic material demands, and he identified a mismatch between human consumption patterns and the ability to satisfy material desires. Unlike later thinkers, such as Theobald and Galbraith, Patten did not advocate an entirely new system of distribution and instead argued that improved education would be necessary to moderate human consumptive behaviours.[16] Nonetheless, Patten explicitly acknowledged the economic inequities caused by new productive capacities, and he proposed a progressive economic system to protect the 'lower classes': 'The process, too, by which a natural evolution is carried through, is a very heartless one. It destroys the weak while it protects the strong. […] In aiding the development of the lower classes, rather than allowing them to be destroyed in the struggle for existence, the motive should be a love for humanity, and not the necessities of social progress. There need be not fear that society will cease to progress.'[17] While Patten's work does not serve as a direct precursor for Galbraith and Theobald's concerns about abundance in the 1960s, his work is an important early example of theorizing the tension between technological improvement and human consumptive patterns.

[14] John Kenneth Galbraith, *The Affluent Society* (Boston, MA: Houghton Mifflin, 1958).

[15] Simon N. Patten, *The Consumption of Wealth* (Pennsylvania, PA: T. & J.W. Johnson, 1889), 62.

[16] Benjamin Kline Hunnicutt, *Work without End: Abandoning Shorter Hours for the Right to Work* (Philadelphia, PA: Temple University Press, 1988), 34.

[17] Patten, *The Consumption of Wealth*, 68.

Building on the work of Patten and Galbraith, Theobald presented abundance as an apt characterization of contemporary American society, rather than a distant utopian future.[18] In *The Challenge of Abundance*, Theobald argued that already-existent abundance in America required a reconsideration of the mechanisms of resource distribution and the nature of economic growth. This view challenged the prevailing Keynesian orthodoxy, which was credited with the postwar economic boom, by suggesting that a system of post-scarcity government intervention was required. In this sense, the abundance argument distinguished itself from a technological eschatology by focusing on the current state of American society and economic productivity rather than emphasizing the potential effects of cybernated change.

Although many critics rejected Theobald's views of abundance as fancifully unrealistic, the idea of an affluent society, in which abundant riches should be distributed more equitably, retained its power throughout the decade.[19] A report of the President's Commission on Income Maintenance Programs from 1969, entitled *Poverty Amid Plenty*, endorsed an income maintenance programme and articulated its justification in language strikingly similar to that of Galbraith and Theobald: 'By approaching this goal in a manner that reaffirms our society's respect for the worth and dignity of all its citizens, we shall have recognized the responsibilities of affluence and, in doing that, we shall have improved the quality of our national life'.[20] Although some in the cybernation camp viewed technological progress as an instrument to create a more just and humane society, others expressed reservation, and even fear about the effects of untrammelled scientific advancement. One author on the subject, Amos Lovenstein, worried that a society without an income guarantee would continue to fracture along the lines of race and class to which the 1960s was witness:

> Even if high levels of unemployment from cybernation were not to occur, the experience of steady redeployment, reallocation, and retraining would

[18] Robert Theobald, *The Challenge of Abundance* (New York, NY: New American Library, 1962), 45.

[19] Michael Harrington, *The Other America: Poverty in the United States* (Harmondsworth: Penguin Books, 1963); Dwight MacDonald, 'Our Invisible Poor', *The New Yorker*, January 19, 1963.

[20] President's Commission on Income Maintenance Programs, *Poverty amid Plenty: The American Paradox. The Report of the President's Commission on Income Maintenance Programs* (Washington, DC: USGPO, 1969), 9.

> constitute a kind of 'disguised' technological unemployment. If a growing economy and increased demand have offset the unemployment from cybernation, still the shock to security will have occurred, even at relatively full employment. Without risking a romantic explanation of history, one can argue tenderly that human beings may sense the threat to survival even when words fail them and statistics are elusive.[21]

Lovenstein's work represented one voice in a growing chorus of theorists and social scientists who viewed technological change as a grave threat to social stability. In the same volume in which Lovenstein published his essay, Robert Davis posited that the only significant check to technological growth was social opposition and cultural norms which could slow the deployment of new cybernetic technologies. For Davis, the conflict between technology and the fabric of human society helped explain both the potential dangers and possibilities of cybernation: 'Unless new, stronger, and more responsible social control is exerted over those who make decisions of this kind, technology rather than human-considerations will set the goals of the society and determine its destiny'.[22] For thinkers like Lovenstein and Davis cybernation offered the opportunity to reconfigure society in a way that placed 'human-considerations' at the centre of social policy.

Concerns about cybernation in the 1960s can be viewed as an extension and intensification of cybernetic thought from the 1950s. In his 1949 book, *The Human Use of Human Beings: Cybernetics and Society*, Norbert Wiener wrote pessimistically about the social effects of cybernetic technology: 'The world of the future will be an even more demanding struggle against the limits of our intelligence, not a comfortable hammock in which we can lie down to be waited upon by our robot slaves'.[23] Throughout the 1950s, Wiener's abstract concerns about cybernetics and automated production became even more concrete, and the businessman John Diebold wrote frequently and even briefed Congress on the topic.[24] It is clear from

[21] Amos Lovenstein, 'Guaranteed Income and Traditional Economics', in *The Guaranteed Income: Next Step in Economic Evolution?*, ed. Robert Theobald (Garden City, NY: Doubleday, 1966), 101.

[22] Robert Davis, 'The Advance of Cybernation: 1965–1985', in *The Guaranteed Income*, ed. Robert Theobald, 35.

[23] Wiener, *Human Use of Human Beings*.

[24] Angus Burgin, 'Market Politics in an Age of Automation', in *Beyond the New Deal Order: US Politics from the Great Depression to the Great Recession*, eds. Gary Gerstle, Nelson Lichtenstein and Alice O'Connor (Philadelphia, PA: University of Pennsylvania Press, 2019).

the widespread interest in Wiener's work and Diebold's keen audience in Congress that worries about automation existed throughout the 1950s. The major distinction, however, between the 1950s-era discourse and the subsequent cybernation discussions of the 1960s was the imminent technological eschatology and the importance given to new social programmes, like a guaranteed income. As noted above, cybernation theorists believed that an automated age had already arrived, whereas Wiener's language explicitly emphasized the future effects of predicted technological change. Further, Wiener and Diebold never went so far as to propose entirely new economic or social programmes to ensure the fair distribution of automated production. In these two senses, discourse around cybernation represented a radical extension of earlier concerns about cybernetic technology that was premised on the need for radical social change and an ongoing revolution in productive capacity.

Debates about automation in the 1960s highlighted the intersection between concerns of affluence and an imminent technological eschatology. The famous chronicler of the 1960s, Theodore Roszak, suggested that countercultural dissent was only possible in the context of an affluent society, but debates about guaranteed income underscore a different dimension of the abundance discourse.[25] Affluence, combined with a mix of fear and idealism, promoted a new form of debate around automation which viewed technology as a potential source of liberation, but also enslavement. As the concerns of cybernation theorists gained an increasingly wide audience, different groups of activists and students seized upon the technological eschatology and explored its ramifications for policy reform.

Concerns around cybernation reached a wide audience throughout the 1960s and even spurred grassroots organizing within an increasingly political and engaged youth population. A primary example of such engagement is found in the Ad Hoc Committee for a Guaranteed Income (AHCGI), which was formed by a group of social work students from the University of Chicago's School of Social Service Administration in the summer of 1966.[26] From 1966 to 1968, the AHCGI published a monthly

[25] Roszak, *The Making of a Counter Culture: Reflections on the Technocratic Society and its Youthful Opposition* (Garden City, NY: Doubleday, 1969), 15.

[26] AHCGI as an abbreviation was never used by the committee itself, but I use this acronym to distinguish it from the Ad Hoc Committee on the Triple Revolution.

newsletter called the 'Guaranteed Annual Income Newsletter' or 'GAIN', which according to its statement of purpose was 'primarily intended for the interested citizen who wishes to learn about a pressing social issue rather than for the specialist'.[27] GAIN's intended audience suggests a different approach to guaranteed income debates from the characterization found in the academic literature. This evidence demonstrates that serious efforts were undertaken to broaden the appeal of an income guarantee by using the newsletter as a vehicle for communication between experts and a wider audience.

Not only did the issues discussed in GAIN address a different audience, they analysed a wider range of justifications for an income guarantee than those found in government agencies. The pages of GAIN comprised an impressive collection of social theorists who approached income guarantees from a range of perspectives and methodological backgrounds. Some of the most notable contributors included Edward Schwartz, Frances Fox Piven, and Richard Cloward, who, despite differing approaches and social concerns, argued for an income guarantee in the pages of GAIN. According to Irwin Garfinkel, a founding member of the AHCGI who was student in Chicago, both a desire for welfare reform and concerns about technological disruptions prompted consideration of the income guarantee.[28] Although the first issue of GAIN cast doubt on the predictions of an imminent technological transformation, the theme of automation appeared repeatedly in subsequent editions of the newsletter. This clearly reflected the influence of Robert Theobald, whose presence at a retreat in April 1966 first instigated interest in developing the newsletter.[29]

Theobald's own writing appeared in the May–June 1967 edition of the newsletter under the title 'Guaranteed Income: Short and Long-Run Issues'. In his article, Theobald remained committed to an income guarantee and he frequently referred to the long-run necessity of such a programme given forecasted economic developments. But unlike earlier works, Theobald approached the predicted chronology of technological change in a different light. In the conclusion of his article, he shifted the

[27] 'Statement of Purpose', *Guaranteed Annual Income Newsletter* 1, no. 1 (June 1966): 2.

[28] Chris Hughes, 'Historical Q&A: Irv Garfinkel on the Guaranteed Income', *Medium*, November 29, 2017, https://medium.com/economicsecproj/historical-q-a-irv-garfinkel-on-the-guaranteed-income-47260c585c20.

[29] 'The Ad Hoc Committee for a Guaranteed Income', *Guaranteed Annual Income Newsletter* 1, no. 1 (June 1966): 1.

debate from the immediate focus on statistics and policy specifics to a more general reflection on the moral state of American society:

> The basic debate must not therefore be permitted to drift into concerns about the details of how we set up measure to provide incomes to the poor: this is largely a technical question capable of largely technical solutions. The profound question is whether we will, or will not, concede the right of each man to participate in the decisions which determine his destiny.[30]

It is interesting to contrast Theobald's moral theorizing from the 1967 issue of GAIN to the more technical forecasts which appeared in earlier works such as *Free Men and Free Markets* and the *Rich and the Poor*.[31] By 1967, a presidential commission on technology, automation, and economic progress had published its report in the year prior to Theobald's article which seriously undermined the credibility of the more radical predictions about automation.[32] As is clear from the GAIN article and Theobald's 1968 book, *Committed Spending*, automation did not disappear from his policy calculus, but his economic critiques became rooted in an updated chronology.[33] Although Theobald never explicitly disavowed his earlier predictions, he couched his policy recommendations in a more abstract idiom as the 1960s progressed. Automation still appeared as a serious threat which required meaningful economic and social redress, but his later theories employed cybernation predictions as justifications for new social policies rather than motivators for immediate action.

The 'Guaranteed Annual Income Newsletter' represents an important, but seemingly forgotten chapter of the debate surrounding income guarantees and automation in the 1960s. The newsletter and its young publishers from the University of Chicago underscore a different form of engagement with social policy that bridged the divide between government bureaucrats and the public. The articles published in GAIN took

[30] Robert Theobald, 'Guaranteed Income: Short and Long-Run Issues', *Guaranteed Annual Income Newsletter*, 2, no. 1 (June 1967): 3.

[31] Robert Theobald, *The Rich and the Poor; a Study of the Economics of Rising Expectations*, (New York, NY: Potter, 1960); Robert Theobald, *Free Men and Free Markets* (Garden City, NY: Anchor Books, 1965).

[32] See chap. 2 and Appendix II in Harold Bowen et al., *Technology and the American Economy, Report of the National Commission on Technology, Automation, and Economic Progress* (Washington, DC: USGPO, 1966).

[33] Theobald, 'Guaranteed Income: Short and Long-Run Issues'.

seriously the question of automation while revealing that debates about cybernation clearly evolved as the 1960s progressed. The imminent threat of economic rupture appears to have waned by the end of the 1960s, but the topics raised by the cybernation frenzy remained salient to discussions of guaranteed income. Robert Theobald's own writings also demarcate an adaptation on the part of cybernation rhetoric which moved away from direct forecasting to more general considerations about the moral requirements of a technological society.

As cybernation theorists probed the relationship between humanity and its technological potential, a growing chorus of opposition had come to view the cybernation camp as a misinformed fringe group of policy theoreticians, who stole attention from the real problems of poverty and welfare reform. Opponents cited a falling unemployment rate during the mid-1960s as evidence that cybernation had not initiated the predicted period of technological unemployment, and one critic invoked the shortcomings of contemporary computer technology, writing in 1964: 'Had he [Theobald] recognized the computer's weakness in adapting itself creatively to unprogrammed problems, he might have come to different conclusions about the obsolescence of man'.[34]

In addition to academic critics, government studies from the 1960s also suggested that the cybernation camp had seriously overestimated the rate of technological change. A 1966 report of the National Commission on Technology, Automation, and Economic Progress entitled 'Technology and the American Economy' acknowledged the 1960s as a period of 'conscious social change', but held that technology was not a primary driver for persistent levels of unemployment. The report also predicted no significant change in economic productivity in the coming decade which would result in serious unemployment, beyond local effects in market sectors particularly well suited to automated technologies.[35] In short, government findings seriously challenged the assertions of Theobald and others by suggesting a rate of technological progress that would have significantly smaller destabilizing effects on employment and aggregate demand.

Existing literature on the cybernation frenzy from the 1960s has omitted crucial responses from writers like Daniel Bell and Robert Heilbroner, who, in the pages of the *New York Review of Books*, wrote extensive

[34] F. M. Scherer, review of *Review of Free Men and Free Markets*, by Robert Theobald, in *Technology and Culture* 5, no. 3 (1964): 483.

[35] Bowen, et al., *Technology and the American Economy* xi.

critiques of the most important works on cybernation theory from the decade. The essays by Bell and Heilbroner formed the basis of a printed debate in which Robert Theobald, Herbert Simon, and other cybernation theorists responded to their critics and challenged new claims to scientific authority. These debates not only offer a new perspective on the reception of cybernation theory, they also shed light on the role of expert authority during a period when claims to knowledge and expertise played an important role in shaping government policy.[36]

In 1965, the work of the Ad Hoc Committee on the Triple Revolution and the writings of Robert Theobald were the subject of a pointed critique by the sociologist Daniel Bell in the *New York Review of Books.* A professor at Columbia, a widely read public intellectual, and chair of the Commission for the Year 2000, Bell had already established himself as an intellectual authority in discussions of social and economic policy by the time he published 'The Bogey of Automation' in August of 1965. Historian Howard Brick has noted that liberal intellectuals, like Bell, had begun the 1960s with a commitment to the social sciences and an attendant belief that modernization theory had the capacity to successfully integrate emergent social sectors into a more unified society.[37] By the middle of the decade, however, violent protests challenged the optimism of liberal intellectuals and threw a menacing shadow over the predictions of social harmony which Bell and others had envisioned. Bell's essay on automation challenged the cybernation theorists on a variety of methodological grounds, but the context of emergent social unrest may help explain Bell's sneering dismissal of the 'specters of automation' as a distraction from 'the really difficult political and economic problems that lie ahead'.[38]

For Bell, forecasts of an automated future like those advanced by the Ad Hoc Committee on the Triple Revolution were methodologically unsound and uselessly provocative in a period of rapid and destabilizing change. In the opening of his essay, Bell somewhat mockingly referred to the Ad Hoc Committee as a 'new "school"', and despite his sardonic characterization, Bell implicitly conceded that the Committee had achieved a measure of popular respectability. By the time of his writing, the Ad Hoc

[36] See Nils Gilman, *Mandarins of the Future: Modernization Theory in Cold War America* (Baltimore, MD: Johns Hopkins University Press, 2003).

[37] Howard Brick, *Age of Contradiction: American Thought and Culture in the 1960s* (Ithaca, NY: Cornell University Press, 2000), 109.

[38] Daniel Bell, 'The Bogey of Automation', *New York Review of Books*, August 26, 1965, https://www.nybooks.com/articles/1965/08/26/the-bogey-of-automation/.

Committee had received coverage in the *New York Times*, and the works of Theobald and others had attracted a wider readership as the cybernation frenzy began to capture public attention.[39] Bell began his attack on the cybernation school by briefly outlining the claims of the Ad Hoc Committee and Donald Michael about the predicted increase in productivity before dismissing their reasoning as something 'based on speculation, not fact'. As evidence, Bell cited a range of statistics from government agencies to undermine such 'speculation' before turning to a broader question about the definition of 'technology'.

For Bell, the crux of the cybernation frenzy lay not in assessing the predictions of opposing camps in the automation debate, but rather in the methodological and scientific frames used to define and measure technological progress. Technology, in Bell's view, could only be understood through the language of economics: 'The most useful view is the one taken by economists, which maintains that technological change is change that increases the efficiency of a given set of productive forces; it is, to put it crudely, a change that gives you more production for less work.'[40] For Bell, productivity was the ideal metric for technological progress, and was easily measured with statistics like national income, labour force participation, and unemployment rates. With this framework, Bell dismissed the contention that automation was to blame for persistently high rates of unemployment by arguing that population growth had outpaced growth of national income. Under Bell's new economic accounting, the belief that technological unemployment lay behind previously inexplicable rates of unemployment was baseless.

The recourse to economic theory and the assertion of social-scientific frameworks as a source of unimpeachable authority offers an interesting example of what one historian has identified as 'the idea of forecasting as a social and political technology for post-industrial mass society'.[41] In this case, Bell used empirical economic claims to justify his argument that technological change could not explain persistent unemployment and was therefore unlikely to cause social rupture. For Bell, achieving high rates of growth would necessitate increases in both productivity and employment in the long run: 'With so many needs to be filled, we must have a rise in productivity that will require not only increased automation but the full

[39] 'Guaranteed Income Asked For All, Employed or Not'.

[40] Bell, 'The Bogey of Automation'.

[41] Andersson, *The Future of the World*, 101.

employment of the entire labour force'.[42] The twinned increase in automation and employment suggests that while Bell genuinely welcomed productivity-improving technologies, he viewed wage labour as necessary to ensure equitable economic and social outcomes. The call for a guaranteed income, therefore, undermined the employment tenet of Bell's vision for future prosperity.

The role of authority in debates about automated futures was taken up in Donald Michael's response to Bell in which he appropriated the language of fact versus speculation. In the opening lines of his response, Michael pointedly rejected Bell's putative factual authority: 'Any popular exploration of a topic as complex as cybernation is bound to be skimpy: to fuse fact and speculation. This includes Daniel Bell's contributions in the issue of August 26.'[43] Michael proceeded to question Bell's facts by citing difficulties in measuring macroeconomic data and challenging head-on the reliability of statistical measures from the Department of Labor and other traditional sources of empirical data. Michael's critique did not highlight alternative measures of productivity or economic growth which were superior to those cited by Bell. Instead, his critiques comprised an effort to undercut the legitimacy of Bell's argument. In this way, Michael charted a different course by accepting that all forecasts of technological progress will entail some amount of speculation:

> At any rate, no report conscientiously estimating the future could assert categorically that computers could be '*only* in offices' in certain industries, or that '*only* 14 of the 36 industries *could possibly use* computers to control production itself' during the coming decade. No available models can adequately, much less precisely, predict the rate at which an industry will cybernate. [...] These assertions are speculations, not facts—and incautious speculations at that.[44]

Michael's response did not precisely defend the cybernation theorists' claims, so much as attack Bell's analytical framework. Michael's argumentative technique called explicit attention to deficiencies in normal predictive metrics, such as those cited by Bell, and in so doing, he positioned the more radical predictions about automation as equally speculative.

[42] Bell, 'The Bogey of Automation'.

[43] Donald N. Michael, 'Automation', *New York Review of Books*, November 25, 1965, https://www.nybooks.com/articles/1965/11/25/automation-1/.

[44] Ibid.

The Bell-Michael debate offers an instructive perspective on the role of rational forecasting versus normative moral judgements in the development of social policy from this period. Historian Irving Kristol has written that left-wing championing of the 'automation scare' prompted a neoconservative retrenchment, which sought to reassert reason and incrementalism as the foundations for social policy initiatives.[45] Bell's response to Michael's 'speculative' claims about future predictions buttresses Kristol's argument that opponents of automation theorists used data and economic reasoning to undermine the validity of more radical claims about a step change in productive capacity. But rejection of the so-called automation scare by the likes of Bell, Leon Keyserling, and others was hardly definitive.[46] In fact, the publications of Herbert Simon, Donald Michael, and Robert Theobald—some of the most ardent exponents of a technological eschatology—continued to be read and receive serious consideration throughout the decade.

Evidence for continued interest in the topic is found once again in the *New York Review of Books* which continued to publish reviews of many significant texts on automation throughout the 1960s. In fact, Bell's August 1965 article was followed by a list of eight 'Recent Books on Automation', notwithstanding serious criticism from some academic circles. In the year following Bell's review, the prominent economist Robert Heilbroner, who was also a cosignatory of the 'Report on the Triple Revolution', published a lengthy review of Herbert Simon's *The Shape of Automation* and Robert Theobald's edited text *The Guaranteed Income* in the *New York Review*.

In Heilbroner's assessment of Simon and Theobald's writings, he accepted from the outset that technological unemployment would remain a prominent if, at times, unseen force in the capitalist future: 'I believe that a persistent cloud of technological displacement will nonetheless hover over the future of capitalism'.[47] But Heilbroner's acceptance of

[45] Irving Kristol, 'American Conservatism 1945–1995', *The Public Interest*, 121.

[46] Leon Keyserling published a short response to 'The Bogey of Automation' which accepted Bell's basic methodological framework but suggested slightly modified statistics about economic growth and productivity advances. See Daniel Bell and Leon H. Keyserling, 'Automation', *New York Review of Books*, November 25, 1965, https://www.nybooks.com/articles/1965/11/25/automation-2/.

[47] Robert L. Heilbroner, 'Where Do We Go From Here?', *New York Review of Books*, March 17, 1966, https://www.nybooks.com/articles/1966/03/17/where-do-we-go-from-here/.

technological unemployment as an inevitable feature of the future economic order did not translate into full-throated support for Simon or Theobald's arguments. Heilbroner's review took aim at Herbert Simon's self-styled moniker, 'technological radical and economic conservative', by suggesting that no form of economic conservatism could be compatible with the radical technological innovations anticipated by Simon's own work. This critique of Simon's view provides the foreground for Heilbroner's own argument that market mechanisms will be unable to ensure a smooth transition away from an economy based on wage labour:

> It is the question whether the market process will be able to supervise the inevitable transition to a society in which less labor will be used. I do not believe it will, nor do I think that the market will serve, at the terminal point of that transition, as an adequate mechanism for the distribution of income to the population in general, or of jobs to those who will work.[48]

Unlike Bell, Heilbroner was not primarily interested in the validity of short-term predictions about changes in productive capacity. Rather, he was centrally concerned about the role of market allocation mechanisms in the long term, and for this reason, he accepted guaranteed income proposals as a 'very useful remedy' to questions of economic distribution in a world of highly automated labour.

Nonetheless, Heilbroner's theoretical acceptance of an income guarantee was qualified in a way that Theobald's was not. Whereas Theobald proposed the prompt enactment of a programme of 'basic economic security', Heilbroner's timescale did not recommend an income guarantee in the near term: 'the long run is still a long way off, and in the meantime we have to operate within the confines of a market economy where technology is only gradually and incrementally making its effects know'. Still, the idea of an income guarantee did make Milton Friedman's negative income tax appear a more practicable alternative with similar benefits, and Heilbroner concluded his essay with explicit support for a form of Friedman's idea. Because Heilbroner accepted an income guarantee on a theoretical level, he came to view the negative income tax as a pragmatic intermediate step on the road to a full income guarantee. Even if the cybernation theorists' predictions or recommendations were not accepted

[48] Ibid.

in toto, their claims were used as different justifications for more incremental reforms, such as the negative income tax.

Several important themes emerge from the critique of cybernation theorists during the 1960s. First, and quite simply, technology and its potential for social change appeared as an important space for methodological, futurological, and ideological exchange during the decade. In addition to the reviews and listed texts which appeared in the *New York Review of Books* from 1965 to 1966, an essay from later in the decade unequivocally stated: 'No other single subject [technology] is so universally invested with high hopes for the improvement of mankind generally and of Americans in particular'.[49] Technology captured the attention of writers for a variety of reasons, but the quintessentially unknowable character of technological progress allowed theorists of different ideological persuasions to inscribe debates about technology with their own normative visions of the future. Some expressed reserved optimism whereas others were more fearful, but in all cases, a technological future represented a changed world that would challenge traditional principles of economic organization.

A second important theme to emerge is the role of scientific authority and expertise. As Theodore Roszak famously argued in *The Making of a Counterculture*, an ascendant technocracy of expert elites was remaking American society through a silent managerial conquest during the 1960s.[50] On first reading, the writings of academics in the *New York Review* appear to conform to Roszak's conception of a malign technocracy, but this ostensible similarity is not borne out upon closer examination. Although Theobald, Heilbroner, Simon, and others were part of an expert elite, they were deeply involved with the New Left and student organizers through their work on the Triple Revolution and GAIN. Further, their critiques of capitalism, market forces, and rejection of traditional economic metrics mirrored the calls for reform found within the broader counterculture. The 'Report on the Triple Revolution', for instance, was signed by leading figures from SDS, and the historian James Miller has noted that calls for

[49] John McDermott, 'A Special Supplement: Technology: The Opiate of the Intellectuals', *New York Review of Books*, July 31, 1969, https://www.nybooks.com/articles/1969/07/31/a-special-supplement-technology-the-opiate-of-the-/.

[50] Roszak, *The Making of a Counterculture*, 19.

renewed democracy in the report evidence the influence of ideas from student organizing.[51]

A final theme to observe from the automation debates is the exclusively American-centric focus of the exchange. Virtually no reference was made to foreign powers or the global implications of technological progress in the many pages devoted to automation. Rapid and destabilizing technological change appeared in these accounts as a uniquely American phenomenon. The almost total absence of reference to the socialist East or even other nations in the capitalist West reveals a deep current of American exceptionalism. The power of postwar growth and the advent of what Lizabeth Cohen has called the 'Consumer Republic' lent American discussions about economic progress a unique character.[52] Heilbroner and Theobald were both deeply critical of capitalist norms, and they questioned the ultimate efficacy of market-based systems, but they never appealed to contemporary examples of socialism in their arguments. Their reticence to invoke geopolitical foes like the Soviet Union is understandable within the context of Cold War discursive norms, but the absence of non-American examples goes further. As John McDermott noted in his 1969 essay, the potential and burden of technological progress was predicted to impact 'Americans in particular'. The lack of non-American references throughout the automation debates ignored important currents in the socialist East, in which communist ideologues and economic planners similarly probed the relationship between technology and socialist progress. Within the United States, concerns about cybernation and labour policies existed in a sphere that was largely disconnected from Cold War geopolitical considerations.[53]

The cybernation frenzy of the 1960s was a volatile space of debate which drew contributions from academics, government policymakers, and student activists. The stakes of this debate were extremely high—nothing less than the legitimacy of the capitalist system hung in the balance—and the rhetorical power of a technological eschatology prompted vigorous responses from both supporters and detractors of the cybernation forecasts. This chapter has argued that discussion that the threat of technological unemployment gave space to a new form of social critique which

[51] Miller, *Democracy Is in the Streets*, 192.

[52] Lizabeth Cohen, *A Consumer's Republic: The Politics of Mass Consumption in Postwar America* (New York, NY: Vintage Books, 2004).

[53] McDermott, 'A Special Supplement'.

questioned the very foundations of the liberal-capitalist state. The wide-reaching ramifications of an obsolete labour force prompted novel reconsideration of the responsibilities of an affluent American state. It was through these critiques that academic experts and student-level organizers came to consider a guaranteed annual income as a response to forecasted technological disruption.

CHAPTER 5

The Other Side of Abundance: Feminist and Ecological Arguments for Guaranteed Income in the United States, c. 1960–1980

Alyssa Battistoni

The decade since the financial crisis of 2008 has seen a proliferation of proposals for remaking systems of economic production and distribution. Among them has emerged steady interest in the idea of a universal basic income (UBI). For its advocates, UBI represents a solution to the persistence of poverty in affluent societies, a response to the threat of automation, and a tool to advance freedom for all. The new interest in UBI coincides with recognition of the ecological crisis of climate change and a resurgence of feminist thought and practice. Yet feminist and ecological arguments for basic income are rarely central to contemporary discussions of it. Rather, each is typically referenced—if at all—as one argument among many comprising the case for UBI, rather than as distinctive accounts of political economy and the role of UBI in it.

In this chapter, I present a history of feminist and ecological thought about proposals for guaranteed income in the United States in the 1960s

A. Battistoni (✉)
Barnard College, New York, NY, USA
e-mail: abattist@barnard.edu

P. Sloman et al. (eds.), *Universal Basic Income in Historical Perspective*, https://doi.org/10.1007/978-3-030-75706-9_5

and 1970s, showing how these guaranteed income supporters analysed and sought to address larger problems of the post-war political economy and welfare state. The guaranteed income proposals in question are not equivalent to universal basic income: guaranteed income refers to any policy which sets a baseline income standard, which may be achieved in various ways (through some combination of wages, benefits, tax credits, etc.), while universal basic income refers more specifically to a guaranteed income provided via universal, unconditional, regular payments. Yet they share enough that debates over the former can, and often do, serve as a guide to considering the politics of the latter.[1] Although feminist and ecological thinkers had different analyses of the guaranteed income, both groups understood the problems of industrialized capitalist society to extend beyond the persistence of poverty or the threat of automation, instead raising more fundamental questions about the organization of the economy, the meaning of work, the use and distribution of resources, and the relationship of economic rights to social oppression. The arguments examined here also complicate two common readings of UBI: one which sees UBI as a mechanism for individual freedom, as advanced by theorists like Philippe Van Parijs, and an emerging strain of intellectual history that characterizes basic income as fundamentally neoliberal in its market-oriented minimalism.

Van Parijs has been one of UBI's most steadfast advocates over the years and has done much to bolster the intellectual credibility of the idea. For van Parijs, the most fundamental argument for basic income is that it represents a commitment to 'real freedom for all'—to the ability of each individual to choose what to do with their own life. The paradigmatic figure of van Parijs's argument for basic income is the surfer, who contributes nothing to society but who, van Parijs argues, should be able to choose his own version of the good life nevertheless.[2]

[1] See the discussion by Philippe Van Parijs, 'A Basic Income for All', *Boston Review* (October/November 2000). Many articles in this volume also reference the history of debates over guaranteed income as important precursors to contemporary discussions of UBI: see in particular Anton Jäger, '"Free of Our Labours and Joined Back to Nature": Basic Income and the Politics of Post-Work in France and the Low Countries'; Daniel Zamora, 'Basic Income in the United States (1940–1972): How a Fringe Idea Went Global'; Andrew V. Sanchez, 'Cybernated America: Specters of Automation and Guaranteed Income in an Affluent Age'.

[2] Phillippe van Parijs, 'Why Surfers Should Be Fed: The Liberal Case for an Unconditional Basic Income', *Philosophy & Public Affairs* 20, no. 2 (Spring 1991): 101–131.

By contrast, Anton Jäger and Daniel Zamora offer a critique of UBI, and the more general conceit of the guaranteed income. In two recent articles, Jäger and Zamora observe that 'guaranteed income's "anti-normative" design … rendered it attractive to the New Left' and argue that interest in the guaranteed income 'grew in close correlation with a deeper subversion of the Keynesian paradigm'.[3] For Jäger and Zamora, guaranteed income should be read as a fundamentally neoliberal project, oriented towards expanding the scope of the market and envisioning freedom as individual consumer choice. They therefore argue that contemporary UBI proposals remain 'firmly rooted in a neoliberal understanding of social justice'.[4] Samuel Moyn makes a similar argument, charging that in the past four decades, campaigners for social justice have 'generally dropped material equality as a goal, prioritizing more basic and minimal aspirations to save the poor'.[5] The movement for human rights, he argues, has focused on sufficiency—provision of a minimum standard of living—rather than equality. The idea of universal basic income exemplifies the former for many of its defenders as well as its detractors: UBI sets a floor beneath which no human being is supposed to sink, regardless of how high some people rise.[6] 'Enough, in this view, is enough', Moyn writes—though his own view is that it is not. Jäger and Zamora agree with Moyn that discussions of a guaranteed income, constituting a 'floor' of social provision, have 'naturally sidelined discussion of building ceilings and the reduction of market dependency'.[7]

I agree with Jäger and Zamora that we must understand basic income as a historically specific phenomenon rather than a transhistorical 'idea', with a neat line drawn from Thomas Paine to Andrew Yang's campaign for the 2020 Democratic presidential nomination.[8] Yet I differ with aspects of their analysis of the historical moment in which basic income emerged.

[3] Daniel Zamora and Anton Jäger, 'One Question: Universal Basic Income', *State of Nature* blog, 30 July 2018, accessed 20 March 2020, https://stateofnatureblog.com/one-question-universal-basic-income/.

[4] Daniel Zamora and Anton Jäger, 'Historicizing Basic Income: Response to Daniel Zeglen', *Lateral* 8, no. 1 (Spring 2019).

[5] Samuel Moyn, *Not Enough: Human Rights in an Unequal World* (Cambridge, MA: Harvard University Press, 2018).

[6] See, for example, Andy Stern's book *Raising the Floor: How a Universal Basic Income Can Renew Our Economy and Rebuild the American Dream* (New York, NY: PublicAffairs, 2016).

[7] Zamora and Jäger, 'Historicizing Basic Income'.

[8] Yang campaigned almost exclusively around the idea of a UBI, which he characterizes as a 'freedom dividend' set at $1,000 per month. See Andrew Yang, *The War on Normal People:*

Jäger and Zamora argue that basic income should be read as 'a response to the decline of the centrality of work and of the post-war welfare state' since the 1960s and 1970s.[9] In my reading of feminist and ecological thinkers, it was at least as significantly a response to the much-touted abundance of the post-war era: both feminist and ecological thinkers presented novel analyses of the foundations of that abundance, arguing that post-war prosperity was built in part on un- and underpaid work performed by women and the overuse of natural resources. If post-war abundance seemed to represent the end of what Keynes had called the 'economic problem' of scarcity, moreover, it also seemed to open up an entirely new set of economic questions: how should this abundance be distributed, and how could it be sustained? These advocates for a guaranteed income, moreover, did not necessarily seek to decentre work. Rather, they presented their own analyses of work and its significance in the post-war economic order, and new accounts of how it should be organized in the future.

My discussion of feminist thought in Part I of this chapter focuses on the welfare rights movement in the United States in the 1960s and 1970s, as understood through organizers and members of the National Welfare Rights Organization (NWRO), a national, member-based organization of welfare recipients active between 1966 and 1975.[10] The thought of welfare rights organizers, I argue, must be seen as an important part of the intellectual history of basic income and taken seriously in its own right.[11] Welfare recipients, after all, received regular payments that were unconnected to specific tasks performed or objectives achieved; although such payments were conditional on need rather than universal, they nevertheless epitomized many of the anxieties about work, reward, and desert that characterize contemporary debates about UBI proposals. Even at the time, many analysts recognized that 'transfer payments', such as disability benefits and unemployment insurance, represented 'a vital, growing area

The Truth About America's Disappearing Jobs and Why Basic Income Is Our Future (New York, NY: Hachette, 2018).

[9] Zamora and Jäger, 'Historicizing Basic Income'.

[10] Although the term 'welfare state' describes an expansive array of social programmes, in the US context the term 'welfare' typically describes the benefits paid to single mothers under the programme Aid to Families with Dependent Children (AFDC).

[11] Although the welfare rights movement is rarely discussed in the philosophical literature on basic income, the work of the feminist political theorist Carol Pateman stands as a notable exception. See Terrell Carver and Samuel A. Chambers, eds., *Carol Pateman: Democracy, Feminism, Welfare* (New York, NY: Routledge, 2011).

where "work" and "pay" are not closely related', and were therefore relevant to discussions of guaranteed income.[12] The NWRO, moreover, declared a guaranteed income to be among its top priorities, and played a prominent role in debates around the version of guaranteed income contained in the Nixon administration's Family Assistance Plan (FAP), first introduced in 1969. Indeed, many of the philosophical arguments for a basic income developed in the 1980s and 1990s by van Parijs and others had been advanced in some form by welfare rights organizers during their campaign. Welfare rights organizers, however, developed these arguments not in the abstract, but in response to the particular conditions under which welfare was made available: women made up the vast majority of welfare recipients, and this shaped the way they understood the guaranteed income and its potential effects.[13]

Welfare rights organizers did not necessarily identify themselves as feminists per se. Although women, and black women in particular, made up the overwhelming majority of the NWRO membership, the organization identified itself as part of the poor people's movement rather than the simultaneously developing women's movement. At times the NWRO, comprised largely of poor black women, was at odds with predominantly white, middle-class feminist organizations. Its organizers' analyses of women's work, family structures, and the bases of women's independence nevertheless resonated with those made by socialist feminists and black feminists, and inspired aspects of the socialist feminist movement, like the Wages for Housework campaign of the 1970s.[14] Welfare recipients organizing with the NWRO framed the family as both a normative and economic institution, pointing to the gendered distribution of labour under Fordism and

[12] Meno Lovenstein, 'Guaranteed Income and Traditional Economics', in *The Guaranteed Income: The Next Step in Economic Evolution?*, ed. Robert Theobald (Garden City, NY: Doubleday & Co., 1966), 113.

[13] For a reading of welfare rights organizers as 'organic intellectuals' of the feminist movement, see Premilla Nadasen, 'Expanding the Boundaries of the Women's Movement: Black Feminism and the Struggle for Welfare Rights', *Feminist Studies* 28, no. 2 (2002).

[14] Guida West, *The National Welfare Rights Movement: The Social Protest of Poor Women* (New York, NY: Praeger, 1981), 232–248. For an analysis of the NWRO as a feminist influence on Martin Luther King, Jr.'s understanding of the guaranteed income, see Shatema Threadcraft and Brandon Terry, 'Gender Trouble: Manhood, Inclusion, and Justice', in *To Shape a New World: Essays on the Political Philosophy of Martin Luther King, Jr.*, eds. Tommie Shelby and Brandon Terry (Cambridge, MA: The Belknap Press, 2018); on Wages for Housework, see Silvia Federici and Arlen Austin, eds., *Wages for Housework: The New York Committee 1972–1977: History, Theory, Documents* (Brooklyn, NY: Autonomedia, 2017).

the limited options available to women working for wages.[15] Whereas basic income is often understood as providing income detached from work, many welfare rights organizers presented the demand for guaranteed income as a way of *recognizing* women's unpaid work. And while they argued that a guaranteed income could advance freedom, the subject they had in mind was not an individual free to choose any lifestyle, as per van Parijs's surfer, but a woman with children who was subject to male domination within the home, and who had few options outside of it, particularly since domestic work was unprotected by New Deal labour law. A gender-neutral guaranteed annual income could serve, somewhat paradoxically, as recognition of and compensation for women's unwaged labour, both in and out of the home; and it could free women from interpersonal forms of dependence, even as they rejected the stigmatized charge of 'dependency'.[16] Welfare organizers did seek to subvert the patriarchal elements of the welfare state, which subjected applicants to humiliating scrutiny of their parenting, backgrounds, and sexual history. But their arguments were not 'anti-normative' so much as 'alter-normative': that poor women should have some measure of autonomy in their lives and should not be subjected to heightened moral scrutiny simply because they were poor. Nor did welfare rights campaigners conceive of a guaranteed income simply as a defence against absolute poverty, but rather, sought an 'adequate' income.

In Part II, I turn to consider the ecological case for guaranteed income. Whereas most mainstream thinkers characterized the post-war period as one of unprecedented abundance, thinkers in and around the emerging environmental movement were troubled by the instability of this abundance, which they argued relied on environmentally destructive forms of production. The environmental impacts of the post-war boom in growth took many forms and generated new forms of politics under the banner of the environmental movement. The environmental impacts of nuclear testing, no longer secret, were put under increasing public scrutiny. Urban sprawl and growing car ownership resulted in worsening air pollution,

[15] Historians generally recognize that the central figure of the post-war economy and its welfare state was the male wage-earner: as Moyn observes, 'no welfare state designed policies that treated [women] equally', instead treating wage-earning men as 'proxies' for their wives and families. One of the central institutions of the post-war economy was the 'family wage'—a wage high enough for a male breadwinner to support a wife and children at home. Moyn, *Not Enough,* 38.

[16] On dependency, see Nancy Fraser and Linda Gordon, 'A Genealogy of Dependency: Tracing a Keyword of the U.S. Welfare State', *Signs* 19, no. 2 (Winter 1994): 309–336.

while untreated municipal sewage and unregulated waste disposal made waterways unfit for public use. High-profile disasters, like a 1966 oil rig blowout off the shore of Santa Barbara and the 1966 Cuyahoga River fire in Cleveland, drew further attention to environmental problems. The New Left criticized American consumer culture, while hippies embraced the 'back-to-the-land' movement. Growing environmental concern culminated in the first Earth Day on 22 April 1970, and in a suite of environmental legislation passed under Richard Nixon's presidency.[17]

In this context, ecological thinkers in the 1960s and 1970s sought to develop economic analyses that took such issues into account, and to propose new policies for addressing environmental problems, of which a guaranteed income was one. Here, I focus on environmental arguments for a guaranteed income made by the ecologist William Vogt and the ecological economist Herman Daly. Although similar in some respects, they emphasized different root causes of the environmental problem: Vogt's analysis centred on population, while Daly's focused on economic growth. Vogt suggested that a guaranteed income could promote ecologically beneficial forms of labour and leisure, but worried about its effects on population growth. His analysis exemplified a broader anxiety about overpopulation that would develop amongst a subset of ecologists, including Garrett Hardin and Paul Ehrlich. Daly, meanwhile, was one of a group of heterodox economists known as ecological economists, who launched a critique of the 'growthmanship' of the 1950s and argued that economics had to take the biophysical world into account. Daly proposed that a guaranteed income could be part of a shift away from the Keynesian growth economy and towards a 'steady state economy', which would necessitate a new structure of work and income. While, in the post-war economy, income was tethered to waged work and full employment was possible only with continued growth, Daly argued for both a floor *and* a ceiling for income, framing this policy as one part of a vision of an entirely different organization of production. A minimum and maximum income, he argued, would help limit inequality, which in turn drove conspicuous consumption and growth. Both Daly and Vogt advocated increased leisure pursued not simply as a matter of individual consumption choice, but as part of a broader social transformation that would reconnect people to the natural world and interrupt the cycle of production and consumption for its own sake. 'Enough',

[17] Robert Gottlieb, *Forcing the Spring: The Transformation of the American Environmental Movement* (Washington, DC: Island Press, 1993).

in their formulation, meant not only ensuring a baseline standard of sufficiency, but recognizing when needs were satiated.

From Welfare Rights to Guaranteed Income

Like most elements of the American welfare system, the first iteration of the benefits typically referred to as 'welfare' was put into place during the New Deal, through a programme then called Aid to Dependent Children (ADC). Part of the 1935 Social Security Act, ADC was modelled on the older tradition of 'mother's pensions'—stipends paid to widowed women with children, intended to support children whose fathers were deceased or otherwise absent from the household. Like other New Deal-era programmes, it was premised on the assumption that households comprised a male breadwinner and female caretaker; it was considered an uncontroversial programme to support the 'deserving poor' and a recognition of the value of motherhood.[18] In 1939, many of the recipients perceived as most 'deserving'—widows of workers who qualified for federal benefits and their children—became eligible for social insurance and received support through that mechanism instead, leaving ADC to provide primarily for unmarried mothers. By the 1960s, public perceptions of ADC, which became Aid to Families with Dependent Children (AFDC) in 1962, had changed drastically: it was viewed as a stigmatized programme for single mothers, and strongly associated with minority recipients.

The suite of programmes implemented under the banner of Lyndon Johnson's Great Society extended the scope of social welfare but did not fundamentally transform this two-tiered system, which allocated some benefits through universal social insurance programmes and others through programmes targeted expressly at the poor. While the former were popular and widely viewed as legitimate, the latter were increasingly stigmatized. Although Johnson proclaimed a War on Poverty in 1964, the bulk of Great Society spending was on universal social programmes that benefited the middle class.[19] Yet it was spending on the poor that captured the most attention. Welfare rolls grew drastically in the 1960s, and the

[18] Brian Steensland, *The Failed Welfare Revolution: America's Struggle over Guaranteed Income Policy* (Princeton: Princeton University Press, 2018).

[19] Thomas F. Jackson, 'The State, the Movement, and the Urban Poor: The War on Poverty and Political Mobilization in the 1960s', in *The 'Underclass' Debate: Views from History*, ed. Michael Katz (Princeton: Princeton University Press, 2018).

'welfare crisis' became the subject of national scrutiny. State and local governments blamed budget shortfalls on a growing number of welfare recipients, and Republicans pointed to anti-poverty programmes as an instance of government overreach.[20] For many observers, the expansion of the welfare rolls augured the rise of 'dependency': instead of utilizing state support temporarily as a safety net, they charged, a growing number of poor people relied entirely on government support for survival.[21] The figure of this problem was the single mother: as New York senator and sociologist Daniel Patrick Moynihan later observed, 'the symbol of welfare dependency was the female-headed family'—and the black female-headed family in particular.[22] Moynihan's own controversial analysis of black poverty famously centred on the dissolution of the black family, which he argued had left many households without a male breadwinner.[23]

At the same time, as the number of welfare recipients grew, a movement to organize them emerged, shaped by confluence of factors in the mid-1960s. As the first phase of the civil rights movement came to an end, many of its leaders turned their attention to questions of poverty and economic justice, while riots and unrest in many Western and Northern cities augured the rise of a new, more militant phase of the black freedom struggle on a national scale. Johnson's War on Poverty augured a sympathetic administration, and broader concern about 'poverty amidst plenty' presented an opening for welfare recipients to articulate their needs. The recognition of poverty as a national issue helped constitute 'the poor' as a group with political force. When the NWRO was founded in 1966, it joined a broader movement of poor people organizing around their needs.

The ostensible crisis of welfare produced a number of proposals for reforming or supplanting the existing welfare system. Richard Nixon criticized the War on Poverty during his presidential campaign, and, once in

[20] Mark McLay, 'A High-Wire Crusade: Republicans and the War on Poverty, 1966', *Journal of Policy History* 31, no. 3 (July 2019): 382–405; Steensland, *The Failed Welfare Revolution*.

[21] See Daniel P. Moynihan, 'The Crises in Welfare', *The Public Interest* 10 (Winter 1968): 3–29; Alice O'Connor, *Poverty Knowledge: Social Science, Social Policy, and the Poor in Twentieth-Century U.S. History* (Princeton: Princeton University Press, 2009); Karen M. Tani, *States of Dependency: Welfare, Rights, and American Governance*, 1935–1972 (Cambridge University Press, 2016); Fraser and Gordon, 'Genealogy of Dependency'.

[22] Daniel Patrick Moynihan, *The Politics of a Guaranteed Income: The Nixon Administration and the Family Assistance Plan* (New York, NY: Random House, 1973), 29.

[23] Daniel Patrick Moynihan, *The Negro Family: The Case for National Action* (Washington, DC: Office of Policy Planning and Research, US Department of Labour, 1965).

office, argued that anti-poverty programmes could be made more effective through reorganization and 'innovation'.[24] Milton Friedman's Negative Income Tax (NIT) constituted one such innovation: Friedman proposed a simple policy wherein any household falling below a certain level of income would, instead of paying income tax, receive a transfer sufficient to bring their income to the minimum standard. Nixon's Family Assistance Plan, introduced in 1969 but never passed, deployed a version of the NIT paired with various conditions, including work requirements.[25] From the left, the social scientists Richard Cloward and Francis Fox Piven proposed 'A Strategy to End Poverty', drawing attention to the fact that a huge number of people eligible for welfare benefits did not actually receive them. If poor people registered for welfare benefits to which they were entitled, Cloward and Piven argued, they would swamp the system and force reforms, ideally culminating in a guaranteed income.[26] The NWRO embraced Cloward and Piven's strategy and adopted the demand for a guaranteed income, which it declared a top priority at its first conference in 1967.[27] Although the guaranteed income could be obtained either through work that paid adequate wages or through social provision for those who could not work, the bulk of NWRO organizing addressed the state provision of income to mothers who did not work outside the home—colloquially, 'welfare'.

Rather than encouraging 'anti-normative' lifestyles or offering income without the expectation of work, however, these guaranteed income proposals were often concerned with stabilizing the family and incentivizing work by the poor. Jäger and Zamora argue that with Friedman's NIT represented a break from 'work requirements and their contractual dimension', shifting away from contractually mandated labour towards the use of incentives to motivate work.[28] Yet it was the existing welfare system that

[24] Richard Nixon, 'Special Message to the Congress on the Nation's Antipoverty Programs', 19 February 1969, *The American Presidency Project*; McLay, 'A High-Wire Crusade', 401.

[25] Steensland, *The Failed Welfare Revolution*. For another discussion of the NIT and FAP, see Zamora, 'Basic Income in the United States'; for a more thorough overview of the differences between the NIT and UBI, see Philippe Van Parijs and Yannick Vanderborght, *Basic Income: A Radical Proposal for a Free Society and a Sane Economy* (Cambridge, MA: Harvard University Press, 2017).

[26] Richard Cloward and Francis Fox Piven, 'The Weight of the Poor: A Strategy to End Poverty', *The Nation*, May 2, 1966.

[27] West, *The National Welfare Rights Movement*, 23–25.

[28] Jäger and Zamora, 'Historicizing Basic Income'; see also Zamora, 'Basic Income in the United States'.

seemed to its critics to offer rewards without work altogether. While guaranteed income proposals took a formally novel approach to encouraging work, therefore, they expressed a work imperative nonetheless. They were also often framed as a response to the moral crisis of female-headed households: as Melinda Cooper argues in her recent book *Family Values* (2017), elements of the demand for a guaranteed income were aimed at shoring up the American family, and the black family in particular.[29] Friedman's NIT proposal aimed to improve financial incentives for transfer recipients to undertake paid work, while Nixon's FAP, particularly in its amended 1972 instantiation, proposed a form of 'workfare' that would require welfare recipients to register for training or labour in order to receive benefits. The FAP also extended benefits to 'male-headed' families, seeking to incentivize not only work but two-parent families.[30]

The NWRO's arguments for guaranteed income differed significantly from both Friedman's NIT and Nixon's FAP. The NWRO sharply criticized the FAP as inadequate to the needs of welfare recipients, and its opposition is usually cited as a significant element in the programme's failure to pass.[31] Yet the NWRO, too, often presented its own case for a guaranteed income by appealing to the value of work and the moral status of the family, even as it challenged conventional meanings of these terms. For a segment of the welfare rights movement, the guaranteed income was intended to function as a 'black family wage': many welfare rights organizers did not disagree with Moynihan's argument that the breakdown of the black family was the origin of black poverty.[32] As Cooper observes, welfare rights defenders like Cloward and Piven advanced a family-centric argument for guaranteed income, arguing that welfare had contributed to the increase in single mothers by denying welfare benefits to households that included an unemployed male. A guaranteed income, they argued, would make it possible for families to stay together while receiving state benefits—a precise echo of Moynihan's argument. In its first few years of operation, the NWRO, led by executive director George Wiley and predominantly male staff, held the view that the existing system of welfare

[29] Melinda Cooper, *Family Values: Between Neoliberalism and the New Social Conservatism* (New York, NY: Zone Books, 2017).

[30] Moynihan, *The Politics of Guaranteed Income;* Cooper, *Family Values;* Felicia Kornbluh, 'Who Shot FAP? The Nixon Welfare Plan and the Transformation of American Politics', *The Sixties: A Journal of History, Politics and Culture* 1, no. 2 (2008): 125–150.

[31] Kornbluh, 'Who Shot FAP?'

[32] Cooper, *Family Values.*

weakened the family and prioritized goals that reinforced rather than challenging normative positions regarding family structure and gender roles. As the historian Premilla Nadasen observes:

> They blamed the welfare system for the rise in single-parent families. One staff person said, AFDC [Aid for Families with Dependent Children] 'does undermine the family structure because in most states a family headed by an able-bodied man cannot get welfare no matter how poor it is. So to get help for his family a father has to leave.' The guaranteed income, available to two-parent and single-parent families, would resolve this problem.[33]

Welfare recipients themselves sometimes echoed this rhetoric as well. Cassie Downer, a welfare recipient and the chair of the Milwaukee County Welfare Rights Organization, a local branch of the NWRO, argued that 'the family is the basis of American society, but we are moving away from the family because people are forced out of the home in order to get an adequate income'.[34] The NWRO advocated the achievement of a guaranteed income via a gendered dual track: access to jobs with adequate wages for men, and guaranteed welfare benefits for women with children. Its platform for the 1968 Poor People's Campaign, for example, called for a minimum guaranteed income of $4000 for every family, and for three million jobs for men specifically.[35]

Yet many NWRO members and organizers took a different tack, explicitly framing a guaranteed income as a way to be free from dependence on a man or to escape oppressive familial and intimate relationships. Welfare claimants were pathologized by critics for their 'dependency' on the state, portrayed as the pathetic, parasitic obverse of the independent wage-earner. They sought to challenge this depiction, pointing out that marriage itself constituted a form of interpersonal dependence—but a socially acceptable one. Women were forced to maintain relationships with men in order to get by.[36] As Nadasen argues, then, 'in fighting for a guaranteed income and higher benefit levels, they also demanded economic

[33] Premilla Nadasen, *Welfare Warriors: The Welfare Rights Movement in the United States* (New York, NY: Routledge, 2004), 165.

[34] Milwaukee Welfare Rights Organization, *Welfare Mothers Speak Out* (New York: W.W. Norton, 1972).

[35] 'NWRO Demands for the Poor People's Campaign', *NOW!*, August 21, 1968; cited in West, *The National Welfare Rights Movement*, 88.

[36] Fraser and Gordon, 'A Genealogy of Dependency'.

autonomy, that is, access to enough money to raise their children independent of men'.[37] Central to this line of argument was Johnnie Tillmon, an African-American woman from California and the first chair of the NWRO, who led a push for welfare recipients to have more power within the organization. Before joining the NWRO, Tillmon—a former union shop steward—had organized welfare recipients in California through the local group ANC [Aid to Needy Children] Mothers Anonymous. ANC Mothers Anonymous had identified welfare as a women's issue specifically and advocated for a 'women's agenda' comprising childcare and access to training and jobs not only for male heads of household, but for mothers who received welfare. In 1972, Tillmon made the case that 'Welfare is a Women's Issue in *Ms.* Magazine, then a central publication of the feminist movement. As Tillmon wrote, 'Society needs women on welfare as "examples" to let every woman, factory workers and housewife workers alike, know what will happen if she lets up, if she's laid off, if she tries to go it alone without a man'.[38] A guaranteed income, she argued, would 'eliminate sexism from welfare'.[39] Access to welfare constituted a form of economic independence for women, one which gave them more control in their relationships with men.[40]

At the same time, Tillmon pointed out, while the welfare state had liberated many women from dependence on an individual man, it had subjected them to different forms of subordination. Tillmon emphasized the sexism at work in the conditions imposed on welfare recipients:

> Welfare is like a super-sexist marriage. You trade in a man for the man. But you can't divorce him if he treats you bad. ... The man runs everything. In ordinary marriage, sex is supposed to be for your husband. On A.F.D.C., you're not supposed to have any sex at all. You give up control of your own body. It's a condition of aid. You may even have to agree to get your tubes tied so you can never have more children just to avoid being cut off welfare.[41]

The state acted as a patriarch more controlling than any individual father, husband, or boyfriend, determining how women could behave. Tillmon

[37] Premilla Nadasen, Jennifer Mittelstadt and Marisa Chappell, eds., *Welfare in the United States: A History with Documents 1935–1996* (New York, NY: Routledge, 2003), 58.

[38] Tillmon, 'Welfare is a Women's Issue'.

[39] Tillmon, 'Welfare is a Women's Issue'.

[40] Nadasen, 'Expanding the Boundaries'.

[41] Johnnie Tillmon, 'Welfare is a Women's Issue', *Ms.* (Spring 1972).

and others argued that they should be able to choose relationships with men on their own terms: they should be able to engage in sexual and romantic relationships as they chose without compromising their access to benefits, and should not be forced to depend on men for support.[42] Though critical of the state, however, Tillmon and other NWRO organizers should not be classified as 'anti-statist': they did not reject the state altogether, but sought to transform it such that it treated welfare recipients with dignity, as it did recipients of social insurance.[43] Instead, in many ways the welfare state functioned more like an employer than a provider of a guaranteed benefit: recipients were scrutinized, examined, and held accountable for their failures to live up to the state's standards of homemaking and morality. Organizers insisted that women should receive public benefits adequate to meet their needs and the needs of their children, without the kind of monitoring to which they were frequently subject. Calls for a guaranteed income did serve as a critique of the prevailing morality then, but not of morality *per se*; rather, welfare recipients criticized the imposition of moral standards exclusively on poor women. Many welfare recipients also articulated a different set of moral values, insisting on the worth—both economic and moral—of their work as mothers in arguing for a guaranteed income.[44] Although 'mothers' were sanctified in the abstract, in reality, only middle-class white women were treated as if they deserved the status of motherhood. Black mothers in particular were vilified for having too many children; yet their insistence on keeping them, rather than giving them up for adoption, was an assertion of 'family values' in its own right.[45]

NWRO organizers also advanced an analysis of the economic value of women's work in the home. One of the sources of women's poverty, they argued, was that the post-war economy and its welfare state did not recognize women's unwaged work as productive, meaning that they were poor *despite* the fact that they worked. They were not freeloaders or parasites, they argued: to the contrary, they did crucial work that went unrecognized and unrewarded. A guaranteed income could effectively serve as payment for that work. Downer argued that 'the greatest thing a woman

[42] Nadasen, 'Expanding the Boundaries'.

[43] For an analysis of anti-statist arguments for guaranteed income, see Jäger, 'Free of Our Labours'.

[44] Nadasen et al., *Welfare in the United States.*

[45] See Annelise Orleck, *Storming Caesar's Palace: How Black Mothers Fought Their Own War on Poverty* (Boston, MA: Beacon Press, 2005).

can do is raise her own children, and our society should recognize it as a job. A person should be paid an adequate income to do that.'[46] Tillmon similarly argued that, if she were President, she would 'issue a proclamation that women's work is real work' and 'start paying women a living wage for doing the work that we are already doing—child raising and housekeeping'.[47] These arguments inspired the socialist feminists associated with the Wages for Housework movement, who saw African-American women struggling for welfare rights as progenitors of their own movement to recognize and wage work performed in the home. The international Wages for Housework campaign built close ties to the NWRO in the latter's waning days, and in 1976, a year after the NWRO had dissolved for lack of funds, the Wages for Housework campaign organized a conference on welfare to discuss resistance to welfare cuts then in motion. The conference framed welfare as a wage won for work: 'Welfare is the first money we women have won directly from the government for the work we do in our homes', a leaflet declared.[48] Welfare should be replaced, they argued, with 'wages for housework' paid to all women. Although they used the language of the 'wage' rhetorically in describing the right of welfare mothers to receive benefits, what they demanded in practice was not wages at all, but the public provision of social needs regardless of actual work performed. Although women's dependence on men and the state bore similarities, Wages for Housework theorist Silvia Federici argued, the difference was politically significant. Welfare brought reproduction out of the individual home and privacy of the family, making it public and political. It gave women a claim on public resources, and a claim to struggle around, as working men had long struggled around the wage paid by their employer: in fact, many in the NWRO described the organization as a 'union' for poor women.

Access to waged work also remained significant in the normative framework deployed by welfare organizers. Many welfare recipients insisted they wanted to work outside the home, but argued that women could not find jobs that paid enough to support their families, that they could not work outside the home without access to affordable childcare, and that if they

[46] Cassie Downer, in *Welfare Mothers Speak Out*, 136.

[47] Tillmon, 'Welfare is a Women's Issue'.

[48] *Come to a Conference Sponsored by the New York Wages for Housework Committee, Saturday, April 25, 10am–6pm*, conference invitation leaflet, emphasis in original (Silvia Federici Archives), cited in Louise Toupin, *Wages for Housework: A History of an International Feminist Movement, 1972–1977*, trans. Käthe Roth (London: Pluto Press, 2018).

did earn money from waged work, they would lose their benefits.[49] The problem was not that poor women did not have a 'work ethic', as was often charged, but that the kinds of jobs they could get were poorly paid, often part-time, and frequently conflicted with their parental responsibilities. The two problems were related: domestic and care work were not valued when they were done in the home, and they were not valued highly when they were waged. Without education and training, those were the only kinds of jobs that most poor women could get. Many women on welfare had previously worked as 'domestics'; they pointed out the absurdity of paying someone else to take care of their children so they could get a low-wage job cleaning someone else's home or caring for someone else's children.[50] As the organizer Beulah Sanders argued, 'If you're going to slave for nine hours a day and get nothing but the same welfare check … you can sit home and take care of your family, instead of paying someone else to take care of them and get the same nothing'.[51] Welfare recipients therefore argued not only for support for women who worked within the home, but for access to education, free childcare, and good jobs with adequate wages for women who worked outside it. Where conservatives argued that welfare payments reduced the incentive to work, welfare recipients pointed to the conditions of work as the real problem. The NWRO thus demonstrated a sophisticated analysis of the limitations of the existing structure of work. Rather than simply arguing for the alleviation of poverty through cash transfers and income support alone, they identified the structural causes of their poverty, and the barriers to 'working their way out of it'. They saw a guaranteed income not as an 'alternative' to increases in the minimum wage, as Friedman and others did, but as complementary elements of a programme to adequately pay for domestic and care work, wherever it was done.[52]

As Frances Fox Piven and Wilson Sherwin observe, welfare rights organizers drew attention not only to their work as mothers, but to 'the

[49] The tension between calling for a guaranteed income obtained through work or welfare was persistent throughout the history of the NWRO. See West, *The National Welfare Rights Movement*; Felicia Kornbluh, *The Battle for Welfare Rights: Politics and Poverty in Modern America* (Philadelphia: University of Pennsylvania Press, 2007).

[50] Orleck, *Storming Caesar's Palace*.

[51] Cited in West, *The National Welfare Rights Movement*, 89.

[52] See Zamora's discussion of the negative income tax as an alternative to minimum wages, this volume.

necessity and relevance of community engagement'.[53] Piven and Sherwin quote the Brooklyn Welfare Organization (B-WAC) organizer Jacqueline Pope describing how welfare organizers 'promoted discussions concerning social or political unsalaried community participation that was as important as salaried work. In essence, people could make contributions to improving the quality of community life regardless of their employment status.'[54] The argument for a guaranteed income can therefore also be seen as resonant with arguments for a 'political economy of citizenship', one that recognizes that time away from work is necessary for political engagement and democratic participation.[55] Years later, the political theorist Carol Pateman would articulate similar arguments in defence of a universal basic income as an element of democratic social reproduction, which seeks to uphold the 'social web of interdependence'.[56] Pateman has described a guaranteed income as a critical element of democratization—which 'would allow individuals more easily to refuse to enter or to leave relationships that violate individual self-government or that involve unsafe, unhealthy, or demeaning conditions'—in terms that echo those of welfare rights organizers.[57]

Welfare, of course, was not a universal benefit; even the guaranteed annual income proposal was not a truly universal basic income. But as welfare rights organizers campaigned for a guaranteed income, they often framed their struggle in universal terms. Tillmon declared that 'welfare is a women's issue', arguing that welfare rights organizers were 'the front-line troops of women's freedom': the economic struggles of poor and working-class women were essential to understanding women's oppression and achieving liberation more broadly.[58] Through their struggles to recognize women's work and dependence on men for income, she suggested, 'maybe we poor welfare women will really liberate women in this country'.[59]

[53] Wilson Sherwin and Frances Fox Piven, 'The Radical Feminist Legacy of the National Welfare Rights Organization', *WSQ: Women's Studies Quarterly* 47, no. 3 (2019): 139.

[54] Cited in Sherwin and Piven, 'Radical Feminist Legacy'.

[55] Michael Sandel, *Democracy's Discontent: America in Search of a Public Philosophy* (Cambridge, MA: The Belknap Press, 1998), 123–5.

[56] Carol Pateman, 'Another Way Forward: Welfare, Social Reproduction, and a Basic Income', in *Carol Pateman: Democracy, Feminism, Welfare,* eds. Terrell Carver and Samuel A. Chambers (New York, NY: Routledge, 2011), 42.

[57] Carol Pateman, 'Democratizing Citizenship: Some Advantages of a Basic Income', *Politics & Society* 32, no. 1 (March 2004): 95.

[58] Tillmon, 'Welfare is a Women's Issue'.

[59] Tillmon, 'Welfare is a Women's Issue'.

Welfare rights organizers often extended their arguments beyond their own labour to encompass other forms of unwaged work: Downer, for example, observed that not only mothers but 'all people contribute to our society in one way or another', arguing that 'a guaranteed adequate income will recognize work that is not now paid for by society'.[60] 'We are not an organization of selfish people and we are not out to get things done just for Welfare Rights or members of our organization', Sanders wrote. 'We, as an organization, want to see some guaranteed adequate income for all people in the United States of America.'[61] Everyone contributed to society, and everyone deserved a guaranteed income. In fact, they pointed out, nearly everyone in America was on welfare already—whether via tax relief for married couples, homeowners' assistance, debtors' aid, corporate subsidies (particularly for oil companies), or student scholarships. In a complex modern society, everyone was dependent in some way: 'independence' was a fantasy. Dependency was a universal condition, they argued: everyone was dependent on the state to some degree, as well as on each other.

Finally, rather than envisioning a guaranteed income as merely a subsistence income, the NWRO emphasized that its demand was for an 'adequate income: a system which guarantees enough money for all Americans to live dignified lives above the level of poverty'.[62] The NWRO defined an adequate minimum income as one that would allow families to 'live in dignity' with their basic needs met, and so demanded a federal guaranteed income of $5,500 in 1969 (approximately $40,000 in 2020) using data from the Bureau of Labor Statistics.[63] Although this demand was for 'enough', it was a definition of 'enough' that exceeded mere subsistence. The call for an 'adequate' income was a call for inclusion in social life, and organizers acted accordingly, insisting that welfare recipients should not simply eke out survival, but should be able to enjoy small luxuries like Christmas presents. This emphasis on an adequate income would subsequently be key to republican justifications of basic income: as Philip Pettit would argue nearly four decades later, any 'satisfactory argument for basic income', assessed on republican grounds, must 'establish a right to an intuitively adequate level of income'.[64] Indeed, the most common objection to

[60] Downer, in *Welfare Mothers Speak Out*, 135.

[61] Nadasen et al., *Welfare in the United States.*

[62] West, *The National Welfare Rights Movement,* 39.

[63] West, *The National Welfare Rights Movement,* 42.

[64] Philip Pettit, 'A Republican Right to Basic Income?', *Basic Income Studies* 2, no. 2 (2007): 1.

the NWRO's guaranteed income proposal was that their suggested guaranteed income would give those on welfare an income on par with that of low-wage workers—that their definition of 'enough' was in fact too much.[65]

Although some NWRO organizers therefore sought to challenge and transform prevailing conceptions of work and family, they did not succeed. In spite of welfare recipients' efforts to portray themselves as representative of a widespread need for government support, they were depicted by critics as distinctively deviant, described by Ronald Reagan and other politicians of the New Right as 'welfare queens' living parasitically off social wealth. Despite receiving a tiny portion of the federal budget, welfare recipients were scapegoated for economic stagnation.[66] In particular, the critique of 'welfare' became a way of enacting the backlash against the civil rights movement. Martin Gilens argues that the expansion of welfare was a crucial factor in 'how the poor became black': public perceptions of poverty shifted from the 'poor rural whites of Appalachia' to poor urban blacks, who were cast as lazy and entitled, even though the majority of AFDC recipients were white women.[67] 'Welfare reform' would take another two decades, culminating in President Bill Clinton's pledge to 'end welfare as we know it' and the passage of the Personal Responsibility and Work Opportunity Reconciliation Act (PRWORA), which ended AFDC and replaced it with 'temporary assistance for needy families' (TANF). TANF set sharp limits on support for single mothers to care for children at home, instead incentivizing waged work—and marriage.[68]

Ecology and Growth

Where welfare recipients argued for a guaranteed income as compensation for unwaged work and a means to women's liberation, some environmental thinkers saw a guaranteed income as part of a programme to jump off the treadmill of production and consumption that had fuelled the post-war economic boom, and whose environmental effects were becoming

[65] Moynihan, *The Politics of Guaranteed Income.*

[66] See Pateman, 'Another Way Forward', 191.

[67] Martin Gilens, 'How the Poor Became Black: The Racialization of American Poverty in the Mass Media', *Race and the Politics of Welfare Reform,* eds. Sanford F. Schram, Joe Soss and Richard C. Fording (Ann Arbor, MA: University of Michigan Press: 2003).

[68] Pateman, 'Another Way Forward'.

increasingly apparent.[69] Rachel Carson's landmark 1962 book *Silent Spring* drew attention to the effects of industrial production, from agricultural pesticides which killed wildlife to smokestacks and internal combustion engines which rendered the air thick with pollution.[70] *Silent Spring* served as a catalyst for the American environmental movement, which joined the New Left in critiquing American consumer society.[71] Anxiety about growth was widespread, and intensified with the 1972 publication of the Club of Rome's report on *The Limits to Growth*, which predicted the end of cheap and widely available natural resources in the near future.[72] The energy crisis of 1973, though not actually caused by biophysical scarcity, gave credence to fears that the Earth was running low on resources. The age of abundance seemed to be coming to a close.

The idea of 'enough' was popular with ecological thinkers, but it did not simply mean that every person should have sufficient resources to ensure bare survival. Rather, the call for 'enough' was meant as a warning against growth for its own sake. 'Enough' meant accepting adequate plenitude and comfort rather than relying on perpetual growth to relieve poverty and social harms. It entailed not only a 'floor' below which no one should fall, but a different view of political economy altogether, one that sought limits to work, production, and inequality—otherwise, desire and consumption could spiral indefinitely. Achieving sufficiency for all without devastating the planet required greater equality. In this context, a guaranteed or minimum income was almost entirely pragmatic, proposed as a way to meet human needs without creating new wants or requiring new production to provide employment. Yet the guaranteed income on its own would not bring about an ecological society, if people used it to engage in resource-intensive activities, avoid ecologically beneficial work, or—for neo-Malthusians—have more children. A guaranteed income was therefore only one part of a broader programme for ecological transformation.

[69] This period is now described as the 'Great Acceleration', comprising both economic growth and increased biophysical impacts. J.R. McNeill and Peter Engelke, *The Great Acceleration: An Environmental History of the Anthropocene Since 1945* (Cambridge, MA: The Belknap Press, 2014).

[70] Rachel Carson, *Silent Spring* (Boston: Houghton Mifflin, 1962).

[71] Gottlieb, *Forcing the Spring*.

[72] Donella H. Meadows, Dennis L. Meadows, Jørgen Randers, William W. Behrens III, *Limits to Growth: A Report for the Club of Rome's Project on the Predicament of Mankind* (Washington, DC: Potomac Associates, 1972).

The ornithologist William Vogt considered contemporary guaranteed income proposals more specifically in relation to ecological questions in his essay 'Conservation and the Guaranteed Income' in Robert Theobald's edited volume *The Guaranteed Income* (1965). Vogt, the author of the 1948 bestseller *The Road to Survival*, had long argued that the growing human population threatened ecological function, and that many efforts aimed at improving human welfare encouraged excessive population growth. Vogt criticized the Food and Agriculture Organization's provision of food aid to India and China, argued that medical care contributed to overpopulation by preventing deaths, and called for 'sterilization bonuses' rather than pro-natalist family allowances. In 1951, he was made National Director of the Planned Parenthood Federation of America.[73] His arguments would help spur a neo-Malthusian revival amongst ecologists, as eventually popularized by the biologist Paul Ehrlich's 1968 bestseller *The Population Bomb*.[74]

Vogt found the prospect of a guaranteed income simultaneously intriguing and worrisome. Foremost among his anxieties was the potential for a guaranteed income to contribute to a population increase. The free goods and services of the welfare state were already pro-natalist, he thought: 'At present "free" schooling, "free" books, "free" school lunches, draft exemption for married men, subsidized, low-income housing and income-tax reductions all favor the larger family', he argued.

> [W]hat the guaranteed income will do—if anything—to birth rates is one of the most important questions that can be asked about it because it might have a fundamental effect on the place of man within his ecosystem ... if the guaranteed income tends to subsidize early marriage and irresponsible procreation, it may not only help to defeat the end toward which it is directed; it may help to bring disaster down upon the country.[75]

The only time the American birth rate had ever decreased was during the Great Depression, he observed; this decline had been 'brought about voluntarily, under economic pressure'.[76] A guaranteed income would relieve

[73] Matthew Connelly, *Fatal Misconception: The Struggle to Control World Population* (Cambridge, MA: Belknap Press, 2008).

[74] Paul Ehrlich, *The Population Bomb* (New York: Ballantine Books, 1968).

[75] William Vogt, 'Conservation and the Guaranteed Income', in *The Guaranteed Income*, ed. Robert Theobald (New York, NY: Anchor Books, 1965), 152.

[76] Vogt, 'Conservation', 142.

that kind of economic pressure, and thus, Vogt thought, would likely cause birth rates to shoot up. Growing population, moreover, created more competition for jobs, thus exacerbating one of the problems that a guaranteed income was intended to solve.

Vogt's analysis of welfare was shared by other ecological critics in the lineage of Thomas Malthus. The ecologist Garrett Hardin's famous article on the 'tragedy of the commons', first published in 1968, focused its analysis not on the oft-discussed problem of grazers sharing a common field, but on the American welfare state. For Hardin, as for Vogt, welfare created an incentives problem: freed by state support from the constraints of survival of the fittest, there was no reason for people not to have more children than they could afford and than the earth could sustain.[77] Welfare payments and child allowances, Hardin and others suggested, might actively encourage people to have more children in order to obtain more income; thus the most significant question regarding a guaranteed income was whether it would do the same. In fact, there was little evidence to suggest that access to welfare increased family size. Many population campaigners nevertheless followed Vogt and Hardin in criticizing the welfare system for encouraging people to have more children than they could support. As one local coordinator for the organization Zero Population Growth argued, 'there is a great deal of resentment about the welfare mothers being able to have as large a family as they want at the taxpayer's expense while the taxpayer is being asked to limit himself to only one or two natural children'.[78]

At the same time Vogt saw many potential benefits to a guaranteed income. He acknowledged that it would create more time for leisure: for people to enjoy the outdoors, to play recreational sports, to not only spend more time in nature but to learn more about it—all activities that would offer opportunities for humans to reconnect to nature. As Vogt argued, 'outdoor recreation under the guaranteed annual income could make an important contribution by letting people in on such secrets as the fact that a marsh is at least as interesting and beautiful as a Picasso'.[79] Others, 'relieved of economic necessity by the guaranteed income, might

[77] Garrett Hardin, 'The Tragedy of the Commons', *Science* 162 (December 1968): 1243–8.

[78] Keith Makoto Woodhouse, *The Ecocentrists: A History of Radical Environmentalism* (New York, NY: Columbia University Press, 2018), 88.

[79] Vogt, 'Conservation', 152.

find great satisfaction in helping with [ecological] research'.[80] For farmers, a guaranteed income might effectively serve as a subsidy allowing them to better manage their woodlots rather than cutting them prematurely for cash.[81] It might encourage resettlements of 'small towns and country life where dollars go further', helping to 'restore many "distressed" areas to social and economic health'; it might encourage the rediscovery of gardening and hunting.[82] Yet in a world organized around work, the challenge of 'coping with leisure' would be significant: 'we, as a people, are not prepared for leisure'.[83] It would be particularly challenging to enjoy leisure in ways that were not environmentally destructive (after all, much outdoor activity involved extensive automobile travel) or stultifying (Vogt feared a nation of people glued to the television).

Yet if leisure might encourage nature appreciation, Vogt also worried that removing the compulsion to work would have negative effects. Some forms of environmentally beneficial work might be encouraged by a guaranteed income—for instance, people supported by a guaranteed income might volunteer to help scientific research or tend to national parks. But other forms of less pleasant work would also need to be done; indeed, many forms of ecologically beneficial work were likely to be labour-intensive. 'Automation is no more suited', Vogt argued, 'to building up food and cover for prairie chickens or grouse than it is for fighting the war in South Vietnam. There will be, for the foreseeable future, hard physical work to be done.'[84] Labour-intensive agriculture was better for the environment than highly mechanized production, for example, but would be rendered impossible by a scarcity of workers; he feared that a small group of people would end up doing the 'noisome jobs' of society, effectively made 'untouchables'.[85] To counter this stratification, he proposed creating a Citizens' Service Corps, which would put young people to work nursing, caring for the sick and elderly, and undertaking conservation projects, perhaps as a requirement of receiving the guaranteed income.

For all the challenges a guaranteed income presented, however, Vogt argued that 'we shall almost certainly need something like it'.[86] For it to

[80] Ibid., 153.
[81] Ibid., 156.
[82] Ibid., 147–8.
[83] Ibid., 149–50.
[84] Ibid., 166.
[85] Ibid., 159.
[86] Ibid., 147.

work, it would have to exist not as a tool to undermine moral consensus, but in tandem with a project of renewed moral development and education, one that would actively seek to rebuild human relationships to nature and reconstruct a society oriented around appreciation for nature, arts, and intellectual life rather than the easy gratification of television. Only embedded in such an overarching societal transformation could guaranteed income satisfy the needs of conservation as well as people.

Vogt's guaranteed income was therefore one element of a broader programme aimed at controlling population and developing a new moral order centred around nature. For the ecological economist Herman Daly, meanwhile, the guaranteed income was part of a more thorough transformation of social and economic structures away from the 'growth economy' of the post-war era. Daly had been a graduate student in development economics when he encountered Nicholas Georgescu-Roegen, a foundational thinker of ecological economics whose book *The Entropy Law and the Economic Process* (1971) sought to ground economics in the laws of thermodynamics. While conducting research in northeastern Brazil in 1967, Daly began to piece together a new theory of economics, drawing on Georgescu-Roegen's study of energy, Carson's attention to ecology, John Stuart Mill's account of the economic stationary state, and his own observations of Brazilian society, most notably the class differential in numbers of children.[87] He began to articulate an account of what he called the 'steady state economy'—an economy which sought to maintain, rather than increase, material throughput.

Achieving a steady state, Daly argued, would require substantial changes to the organization of production and distribution, and hence in the organization of work and income. Full employment, one of the pillars of the post-war social contract, relied on economic growth, and economic growth relied on a cycle of production and consumption that resulted in environmental degradation. To break this cycle and stave off ecological catastrophe would require a new relationship of production to income. As Daly wrote in a 1971 essay:

> Growth is necessary to maintain full employment. Only if it is possible for nearly everyone to have a job can the income-through-jobs ethic of distribution remain workable. ... Why do people produce junk and cajole other

[87] Herman Daly, 'Ecologies of Scale', Interview by Benjamin Kunkel, *New Left Review* 109 (January–February 2018).

> people into buying it? Not out of any innate love for junk or hatred of the environment, but simply in order to earn an income. ... We need some principle of income distribution independent of and supplementary to the income-through-jobs link.[88]

Daly's argument for a guaranteed minimum income would be cited in the 1972 *Limits to Growth* report: in a 'long-term equilibrium state' that could reverse the trend of unlimited growth, the report suggested, a minimum level of material provision 'would have to be set so that there would be enough food and material production to maintain everyone at (at least) a subsistence level'.[89]

In his 1977 book *Steady State Economics*, Daly developed his critique of growth and account of the steady-state economy more fully. A 'steady state economy' was one that maintained 'stocks of physical wealth and people' at a stable level instead of seeking to grow them in perpetuity. This, in turn, required new systems for producing and distributing goods. Daly was particularly concerned with inequality, not as a matter of unfairness or injustice, but as a practical matter: inequality drove growth, and inequality required growth to take pressure off of distributional conflicts. 'We are addicted to growth', Daly argued, 'because we are addicted to large inequalities in income and wealth'.[90] Inequality tended to increase consumer desires and fuel growth via an endless cycle of social jockeying through the acquisition of commodities that conferred status—what the sociologist Fred Hirsch would describe as the quest for 'positional goods'.[91] Scarcity was not merely a biophysical phenomenon but a social one; addressing 'growthmania' therefore required social interventions. Yet while growth could not continue forever, if it ended, inequality would appear even starker. The critique of growth and analysis of the steady-state economy thus suggested that 'redistribution is the only cure for poverty, because growth simply cannot do the job'.[92] Writing in the aftermath of the debate over Nixon's guaranteed income proposal, Daly observed that the idea of a minimum income had considerable political support, yet

[88] Herman Daly, 'Introduction to Essays Toward a Steady-State Economy', in *Valuing the Earth: Economics, Ethics, Ecology*, eds. Herman Daly and Kenneth Townsend (Cambridge, MA: MIT Press, 1993), 38.

[89] Meadows et al., *Limits to Growth*, 178–179.

[90] Daly, *Steady State Economics*, 103.

[91] Fred Hirsch, *Social Limits to Growth* (Cambridge, MA: Harvard University Press, 1976).

[92] Daly, *Steady State Economics*, 38.

pointed out that there had been no discussion of a maximum income or of an upper limit on wealth. He thought that both, however, were essential to a steady-state economy, which would stabilize incomes within a relatively narrow band of income distribution. The distributive programme of the steady-state economy therefore called for 'minimum and maximum limits on income and the maximum limit on wealth'.[93]

Yet although Daly's anti-growth position rendered him a radical in one respect, in other ways he was orthodox. Daly looked to markets as a means of allocating goods, including birth licences and biophysical resources, and thought that a maximum and minimum income would make markets work better: 'exchange relations are mutually beneficial between relative equals', Daly argued, whereas 'exchange between the powerful and the powerless is often only nominally voluntary and can easily be a mask for exploitation, especially in the labor market, as Marx has shown'.[94] A maximum income would eliminate incentives towards monopoly, while minimum income would render unions superfluous 'as a means of confronting the power of concentrated wealth, since wealth would no longer be concentrated'.[95] A minimum and maximum income, he thought, might even play a role in 'legitimating the free market, since most of our blundering interference with the price system (e.g. farm program, minimum wage, rent controls) has as its goal an equalizing alteration in the distribution of income and wealth'.[96] Natural resources had to be priced more highly to reflect their scarcity and worth, but without attention to income distribution, the burden of this pricing would fall on the poor. A minimum income could help offset the higher costs of goods. Daly thus claimed that his plan for distribution was 'based on impeccably respectable premises: private property, the free market, opposition to welfare bureaucracies and centralized control'.[97]

Daly's version of a minimum income thus had some elements in common with the NIT proposed by neoliberal economists like Friedman,

[93] Herman Daly, *Steady State Economics: The Economics of Biophysical Equilibrium and Moral Growth* (New York, NY: W.H. Freeman & Co., 1977), 53. By the late 1980s, however, Daly had dropped the maximum income requirement. See Herman Daly and John Cobb, *For the Common Good: Redirecting the Economy Toward Community, the Environment, and a Sustainable Future* (Boston, MA: Beacon Press, 1989).

[94] Daly, *Steady State Economics*, 54.

[95] Ibid., 56.

[96] Ibid., 54.

[97] Ibid., 71.

insofar as it was hostile to state control and 'welfare bureaucracies', and favourable to markets. But, in other respects, Daly's worldview sharply departed from Friedman's. In particular, the limits to wealth acquisition imposed by the maximum income stood in distinct opposition to neoliberal emphases on personal responsibility and reward. Daly himself saw the market socialist Oscar Lange as an exemplar in attempting to combine 'some socialist principles of distribution with the allocative efficiency advantages of the market system'.[98] In Daly's account, limits to personal wealth were necessary not only to prevent wasteful resource use, but to restore decentralized decision making and 'perhaps revive our populist heritage'.[99] Rather than being anti-normative in his moral orientation, moreover, Daly was deeply moralistic, arguing that a steady-state economy required the recovery of an objective morality alongside the recognition of biophysical reality. Subjective wants were infinite, but objective needs were not, and a consensus around the good was necessary to decide how limited resources ought to be used. Economics had erred, he thought, in deeming ethical questions simply matters of personal preference and taste.

Conclusion

Neoliberalism may have taken the place of the Keynesian social order, but it was not the only response to it. Many of those offering support for guaranteed income programmes articulated critiques of the post-war American economy, assessed in both moral and economic terms, while offering alternative visions that did not come to pass. Yet their calls for guaranteed income did not create the crisis of Keynesianism that began in the 1960s, and many of the criticisms they launched of the existing structure of work and income were grounded in real problems.

Socialist feminists and welfare rights organizers did not call for a guaranteed income 'against the New Deal order' nor advance an explicitly 'post-workerist' project.[100] Rather, they pointed out that the work they did as part of that economy was not recognized, and construed the guaranteed income as a form of support for unwaged work, from childcare to community organizing. A guaranteed income could be a tool for economic justice and freedom from oppression, offering women the

[98] Daly, 'Introduction to Essays Toward a Steady-State Economy'.

[99] Ibid., 73.

[100] Zamora, 'Basic Income in the United States', Jäger, '"Free of Our Labours"'.

possibility of freeing themselves from dependence on intimate relationships. Although they criticized state paternalism, they did so not in order to undermine the state altogether, but to push it towards more universal and unconditional forms of public provision. Welfare organizers also argued that they were entitled to more than bare subsistence, calling for an adequate income for all. Although feminist scholars have engaged these arguments and positions, they have often been relegated to a footnote in academic work on basic income.[101] Yet their criticisms and demands deserve to be taken seriously by scholars of basic income more broadly. Indeed, the place of unwaged care work is increasingly part of political arguments for basic income. As the journalist Annie Lowrey argues in her recent book *Give People Money* (2018), 'part of the promise of a UBI would be for society to compensate women for their unpaid labor … a UBI is a powerful rejection of the notion that people who toil without pay do not contribute'.[102] The history of similar arguments made by welfare rights organizers can illuminate the strengths and weaknesses of contemporary arguments in this vein.

Ecological thinkers, meanwhile, thought that the freedom granted by a guaranteed income must be part of a broader reorganization of economic life and guided by a new normative orientation towards nature. Here, too, we should take seriously the critiques of growth and its necessity to support full employment made by ecological thinkers and their search for new ways of organizing production and distribution. And here, too, arguments initially made by ecological thinkers on the fringes of mainstream debate are increasingly present in arguments for basic income. One proposed climate policy, known as 'cap-and-dividend', proposes, to tax carbon emissions and distribute the revenue equally and universally comprising a small UBI modelled after Alaska's Permanent Fund.[103] Advocates of 'degrowth',

[101] For feminist arguments in support of universal basic income, see Pateman, 'Another Way Forward'; Lindsey McDonald, 'We are All Housewives: Universal Basic Income as Wages for Housework', *Lateral* 7, no. 2 (2018); Tai Neilson, 'Response to Lindsey McDonald, "We are All Housewives: Universal Basic Income as Wages for Housework"', *Lateral* 7, no. 2 (2018); Kathi Weeks, *The Problem with Work: Feminism, Marxism, Antiwork Politics, and Postwork Imaginaries* (Durham, NC: Duke University Press, 2011).

[102] Annie Lowrey, *Give People Money: How a Universal Basic Income Would End Poverty, Revolutionize Work, and Remake the World* (New York, NY: Crown, 2018), 152–3; see also Judith Shulevitz, 'It's Payback Time for Women', *The New York Times*, January 8, 2016, and brief discussions in Daniel Raventós, *Basic Income: The Material Conditions of Freedom*, trans. Julie Wark (London: Pluto Press, 2007) and Van Parijs and Vanderborght, *Basic Income*.

[103] See the initial articulation of this idea in Peter Barnes, *Who Owns the Sky? Our Common Assets and the Future of Capitalism* (Washington, DC: Island Press, 2003).

following in the tradition of ecological and steady-state economics, have embraced both a basic income and a maximum income in recent years.[104] And European green parties have been among the most consistent supporters of a basic income, justified on grounds similar to those advanced by Daly: a basic income would facilitate leisure in place of commodity consumption; assert 'common ownership of the earth' and its resources; and function as a 'systemic curb on growth' while also tackling the problem of unemployment.[105] Yet for green UBI advocates, as Philippe Van Parijs and Yannick Vanderborght observe, a basic income can only function in the name of sustainability if it is paired with a 'commitment to "post-materialist values" ... a primacy of the spiritual over the material' and a recognition that the point of abundance is to 'emancipate people rather than to maximize their consumption potential'.[106] Again, basic income is not presented as an 'anti-normative' institution, but envisioned as one part of a larger economic and social transformation underpinned by a deeply normative vision of the good life.

A universal basic income is not, of course, the only way of addressing the problems outlined by the thinkers examined in this chapter; indeed, there is good reason to be sceptical of contemporary enthusiasm for UBI, as I have argued elsewhere.[107] Yet the distinctive analyses and ideas put forth by feminist and environmental thinkers should be considered in their own right, rather than through the lens of the neoliberal project. The ideas and arguments discussed here remain relevant not only to contemporary discussions of UBI, but to more general considerations of how production and distribution might be organized in the twenty-first century. The questions they raise—about what constitutes work and how it should be rewarded; about how abundance can be shared and sustained; about the centrality of growth to economies—remain very much with us.

[104] Samuel Alexander, 'Basic and Maximum Income', in *Degrowth: A Vocabulary for a New Era*, eds Giacomo D'Alisa, Federico Demaria and Giorgos Kallis (New York, NY: Routledge, 2015), 146–51.

[105] Van Parijs and Vanderborght, *Basic Income*, 201.

[106] Ibid., 202.

[107] Alyssa Battistoni, 'The False Promise of Universal Basic Income', *Dissent* 64, no. 2 (Spring 2017): 51–62; see also Aaron Benanav, 'Automation and the Future of Work: Part 2', *New Left Review* 120 (November–December 2019).

PART II

Basic Income and the Politics of Work in Post-Industrial Europe

CHAPTER 6

'Free of our labors and joined back to nature': Basic Income and the Politics of Post-Work in France and the Low Countries

Anton Jäger

On April 30, 1983, a group of Dutch left-wing radicals based in Amsterdam's Pijp-quarter undertook preparations for their country's annual May Day. As the Pentecost of the global workers' movement—the initial 'holiday outside all calendars', as Eric Hobsbawm once put it—the date was one of the few festive days without clear Christian precedents.[1] It was also the proud achievement of one century of class struggle. In 1884 the American trade unionist Samuel Gompers—later head of the American Federation of Labour—called for a demonstration for an eight-hour

[1] Eric Hobsbawm, 'Birth of a Holiday: The First of May', in Philip S. Foner, ed, *May Day: A Short History of the International Workers' Holiday, 1886–1986* (New York, NY: International Publisher, 1986).

A. Jäger (✉)
University of Cambridge, Cambridge, UK

Université Libre de Bruxelles, Brussels, Belgium

P. Sloman et al. (eds.), *Universal Basic Income in Historical Perspective*, https://doi.org/10.1007/978-3-030-75706-9_6

working day on May 1, 1886. After violent clashes between police and protesters, the first unofficial May Day demonstrations later ended with a bloody bomb attack at Haymarket Square in Chicago, killing twelve and maiming dozens.

In 1983, however—a near century after Gompers' call—the Dutch group thought the name 'Labour Day' somewhat obsolete.[2] Some even thought it positively damaging. Instead, they proposed rebaptizing it as the 'Day Against the Work Ethic' (*Dag tegen het arbeidsethos*), celebrating the advent of a world in which humanity would be exempt from the 'duty to labour' altogether. Members were to gather in the Amsterdam cinema Rialto for the foundation of a consortium that would represent what they called the 'conscientiously unemployed' (*bewust werklozen*). This would happen under the name 'Dutch Council Against the Work Ethic' (*Nederlandse Bond Tegen het Arbeidsethos*). The night featured talks, documentaries, and poetry readings, with a screening of Charlie Chaplin's 1936 classic *Modern Times* following a lecture by Dutch philosopher Hans Achterhuis.[3] The mood was easy-going but excitable (Fig. 6.1).

Founded by the Dutch pacifist Bo 'Bingel' Baden, the anti-work grouplet was first conceived in 'an empty space, with two old bureaus placed against each other'.[4] Ironically, the Council's founding meeting was left underattended, with not a single external member showing up. This was not too last, however. When Baden took to the airwaves on a local radio station and announced the founding of the group, a large squadron of squatters (*krakers*) and former hippies quickly trickled in. Soon, journalists also expressed their interest, while angry members of the Labor Party (*PvdA*) and unionists voiced their discontentment. Despite its official status as a union of the 'jobless', figures in the mainstream labour movement disagreed with plans to halt the re-integration of the Dutch 'army of

[2] For overviews and documents of the movement, see Hans Achterhuis, *Arbeid: een eigenaardig medicijn* (Amsterdam: Ambo, 1981), 54–55; Frank van Luijk, *Waarom werken wij? De betekenis van werken 1983–2008/2009* (PhD diss., Free University of Amsterdam, 2009), 24–25; René Didde, 'Brandende trams en Bhagwan', *De Volkskrant*, April 11, 1998; K.G. Boon et al., *Het boek van de arbeid* (Amsterdam: De Arbeiderspers, 1957); H.G. Haaker, ed., *Arbeid, beroep en samenleving* (Assen: Van Gorcum, 1981).

[3] See Rob Van Essen, *Kind van de verzorgingsstaat: opgroeien in een tijdlos paradijs* (Amsterdam: Atlast Contact, 2016), 211; Herman Wigbold, *Bezwaren tegen de ondergang van Nederland* (Amsterdam: Arbeiderspers, 1998); Robert C. Kloosterman, 'Amsterdamned: The Rise of Unemployment in Amsterdam in the 1980s', *Urban Studies* 31, no. 8 (October 1994): 1325–1344.

[4] Cited in Bidde, 'Brandende trams'.

Fig. 6.1 'Night Against the Work Ethic' (*Nacht tegen het arbeidsethos*), 1982. Source: Dutch National Archives (open copyright)

unemployed'. Work was to remain central, the labourites claimed, and the Council was playing a dangerous game.

Adversity from the established left, however, did little to cool off Baden's ambitions. 'We refuse to accept', one of the first issues of his magazine *Luie Donder!* (Lazybones) proclaimed in 1984, 'that labour, however dignified for man and his environment, can ever be humanity's highest value'.[5] The issue strutted a front page emblazoned with the

[5] Cited in ibid.

slogan 'Desecrate Labour!' (*Ontheilig de Arbeid!*), after which the Council asserted 'that as long as we live in a society in which wage labour is central, there will always and by definition exist large groups of people who will opt out and who will be degraded to a societally inferior position'. As a result, the magazine advised a radical departure from policy orthodoxy. In an article entitled 'Duty to Labour—Yuck!' (*Arbeidsplicht … bah!*), for instance, the Council's members investigated the possibility of replacing current social security system with a more streamlined version.[6] Disgusted by the so-called obligation to look for work (*sollicitatieplicht*), they called for a 'right to autonomy vis-à-vis one's own labour and life' and insisted on seeing their current unemployment benefits as a substitute for a permanent, discretionary grant. The 'permanently unemployed', they claimed, 'have much to benefit when we transcend the society of the "animal laborans" and abolish wage labour … we thus have to decouple labour and income'. As the text finished: 'Long live the basic income!' (*Lang leve het basisinkomen!*).[7]

The Council's plea was not the first official Dutch call for a basic income. In the 1930s, Dutch socialists had already drawn on French and English precedents to think out grants that could remedy the country's roiling economic crisis. The word 'basisinkomen' (originally 'basis-inkomen') was introduced into Dutch vernacular on this occasion, coined somewhere in the middle of the decade.[8] Its inventor was the Dutch economist Jan Tinbergen, then a member of the Dutch Social-Democratic Workers' Party (*Sociaal-Democratische Arbeiders Partij*). In a 1934 commentary on the party's 'workers' plan' (*Plan van de Arbeid)*—conceived on the model of Henry De Man's own 'Plan De Man'—Tinbergen had tried to convince his colleagues to include a version of a permanent grant based on his prior readings of G. D. H. Cole's writings on the 'basic income'. The absence of a work requirement worried other members, above all, mainly since it carried the risk of alienating classical socialist electorates. Similar worries surfaced in France. Personalist writers such as

[6] See Bo Bingel, 'Achterhuis: Arbeid 'n vreemde ziekte', *Luie donder* 2 (1984): 19–20. Available at Collectif Charles Fourier Archives, Université Louvain-la-Neuve, Box 22, Folder 1981, and the International Institute for Social History, Amsterdam. All the quotations of the sources originally in French or Dutch are translated by the author.

[7] See Greetje Lubbi, 'Wie zijn de werkelijke luchtfietsers?', in *Naar scheiding arbeid en inkomen* (Brussels: Werkgroep Arbeid en Milieu, 1985), 13–16.

[8] Tinbergen took the term from G. D. H. Cole, whose own term 'basic income' was used regularly in the 1930s—hence the original hyphenation.

Alexandre Marc or Emmanuel Mounier had tried to institute the proposal in the 1930s as an alternative to state-centred and centralized social policies, carefully insisting that the grants had to be coupled with a 'labour contract'.[9] In his *Personalist Manifesto* (1936), for instance, Mounier argued that the 'first right of the economic person is a right to a vital minimum'. While such authors anticipated the theoretical orientation of some of the advocates of UBI in the mid-1960s, their theories remained intimately tied to a notion of 'work' as the basis of human sociability.[10]

The grip of workerist dogma had become much weaker by 1983, however. Starting in the late 1960s, social reformers, politicians, and activists had already begun to rethink parts of the Dutch social security system to decrease its work-centredness. This debate acquired particular gravitas in the early 1980s in the wake of the oil crisis. Dutch unemployment skyrocketed to over 10 per cent coupled with high inflation, pushing a large portion of the Dutch workforce on unemployment rolls. This tendency was particularly pronounced in cities such as Amsterdam, the base of the Council, swiftly earned itself the term 'Amsterdamned' for its status as a jobless hub.[11] Ad hoc remedies were proposed, including public works programmes, job-sharing initiatives, reduced working hours, and municipal job guarantees. Dutch crisis fighting could never secure a permanent solution to the joblessness problem, however. Many younger workers remained locked out of employment circuits and became indefinitely dependent on the dole, driving up social security costs. When profit rates were restored some years later, effects on employment rates were minimal

[9] Christian Roy, 'Revolution, Work, Resistance: French Personalism's Connections with Eugen Rosenstock-Huessy', in *Culture, Theory and Critique* 56, no. 1 (January 2015); Jean-Louis Loubet del Bayle, *Les non conformistes des années 30* (revised and updated edition, Paris: Seuil, 2001), 415–433; John Hellman, *The Communitarian Third Way: Alexandre Marc and Ordre Nouveau 1930–2000* (Montréal: McGill-Queen's University Press, 2002).

[10] See Hans-Georg Betz, *Postmodern Politics in Germany* (London: Macmillan, 1991), 36–37; François Dosse, *Gilles Deleuze & Félix Guattari: Intersecting Lives* (New York, NY: Columbia University Press, 2007), 294.

[11] Another important catalyst to a left anti-work and anti-state sensibility was the 1972 publication of the Club of Rome's 'Limits to Growth' report, issued on the eve of the global oil-shock and the consequent financial slump. E.F. Schumacher's 1973 book, *Small Is Beautiful,* for instance, a call for decreased and decentralization production was coupled with an incentive to look for 'work that really needs to be done, namely, the development of technologies by which ordinary, decent, hardworking, modest and all-too-often abused people can improve their lot'. Cited in Christopher Lasch, *The Minimal Self: Psychic Survival in Troubled Times* (New York, NY: W. W. Norton and Company, 1987), 89.

and unevenly distributed. 'The economy might be getting out of its slump', one writer diagnosed in 1983, 'but the effect on employment is nil'. Instead, 'guaranteeing an income to everyone' seemed a more elegant solution, which would disregard people's place in a productive hierarchy. Although it was an uphill battle, this was a distinct contrast with the solitary advocacy of Tinbergen's 'basisinkomen' in 1934.

Some sensitive parameters had shifted since the Great Depression, and a distinctly new vision of 'emancipation' was at the root of the basic income defended by the Council in the 1980s. This vision has gone by many different aliases in the literature—the 'post-labor thesis', 'cybernetic socialism', 'the consumptionist critique', '73 thought', 'anti-Fordism', or 'post-productivism'.[12,13] This chapter draws together these literatures to investigate the intellectual preconditions that first made possible mass UBI advocacy on the Dutch Left. Examining the European left's response to the stagflation crisis, it argues that two parameters had to be in place for a new UBI to strike root: a left-wing antistatism which cast doubt on the organizational capacities of party democracy and a philosophical post-workism which questioned 'labour' as a source of emancipation. Both these trends destabilized the centrality of the 'producer' in the socialist tradition and explicitly pitted themselves against a commandeering centralized state. They also shared roots in the American basic income debate of the 1960s. These had provided the outlines for the original Negative Income Tax and Guaranteed Income plans put forward by the Council and other Dutch activists. Most prominently, however, its conceptual groundwork was laid in the wake of the French 1968, in which a generation of left-wing thinkers influenced by cybernetics rethought notions such as 'labour', 'state', and 'welfare' against the existential crisis of the Fordist regime. Cybernetic languages played a key role in both. Applied to labour-saving technology, cybernetics would eliminate the need for human

[12] See, inter alia, Richard Barbrook and Andy Cameron, 'The Californian Ideology', *Science as Culture* 6, no. 1 (January 1996): 44–72.; Jasper Bernes, *The Work of Art in the Age of Deindustrialization* (London: University of California Press, 2016); Katja Diefenbach, 'Alles läuft gut: Warum eine Politik des Wunsches nichts damit zu tun hat, sich etwas zu wollen', *diskus* (March 2003): 35–37; Benjamin Noys, *Malign Velocities: Accelerationism and Capitalism* (Winchester, UK: Zero Books, 2013), 5–6; Benjamin Noys, *The Persistence of the Negative: A Critique of Contemporary Continental Theory* (Edinburgh: Edinburgh University Press, 2011); Russell Jacoby, *Dialectic of Defeat: Contours of Western Marxism* (Cambridge: Cambridge University Press, 2002).

[13] Ibid., 327.

labour in the factory, bringing forth 'machines controlling machines'. As a counterweight to bureaucracy, however, it also opened up vistas towards less state-centred forms of decision-making and decreased the arbitrary power of bureaucrats. This cybernetic synthesis thus constituted a double manoeuvre against both an 'Old Left' and the 'Old Right', which had supposedly entered into an unholy 'statist' alliance in 1970s. It was also this dual revolution—variably performed by thinkers such as Herbert Marcuse, Michel Foucault, Ivan Illich, Bram Van Ojik, Roel Van Duijn, Félix Guattari, Toni Negri, André Gorz, and Philippe Van Parijs—that really lay the groundwork for the first European UBI wave.

'Work' Versus 'Labour': The End of Producer Sovereignty

The Dutch Council Against the Work ethic held its first 'anti-May Day' in 1983. Nearly a decade before, however, a French group had already held a remarkably similar event. On 1 May 1 1975, the French *Union ouvrière* circulated pamphlets scripted with the words 'Down with the Festival of Alienated Labour' amongst Parisian workers gearing up for their annual May Day celebration. Their tone was duly iconoclastic. 'Mandatory planning, collective ownership of the means of production, proletarian ideology', the organization proclaimed, had simply 'nothing communist about'.[14] Workers' unions in turn had become little 'but the tools of the bosses', and workers had become 'thick-headed to think that one would in your thousands demand to lose your life … through labour'. As the leaders saw it, 'union strategists"' were 'not saying: "Death to labour, never work, let's abolish wage slavery, right to laziness, death to survival"'. Instead, they were out to strengthen the class compact, further locking the proletariat in its corporate cage.

With its call to a general anti-work insurrection, the *Union ouvrière* was only part of a wider transnational movement. In the late 1960s, Northern Italy's industrial centres already experienced a convulsive wave of strikes, in which workers refused to honour the promises of productivity of the post-war settlement. Inspired by the events, 1970s German radicals then organized the Tunix ('Do Nothing') collective under the credo of the

[14] Cited in Alastair Hemmens, 'The New Spirit of Capitalism and the Critique of Work in France Since May '68', in *The Critique of Work in Modern French Thought* (London: Palgrave, 2019), 182–183.

'Great Refusal', hosting conferences with speakers such as Michel Foucault, Gilles Deleuze, and Félix Guattari.[15] Later, members of the Tunix joined 'Happy Unemployed' groups, who set up action circles that ridiculed the 'love of labour' adhered to by social democrats. Former members of Tunix became enthusiastic proponents of the basic income in the 1980s, contraposing them to classical unemployment schemes. In 1985, the Dutch Council Against the Work Ethic thus joined a lively European scene with French unemployment unions, German anti-work activists, and Italian post-operaists.

All these organizations also served as representatives of a new cybernetic left that had arisen in the 1960s and 1970s, with intellectual tutors such as Herbert Marcuse, Toni Negri, André Gorz, and Félix Guattari. All of these authors discerned the profoundly destabilizing consequences of new cybernetic techniques both on notions of state and labour. These also proved a handy tool to destabilize the post-war Fordist order. This was an order, as observers noted, that stood out by 'a strong state, robust unionism, or the normative order of a heterosexual patriarchy'.[16] Centred around two nodes—the family and the workplace—post-war Fordism thus glorified the 'breadwinner and family man' who 'circulated his wages and other social benefits back into the family as a basic social reproductive unit', serving as the 'basis for state policy in matters of employment, welfare, and development'.[17]

America again set the precedent here. It was within Ford's own Detroit factory, overall, that post-Fordism's first symptoms first manifested themselves. In 1946, American managers decided to ramp up labour-saving machinery in the aftermath of a series of boisterous strikes. The measure led specialists to coin the term 'automation' and the foundation of Ford's very own 'Automation Department'.[18] Social science paid close attention. In 1957, for instance, the German sociologist and Frankfurt School adept Friedrich Pollock surveyed the wave of robotization sweeping the

[15] See Joachim Häberlen, *The Emotional Politics of the Alternative Left: West Germany, 1968–1984* (Cambridge: Cambridge University Press, 2018), 240.

[16] Andrea Muehlebach and Nitzan Shoshan, 'Post-Fordist Affect', *Anthropological Quarterly* 85, no. 2 (Spring 2012): 317.

[17] Ibid., 317.

[18] See Carroll Pursell, ed., *A Companion to American Technology* (London: John Wiley & Sons, 2008), 65; David Noble, *Forces of Production* (New York, NY: Knopf, 1984). Peter Drucker situates the coinage in 1951, although other reports situate it earlier. See Peter Drucker, *Innovation and Entrepreneurship* (London: Routledge, 2012), 99.

American industrial landscape.[19] He here extended his 1938 'integration thesis', which had first proclaimed the integration of the masses into government through the 'the authoritarian state'.[20] In Pollock's 'post-liberal' economy, the market had been abolished and planning had been instituted, mainly through corporate mergers and cartelization. Political freedom under integration, however, was an illusion. This process was only furthered through the invention of automation in the post-war period, in which increases in productivity could be used to buy off pacified working classes threatened with increasing redundancies and permanent technological unemployment.

Pollock's writings on automation and the 'integration thesis' provided the impetus for the most eloquent proponents of the post-work thesis in the 1960s. Herbert Marcuse, for instance, worked out his 1964 American version of *One-Dimensional Man* with a keen eye on the effects of the 'cybernetic' revolution and how it restructured labour practices. Cybernetics and 'automation' had steadily fused into 'cybernation'. These had been a topic of interest to philosophy in the 1950s and some Marxists, but few had taken stock of its cultural effects on the Western work ethic. Marcuse's own reconsideration of Marxian views of labour went back to the 1930s, drawing on the writings of Lewis Mumford.[21] It was mainly in the 1950s, however, that he began to reconsider the socialist tradition's classical emphasis on the 'dignity of labour'.[22] This was analogous to his

[19] Friedrich Pollock, *Automation: A Study of its Economic and Social Consequences* (New York, NY: Praeger, 1957). Pollock already foresaw the presumed necessity of basic income schemes, referencing Walter Reuther's worries. See also John Diebold, *Automation: The Advent of the Automatic Factory* (New York, NY: 1952).

[20] Friedrich Pollock, 'State Capitalism: Its Possibilities and Limitations', in *Critical Theory and Society: A Reader*, eds, Stephen Bronner and Douglas Kellner (New York, NY: Routledge, 1989): 115–120; Friedrich Pollock, 'Is National Socialism a New Order?', *Studies in Philosophy and Social Science* 9, no. 3 (1942): 453. See also Moishe Postone and Barbara Brick, 'Critical Pessimism and the Limits of Traditional Marxism', *Theory and Society* 11 (September 1982): 617–658, for a discussion.

[21] J. Jesse Ramirez, 'Marcuse Among the Technocrats: America, Automation, and Postcapitalist Utopias, 1900–1941', in *Amerikastudien/American Studies* 57, no. 1 (January 2012): 31–50. See also Harry Braverman, *Labor and Monopoly Capital: The Degradation of Work in the Twentieth Century* (New York, NY: Monthly Review Press, 1974), for a discussion of this trend.

[22] See Frederick Harry Pitts, 'Escape by Approximation: The Contemporary Relevance of Marcuse's Conceptualization of Labor', *Telos Scope*, July 17, 2012. For the original, see Douglas Kellner, 'Introduction to "On the Philosophical Foundation of the Concept of Labor"', *Telos* 16 (Summer 1973): 2–8. Herbert Marcuse, 'On the Philosophical Foundation

colleague Hannah Arendt—with whom Marcuse had studied under Heidegger in the 1920s—distinction of labour as a purely 'reproductive' activity (*labor*) and spontaneous and self-determined 'action' (*work*), although Marcuse cast an even wider net for his notion of 'labour'.[23] *All* of human activity, he thought, was deserving of the label, erasing the boundary between 'work' and 'play' prevalent in the socialist tradition before. It was this 'ontological' notion of labour, above all, that capitalist societies seemed incapable of providing, although its technical tendencies constantly pushed towards obsolescence. This teased out a fresh contradiction in late industrial societies. Instead of offering European working classes their deserved leisure, Marcuse saw how capitalism blackmailed workers into deferring their gratification for higher consumption rates.

Automation would undo this delicate balancing act, however. The robotization ushered in by the 1950s, as Marcuse saw it, led to the end of the working class as the 'living contradiction of established society' and opened up space for models beside the male wage earner.[24] The 'self-organizing' aspects of cybernetics again proved central here. If machines could create machines, labour was no longer an exclusively human affair, and the working class lost its prerogative as the 'making class'. Marcuse thus interpreted the aggressive automation of the 1950s and 1960s as a cue for humanity's final jump for the sphere of 'necessity' to a new 'freedom', freeing up the sexual energy previously suppressed of the bourgeois work ethic. Against the 'automation hysteria' of the 1950s, Marcuse thought that automation was radically altering the balance between 'freedom' and 'necessity' itself. The two had undergone a sudden dislocation—and socialism would move from Marx back to Fourier.

In 1966, Marcuse's Frankfurt colleague Erich Fromm postulated that his jump could be instantiated in the form of a universal grant—a policy

of the Concept of Labor in Economics', *Telos* 16 (Summer 1973). See also Rakesh Bandari, 'On the Continuing Relevance of Mattick's Critique of Marcuse', *International Journal of Political Economy* 29 (Winter 1999/2000): 56; Paul Mattick, *Critique of Marcuse* (New York, NY: Herder and Herder, 1972); Howard Brick, *Transcending Capitalism: Visions of a New Society in Modern American Thought* (New York, NY: Cornell University Press, 2015).

[23] Philip Walsh, *Arendt Contra Sociology: Theory, Society and its Science* (London: Routledge, 2016), 140.

[24] Cited in Bernes, *The Work of Art*, 161. For original, see Herbert Marcuse, *Eros and Civilization* (New York, NY: Beacon Press, 2015), 156.

that would destabilize the link between income and work.[25] Although Marcuse never explicitly endorsed the proposal, his philosophy twined elegantly with the New Left's search for a new, non-normative form of welfare. 'Freed from this enslavement', he thus claimed, productivity would shed 'its repressive power and impel the free development of individual needs. ... The more complete the alienation of labor, the greater the potential of freedom: total automation would be the optimum.'[26] Marcuse's rebuke to the integration thesis was thus to wake the proletariat from its 'social sleep' by calling in other actors and awaiting automation's disruptive effects.

The late 1950s had seen the steady transfer of this integration thesis into a French frame.[27] Works inspired by the American and British sociology such as those by Serge Crozier or, later, Jean Baudrillard's 1969 *The Consumer Society* were prominent examples.[28] The latter diagnosed the waning of the 'worker' as the prime figure in capitalism, together with its concomitant 'mythology of production'. Drawing on James Galbraith's work on the 'affluent society', Baudrillard argued that the 'fundamental problem of contemporary capitalism' was no longer between the 'maximization of profit' and the 'rationalization of production conceived from the point of view of the producer'.[29] Rather, it had moved to a 'contradiction

[25] See Erich Fromm, 'The Psychological Aspects of the Guaranteed Income', in *The Guaranteed Income*, ed. Robert Theobald (New York, NY: Doubleday & Co., 1966). Herbert Marcuse, *One Dimensional Man* (London: Routledge, 2002); Charlotte Mohs, Marco Bonavena and Johannes Hauer 'Abschied von der Klassenmetaphysik: Formwandel der Klassengesellschaft, Paralyse der Kritik', *Phase* 2 (2018): 51–52; Alberto Toscano, 'Liberation Technology: Marcuse's Communist Individualism', *Goldsmiths Working Papers* (2005): 6–22; R. Moore, 'Eros and Civilization for a Jobless Future: Herbert Marcuse and the Abolition of Work', *Heathwood Journal of Critical Theory* 1 (2016): 2; Bernes, *The Work of Art*, *passim*.

[26] Cited in Kevin Anderson, ed., *The Dunayevskaya-Marcuse-Fromm Correspondence, 1954–1978: Dialogues on Hegel* (London: Lexington Books, 2012), xxxiii; Herbert Marcuse, 'The End of Utopia', in 'Psychoanalyse und Politik', Lecture delivered at the Free University of West Berlin, July 1967.

[27] Especially popular at that time was the work of John Goldthorpe: John Goldthorpe and David Lockwood, *The Affluent Worker: Political Attitudes and Behaviour* (Cambridge: Cambridge University Press, 1963). Later exponents include Daniel Bell and his own 1976 classic *The Coming of Post-Industrial Society*, where Marx's 'labour theory of value' was declared historically obsolete in the age of the supercomputer and mass automation.

[28] Serge Crozier, 'L'ère du prolétariat s'achève', *Arguments* 12–13 (February–March 1959). Jean Baudrillard, *The Consumer Society* (London: Sage, 2016), passim.

[29] Ibid.

between a virtually unlimited productivity' and 'the need to dispose of the product', thus bringing about a decline in the centrality of the work ethic. This implied the fading away of the working class as the subject of history, and its replacement by a post-historical consumer caste. 'The idea of a transcendent exteriority of force to the system', Jean-Francois Lyotard claimed in his 1973 *Libidinal Economy*, now appeared ''o be dangerously threatened by the actual state of capitalist production'.[30] The question for radicals thus became how to reawaken a quiescent working class by subverting their cultural commitment to the work ethic, assisted by recent advances in cybernetic thinking.

How this sentiment could best be tied to an anti-work ethic was spelled out by the Belgian Situationist Raoul Vaneigem in the lead up to the 1968 revolt. 'The obligation to produce', Vaneigem claimed in his 1967 *The Revolution of Everyday Life*, 'alienate(d) the passion to create', while 'productive labour only reinforced the forces of order'.[31] 'From the Nazi *Arbeit macht frei* to Henry Ford to Mao', he noted, the 'cult of labour' had now become a universal fact in the communist and capitalist worlds alike. The 1960s, however, would see automation cause 'mass replacement of workers by mechanical slaves'.[32] The rise of this machine would reveal the superfluity of labour to social reproduction, thereby betraying 'its adherence to the barbarous procedures of the established order'. 'The trickery of work has been exhausted', Vaneigem finished in 1967, and 'there is nothing left to lose, not even the illusion of work itself'.

Cybernetics again proved a capacious tool to counter this pro-work consensus. Since the mid-1940s, a growing body of literature had begun to fantasize over the usage of cybernetic techniques to heighten France's industrial output. To writers such as Jean Fourastié—inventor of the term of *Les trente glorieuses*—cybernetics could drastically ramp up productivity, undo workplaces of coercive elements and expand free time.[33] Other writers foresaw the advent of a 'governing machine' which would dispense with the need for human governance altogether.[34] Vaneigem and other

[30] See Jean-Francois Lyotard, *Libidinal Economy* (New York, NY: A & C Black, 2004), 211.

[31] Raoul Vaneigem, *The Revolution of Everyday Life* (New York, NY: PM Press, 2009), 39. See also Anselm Jappe, *Guy Debord* (London: PM Press, 2017), for an overview of the movement.

[32] Vaneigem, *Traité*, 36.

[33] Jean Fourastié, *Les 40.000 heures* (Paris: Denoël, 1965).

[34] See Miriam R. Levin, ed., *Cultures of Control* (London: Routledge, 2005), 249. The phrase was coined by the Dominican Friar Père Dubarle, who reviewed Norbert Wiener's book in *Le Monde* in 1948.

Situationist writers took issue with the technocratic of this literature, whose interest in cybernetic technologies seemed secondary to their desire to neutralize class conflict—'cybernetic rascals' (*canaille cybernétique)* was Vaneigem's expression for them.[35]

Like a sorcerer's apprentice, however, French technocrats had conjured up a spirit that was difficult to control. The new 'science of systems' would not only prove detrimental to class consciousness. It would also allow for a radical expansion of the sphere of leisure and open up vistas for a world beyond work from the left. 'Snatched from its masters', Vaneigem claimed in his *Traité du savoir à l'usage des jeunes générations* (a tract with considerable influence on the 1968 movement) 'cybernetics will liberate human groups from work and social alienation', and complete 'the project of Charles Fourier in an age when utopia was still possible'. Countering the 'Cybernetic State' proposed by right-wing technocrats—'Stalino-cyberneticians', as Vaneigem called them—he hoped for a revolutionary repurposing of automation. 'In founding a perfect form of power', Vaneigem saw, 'the cyberneticians will promote the emulation and perfection of refusal ... their programming of new techniques will be twisted by another organization—a revolutionary one'. Although the working class had missed its appointment with history, capitalism still produced fresh gravediggers.

Such moves were mirrored by other sectors of the New Left. Developments within Marxology, for instance, seemed to push in a similarly work-sceptic direction. In 1964, the English historian Eric Hobsbawm had put out the first snippets of a list of unedited manuscripts by Karl Marx assembled as *Pre-Capitalist Economic Formations*; in 1968, the Canadian Germanist Martin Nicolaus published a longer introduction to the new batch of manuscripts in the *New Left Review*, in which he hinted at the newly assembled pieces as the *Grundrisse* (Marcuse had already encountered parts of the manuscript in the early 1950s).[36,37] As noted by Mike Davis, the book 'considerably levelled the playing field for

[35] See Raoul Vaneigem, *Traité de savoir-vivre à l'usage des jeunes générations* (Paris: Gallimard, 1967); Alexandre Moatti, 'Vocabulaire et controverses autour de la cybernétique et du transhumain, années 1960–1970', in *L'Homme et la société* 205 (2017).

[36] See Ramirez, 'Marcuse and the Technocrats', 188.

[37] Cited in Herbert A. Applebaum, *The Concept of Work: Ancient, Medieval, and Modern* (New York, NY: SUNY Press, 1994), 446. For the original, see Marx, *Grundrisse*, 705.

non-German readers', also adding '900 pages of required study to the several thousand pages of the four volumes of *Capital*'.[38]

The Marx unearthed by Nicolaus proved a creative shock to Europe's left's milieu. Most of this concerned the distinctly new vision of emancipation the thinker seemed to offer in the manuscripts (which were less staunchly pro-work than had been presumed), and his insights into recent post-industrial trends. In several passages in the *Grundrisse*, Marx predicted the progressive elimination of the need to labour, instantiated in a notion on the 'general intellect'. 'To the degree that large industry develops', Marx's text read, 'the creation of real wealth comes to depend less on labour-time and on the amount of labour employed' than upon 'the general state of science and on the progress of technology'.[39] At this point, the 'surplus labour of the mass' would cease 'to be the condition for the development of general wealth', just as 'the non-labour of the few has ceased to be the condition for the development of the general powers of the human mind'.[40] Consequently, time for 'the artistic, scientific etc. development of the individuals' would be freed up and 'the measure of wealth would then not any longer, in any way, labour time, but rather disposable time'.[41]

Nicolaus' Marx had both practical and theoretical effects. In Germany, the publication of the manuscripts kick-started the growth of the so-called New Reading of Marx, with interpreters like Hans-Georg Backhaus and Moishe Postone, who undertook a profound re-reading of previous 'labour-centric' readings of the thinker.[42] In Italy, the discovery of the so-called Fragment on Machines in Marx's *Grundrisse* stimulated the rise of 'post-operaismo', where, in the aftermath of the country's hot summer of 1969, the emphasis shifted from a 'struggle within factories' to a

[38] See Mike Davis, *Old Gods, New Enigmas: Marx's Lost Theory* (London: Verso Books, 2017), 111. For overviews, see Frederick Harry Pitts, *Critiquing Capitalism Today: New Ways to Read Marx* (London: Springer, 2017); Jan Hoff, *Marx Worldwide: On the Development of the International Discourse on Marx since 1965* (London: Brill, 2016); Ricardo Bellofiore, *Re-reading Marx: New Perspectives After the Critical Edition* (London: Palgrave Macmillan, 2009).

[39] Ibid., 705.

[40] See Frederick Pitts, *Critiquing Capitalism Today*, op. cit., 144–149.

[41] Antonio Negri, *Marx Beyond Marx: Lessons on the Grundrisse* (London: Autonomedia, 1991), 211. See also his *Revolution Retrieved: Writings on Marx, Keynes, Capitalist Crisis, and New Social Subjects (1967–83)* (London: Red Notes Italian Archive, 1977).

[42] Postone would later come out as a UBI supporter in the 1990s. See Moishe Postone, *Time, Labor, and Social Domination: A Reinterpretation of Marx's Critical Theory* (New York, NY: Cambridge University Press, 1995), 21, where he drew on Gorz.

contestation within society as a whole, conceived as the field of 'social production'.[43] In his 1978 *Marx Beyond Marx: Lessons from the 'Grundrisse'*, Negri already claimed that 'non-work, the refusal of work becomes the worker's point of view, the basis from which the law of value can be inverted and the law of surplus value reinterpreted'.[44] The argument would later serve as a handy justification for Negri's own version of the basic income—the ideal welfare for the post-industrial worker.

The new Marx also had a profound impact on the French Marxist André Gorz.[45] Born in Vienna 1923 to a Jewish mother and Catholic father, Gorz ended up on the editorial board of Sartre's *Les temps modernes* after publishing his first work in the early 1960s. Quickly, he became known as the head of the so-called Italian tendency at the magazine. Gorz himself had commented on passages from the *Grundrisse* in the course of the 1960s, translating it into French. He casted them as messages in a bottle for a 'post-industrial' left.[46] His primary drivers, however, were again political. In the midst of a debate on the 'society of affluence' and 'end of class', he held steadfast to a classical socialist line in the early 1960s, questioning the 'integration thesis' which held sway in some left-wing circles. In a text entitled 'the Belgian Denial' (*Le démenti belge*), published in *Les Temps modernes*, Gorz claimed that the integration thesis now stood debunked, stating that if 'high salaries and advanced social legislation should provoke the gentrification (*embourgeoisement*) of the workers, Belgian workers should be amongst the most gentrified all of workers in Europe'.[47] The piece followed the 'strike of the century', where Belgian workers struck for almost two months in the harsh winter of 1960–1961 and mobilized thousands in quasi-insurrectionist fashion.

[43] See André Gorz, 'Le démenti belge', *Les Temps Modernes* 178 (February 1981), 1055

[44] Cited in Scott Lasch, *The End of Organized Capitalism* (London: John Wiley, 2018), 210.

[45] In the mid-1960s, André Gorz would become one of the first editors to put out a more elaborate version of the text. See Helmut Reinicke and Moishe Postone, 'On Nicolaus "Introduction" to the Grundrisse', *Telos* 22 (Winter 1974–75), 130–48; Martin Nicolaus, 'The Unknown Marx', *New Left Review* 48 (March–April 1968); Finn Bowring, *Andre Gorz and the Sartrean Legacy: Arguments for a Person-Centred Social Theory* (New York, NY: Springer, 2000).

[46] Ibid., 210.

[47] Mateo Alaluf, 'Qu'est-ce que les grèves de 1960–1961 ont fait à la sociologie?', in *Mémoire de la grande grève de l'hiver 1960–1961 en Belgique*, eds. B. Francq, L. Courtois, P. Tilly (Brussels: Le cri, 2011), 187–195; F. Perroux and H. Marcuse, *François Perroux interroge Herbert Marcuse... qui répond* (Paris: Aubier, 1969), 1976.

In the late 1960s and early 1970s however, Gorz made a volte-face on the integration thesis. Visits to America awakened an interest in the politics of Black Powerism and anti-poverty discourse, who were outright about their commitment to organizing the 'poor' rather than the 'working class'. In the aftermath of May 1968, Gorz was one of the first loudest voices proclaiming the decreased possibility for revolution in European societies. 'More than anyone anticipated', he claimed, 'capital has succeeded in reducing workers' power in the productive process', while increasing 'the technical power and capacities of the proletariat as a whole and the impotence of proletarians themselves'.[48] As a consequence, the class 'collectively … responsible for developing and operating the totality of the productive forces' had become 'unable to appropriate or subordinate' this totality.[49] The increasing stratification of the French workforce between a highly paid unionized sector and precarious 'surplus workers' proved that 'producerist' rhetoric had become a political peril.

This shift also tied in with Gorz's changing readings of the *Grundrisse*. While Marx's 'fragment on machines' had seemed to presage a 'polytechnic' class of workers—able to tend production without managerial authority—Gorz now realized that this 'hyper-specialisation' might occur at the cost of a deskilling of lower ranks of workers. The polytechnician of the *Grundrisse* thus relied on the new serf of the factory floor, first introduced by Taylorism.[50] This underclass had ever little to gain from work, Gorz noted in 1973. Instead they 'had been promised a bourgeois privilege, they had gone into debt to acquire it, and now they saw that everyone else could also get one'.[51] Drawing on the cultural critic Ivan Illich, Gorz noted how 'a good part of each day's work goes to pays for the travel necessary to get to work', while it cut 'a person into slices, it cuts our time, our life, into separate slices so that in each one you are a passive consumer at the mercy of the merchants', obscuring that 'work, culture, communication, pleasure, satisfaction of needs, and personal life can and should be one and the same thing: a unified life, sustained by the social fabric of the community'.[52]

[48] André Gorz, *Ecology as Politics* (New York, NY: Blackrose Books, 1980), 77.

[49] Cited in Conrad Lodziak and Jeremy Tatman, eds., *André Gorz: A Critical Introduction* (London: Pluto Press, 1997), 66.

[50] See Alain Lipietz, 'André Gorz and Our Youth', *Vlaams Marxistisch Tijdschrift* 46 (2012): 88, for a powerful reflection on this turn in Gorz's thinking.

[51] André Gorz, *Farewell to the Working Class*, 67.

[52] Ibid.

In the course of the 1970s Gorz increasingly inched towards a more openly sceptical attitude towards the left's work-centric socialism.[53] The effects of the information revolution, he claimed, were creating an increasingly stratified work force beyond the purview of left-wing organizations. 'Productive activity' had thus 'been emptied of its meaning, of its motivations and its object simply to become a way to earn a salary. It has stopped being part of "life", simply to become a means to "make a living"'.[54] As Gorz noted in what would become one of his most influential books, *Farewell to the Working Class*, this cast doubt on salvation within the 'proletarian condition' itself:

> As long as workers own a set of tools enabling them to produce for their own needs, or a plot of land to grow some vegetables, and keep a few chickens, the fact of proletarianization will be felt to be accidental and reversible. For ordinary experience will continue to suggest the possibility of independence: workers will continue to dream of setting themselves up on their own, of buying an old farm with their savings or of making things for their own needs after they retire. In short, 'real life' lies outside your life as a worker, and being a proletarian is but a temporary misfortune to be endured until something better turns up.

The natural conclusion was that the 'Marxist conception of "liberation *within* work"' as 'the necessary prerequisite for "liberation *from* work"', had become an "unsustainable utopia". '"For workers", he claimed, it was "no longer a question of… putting themselves in control of work, or seizing power within the framework of their work'. Rather, the point was now 'to free oneself from work by rejecting its nature'.

Gorz's writings also provided the main point of inspiration to the Dutch post-work left. In a 1982 electoral pamphlet for his own 'Political Party of Radicals' (*PPR*, or *Politieke Partij der Radicalen*), for instance, the Dutch politician Bram Van Oijk placed a bold bet on his electoral fortunes. He came out as a supporter for a relatively new proposal known as the 'basisinkomen'. Launching the plan, he opened with a translation of a

[53] Michel Bosquet (André Gorz), *Capitalism in Crisis and Everyday Life* (London: Harvester Press, 1977), 22. See also Michael Scott Christofferson, *French Intellectuals Against the Left: The Antitotalitarian Moment of the 1970s* (London: Berghahn Books, 2004), 42–50.

[54] André Gorz, *Farewell to the Working Class* (London: Pluto Press, 1982), 35.

haunting question first posed by André Gorz in his *Farewell to the Working Class* (1980):

> Will the third industrial revolution … lead to a new golden age, where we shall work less and have a large mass of riches at our disposal, or will some be condemned to joblessness and others to over productivity?[55]

Founded in 1968, Van Ojik's PPR had enjoyed a mild ascent in the early years of the decade while drawing on disaffected voters from the mainstream left. In 1982 it still had a penchant for provocation. Referring to a 'little-known' American thinker named Robert Theobald, the party's head sought to demonstrate that the economic predicament faced by the Netherlands in 1982 was far from unprecedented in Western history.[56] Already in the early 1960s, he claimed, Theobald had detected a growing 'chasm' between 'fallow labour power' and a 'variety of unmet needs'.[57] Since 'labour' and 'income' were 'to a very high degree already uncoupled in the Netherlands', Van Ojik proposed a partial version of basic income, pegged to an acceptable minimum, yet without any concomitant duties for job-seeking.[58]

Van Ojik already had a sizeable Dutch literature to draw on when compiling this pamphlet. In the mid-1970s, a fresh version of the 'basisinkomen' was making headway in Dutch and European debates with inspiration from American precedents. In 1967, for instance, a Dutch translation of Theobald's work was published in Antwerp under the title 'Guaranteed Income in a Free Society; Economic and Social Consequences of Automation'.[59] Milton Friedman's plan officially entered Dutch policy debates in 1970, when the Catholic fiscal specialist Ferd Grapperhaus contemplated it as a more 'socially just' response to labour market rigidity after increasing automation, an argument later repackaged in a parliamentary

[55] See Bram Van Ojik, *Basisinkomen* (Amsterdam: Politieke Partij Radikalen Studiestiching, 1982), title page. Later examples include Bram Van Ojik, 'Basisinkomen en arbeidstijdverkorting', in *Socialisme en democratie* 10 (1983): 25–30.

[56] Ibid., 15.

[57] Ibid.

[58] See Jan-Pieter Kuiper, 'Volwaardige arbeid ook voor minder-validen', *AVO* (December 1976): 9. See also Loek Groot et al, *Basic Income on the Agenda: Policy Objectives and Political Chances* (Amsterdam: Amsterdam University Press, 2011), 219.

[59] Robert Theobald, *Gewaarborgd inkomen in een vrije maatschappij* (Antwerpen: Werkgroep 2000, 1967).

report.[60] 'It is not unthinkable', Grapperhaus claimed in 1970, 'that increasing automation can have the consequence that certain groups in the population ... will be permanently shut out of the labour process'.

By Van Ojik's time, however, the Dutch debate on the scheme had already acquired a more prominent protagonist. This was the Dutch ex-missionary and company physician Jan-Pieter Kuiper. Kuiper had read Theobald's tract in the late 1960s and was one of the first voices to plead for a decoupling of 'labour' and 'income' in a Dutch context. 'In the last couple of decades', Kuiper claimed in 1977, 'many attempts have been made to restructure work (*herijken*) and to give the negotiation between capital and labour (*arbeidsonderhandelingen*) more content'.[61] Although he was 'obviously sympathetic to these initiatives, he now asked himself the question 'whether we are right to do so'.[62] Kuiper's plea gradually put the UBI at the forefront of Dutch policy debates. Although the proposal stalked these debates under a variety of homonyms—'guaranteed income' (*gewaarborgd inkomen*), 'free income' (*vrij inkomen*), or 'life income' (*levensinkomen*)—the appellation of a 'basic income' gradually settled as a stock phrase, in spite of differences in technical design. This debate culminated in a 1981 call by a subsection of the largest union federation—*Voedingsbond FNV*, charged with representing food sector workers—who came out in favour of a provisory basic income, mainly to alleviate budgetary pressures on unemployment funds. Although most union members were hostile to the measure, a New Left steadily rallied to its defence.

A representative spokesman for this New Left was the former 'provo' writer Roel Van Duijn. Van Duijn was a later member of Van Ojik's PPR and a founder of the so-called Kabouter movement ('Gnome movement').[63] In the 1960s he had already prognosed the declining militancy of mainstream socialist organizations, including their integration into the

[60] F. H. M. Grapperhaus, *Is de negatieve inkomstenbelasting een schrede vooruit op de weg naar de sociale rechtvaardigheid?* (Deventer, 1970).

[61] See Jan-Pieter Kuiper, 'Arbeid en inkomen: twee rechten en twee plichten', *Sociaal Maandblad Arbeid* (1976): 503–512; Jan-Pieter Kuiper, 'Inkomen ontkoppelen van arbeid?', *Gids personeelsbeleid* 18 (June 1977): 477. See also Robert J. van der Veen, *Between Exploitation and Communism: Explorations in the Marxian Theory of Justice and Freedom* (Amsterdam: Wolters-Noordhoff, 1991), 352.

[62] R. Balkker, 'Han Schilperoord: wij willen de handen vuil maken', *Noordnederlandse Dagblad*, 13 (March 1971).

[63] Roel van Duyn, 'The Kabouters of Holland', in Marshall D. Shatz, *The Essential Works of Anarchism* (New York, NY: Bantam, 1971).

corporatist structures. 'The masses', Van Duijn remembered, where those 'who we can't and barely want to convince'.[64] Instead of proletarian militancy, however, a diffuse group of new social actors—students, outcasts, bohemians—could take on a fresh mandate under the moniker of the 'provotariat'.[65] As a member of the Kabouter-movement Van Duijn proposed replacing the existing union structure with a network of self-managed firms which could connect and dose production with the usage of cybernetic technology. He did so by celebrating American variants of 'cybernetic socialism', once imagined by the American poet Richard Brautigan in his 1967 'All Watched over by Machines of Loving Grace':

> I like to think
> (it has to be!)
> of a cybernetic ecology
> where we are free of our labors
> and joined back to nature,
> ... all watched over
> by machines of loving grace.[66]

Brautigan's vision fascinated Dutch neo-leftists, led by its anti-authoritarian bent. 'The new society', Van Duijn claimed in 1971, 'has nothing do with the centralized socialism of yore'. Rather, it would be 'decentralized' and 'anti-authoritarian' and would leave all decisions to 'people where they find themselves'.[67] Inspired by Peter Kropotkin's anarcho-communism, Van Duijn fantasized of a society that would 'not be governed' and 'would instead steer itself' through 'self-directing councils', doing away with a 'formalistic, bureaucratic officialdom' that currently occupied the state.[68]

[64] Editors, 'Het is weer Amsterdam tegen de provincie', *Trouw* (March 2004).

[65] See Roel Van Duijn et al., 'Wat willen we nu eigenlijk?', *De Kabouterkrant* 2 (May 1971): 1.

[66] Cited in Richard Brautigan, *Richard Brautigan's Trout Fishing in America; The Pill Versus the Springhill Mine Disaster; And, In Watermelon Sugar* (New York, NY: Houghton Harcourt, 1989), 1. Brautigan's poems were translated into Dutch in the 1970s, including an edition of *Trout Fishing* under the name of 'Forel vissen'. They continued to exert an influence on Dutch counter-cultural circles in the 1980s, including the Council Against the Work Ethic.

[67] See Roel Van Duijn, *Provo. De geschiedenis van de provotarische beweging 1965–1967* (Amsterdam: Meulenhoff, 1985), 181.

[68] Ibid., 134.

Closely aligned with the French Situationists, Van Duijn later became an eloquent BI-advocate.[69]

Throughout his career Van Duijn also operated as an intellectual broker for French anti-state politics. In the 1970s he featured in collections with Guattari, Foucault and Deleuze and French *autogestionnaire* literature.[70] Following these exemplars, he celebrated the advent of a new 'molecular' revolution, where social change was reconceived as the proliferation of alternative lifestyles next to state-and party-structures. This inflected his view of 'labour' as well. Dutch social democrats and communists, in his view, 'thought that automation was dangerous'.[71] What followed were 'atrocious attempts' to 'workerise' the student into a '*jeune travailleur intellectual*', evinced by the tortured ritualism of French Maoism. All these views, however, were nothing but 'branches on the tree planted by Marx himself', whose central idea was that 'humans only become humans through their labour and that the alienation of labour was therefore humanity's greatest evil'. In contrast, however, Van Duijn thought that the 'cybernetic revolution' would 'rip labour out of the hands of the worker' and 'blow the bottom out of our work-based morality', leading to a world where 'automatic factories' would 'produce everything men needed'. [72] As he put it:

> Automation will give a new impulse to class struggle. The proletariat will be shaken from its apathy, since automation brings with increasing unemployment; what the worker used to do is now done by the machine or the computer.[73]

One of the most explicit models of such a cybernetic utopia had been drawn up by the Dutch Situationist Constant Nieuwenhuys in 1965 under the name 'New Babylon'. Conceived as a city in which work and physical exertion would be superfluous, New Babylon served as a blueprint for a

[69] See R. J. L. Visser, 'Discussie over de betogen met reacties van Vogels en Van Duijn', in *Natuur en cultuur op gespannen voet. Groen licht voor een nieuw denken?*, ed. Rob Visser (Utrecht: Studium Generale Reeks, 1994), 48.

[70] See Roel Van Duijn, Michel Foucault, Herbert Marcuse, Gilles Deleuze & Félix Guattari, *Morgen is het misschien zover. Het nieuwe denken over onze tijd* (Amsterdam: Het Wereldvenster, 1973).

[71] See Constant Nieuwenhuis, *New Babylon* (New York, NY: Notbored, 2009), 3.

[72] Ibid., 134.

[73] Ibid., 133. One of the first editions of 'Provo'—the movement's magazine—carried an entire header on the 'New Babylon' scheme, including references to cybernetics.

future in which cybernetics would do away with the need for authoritarian guidance and interaction would happen on a purely spontaneous basis.[74] 'Let us suppose', Nieuwenhuys claimed in an explicatory text, 'that all nonproductive work can be completely automated; that productivity increases until the world no longer knows scarcity; that the land and the means of production are socialized … in other words, that the Marxist realm of freedom is realizable'.[75] Van Duijn drew heavily on Nieuwenhuys, hoping that his 'provotarian' revolution would make possible the building of the latter's cosmopolis. The city's cybernetic technologies would 'wipe away utilitarianism' and render 'valuable' a whole list of activities previously not considered work. 'A different value', he finished, would now 'have to give content to human lives'.[76]

In 1985, however—the year in which Van Duijn issued his call—this was easier said than done. Most party members stuck to a more workerist line. In a 1982 pre-conference report named 'Resolution on Arbeid' (*Resolutie arbeid*), for instance, the Labour Party pronounced itself in favour of a rekindled full employment-strategy, reclaiming the dignity of the workerist subject. 'Labour', the text claimed, was an 'irreplaceable part of human existence', and remained a 'prime means for self-development'.[77] Rather than giving handouts to the unemployed, the resolution proclaimed the need for reskilling and education reform, which would 'raise possibilities for recurring learning (*wederkerend leren*)'.[78] Prominent politicians such as minister Jaap van der Doef then castigated basic income schemes as injurious and far-fetched, stating that the party 'ought not to

[74] Ibid., 133. See Ali Dur and McKenzie Wark, 'New New Babylon', *October* 138 (Fall 2011): 37–56; Mark Wigley, *Constant's New Babylon: The Hyper-architecture of Desire* (Rotterdam: 010 Publishers, 1998); Mark Wigley and Catherine de Zegher, eds., *The Activist Drawing: Retracing Situationist Architectures from Constant's New Babylon to Beyond* (Cambridge, MA: The MIT Press, 2002). Wark and Dur emphasize the influence of Norbert Wiener on Nieuwenhuy's plans, while even Henri Lefebvre—classically a critic of cybernetics—showed enthusiasm.

[75] Cited in Robert J. van der Veen, *Between Exploitation and Communism: Explorations in the Marxian Theory of Justice and Freedom* (Amsterdam: Wolters-Noordhoff, 1991), 352. Also explored in Cor Schavemaker and Harry Willemsen, *Over de arbeid van de mens* (Amsterdam: Samsom, 1984), a book used by Hans Achterhuis at the University of Amsterdam during his interactions with the Council.

[76] See 19^{e} Kongres van de Partij van de Arbeid, 'Resolutie Arbeid', April 23, 1983, 13.

[77] Cited in Frank Empel en Flip Vuijsje, 'Jaap van der Doef en de herverdeling van de arbeid—"Werk moet een recht blijven"', *De Haagse Post*, May 22, 1980: 2.

[78] See Roel Van Duijn, *Message of a Wise Kabouter* (New York, NY: Duckworth, 1972), 31.

accept that 500.000 people are placed beyond paid employment', mainly 'since work is much more than a means to employment for people'.[79] Moreover, new leftists like Van Duijn had, in contrast to the classical statist perspective of the party a strong suspicion of bureaucracy and industrial welfare programmes. Criticizing the 'state-centrism' of Dutch socialists, he traced their political project back all the way to Thomas Hobbes. Since the state 'took away the autonomy and rights from the guilds', the 'increase in responsibilities of the citizen towards the state decreased their mutual obligations and possibility for reciprocal aid'. If the UBI was to work, it had to reshape old political oppositions. For the New Left, rethinking labour required a deeper rethinking of the state—a task where French precedents again offered succour.

Antistatism Against Social Rights

In his 1977 movie *A Grin Without a Cat*, the French filmmaker Chris Marker gave a personal account of the struggles that shook France from 1967 to 1977 and, more generally, the hopes of the generation that matured around May 1968.[80] Marker claimed that the decade in question had profoundly transformed the self-understanding of European societies, mainly on their left flank. As he put it, 1968 had redrawn the contours of the left itself, reversing its existential destiny and purpose. A new 'kind of problematic' emerged, he wrote, 'dealing blows to every branch of orthodoxy, right or left'.[81] 'There was the barrage of the police, which was one order, and the security service of the union, that was another order. In between there was a space to capture', which 'meant a new kind of struggle'.[82]

For a substantial part of the 1968 generation, this new mode also meant an escape from an older one. This was what leading figures of the French 'Second Left' called the 'social-statism' of the post-war political order. This 'second left' acquired its name from a famous speech of the socialist

[79] See Roel Van Duijn, *De boodschap van een wijze kabouter: Een beschouwing over het filosofische en politicke werk van Peter Kropotkien in verband met onze huidige keuze tussen katasrofe of kabouterstad* (Amsterdam: Meulenhoff, 1969), 60–61. Van Duijn also postulated that cybernetics had replaced dialectics as society's science of change, using the example of a free grid on which users with bikers could circulate.

[80] Chris Marker, *A Grin Without a Cat*, 1977.

[81] Chris Marker, 'Sixties', *Critical Quarterly* 50, no. 3 (October 2008), 26–32.

[82] Ibid.

leader (and later prime minister) Michel Rocard at a 1977 congress of the Socialist Party, where he first drew a distinction between these two lefts.[83] To Rocard, both the 'Old Left' united under the 'common programme' and the old Gaullist right were part of the problem, conceiving of social change exclusive through the lens of a centralized state.[84]

Rocard had tapped into a deeper mood with his speech. 'What do we gain by replacing an employer's arbiter by a bureaucratic arbiter?' André Gorz would ask in the mid-1970s.[85] This centrality of the state in political parties of the left and right was what Pierre Rosanvallon and Patrick Viveret referred to as the dominant 'political culture'.[86] Such a culture—either 'from the left or the right [...] and for which the central element is the state, considered at the same time as the object of the struggle and the space of social transformation'—had become, since the war, the encasing paradigm for all political discussion. A shared enemy was now marked out: 'the old social-statist political culture'.[87] The goal of the Second Left was thus to 'de-stateify French society'. In France this hostility culminated in what Pierre Bourdieu had called an 'anti-institutional mood', with the welfare state increasingly being depicted as a disciplinary tool.[88] This critique turned social security systems into 'a true exercise in stigmatisation for the behaviours and components of their situation, an authentic politics of disciplinarisation and normalisation'.[89]

But there were alternatives. Milton Friedman's negative income tax, for instance, appeared in French public debates as early as 1973, mainly through Lionel Stoléru's book *Overcoming Poverty in Rich Countries.* Stoléru was a high state official sent by President Giscard in the early

[83] See Michel Rocard, 'Un puissant parti socialiste: intervention à la Convention nationale du parti socialiste le 25 novembre 1978', in *Parler Vrai* (Paris: Seuil, 1979), 176.

[84] Pierre Rosanvallon and Patrick Viveret, *Pour une nouvelle culture politique* (Paris: Seuil, 1977).

[85] Michel Bosquet, Occupons le terrain, *Le nouvel observateur* 166 (August 1976): 23.

[86] See Pierre Rosanvallon, 'L'état en état d'urgence', *Le Nouvel Observateur* 670 (September 1977): 49. See in particular Behrent, 'Liberalism without Humanism', 539–568; Claude Mauriac, *Le Temps Immobile VII. Signes, rencontres et rendez-vous* (Paris: Grasset, 1983). Julian Bourg, *From Revolution to Ethics: May 68 and Contemporary French Thought* (Montreal and Kingston: McGill-Queen's University Press, 2007).

[87] Ibid., 49.

[88] See Michael Grenfell, *Pierre Bourdieu: Agent Provocateur* (London: A&C Black, 2004), 171.

[89] Michel Messu, 'Pauvreté et exclusion en France', in *Face à la pauvreté*, ed. F. Merrien (Paris: éditions de l'Atelier, 1994), 148.

1970s to study at the Brookings institute in Washington and transposed Friedman's proposal into a French setting. When Giscard was elected president and as economic adviser, Stoléru argued that an NIT would be more efficient to struggle against deprivation in a capitalist economy. The quest for equality of the post-war period Stoléru argued, only 'removed from the competitive economy both the compass that directs it and the spring that pushes it forth, which meant that it is taken into the hands of the state'.[90]

The idea missed implementation during the Giscard-presidency. Foucault, himself, however, retained interest in the proposal, mainly in academic settings. On March 7, 1979, he focused his Collège de France lecture on the proposal first launched by Friedman in the early 1940s. In Foucault's eyes, Friedman and Giscard's proposal presented a stark caesura with classical models of welfare, which were too firmly centred around a notion of the 'labouring subject' as its definitive normative model. The negative tax system, Foucault claimed, implied 'the formation of an economic policy which is no longer focused on full employment', and which could 'only be integrated in the general market economy by abandoning ... centrally planned growth'.[91] Ultimately however, with the NIT, it became 'up to people to work if they want or not work if they don't', including 'the possibility of not forcing them to work if there is no interest in doing so'.[92]

The most harmonious marriage of French anti-workerism and anti-statism, however, again was the work of André Gorz. In the late years of the decade, Gorz went as far as to advocate a front between neoliberals and 'neosocialists' against the combined forces of French statism. A series of articles written for the French weekly *Le Nouvel Observateur* under the pseudonym of Michel Bosquet claimed that the left might benefit from thinking of workers in terms of 'enterprises' rather than 'producers'.[93] Gorz discerned an occasion in the rise of French neoliberalism to rethink the contours of the left's project as a whole. As he puts in a text of 1976, 'it is clear that Giscard is of the right. But it does not follow from that, that

[90] Lionel Stoléru, *Vaincre la pauvreté dans les pays riches* (Paris: Flammarion, 1974), 289.

[91] Michel Foucault, *The Birth of Biopolitics: Lectures at the Collège de France, 1978–79* (London: Palgrave, 2008), 115.

[92] Michel Bosquet, 'Plaidoyer pour l'entreprise', *Le nouvel observateur* 684 (December 1977): 19–24.

[93] Bosquet, 'Occupons le terrain', op. cit., 23.

the liberalization of society is necessarily a right-wing project and that we should abandon that to the Giscardians.'[94]

Gorz underlined that 'everywhere in Europe there is now, between neoliberals and neo-socialists, exchange and partial osmosis'. Exchanges between the New Left and the New Right were not so much about increasing corporate power but were about a struggle against a common enemy: the state. 'If Giscard succeeds in disengaging central power and freeing new spaces where we can exercise collective initiative, why not profit from it?'[95] In this optic, the retreat of the state provoked by neoliberalism presented an ideal occasion for an anti-statist left to 'occupy the field left vacant by the power'. Gorz concluded with a question:

> Does the left want a society where everyone relies on the state for everything: the pollution of the shore, food additives, architecture, abusive lay-offs, work accidents, etc.? In that case we will only replace private carelessness by administrative carelessness, an employer's arbiter by a bureaucratic arbiter.[96]

Social-statism had created a group of permanently dependent welfare claimants, Gorz claimed, and 'weakened civil society so that disconnected individuals call on the state to compensate, by an even greater social presence, for the disappearance of their capabilities to help each other'.[97]

Gorz and other *autogestion* writers also proved a reliable inspiration to the Dutch anti-state left. The country had been at the forefront of the anti-poverty revolution in the 1960s with the so-called assistance law (*bijstandwet*), which put previously private provision in the hands of the state and stipulated unconditional grants. Even in 1985, however, the mainstream Dutch left had difficulty accepting the proposal. In that year, the Dutch Socialist Party (PVDA) set up a working group on the topic, with prominent party figures such as Dutch minister Sicco Mansholt claiming that the 'introduction of a basic income had become' nothing less than 'a necessity'.[98] In his view, a 'reduction of labour time' was

[94] Ibid., 23.

[95] Ibid.

[96] André Gorz, *Ecology as Politics* (London: Black Rose Books, 1980), 37.

[97] Ibid, 37.

[98] See Sicco Mansholt, 'Invoering van een basisinkomen een noodzakelijkheid', in *Werkgroep PvdA Voor Basisinkomen* (1986), 1. Available in the archives of Collectif Charles Fourier.

'impossible' without the introduction of a basic income. Countering the excessively normative leanings of figures such as van der Doef, Mansholt stated that the claim that the basic income would lead to 'idleness' was 'nonsense'.[99] People, he saw, 'would always want to perform labour', yet today, 'not all available work was compatible with existing wishes'.[100]

Things took another interesting turn at the end of 1985. In the middle of the year, a prominent Dutch think tank put out a report on the institutional inevitability of a basic income. In a statement entitled 'Warrants for Security' (*Waarborgen voor zekerheid*), the Dutch Scientific Council for Governmental Policy or 'WRR' (*Wetenschappelijke Raad voor Regeringsonderzoek)* proposed a partial and 'low' basic income of 30 per cent of the social minimum for cohabitants, pegging its proposal at 5000 guilders per annum or 450 per month.[101] It was not the first engagement on behalf of the council with the intricacies of the basic income; in 1981, the group had already put out their first musings on the subject.[102] In 1985, however, a more strongly neoliberal accent became visible: the report proposed the abolition of minimum wage legislation together with its basic income scheme. As the report concluded, 'to assure a better functioning of the labour market', 'an abolition of the legal minimum wage should be given due consideration'. This, they claimed, would 'stimulate employment', and would finally get rid of the 'complexity' of the current Dutch welfare state.[103]

One thinker swiftly recognized the importance of these Dutch debates for the European BI movement as a whole. In a text written in 1988, Belgian philosopher Philippe Van Parijs surveyed recent developments in Dutch social policy for the French *Saint Simon* think tank. As he saw it, the Dutch had been veritable trendsetters when it came to the fight for a 'vital minimum', visible in their early adoption of the assistance law in 1965 and later debates about the basic income scheme. 'There was no need', he claimed, 'to adhere to unilinear evolutionism to see that the frustrations, uncertainties, hopes and conflicts that have given rise to the Dutch debate might come to prefigure those which are only coming into

[99] Ibid., 1.

[100] Ibid.

[101] Wetenschappelijke Raad voor Regeringsadvies, *Waarborgen voor zekerheid: een nieuw stelsel van sociale zekerheid in hoofdlijnen* ('s Gravenhage: Staatsuitgeverij, 1985).

[102] Wetenschappelijke Raad voor Regeringsadvies, *Vernieuwingen in het arbeidsbestel* (The Hague, 1981).

[103] Ibid., 181.

shape in other countries'. As he saw it, the frame for the UBI was intrinsically transnational, global even. 'What is at stake in this debate', Van Parijs finished, 'is different and much more than the choice of an "adjustment strategy" for social security to our current "crisis"'. Rather, the question was whether the central socio-economic objective of 'progressive forces can and should be radically reformulated'. This reformulation, he claimed, concerned the promise 'to guarantee liberty to all through the installation of a maximal basic income'.[104]

Conclusion: Losing the Battle, Winning the War

From 1968 to 1994, Europe's basic income movement had come a long way. It had transformed the proposal from an exotic export product to a full-fledged alternative for the post-industrial left. Underlying this success was a double conceptual revolution in European left-wing thought. This revolution reoriented debates on social policy from 'inequality' to 'poverty' and reclaimed society as a sphere of liberty beyond the state. This twin revolution had natural critics. As the French philosopher Pierre Rosanvallon noted in his 1995 *La nouvelle question sociale*, the BI owed part of its popularity to an unholy alliance crafted between neoliberals and neo-leftists in the 1980s. To Rosanvallon, it represented 'the pernicious and paradoxical aspect of the end of the classical conception of the welfare state' and a 'symptom of the increasing separation between economic activity and solidarity, and of a surprising convergence between a libertarian and utopian-socialist viewpoint'.[105] 'By radically dissociating the economic from the social' and in their striving for a '"postlabor" society', he claimed, basic income schemes allowed 'the issue of employment to be pushed into the background'.[106]

However hostile, Rosanvallon's statement did get at the specificity of the new UBI put forward in the 1980s. A new version of Tinbergen and Friedman's model initiated a retreat from the 'producerist subject'

[104] Philippe Van Parijs, 'Pays-bas: le débat sur l'allocation universelle, ou l'au-delà du revenu minimum garanti', *Revue belge de sécurité sociale* 30 (1988): 675–684. The text was later reprinted in *Notes de la Fondation Saint Simon*, September 1, 1988, 15–23.

[105] Ibid., 684.

[106] See Pierre Rosanvallon, *The New Social Question—Rethinking the Welfare State* (Princeton, NJ: Princeton University Press, 2000), 64–65. Rosanvallon's original work appeared in 1992 and featured a discussion of Van Parijs' plans as well. Rosanvallon himself did share the attempt to modernize social security in the course of the 1980s and 1990s.

prevalent in the post-war labour movement, transcending someone's mere 'work function'. It also worked on the individualist sensibility of the post-68 generation, who preferred discretion when it came to life choices and shied away from the overtly 'biopolitical' dictates of the welfare state. In 1993, an affiliate of the Flemish Green party summarized this point by casting the BI as a 'post-utopian utopia':

> The proposed model (*basic income*) is a middle way between two utopias. It leaves the market intact but deals with the consequences of market failure. At the same time, it limits state intervention to the creation of a framework wherein those that have become the victim of those failures receive a veritable and humane—but not utopian or ideal—solution for this failure.[107]

It was precisely this acquiescence that critics found alarming. Four years later, when the basic income movement was steadily globalizing itself, the English critic James Heartfield criticized the movement for its tendency to accept the current 'retreat from the sphere of production'.[108] The 'non-class of non-workers' which Gorz had cast as the subject of the post-industrial age, he claimed, simply accepted the 'stagnation of the productive sphere', while the realm of 'material production' was now 'seen as a hang-over from the past'. After neoliberals had successfully redefined work as 'disutility', Heartfield saw that the 'conflictual character of the contest over needs that so heavily marked the first seventy-years of the century' became 'submerged in a civil peace where basic needs are no longer a matter of public debate'. In 'identifying a minimum', the BI would not necessarily have the effect of forcing incomes up. Instead, it might simply induce 'a downward pressure on pay-claims' and further individualize wage bargaining.[109] The left-wing critic George Caffentzis similarly claimed that left's BI-campaign ultimately fell prey to 'a failed politics' because it tried 'to convince both friend and foe that, behind everyone's back, capitalism (had) ended'.[110] In the end, few things would prove more dispiriting than 'work' disguised 'leisure'.

[107] Ibid., 65.

[108] See Wilfried De Vlieghere, 'Herverdeling van werk of basisinkomen?', *EcoGroen* 8 (October 1993): 25.

[109] See James Heartfield, *Need and Desire in the Post-Material Economy* (Sheffield: Sheffield Hallam University Press, 1998), 76.

[110] See George Caffentzis, 'The End of Work or the Renaissance of Slavery?', in *In Letters of Blood and Fire: Work, Machines and the Crisis of Capitalism* (New York, NY: PM Press, 2013), 81.

Ironically, the Dutch Council Against the Work Ethic became the best example of this paradox. Founded in 1982, the group almost disbanded after no more than two years of service. The reasons given by participants for the group's near dissolution certainly were ungainly. The Council, as one former observant claimed, simply found the whole endeavour 'way too much toil'.[111] As the Dutch philosopher Hans Achterhuis reported, himself an early contributor to the Council:

> The campaigners themselves were more firmly gripped by the work ethic than their constituency. Their working weeks occasionally went beyond the double of a regular working week and their working discipline was exemplary. ... It was for a worthy cause, they claimed, and it allowed one to be one's own boss.[112]

In their attempt to abolish 'labour', the post-workerists had nearly worked themselves to death.

[111] Van Essen, *Kind van de verzoringsstaat,* 55.

[112] Hans Achterhuis, 'Neem de tijd—Gevangen in de tredmolen als hamsters', *Trouw*, May 19, 2012.

CHAPTER 7

Activating the Unemployed or Liberating the Employed? Universal Basic Income in the French Welfare Reform Debate

Marc-Antoine Sabaté

One of the political consequences of the 2008 financial crisis—and the austerity politics that followed—was the global resurgence of universal basic income (UBI) advocacy.[1] In France, this new wave of support dramatically took off in 2017 when the socialist presidential candidate, Benoît Hamon, ran his campaign on a UBI platform. Although his *revenu universel* proposal initially succeeded in attracting the urban youth vote, allowing him to win the Socialist Party primaries, Hamon eventually failed to unite the Left and suffered a crushing defeat in the first round of the election.[2] In spite of this, however, UBI is now well settled in the French political agenda. In November 2017, for example, thirteen left-wing presidents of *départements* (i.e. French counties) joined to demand the set-up of local trials. After a year of public consultations, the project was, however,

[1] See Jurgen De Wispelaere, 'Basic Income—Have Austerity's Chickens Come Home to Roost?, *ISRF Bulletin* 13 (June 2017): 22–27.

[2] With a score of 6.35%, he recorded an all-time low for the Parti Socialiste.

M.-A. Sabaté (✉)
Université Libre de Bruxelles, Brussels, Belgium

P. Sloman et al. (eds.), *Universal Basic Income in Historical Perspective*, https://doi.org/10.1007/978-3-030-75706-9_7

eventually and quite contemptuously dismissed by the presidential majority in the *Assemblée Nationale*. The 'Macronists' were indeed already committed to their own guaranteed income reform plan. President Emmanuel Macron had announced in September 2018 that by 2020 all existing social assistance schemes would be merged into a single benefit—incidentally, named *Revenu Universel d'Activité*. In spite of its wilful consonance with Hamon's proposal, this single unified benefit, means-tested and highly conditional, could hardly be definable as a form of UBI.[3] Just as a 'genuine' UBI, however, whose only distinctive character lies in it being unconditional, it would nevertheless amount to yet another step in a continuous process of welfare reform that, since the 1970s, has seen the introduction of conditional cash transfer programmes (*minima sociaux*) to alleviate poverty and encourage work.

The extent to which unconditionality would cause an inflection in this trajectory of welfare reform has been one of the main issues in UBI debates for decades. On the one hand, supporters argue that its implementation would answer 'the multiple defects of the current system of minimum social benefits' (from non-take up to so-called unemployment traps).[4] On the other, that it would free us from the 'employment trap', that is, empower us with the freedom to 'say no' to lousy or unfulfilling jobs.[5] To put it otherwise, UBI would paradoxically strengthen a weakening and 'passive' welfare state and, at the same time, pave the way for a post-welfarist society where employment would no longer be the sole base of one's social identity and citizenship. In recent years, however, there has been a significant tendency to present UBI as a 'new pillar' of the welfare state.[6] Admittedly, UBI has rarely been (explicitly) proposed as a tool to dismantle the welfare state, but the various proposals formulated in the French debate during the 1980s and 1990s were more strikingly committed to alternative social ideals that were at odds with 'welfare capitalism' or called for an 'Exodus' from the 'work-based society'.[7] No doubt, the long-

[3] Indeed, the system would actually be closer to the controversial British 'Universal Credit' system.

[4] Mouvement Français pour un Revenu de Base, *Pour un revenu de base universel. Vers une société du choix* (Paris: Éditions du Détour, 2017), 23.

[5] Philippe Van Parijs and Yannick Vanderborght, *Basic Income: A Radical Proposal for a Free Society and a Sane Economy* (Cambridge, MA: Harvard University Press, 2017), 21–23.

[6] MFRB, *Pour un revenu de base universel.*

[7] André Gorz, *Reclaiming Work: Beyond the Wage-Based Society*, trans. Chris Turner (Cambridge: Polity Press, 1999), 1.

ing for a post-welfarist society is still alive among current French UBI supporters.[8] But one cannot help but notice the peculiar insistence with which many are now framing it as a way to renew the radical post-war experience of implementing the welfare state.[9] This is especially interesting as it is precisely 'in the name of welfare' that UBI has been, and still is, largely rejected by many on the Left.[10]

This chapter will place these debates in historical perspective. Up to now, the history of UBI has essentially been built as a compilation of antecedents—it has been a matter of identifying in the past proposals that are reminiscent of the current one.[11] Such a narrative of origins, however, tells us little, if anything, about UBI's historical conditions of possibility.[12] If it is, indeed, far from being a new idea, then how come it has never found its way towards implementation? Conversely, how come we are now closer than ever to its supposedly long-awaited accomplishment? These are the questions that matter and for which historical investigation is deeply needed. What is needed, in other words, is a critical understanding of how both support for and rejection of UBI are presently structured by the past, that is, an investigation of the 'problematical configuration' through which it came to appear as a relevant policy proposal.[13] How have issues such as poverty, unemployment, or automation been recognized and constructed as social problems, thus calling for some solution while excluding others? To answer this, one could of course go back to the dawn of the *question sociale*—say, to the French Revolution or to the Speenhamland system. In what follows, I focus on a much more recent problematical configuration, or rather a reconfiguration, that changed—both institutionally and intellectually—the course of welfare history.

[8] See for example Abdenour Bidar, *Libérons-nous! Des chaînes du travail et de la consommation* (Paris: Les Liens qui Libèrent, 2018).

[9] 'We had the courage to create the *Sécurité sociale* in 1945; let us now have the courage to implement this new pillar of social protection.' MFRB, *Pour un revenu de base universel*, 31.

[10] Robert Castel, *La montée des incertitudes. Travail, protections, statut de l'individu* (Paris: Seuil, 2009), 187.

[11] For a striking example of this approach, see in particular Van Parijs and Vanderborght, *Basic Income*, 51–98.

[12] For a discussion of this argument, see Daniel Zamora, 'Histoire et genèse d'une idée néolibérale', in *Contre l'allocation universelle*, eds. Mateo Alaluf and Daniel Zamora (Montréal: Lux, 2016), 14–36.

[13] Robert Castel, 'Penser le changement: le parcours des années 1960–2010', in *Changement et pensées du changement. Échanges avec Robert Castel*, eds. Robert Castel and Claude Martin (Paris: La Découverte, 2012), 37–39.

The narrative is well known. It was articulated as early as the 1970s. Confronted by massive unemployment, ageing populations and a slowdown in economic growth, western welfare states entered a 'crisis' that was not only about financial stability but challenged their very legitimacy. As a growing number of people slipped through the net of welfare programmes, the post-war social contract that linked social protection to waged labour seemed to be overwhelmed, and a 'new social question' was formulated through the identification of new forms of poverty and social exclusion.[14] The underlying hypothesis of the chapter is that UBI, in France, *only became justifiable in the wake of this reconfiguration.* In particular, two aspects of the 'welfare state crisis' narrative are of critical importance in order to grasp UBI's historical conditions of possibility. First, the implementation of various active labour-market policies, incentivizing or disciplining recipients in order to get the unemployed back to work. Second, the renewed questioning of the integrative and emancipatory function of work—an idea that, especially in the French case, played a foundational role in the institution of social rights. I will argue that a historically informed understanding of these twofold 'metamorphoses of work' fruitfully sheds light on a still decisive paradox, that is, that UBI is proposed, at the same time, as a way to *activate the unemployed* and as a way to *liberate the employed.*

At a time when UBI is increasingly being put forward by the social-democratic and socialist Left, what is needed is what French sociologist Robert Castel understood as an 'effort to reconsider the upheaval of the most contemporary circumstances by reconstructing the transformations that our current conditions have inherited'.[15] Only in this way can one hope to answer what is, in my view, a crucial, if not the most crucial, issue: how could UBI actually bring about something like an 'emancipatory form' of activation?[16]

[14] For an illustration of this crisis narrative, see Daniel Béland and Randall Hansen, 'Reforming the French Welfare State: Solidarity, Social Exclusion and the Three Crises of Citizenship', *The Journal of Economic History* 23, no. 1, (January 2000): 47–64.

[15] Robert Castel, *From Manual Workers to Wage Labourers: Transformation of the Social Question*, trans. Richard Boyd (New Brunswick: Transaction Publishers, 2002), xiv.

[16] Van Parijs and Vanderborght, *Basic Income*, 26.

Welfare and Social Citizenship in France: From Universalism to Dualism?

The French *Sécurité sociale* essentially fits in with the Bismarckian or 'conservative-corporatist' world of welfare: it fundamentally aims at insuring workers against the occurrence of social risks (i.e. accidents, illness, unemployment, and old age) and it is, therefore, based on social insurance.[17] In the post-war years, public assistance—that is, in the French case, non-contributory and state-managed benefits as opposed to contributory and union-managed programmes—was, on the contrary, supposed to become residual and eventually unnecessary. More, it was politically discarded. It was as workers, not as poor, that citizens were to exercise their right to social security.[18] Robert Castel prominently called this the birth of the 'wage-earning society' (*la société salariale*)—a society where, 'instead of trying to *assist* the victims of the most demeaning situations, it will now be about *securing work itself*'.[19] French historians have long debated whether the original ambition of the system was universal in the sense that the Beveridge plan was generally considered to be. What is certain is that universality was restricted to the male breadwinner—only through their relationship with a working *père de famille* could women, children, or non-workers be included in social citizenship.[20] Excluding women, the system nevertheless remained theoretically opened to their inclusion. Although still largely incomplete, a feminist universalization of social citizenship was therefore possible through women's access to employment. Post-war universalism, in this respect, mainly relied on the ongoing universalization of the 'wage-earning condition'. And the French understanding of social citizenship therefore paradoxically based the universal extent of rights upon the interdependent particularities of occupational

[17] For a synthetic and careful presentation of the French welfare system, see Bruno Palier, 'The Dualizations of the French Welfare System', in *A Long Goodbye to Bismarck? The Politics of Welfare Reform in Continental Europe*, ed. Bruno Palier (Amsterdam: Amsterdam University Press, 2010), 73–100.

[18] See in particular Henri Hatzfeld, *Du paupérisme à la Sécurité sociale 1850–1940. Essai sur les origines de la Sécurité sociale en France* (Nancy: Presses Universitaires de Nancy, 1989), 25–32.

[19] Robert Castel, 'La propriété sociale: émergence, transformations et remise en cause, *Esprit* 347 (August/September 2008): 179.

[20] According to Palier, it was in the end Beveridge's universal principles that were followed through Bismarck's insurance methods. Bruno Palier, *Gouverner la Sécurité sociale* (Paris: Presses Universitaires de France, 2005), 101–106.

activities—a peculiarity that is too often neglected by political scientists' categorizations of welfare regimes, and that one could refer to as 'occupational universalism'.

In Castel's view, this resulted in a 'differentiated continuum of social positions' that, 'in principle, and to the extent that the system works',[21] includes everyone in the 'wage-earning society'. *In principle, and to the extent that the system works.* That is, indeed, the crux of the problem. Because for the system to work, all citizens need to be workers. The 'welfare crisis' narrative tells us that when unemployment started to rise it became necessary to set up a new tier of assistance below the main insurance safety net. Though essentially valid, this narrative overlooks two crucial points. First, as I explain further below, the need for new assistance programmes as a palliative was crucially driven by the tightening of eligibility for unemployment benefits. Second, the fact is that assistance had actually never disappeared and that the undeniable generalization of social protections rather happened through a growing 'interpenetration' of insurance and assistance programmes.[22] The much-debated 'rediscovery of poverty' that gradually brought back the old figure of the poor as the subject of social policy was, therefore, as important as unemployment rates in the diagnosis of the crisis.[23] Indeed, the 'complementarity of action' of insurance and assistance could only function as long as the recipient population was not (or was not seen as) the poor. Until the 1970s, 'social aid' recipients were essentially seen as 'working families who were certainly experiencing difficulties, but accidentally, and who could be reintegrated into the world of work'. Admittedly, assistance had not become as residual as had been expected, historian Colette Bec explains, but it had been integrated into the producer-consumer model—it was used to reduce inequalities *within* the wage-earning continuum.[24]

[21] Castel, *La montée des incertitudes*, 159–160.

[22] Whatever the original universal ambition of the system was, the fact is that the generalization of coverage was carried out through professional segmentation and, as a result, that it could not be achieved through insurance mechanisms alone. See Colette Bec, *L'assistance en démocratie. Les politiques assistantielles dans la France des XIXe et XXe siècles* (Paris: Belin, 1998), 96.

[23] For an engaging discussion of this issue, connecting the American and European 'new poverty' debates, see Daniel Zamora, *De l'égalité à la pauvreté. Une socio-histoire de l'assistance en Belgique (1895–2015)* (Bruxelles: Éditions de l'Université de Bruxelles, coll. 2017), esp. 53–57.

[24] Bec, *L'assistance en démocratie*, 102–103.

In the post-war years poverty had essentially been understood in France through the issues of old age and inadequate housing.[25] But those who came to be called the 'new poor' in the 1970s were not exactly the residual population of destitutes that welfare programmes had not *yet*, or so it was thought, succeeded in integrating to the wage-earning society. They were rather a diverse population of previously employed, potentially 'employable', or presently underemployed people that were increasingly dropping out of the labour market. The troubling nature of the new poverty phenomenon was, in other words, that low-skilled, young, and single-mother workers were increasingly trapped in poverty. Welfare programmes had essentially been designed to cover for temporary loss of earning capacity. The 'new poor', on the contrary, seemed to be durably excluded from the stable employment-social protection nexus. These 'new problems', therefore, 'seemed unmanageable by the existing programmes of the *Sécurité sociale*', and the main institutional response consisted of introducing a range of guaranteed income schemes—a response that progressively led to a dualization of the welfare system.[26]

Two moments can be identified in this process. Following Laurent Geffroy, one can distinguish between a 'liberal importation' of, and a 'socialist conversion' to the idea of guaranteed income.[27] The former (c. 1970) was essentially concerned with poverty and put forward the negative income tax as a potential solution. The latter (c. 1980) was more specifically focused on social exclusion and republican solidarity, and resulted in the introduction of a minimum-income scheme called *Revenu Minimum d'Insertion* in 1988. Both shaped a debate in which UBI later emerged as a viable alternative.

A Neoliberal Breakthrough: The 'Safety Clause for the Player'

Two books are generally highlighted as channels for the publicization of 'new poverty' in the French debate. In 1974, a senior public servant named René Lenoir referred to the 'other France' in order to highlight the

[25] See Serge Paugam, *La société française et ses pauvres. L'expérience du Revenu Minimum d'Insertion* (Paris: Presses Universitaires de France, 2002), 27–50.

[26] Palier, *Gouverner la Sécurité sociale*, 305.

[27] Laurent Geffroy, *Garantir le revenu. Histoire et actualité d'une utopie concrète* (Paris: La Découverte/M.A.U.S.S., 2002), 19–55.

persistence of 'social inadaptation'. He argued that a necessary politics of prevention had for too long been neglected and, in a vein that echoed the communitarian aspects of the US 'War on Poverty', concluded that, in order to achieve social normalcy, the 'excluded' and the 'ill-adapted' needed not only relief but what one might call help for self-help.[28] The same year, Lionel Stoléru, himself a public servant (working as an economic adviser to the then Minister of Finance and soon-to-be President, Valéry Giscard d'Estaing), imported the American debates on poverty in affluent societies as well as a potential solution: the negative income tax.[29]

Stoléru's argument relied on two fundamental assumptions. First, and as far as social policy is concerned, *poverty is nothing else than a lack of resources.* The politics of prevention was dismissed: 'Better safe than sorry', he agreed, but that is 'not enough'. We should first of all 'take care of those who, for one reason or another, are in need'. And what is need, he asked, if not a lack of income? While the lack of income was certainly not the 'only aspect' of poverty, and 'just an aspect, not a cause', for Stoléru it was the most relevant way of conceptualizing the issue for the purposes of policy-making. Hence the justification of cash transfers—if money is what the poor need, would not the best approach be to give them some? The second assumption was that what should matter to policy-makers was not relative but absolute poverty. Social transfers should aim to guarantee a sufficiency threshold, not equalize the wage scale—in other words, 'end poverty' rather than 'reduce the gap between rich and poor'. For if 'almost everyone agrees' that unjust market outcomes ought to be 'corrected' by the state, one had to acknowledge that the 'market economy' cannot 'digest' any recipe. The 'distinction between absolute and relative poverty', Stoléru concluded, 'is, in fact, the distinction between capitalism and socialism'.[30]

[28] René Lenoir, *Les exclus. Un Français sur dix* (Paris: Seuil, 1974).

[29] In the foreword of his book, Stoléru indicated that he had the opportunity to visit the Brookings Institution during the summer of 1973 to study the negative income tax and 'the political implications of such a reform'. Lionel Stoléru, *Vaincre la pauvreté dans les pays riches* (Paris: Flammarion, 1977), 5. He later explained that this research trip was decided in agreement with Giscard, with the intention of understanding why Richard Nixon had failed to introduce it in 1969–1972: Daniel Zamora, Personal email communication with Lionel Stoléru, May 2, 2015.

[30] Lionel Stoléru, *Vaincre la pauvreté dans les pays riches* (Paris: Flammarion, 1977), 119–120, 241, 292–295.

Stoléru's plea was, in this respect, a typical 'sufficiency *vs.* equality' argument—he even went so far as to say that all the viable social achievements of the century were actually sufficientarian in essence, or else they would have been a 'tragedy for the competitive economy'.[31] Samuel Moyn's account of the historical articulations of sufficiency and equality in the building of the welfare state has shown how untenable this position is.[32] On the other hand, it gives a taste of the intellectual context of the 'Giscard years': that of a neoliberal breakthrough in French politics.[33] From that point onwards, the welfare state was increasingly pointed out as placing too great of a burden on the economy and the old liberal-conservative rhetoric of *perversity*—that is, the idea that 'any public policy aiming to change market outcomes ... automatically becomes noxious interference with ... the self-regulating market'—was thus reactivated.[34] But more importantly, perhaps, the Giscardians' economic *credo* was that governments should 'completely separate that which corresponds to the needs of economic expansion from that which corresponds to the concern for solidarity and social justice'.[35] This, Michel Foucault argued in his famous 1978–1979 lectures at the Collège de France, was a 'major idea' of neoliberalism in France as elsewhere: 'the economy must have its own rules and the social must have its specific objectives, but ... they must be decoupled so that the economic process is not disrupted or damaged by social mechanisms'.[36]

But how could this 'separation between the economic and the social' work in practice? There is, according to Foucault, a 'principle' that is 'common' to all forms of neoliberalism, that is, 'the idea that the economy is basically a game ... and that the essential role of the state is to define the economic rules of the game and to make sure that they are in fact applied'. Yet, these rules should only apply on the proviso that a 'supplementary

[31] Ibid., 294.

[32] Samuel Moyn, *Not Enough: Human Rights in an Unequal World* (Cambridge, MA: Belknap Press of Harvard University Press, 2018).

[33] For an exhaustive depiction of the atmosphere of the time, see Serge Audier, *Penser le «néolibéralisme». Le moment néolibéral, Foucault et la crise du socialisme* (Lormont: Le Bord de l'Eau, 2015).

[34] Albert O. Hirschman, *The Rhetoric of Reaction: Perversity, Futility, Jeopardy* (Cambridge, MA: Harvard University Press, 1991): 27. For a typical illustration of this reactionary argument in the French context, see Alain Minc, *La machine égalitaire* (Paris: Grasset, 1987).

[35] Valéry Giscard d'Estaing, quoted in Michel Foucault, *The Birth of Biopolitics: Lectures at the Collège de France, 1978–1979* (Basingstoke: Palgrave Macmillan, 2008), 206.

[36] Ibid., 201

and unconditional rule' is satisfied, 'which is that it must be impossible for one of the partners of the economic game to lose everything and thus be unable to continue playing'. Foucault called it a 'safety clause for the player'—a safeguard, keeping 'players from being excluded from the game', that ought to be 'the only point of contact between the economic and the social'. And what better way to do that than to implement a negative income tax? For it 'ensures as it were a general security, but at the lowest level', and thus allows 'the economic mechanisms of the game … to function in the rest of society'.[37]

Even Foucault therefore reckoned that the negative income tax embodied the neoliberal project of a 'society formalized on the model … of the competitive enterprise'. Yet, he admitted, its French version was not as 'drastic' as the American one.[38] For one thing, Stoléru explicitly ruled out the 'simple' solution of a negative income tax replacing all other welfare expenditures.[39] Besides, there was a genuine ethical ambition in his argument. While one could argue that such a system would merely alleviate the effects of poverty without tackling its structural causes, he would answer that this is precisely the point: 'For some, social assistance must be motivated by the causes of poverty: illness, accident, inability to work or to find employment during recession periods, etc. For others, social assistance must only be motivated by the effects of poverty: every human being has basic needs, and society must help him to meet them when he cannot do so by himself.' The negative income tax 'is thus totally incompatible with the social conceptions that want to know why there is poverty before providing assistance'. In doing so, however, it does away with the burden of proof on both sides—it does not matter whether poverty is 'suffered' or 'deserved', nor that social assistance eliminates 'individual responsibility' or encourages the 'unscrupulous' to 'take advantage of the system'. Society, he concluded, should 'prioritise justice over efficiency'.[40]

In a nutshell, Stoléru's negative income tax proposal is fundamentally aimed at giving people freedom of choice.[41] It seems crucial to outline this

[37] Ibid., 201–202, 206.

[38] Ibid., 206, 204.

[39] He also admitted that, regarding 'fundamental needs' like 'education' or 'healthcare', cash transfers were not 'substitutable' to 'in-kind' services. Stoléru, *Vaincre la pauvreté*, 146.

[40] Ibid., 242, 205–206, 243–245.

[41] Stoléru illustrated it by recalling a famous Chinese proverb—*give a man a fish and you feed him for a day, teach a man how to fish and you feed him for a lifetime.* His interpretation, however, substantially deviated from the usual maxim: 'Duly understood, the Chinese prov-

ethical stance, if only to understand how UBI would later take over this aspiration. In Stoléru's view, for instance, this ethics of choice unequivocally justified the possibility of 'freely-chosen exclusion'. While some may see it as 'society's failure', one should rather recognize 'the right to be oneself' as 'one of the most advanced forms of fundamental rights'. Which is not to say that he advocated idleness—the negative income tax, he explained, would certainly benefit 'those who work little or not at all', but it should not and, he believed, would not create incentives not to work. For if 'it does not compel anyone to work', it nevertheless '*makes work pay*'.[42] The negative income tax, as Foucault understood, should indeed contribute to making the economic game 'as active as possible'. 'Ultimately', however, 'it is up to people to work if they want or not work if they don't. ... They are merely guaranteed the possibility of minimal existence at a given level, and in this way the neo-liberal policy can be got to work.'[43]

A Republican Activation: '*L'Insertion*'

A negative income tax was never implemented in France. Stoléru entered the government after Giscard d'Estaing's victory at the 1974 presidential election, but his proposal was eventually dropped—Giscard judged that 'people are not yet ready for such a deep transformation'.[44] Yet its influence on the French trajectory of reforms is clear: categorical cash transfers (for the elderly, the disabled, or the widowed) were progressively implemented and the idea of a unified social assistance scheme took hold. The idea of a guaranteed income, however, was firmly opposed by the French Left during this period. Too closely related to economic liberalism, it seemed at odds with full employment policies and, more generally, with the traditional politics of socialism that essentially aimed at changing

erb actually reads: "Teach him how to fish, he will always eat *fish*", and there lies the essential flaw of in-kind services—they predeterminate the poor's needs instead of letting him assume the responsibility of defining his needs and choosing the means to satisfy them himself. "Give him money, and he will learn how to fish, hunt, or farm, according to his tastes", this is the philosophy of the social strategy of income, much more respectful of the individual's freedom of choice.' Ibid., 256–257.

[42] Ibid., 245, 138–141.

[43] Foucault, *The Birth of Biopolitics*, 207.

[44] Valéry Giscard d'Estaing, *Démocratie française* (Paris: Fayard, 1976), 59, quoted in Geffroy, *Garantir le revenu*, 27.

society from within the wage relation.[45] In Lionel Jospin's closing speech to the Socialist Party's 1983 convention, for example, the then First Secretary openly criticized guaranteed income supporters—'how could we not believe', he asked, 'that they might dismantle social security and establish a two-tier system: assistance for the poor, insurance for the rich?'[46] Nevertheless, it was under François Mitterrand's Socialist presidency that a comprehensive guaranteed income was ultimately introduced. How did this 'conversion' happen?

Firstly, and mainly, it depended on the growing influence of the 'Second Left' that, as Michel Bosquet (i.e. André Gorz's journalistic pseudonym) wrote in 1976, saw the 'liberalisation of society' as a valuable project that the Left should not 'abandon … to the Giscardians'.[47] Led by Michel Rocard with the support of the CFDT union, this anti-statist Left praised the idea of *autogestion* and pushed for a reappreciation of local solidarity against the 'bureaucratic' national solidarity.[48] Perhaps the clearest statement of this position was Pierre Rosanvallon's seminal 1981 essay on the 'crisis of the welfare state'. While diagnosing a 'financial impasse', the French historian reckoned that this crisis was not about the 'burden of public spending' *per se*, but rather about the 'mechanical and cold development of the welfare state' through the 'disembeddment' of spontaneous social solidarity. In his view, the state was essentially unable to accommodate the needs and expectations of those whose individual circumstances did not match the 'rigidity' of welfare programmes.[49] To

[45] Ibid., 37–39.

[46] Quoted in ibid., 46.

[47] Michel Bosquet, 'Occupons le terrain', *Le nouvel observateur* 116, (August 1976): 23, quoted in Daniel Zamora, 'Finding a "Left Governmentality": Foucault's Last Decade', in *Foucault, Neoliberalism, and Beyond*, eds. Stephen W. Sawyer and Daniel Steinmetz-Jenkins (London: Rowman & Littlefield, 2019), 65–66.

[48] As Donald Sassoon noted, *autogestion* could be broadly defined as 'the self-government of the masses'—it combined aspirations to an 'industrial democracy' and to a 'decentralised economy'. But the concept has always 'remained vague and ill-defined'. Donald Sassoon, *One Hundred Years of Socialism: The West European Left in the Twentieth Century* (New York: The New Press, 1996), 538–540. Besides, its supporters certainly constituted more of a 'galaxy' of groups than a coherent movement. One could, however, identify a common set of principles as follows: 'an existential concern, that of *autonomy*, a will to be embedded in society, expressed by an *anti-statism*, a civilisational rejection, that of *productivism*, and lastly a constant demand to *reduce working hours*'. Willy Gianinazzi, *André Gorz. Une vie* (Paris: La Découverte, 2016), 162.

[49] Pierre Rosanvallon, *La crise de l'État-providence* (Paris: Seuil, 1992), 13, 31–32, 47, 114.

overcome these 'limits of mechanical solidarity', Rosanvallon set out a 'post-social-democratic' programme focused on 'bringing society closer to itself', that is, dropping a 'binary' vision of society—either 'the market or the state', but nothing in between—to embrace an 'autonomisation' and a 'thickening' of 'civil society'. To this end, he concluded, the government should 'reduce demand for the state' and 'reintegrate individuals in direct solidarity networks'.[50]

Secondly, the 'socialist conversion' was crucially influenced by the mobilization of local actors. In that respect, Rosanvallon's programme not only illustrated the Second Left calls for a 'new political culture' ('critical of centralised management' and committed to 'bottom-up social change'[51]), it resonated with the multiplication of social experiments set up by NGOs to fight poverty at the local level.[52] It was, in the end, the 'dramatization of new poverty' organized by civil society's 'moral entrepreneurs' that overcame the widespread political scepticism.[53] The broad media coverage devoted to ATD Quart Monde or to the *Restos du Coeur* put the notion of 'dignity' at the centre of the public debate and 'contributed to a general feeling of generosity and solidarity'.[54] Against this

[50] Ibid., 31, 109–130.

[51] Ibid., 132. See also Pierre Rosanvallon and Patrick Viveret, *Pour une nouvelle culture politique* (Paris: Seuil, 1977).

[52] See in particular Frédéric Viguier, 'Le rôle des associations de lutte contre la pauvreté dans la protection sociale française depuis 1945: le cas d'ATD Quart Monde', *Revue d'Histoire de la Protection Sociale* 6 (2013): 12–34.

[53] Paugam, *La société française et ses pauvres*, 65–70; Matthieu Tracol, 'Trente ans après, retour sur la genèse du RMI', *Fondation Jean Jaurès*, November 30, 2018, https://jean-jaures.org/nos-productions/trente-ans-apres-retour-sur-la-genese-du-rmi. See also Laurent Cyterman and Cécile Dindar, 'Les grandes étapes de l'histoire du RMI', in *RMI, l'état des lieux 1988–2008*, eds. Michèle Lelièvre and Emmanuelle Nauze-Fichet (Paris: La Découverte, 2008), 26–27.

[54] Before the 1988 presidential election, sociologist Serge Paugam explained, 'nine French out of ten took a stance in favour of a minimum income guarantee for the least well-off': Paugam, *La société française et ses pauvres*, 68. The *Restos du cœur* were created by the renowned French comedian Coluche in 1985–1986 to provide food, hot meals, access to sanitary facilities and housing to people in need. The NGO ATD Quart Monde was involved in setting up local experiments of the guaranteed income in the 1970s and 1980s. Its founder, the Catholic priest Joseph Wresinski, published a highly publicized report on poverty in 1987, in which he urged public officials to introduce a comprehensive minimum-income scheme. On this topic, see Frédéric Viguier, *La cause des pauvres en France* (Paris: Presses de Sciences Po, 2020).

background, and after years of internal debates, the idea was eventually adopted by the socialists.[55]

A few month later, on 1 December 1988, the French National Assembly unanimously passed a bill establishing the *Revenu Minimum d'Insertion* (RMI). Just one year before the highly celebrated bicentenary of the French Revolution, the debates were conducted in an atmosphere charged with references to the *Déclaration des droits de l'homme et du citoyen* of 1789—it was a matter of 'taking the final step', new Prime Minister Michel Rocard claimed.[56] The RMI was explicitly put forward as a symbolic refoundation of the republican social contract, and a commitment not to let anyone fall by the wayside: 'France, the country of human rights, could not allow for the 'new poverty' to further develop'.[57] Still, the socialist legislators took a great deal of effort to distinguish their project from 'the liberal principle of *assistance*'. The RMI was not to be seen as mere poor relief, but rather as 'the very condition of *solidarity*'.[58]

And yet, it nonetheless fitted in with the long history of assistance. From the outset, the legislative debate focused on the means to 'reconcile two conflicting demands': the will to institute a genuine right to income, on the one hand, and the worry that the latter might encourage recipients to settle for dependency, on the other—that is, that recipients might not make adequate efforts to provide for themselves.[59] The legislators thus expressly held to the old principle of less eligibility: the RMI was eventually set at a level deemed high enough to meet basic needs but low enough so

[55] In the *Lettre à tous les français* he published on 7 April 1988 as part of his reelection campaign, Mitterrand himself eventually endorsed an idea which was originally Rocard's, his socialist rival, writing that 'a means of living or rather of surviving must be guaranteed to those who don't have anything, who cannot do anything, who are nothing'. Cyterman and Dindar, 'Les grandes étapes de l'histoire du RMI', 28.

[56] 'Solidarity', the Prime Minister added, 'is not the consolation prize of modernisation, it is the condition of its success. Because it gives its very significance to mutual respect, and to the respect of human dignity': *Déclaration de politique générale du gouvernement de M. Michel Rocard*, Sénat, Annexe au procès-verbal de la séance du 29 juin 1988, http://www.senat.fr/dep/1987-1988/i1987_1988_0302.pdf.

[57] Paugam, *La société française et ses pauvres*, 81. In his masterful history of European socialism, Donald Sassoon lists the defence of a guaranteed income as one of the illustrations of a convergence, confirmed by the 1988 election, between Right and Left on economic issues. Differences could now mostly 'be found at the level of values, symbol and language'—'republican values', in particular, provided the Left 'with a radical flourish with which to cover the abandonment of [the] socialist ambition to "break with capitalism"'. Donald Sassoon, *One Hundred Years of Socialism*, 569, 560.

[58] Geffroy, *Garantir le revenu*, 46–47.

[59] Paugam, *La société française et ses pauvres*, 82.

that it would not discourage work.[60] But the main issue of the debate was how to put the buzzword of *insertion* into practice. The RMI consisted of a means-tested benefit, open to anyone over twenty-five years of age, conditional on the signing of a contract by which recipients committed themselves to 'take part in a re-insertion programme' set at the local level, and which could 'entail job seeking, vocational training or activities designed to enhance the recipient's social autonomy'.[61]

In that respect, it seemingly perpetuated other traditions of assistance. The focus on the local level, first, which paradoxically brought up to date the historical construction of poor laws as 'protections of proximity', 'forcefully reinstating a fixed structure upon those who have been disconnected'[62] and, at the same time, constituted a crucial aspect of the 'autogestionary' decentralization strategy.[63] Second, the division between the able-bodied and the disabled poor—'the irrefutable principle that the able-bodied poor must only be aided by the means of labour'[64] is, indeed, certainly the most fundamental axiom of social policy, and the right to existence has admittedly never been anything else than a *right to exist through work*. The French revolutionaries themselves, Robert Castel emphasized, consecrated it while recognizing that the 'fundamental truth of all society' is that '*all men have a right to subsistence*'.[65] Even the 'Jacobin' Declaration of Rights of 1793, in its article 21, states: 'Public relief is a sacred debt. Society owes subsistence to unfortunate citizens, either procuring work for them or in providing the means of existence for those who are unable to work.'[66] This is almost exactly the claim that was made in 1988. Article 1 of the RMI bill states: 'Every person who, because of age,

[60] Its amount was first set at 80% of the minimum wage. Cyterman and Dindar, 'Les grandes étapes de l'histoire du RMI', 29. Today, it is less than half the full-time equivalent minimum wage.

[61] Palier, 'The Dualizations of the French Welfare System', 84.

[62] Castel, *Transformation of the Social Question*, 9, 50. In Castel's view, the local management of the RMI provided the 'genuinely social and political' meaning of the idea of insertion: 'What could this be, indeed, other than the actualisation ... of a 'national imperative' of solidarity ... through the mobilisation of the resources of local communities to rebuild the social bond in a newly rediscovered relationship of proximity?' Ibid., 167.

[63] On the complex issue of how the implementation of a state-managed and centralized assistance system in France also supported a decentralizing political agenda, focused on the concept of *territoires*, see Palier, *Gouverner la sécurité sociale*, 310–322.

[64] Camille Bloch and Alexandre Tuetey, *Procès-verbaux et rapports du Comité de mendicité de la Constituante (1790–1791)* (Paris: Imprimerie nationale, 1911), quoted in Castel, *Transformation of the Social Question*, 162.

[65] Bloch and Tuetey, *Procès-verbaux*, quoted in ibid., 160.

[66] Quoted in ibid., 165.

physical or mental condition, or because of the economic and employment situation, finds herself unable to work, has a right to get a decent means of existence from society. The social and professional integration of people in need constitutes a national imperative.'[67]

Almost, that is, but not exactly—because the newly articulated 'right to insertion' differed greatly from traditional understandings of the right to public relief. To be sure, the able-bodied had to behave responsibly and abide by the terms of their insertion contract, but the very reference to the 'economic and unemployment situation' in the eligibility criteria stressed that poverty and social exclusion were seen as a collective responsibility. In this regard, sociologist Serge Paugam argued, the RMI was not distinguishing *a priori* between the deserving and the underserving poor—anyone, able-bodied or not, was entitled to the benefit provided she fell below the given threshold, and everyone thus had a 'right to participation'.[68] This does not mean, however, that the benefit was seen as being unconditional. The legislative debates were heated on this issue—some put forward insertion as a strict condition while others, especially the bill's drafters, argued that the insertion contract and the payment of the benefit should be two separate issues—but unconditionality *per se* was expressly rejected on both sides of the assembly. The fact remains, however, that sanctions were explicitly limited and remained exceptional—in other words, 'the right to participation prevailed over the logic of conditionality'.[69] In this sense, the RMI can be seen as an activation policy of a particular kind, that one could term a *republican activation*.

France's Two Worlds of Welfare: Insurance Versus Solidarity

The RMI, however, did not entirely live up to expectations. The number of recipients rapidly exceeded original projections, reaching over a million by 1994.[70] As mentioned above, this was largely the consequence of a series of restrictions on unemployment benefits: as eligibility criteria were

[67] Quoted in Palier, *Gouverner la sécurité sociale*, 323.

[68] Paugam, *La société française et ses pauvres*, 107.

[69] Ibid., 110. One should therefore speak of '*ex post* conditionality'. Geffroy, *Garantir le revenu*, 56.

[70] See Philippe Cordazzo, 'Les bénéficiaires du RMI: évolution et renouvellement des effectifs (1989–2002)', *Recherches et prévisions*, no. 74 (2003): 71–79.

tightened, more and more uninsured unemployed turned to the RMI.[71] Furthermore, as it was possible for people earning less than its amount to supplement their income up to the RMI level, it became a last resort safety net not only for the unemployed but also for the working poor.[72] In this regard, and because this evolution came hand in hand with the '*jeopardization* of labour', one could argue that the real innovation of the RMI—less in its design than in its actual functioning—was the collective choice to assist in-work poverty, that is, certainly, to provide a welcomed support to atypical workers but also, and perhaps more fundamentally, to encourage the perpetuation of precarious employment.[73] While proving to be a matter of 'survival' for millions, it therefore ended up fostering greater 'social insecurity'.[74] But there is more to it. The RMI also went hand in hand with a double process of 'fiscalization' (the move from a contribution-based to a tax-based system) and 'statization' (the move from a union-managed to a state-managed system) of welfare.[75] The eventual result of

[71] Eligibility requirements had already been tightened under Giscard, but the key reform was adopted in 1984, during François Mitterrand's first term. The unemployment benefit system was reorganized according to a dual logic, distinguishing between 'insurance' (selective unemployment benefits) and 'solidarity' (non-contributory cash transfers). This new regime of solidarity therefore paved the way for the RMI—before its introduction, many, especially the long-term unemployed, remained excluded from the solidarity benefits, and further cuts during the 1990s later pushed recipients to fall back on it. See Jean-Luc Outin, 'Le RMI et l'indemnisation du chômage', in *RMI, l'état des lieux*, 101–117.

[72] An incentives component was even added, in 1998, which further allowed recipients to cumulate the RMI with a low-paid job. In 2008, it was estimated that about half of the recipients were uninsured job seekers, and that another third were working for a wage lower than the RMI threshold. Jean-Luc Outin, 'Le RMI et l'indemnisation du chômage', in *RMI, l'état des lieux*, 108–109. See also Cyterman and Dindar, 'Les grandes étapes de l'histoire du RMI', in *RMI, l'état des lieux*, 35–36.

[73] Castel, *Transformation of the Social Question*, 380. As sociologist Nicolas Duvoux explains, 'public policies to combat unemployment have multiplied labour law exemptions': Nicolas Duvoux, *Le nouvel âge de la solidarité. Pauvreté, précarité et politiques publiques* (Paris: Seuil/La République des Idées, 2012), 41–42. Besides the flexibilization of work contracts and working times, another key element has been the cuts in employers' contributions on low-paid and part-time jobs in order to provide incentives for companies to hire specific categories of excluded workers: see Palier, *Gouverner la sécurité sociale*, 348.

[74] Nicolas Duvoux, 'Trente ans de RMI. La réforme perpétuelle de l'assistance sociale', *La Vie des Idées*, November 27, 2018, https://laviedesidees.fr/Trente-ans-de-RMI.html.

[75] In 1988, it was argued that the additional cost induced by the RMI's expenses would be indirectly covered by the reinstitution of a 'solidarity' wealth tax. The decisive step in the fiscalization and statization process, however, consisted in the creation by the Rocard government in 1991 of a new flat-rate tax, the *Contribution Sociale Généralisée* (CSG), which has

this, Bruno Palier explains, has been the division of 'French welfare and society into two worlds: those still insured by an increasingly contributory complex of public and private insurances, and those dependent on a new tier of basic social protection'.[76]

Moreover, the building of this new institutional framework cannot be divorced from the emergence of new theories of the welfare state. Particularly salient, in this regard, has been the growing distinction between insurance and solidarity. In the wake of François Ewald's massive 1986 genealogy of the welfare state as the vehicle of an 'insurance society', the idea that insurance was 'the inseparably technical and philosophical basis of the welfare state' became a commonplace among French intellectuals. And yet, it was increasingly suggested that this 'insurance paradigm' had entered a crisis.[77] In his 1995 essay *The New Social Question*, for instance, Rosanvallon highlighted the central historical role of insurance but argued that social risks were no longer 'unpredictable' or 'equally distributed', among the population. In an age filled with 'phenomena of exclusion, such as long-term unemployment', he contended, 'the unifying category of risk has lost a great deal of its relevance', and the 'veil of ignorance' historically underlying the 'social contract' is, as a result, 'irreparably torn'.[78] Following Rosanvallon, it was therefore as though it was sociologically not possible to guarantee universal social insurance coverage anymore. For there could be no solidarity between individuals knowing they are not facing the same risks, social insurance would now be, all at once, foundational and inadequate.

For Ewald, it followed that we, as a society, had to embrace the growing individualization of risks. Actively involved in setting the intellectual agenda of the main French employers' organization in the 1990s, Foucault's disciple indeed called for an extension of the rationality of (private) insurance that would go so far as to 'commodify welfare services'.[79]

today become the second largest source of revenue in the French fiscal system, after VAT. As a result, social contributions which then used to account for about 80% of social security revenues now only represent about half: see Palier, 'The Dualizations of the French Welfare System', 85–86.

[76] Ibid., 73.

[77] Pierre Rosanvallon, *The New Social Question. Rethinking the Welfare State*, trans. Barbara Harshav (Princeton: Princeton University Press, 2000), 16. See also François Ewald, *The Birth of Solidarity: The History of the French Welfare State*, trans. Timothy Scott Johnson, ed. Melinda Cooper (Durham, NC: Duke University Press, 2020).

[78] Rosanvallon, *The New Social Question*, 16–17, 21. The reference to John Rawls's famous 'veil of ignorance' is explicit.

[79] François Ewald, 'La société assurancielle et son avenir', *Le Débat* 157 (2009): 94–95.

It was, in his mind, a matter of putting everyone in the position to take risks, 'for this is, since the dawn of time, the principle of human dignity'.[80] In the end, his concept of insurance was not to be understood as a means to the end of organizing a universal social solidarity but rather as an end in itself: the very ordering principle of a society of risk-friendly individuals.[81]

Rosanvallon, for his part, did not support such a drastic promotion of insurance as an 'alternative and self-sufficient system'.[82] For left-wing intellectuals, the watchword of the time was rather to rethink solidarity. But what else could be left for solidarity, other than, precisely, human dignity? Solidarity, historian Marie-Claude Blais argued, resurfaced as a 'magic term for justifying the welfare state when its original foundations were missing'.[83] Far from a solidarity between workers, solidarity thus became a moral, compassionate, and quasi-humanitarian commitment to take care of those who were excluded from the 'insurance society'. Seen from this angle, the RMI was indeed, and just as much as the negative income tax, about establishing a sufficientarian floor. But the outpouring of generosity that accompanied its introduction did not last long. An 'exhaustion of compassion' was eventually diagnosed—with, for example, 53% of respondents in a 2003 survey considering that the RMI's recipients were not encouraged to look for a job—and it became associated with a so-called culture of dependency, as illustrated by the coining of the demeaning expression *Rmistes* to refer to the recipients.[84]

Solidarity as a mere moral duty was simply too fragile to support the establishment of a new social right. This is precisely why 'insertion' was such a crucial concept, and it is why Rosanvallon's 1995 essay eventually presented an argument for an 'active welfare state'. Contradicting his own 'insurance paradigm' argument, the Second-Left intellectual reminded his

[80] François Ewald and Denis Kessler, 'Les noces du risque et de la politique', *Le Débat* 109 (2000): 71.

[81] On Ewald's significance in the French intellectual debate, see Michael C. Behrent, 'Accidents Happen: François Ewald, the "Antirevolutionary" Foucault, and the Intellectual Politics of the French Welfare State', *The Journal of Modern History* 82, no. 3 (September 2010): 585–624.

[82] Colette Bec, *La Sécurité sociale. Une institution de la démocratie* (Paris: Gallimard, 2014), 209.

[83] Marie-Claude Blais, *La solidarité. Histoire d'une idée* (Paris: Gallimard, 2007), 320–330.

[84] Marie-Thérèse Espinasse and Olivia Sautory, 'Les opinions des Français sur la pauvreté et le RMI', in *RMI, l'état des lieux*, 254. On the 'exhaustion of compassion' issue, see Julien Damon and Georges Huatchel, 'Fatigue de la compassion et contestation suspicieuse', *Informations sociales* 98 (2002): 32–39.

readers that 'insurance is a technique, while solidarity is a value', and warned against the threat of a dual society inherent in the normative distinction between the two. Solidarity, thus defined, was in his mind too dependent on a 'passive' logic of 'compensation', which could only end up with 'the temptation to pay wages of exclusion' unless something were to be done to 'transform passive expenses into active ones'. The RMI, Rosanvallon admitted, was already a 'profound' and welcome 'break' with the traditional welfare model, but it was still in need of a 'clear social philosophy'—which meant accepting that 'the welfare state can no longer merely distribute allowances and administer universal rules'.[85] Not unlike Anthony Giddens's call for a 'social investment state', Rosanvallon's 'soft workfare' argument came down to two principles: ***individualization*** and ***obligation***.[86] Solidarity was to be rethought with 'clearer knowledge of the situation and chances of each individual', and social rights were to be 'reinterpreted as a contract articulating rights and obligations'. This, he concluded, was the only way towards an 'individualization of society' that would not involve a 'return to an archaic paternalism'.[87]

Pleading for an 'inclusive society', Rosanvallon actually was comfortable with the fact that, 'since neither the market (because of modernization) nor the state (because of deficits) can create social activities beyond the passive welfare state', activating the unemployed essentially meant subsidizing 'third-sector' jobs, that is, both—and ambiguously—'noncommercial' activities in the voluntary sector and a 'new economy of services'. But this 'intermediary economy' was supposed to remain transitional, defining 'a space for resocialization and professional retraining'.[88] Rosanvallon's hopes, however, were disappointed—activation policies and labour-market deregulation fostered the constitution of a 'second labour market, largely disconnected from the first', and which does not 'provide a springboard to stable employment'.[89] One could even go so far as to establish a 'parallel' between 'the multiplication of means-tested minimum benefits' and 'the multiplication of part-time and (very) low-income

[85] Rosanvallon, *The New Social Question*, 108, 43, 61–62, 57, 84.

[86] Anthony Giddens, *The Third Way: The Renewal of Social Democracy* (Cambridge: Polity Press, 1998).

[87] Rosanvallon, *The New Social Question*, 87, 105–106.

[88] Ibid., 82, 87, 95.

[89] 'In many *insertion* programmes, Nicolas Duvoux argues, access to the "dignity" of work and to a payslip is in itself a sufficient purpose, regardless of the status or qualification of the work performed.' Duvoux, *Le nouvel âge de la solidarité*, 40–41.

jobs'.[90] In the end, sociologist Nicolas Duvoux argues, the active welfare state only mitigated social exclusion by replacing what Castel had called a 'continuum of social positions' by a 'continuum of vulnerability'.[91]

From Obligation to Emancipation: UBI and the 'End of the Labour Society'

As we have seen, the introduction of the RMI represented a crucial change in the trajectory of French welfare reform. A change which made it possible for UBI to appear as a radical but legitimate alternative. Indeed, it seems to me that the latter only starts to sound genuinely appealing when one both assumes that universal coverage can no longer be achieved through social insurance alone—which means that it is necessary to have a non-contributory safety net—and nevertheless believes that conditional and means-tested benefits inevitably have unwelcome consequences. This is, in fact, precisely the argument presented by Philippe Van Parijs and Yannick Vanderborght in their 2017 book on UBI. Once one acknowledges the need to introduce a guaranteed income of some sort, they write, there are basically two solutions. One 'is very unattractive'—it 'consists of expanding the old model of public assistance first born in the sixteenth century and instantiated by today's guaranteed-minimum-income schemes of a conditional sort'. The other also 'require[s] a minimum-income scheme, but of an unconditional sort'. In their mind, however, the 'conviction that the growing jobless population must be provided with some means of livelihood' actually stems from an underlying socio-economic assumption: the 'expectation that meaningful work will be lacking' in the near future.[92]

Here we touch on the last piece of the puzzle: while it justified activation, the formulation of a 'new social question' also renewed the questioning of the very social model that active policies such as the RMI were supposed to preserve. It is, indeed, widely acknowledged that the (re-) emergence of UBI proposals in 1980s Europe came along with the diagnosis of a crisis of the 'labour society'. In France, this was prominently advocated by André Gorz who, in his 1980 book *Farewell to the Working Class*, claimed that social emancipation was 'no longer a question of

[90] Palier, *Gouverner la sécurité sociale*, 337–338.

[91] Duvoux, *Le nouvel âge de la solidarité*, 28.

[92] Van Parijs and Vanderborght, *Basic Income*, 7–8.

winning power as a worker, but of winning power no longer to function as a worker'.[93] For the history of capitalist societies, he thought, had 'dismembered what Marx's vision made whole', that is, the idea that the 'liberation *within* work' would support a 'liberation *from* work'[94]: 'The point now is to free oneself *from* work by rejecting its nature, content, necessity and modalities'.[95] His argument, however, was not an 'end of work' argument in the generally accepted sense. It was, first and foremost, a critique of the welfare state which—because it did not challenge the *economic rationality* inherent to wage-labour—only 'filled in for the decay of social bonds and solidarity', and thus failed to remedy the 'divorce between working and living' induced by the capitalist labour regime. The issue was therefore less a supposed disappearance of work than the fact that automation makes it clear that *economic reason* fundamentally prevents the 'identification with one's work'. As Gorz wrote, 'a job whose effect and aim are to save work cannot, at the same time, glorify work as the essential source of personal identity and fulfilment'. In the end, the society in which a guaranteed income eventually seems to be an unavoidable outcome is not so much a fully automated, workless society than it is a society in which the reduction of socially necessary labour makes the ideal of full-time employment for all materially impossible; a society, in other words, where 'work can no longer serve as the basis for social integration'.[96]

At first, however, Gorz strongly rejected UBI, as Walter van Trier shows in Chap. 8. He argued for a 'social income' scenario (also known as the 'second cheque' strategy) that would not be independent from work *per se*, but rather independent from working hours—in his words, a 'continuous income for a discontinuous work'.[97] It was not until the late 1990s that he changed his mind and took side with the advocates of 'strong unconditionality'.[98] To be sure, Gorz's conversion was deeply influenced

[93] André Gorz, *Farewell to the Working Class: An Essay on Post-Industrial Socialism*, trans. Michael Sonenscher (London: Pluto Press, 1982), 67.

[94] André Gorz, *Critique of Economic Reason*, trans. Gillian Handyside and Chris Turner (New York: Verso, 1989), 91–93.

[95] Gorz, *Farewell to the Working Class*, op. cit.

[96] Gorz, *Critique of Economic Reason*, 132, 31, 88, 70.

[97] André Gorz, 'Sortir de la société salariale', *Transversales Science Culture* 25 (1994): 16.

[98] See Gorz's correspondence with Van Parijs in Philippe Van Parijs, 'De la sphère autonome à l'allocation universelle', in *André Gorz. Un penseur pour le XXIe siècle*, ed. Christophe Fourel (Paris: La Découverte, 2012): 163–177.

by post-Fordist theories of 'cognitive capitalism'—he eventually saw the 'right to a sufficient, unconditional and universal income' as a 'pooling of part of what has been produced in common, deliberately or not'—but the arguments he developed in the 1980s and early 1990s had already resonated with UBI justifications.[99] Even before the RMI was introduced, for example, Gorz argued that employment policies (such as early retirement schemes) amounted 'to a *de facto* recognition that the right to an income can no longer be made dependent on having a job'—though the French government simultaneously treated the unemployed 'as though full-time jobs were and should remain the rule'.[100] Hence the need to 'bring the law into line with the facts'—an argument that would later be repeated by Alain Caillé, founder of the MAUSS collective, who believed the RMI had already disconnected the right to an income from the duty to work.[101] Hiding this fact behind the obligation of insertion, Caillé argued, was maintaining a 'double bind' for recipients who were basically told 'you have a right not to work provided that you do work'; 'you have to look for a job that everybody knows does not exist'.[102]

In the light of this, historian Laurent Geffroy introduced a threefold typology of guaranteed income policies—'incentive income', 'obligation income', and 'emancipation income'—which captures the defining characteristics of the negative income tax, the RMI, and UBI. Both the incentive and the obligation versions of the guaranteed income could be seen as activation policies, albeit in very different ways; the emancipation income, by contrast, would institute an 'explicit disconnection between income and work'.[103] But how far was UBI actually different from activation policies, whether based on incentive or obligation? This was, to a large extent, the main issue of the UBI debates that eventually materialized in the 1990s.

[99] André Gorz, *L'Immatériel. Connaissance, valeur et capital* (Paris: Galilée, 2003), 100–101.

[100] André Gorz, *Paths to Paradise. On The Liberation From Work*, trans. Malcom Imrie (London: Pluto Press, 1985), 34.

[101] André Gorz, 'Allocation universelle: version de droite et version de gauche', *Bulletin du M.A.U.S.S.*, no. 23 (1987): 31; Alain Caillé, 'Pour en finir dignement avec le XXe siècle. Temps choisi et revenu de citoyenneté', *Revue du MAUSS Semestrielle* 7 (1996): 144.

[102] Ibid., 138.

[103] Geffroy, *Garantir le revenu*, 12–13.

An 'Emancipatory Form of Activation'? The Paradoxes of UBI

At first sight, UBI may genuinely seem at odds with the will to activate the unemployed. This was, for example, outlined by Rosanvallon who saw it as 'the extreme limit of the society of indemnification': a 'pernicious and paradoxical aspect of the end of the classical conception of the welfare state' and a way to finally give in to 'the temptation to pay wages for exclusion'. UBI, because it comes no strings attached, would push 'the issue of employment … into the background' and, as a result, 'radically' deepen the dualization of society.[104] And Rosanvallon was not the only one to say so. Among the first to draw attention on the 'splitting of society into one section who are by rights permanent workers and another which is excluded', Gorz considered for a long time that 'the guaranteed minimum functions as the wages of marginality and social exclusion',[105] and that it would inevitably lead to a society where 'unemployment would no longer be a problem to solve'. Gorz's 'political dispute' with UBI supporters thus reflected a shared feeling on the Left that waving the flag of the right to income meant not only rejecting the duty to work but also, and more problematically, giving up on the right to work.[106] Rather, he argued, the 'indissoluble unity' of both rights forms 'the basis of citizenship for every man and woman'.[107]

This charge was, in fact, partly accepted by French UBI advocates—especially those revolving around MAUSS—who made a virtue of its incompatibility with the activation agenda. In their mind, there was something fundamentally coercive in the belief that 'citizenship would be under threat if the reciprocal link between rights and duties was broken'.[108] That being said, they nevertheless firmly rejected the idea that it meant giving up on the right to work. Things were actually the other way around. 'As long as work is an obligation, it is not a right', philosopher Jean-Marc Ferry wrote. UBI would therefore not merely foster 'the negative freedom of choosing not to work', it would provide everyone with a 'positive' freedom of choice and thus support the development of a variety of activities

[104] Rosanvallon, *The New Social Question*, 62–65.

[105] Gorz, *Critique of Economic Reason*, 205.

[106] Gorz, 'Allocation universelle', 39, 31.

[107] Gorz, *Critique of Economic Reason*, op. cit.

[108] Philippe Chanial, *Justice, don et association. La délicate essence de la démocratie* (Paris: La Découverte/M.A.U.S.S., 2001), 356.

currently hidden by both the market and the state.[109] Far from contradicting the aspirations of the RMI Left, UBI would, in fact, materialize the ideals of the *autogestion* movement. It would bring about what the early Rosanvallon had pictured as a 'multidimensional' and 'pluralistic' society: substituting the goal of 'full activity' to the one of 'full employment' and distributing the power of self-management through the achievement of what Gorz had called a right to 'chosen time'.[110]

Yet, from another perspective, UBI may also be seen as a particular type of active policy. Van Parijs, for example, always combined the picture of a free society, where anyone could live like the Malibu surfers, with the argument that, by making work pay, UBI would remove the welfare trap. 'Activating while liberating' was his argument from the start.[111] Likewise, Ferry's ambition was not so much to encourage 'autonomous activities' in Gorz's sense—that is, activities 'which are done for their own sake alone'—as to stimulate 'initiative' and 'enterprise'.[112] He even went so far as to repeat the safety clause for the player argument, and explained that, thanks to UBI, 'one could take entrepreneurial risks' and still 'be sure to get an income to live'.[113] For critics like Castel, however, the issue was that UBI would rather accelerate the ongoing 'development of in-work poverty', forcing people to supplement their meagre allowance through 'precarious' jobs.[114] Even the later Gorz, despite his U-turn, reckoned that an insufficient amount would result in a 'disguised subvention to the employers', allowing them to perpetuate 'undignified working conditions'.[115] In other words, both of them worried that UBI would simply be another way to force the post-Fordist 'new reserve army of labour' into accepting any

[109] Jean-Marc Ferry, *L'Allocation universelle. Pour un revenu de citoyenneté* (Paris: Cerf, 1995), 47, 96. These unrecognized activities, Ferry argued, could be seen as constituting a 'quaternary sector' of the economy, which could be distinguished from the first three in that it gathers 'non-mechanisable activities'. See ibid., 104–108.

[110] Pierre Rosanvallon, *L'Âge de l'autogestion. Ou la politique au poste de commandement* (Paris: Seuil, 1976), 175–180. See also André Gorz, 'Political Ecology: Expertocracy versus Self-Limitation', *New Left Review* 202 (November/December 1993): 55–67.

[111] Philippe Van Parijs, 'Basic Income: A Simple and Powerful Idea for the Twenty-First Century', in *Redesigning Distribution: Basic Income and Stakeholder Grants as Cornerstones for an Egalitarian Capitalism*, ed. Erik Olin Wright (London: Verso, 2006): 19.

[112] Gorz, *Reclaiming Work*, 163; Ferry, *L'Allocation universelle*, 95.

[113] Ferry, *L'Allocation universelle*, 110.

[114] Robert Castel, 'Quels droits pour un plein accès à la citoyenneté?', *Mouvements* 73 (2013): 112.

[115] Gorz, *L'Immatériel*, op. cit.

job.[116] Waiving the right to work would, in fact, do nothing but strengthen the need and thus the duty to work (at least for the poor)—that was ultimately the objection.

A paradox therefore appears: while it is unquestionable that UBI emerged as a response to the growing conditionality of social rights, critics argue that its unconditionality would ironically be the Trojan horse of workfare conditionality. Of course, UBI supporters have always rejected the accusation. Nevertheless, how could one consistently claim that it would both activate the unemployed and liberate the employed from wage-labour? The answer is in a way quite simple: just as the negative income tax, UBI is, before anything else, about freedom of choice. As Van Parijs forcefully argued in his 1995 'real-libertarian' theory of justice, the aim is indeed 'not to discourage as much as possible waged labour or a career-dominated existence, but to do as much as can be done in order to provide everyone with a genuine opportunity to make different choices'.[117] This was also illustrated by Ferry, for whom the repudiation of the 'labourist ideology of full-employment' was not the first step towards a post-work society but the necessary condition for a society where the 'positive freedom to shape one's social activity' would be equally distributed.[118] One must therefore admit that, for all its radicalism, Gorz's call for an exodus from work was a marginal position. And yet, could not one argue that, by incentivizing people to take a part-time job, UBI would, in a way, achieve what the latter pictured as 'the transition from a productivist work-based society to a society of liberated time in which the cultural and the societal are accorded greater importance than the economic'?[119] This was, in the end, the genuine belief behind the 'emancipative activation' argument.

Conclusion

While it is true that UBI is, at present, more clearly presented as a '*nouvelle Sécurité sociale*' than it used to be, one can also see that the current French debate is in many respects a reprise of the debate of the 1980s and 1990s.

[116] Robert Castel, 'Salariat ou revenu d'existence. Lecture critique d'André Gorz', *La Vie des Idées*, December 6, 2013, https://laviedesidees.fr/Salariat-ou-revenu-d-existence.html.

[117] Philippe Van Parijs, *Real Freedom for All: What (If Anything) Can Justify Capitalism?* (Oxford: Oxford University Press), 33–34.

[118] Ferry, *L'Allocation universelle*, 51, 122.

[119] Gorz, *Critique of Economic Reason*, 183.

Arguably, the only substantial difference is that its main advocates are now in the ranks of the socialists.[120] So what difference does it make? Reflecting on Benoît Hamon's 2017 UBI campaign, Antonio Negri found it 'impressive that a Socialist has proposed it, for this proposal is an attempt to refound politics beyond work, against work. An attempt to transcend the centuries-long ontology of socialism itself.'[121] I do not wish to pronounce on such a complex question as Negri's theory of the multitude (nor UBI's potential role in uniting it), but it seems to me that this is a misinterpretation. During his presidential run, Hamon certainly emphasized the 'digital revolution' and the alleged 'rarefaction' of work. The conclusion he drew from it, however, was that 'work is a source of fulfilment' and that 'it must be even more fairly distributed now that it is getting scarce'.[122] Therefore, and just as in the 1990s, what is currently at stake in the French debate is arguably less the end of work than the means to better achieve the right to work.

If this is the case, however, then how did the French Left manage to overcome its traditional suspicion of unconditionality? To begin with, the ever-increasing activation of welfare certainly has a lot to do with it. Critics from the Left used to believe there was no need for UBI because social rights were already unconditional—'unconditionally delivered to those who qualify for them', as Castel quite remarkably wrote[123]—and would remain so as long as the occupational conditions could be satisfied, that is, as long as there remained a reasonable expectation that everyone could find sustainable employment. Three decades later, however, this fragile equilibrium—well described by Étienne Balibar as the 'paradox of a citizenship that can be demanded unconditionally and *yet* is subject to conditions'[124]—seems to be irretrievably broken. Not so much because

[120] The previous debate arguably peaked in the early 2000s with a public report commissioned by Jospin's socialist government and directed by the former recorder of the RMI bill, Jean-Michel Belorgey. In this report, UBI was considered as a serious policy proposal but unambiguously dismissed, 'both for reasons of public spending efficiency and people's dignity at work': Jean-Michel Belorgey, ed., *Minima sociaux, revenus d'activité, précarité* (Paris: Commissariat Général du Plan, 2000), 169.

[121] Antonio Negri, 'Benoît Hamon and Universal Income', *Verso Blog*, February 27, 2017, https://www.versobooks.com/blogs/3109-benoit-hamon-and-universal-income.

[122] Benoît Hamon, *France Inter*, January 8, 2017, https://www.franceinter.fr/emissions/questions-politiques/questions-politiques-08-janvier-2017.

[123] Castel, *La montée des incertitudes*, 212–213.

[124] Étienne Balibar, *Equaliberty: Political Essays*, trans. James Ingram (Durham: Duke University Press, 2014), 110.

occupational conditions could then still be restricted to full-time employment and now no longer could. Rather, and quite simply, because in the process of activation, conditions and duties eventually got the upper hand over rights—a movement which Palier describes as a transition from the ambition of *decommodification* to the one of *recommodification*.[125] UBI, as a result, would in no way threaten the reciprocity of rights and duties; on the contrary, it might in fact offer a way to rebalance the relationship between the two. And even Left sceptics may agree that, in a context where the dualization, fiscalization, and statization of the welfare system has become almost complete, and where a break with path dependency might therefore seem beyond reach, UBI represents a second-best solution, the least bad option to make do with the new world of welfare.[126]

So much for what one might call, from a Polanyian perspective, the defensive aspect of the socialist case for UBI. But what about the offensive one? Unsurprisingly, Hamon's fundamental take on UBI was that it would offer a way to 'manage' the growing scarcity of work 'in such a way that individuals might freely and autonomously choose to reduce their working hours'.[127] It is true that, under the advice of Thomas Piketty, his campaign ultimately tried to shift the focus to the issue of a 'just wage'—the 'automatic inclusion of the basic income on pay stubs', the economist argued, would link the 'idea to a vision of the just society based on the

[125] Palier, *Gouverner la sécurité sociale*, 298. Since 2001, for instance, recipients of unemployment benefits have to be actively looking for a job or be subject to sanctions. See ibid., 225–228. Elected President in 2007 with the slogan 'work more to earn more', Nicolas Sarkozy then introduced a reform of the RMI—renamed *Revenu de Solidarité Active* (RSA)—which extended the logic of incentives and tightened job search requirements. See Duvoux, *Le nouvel âge de la solidarité*, 71–84.

[126] The contemplated merging of all existing *minima sociaux* into a single unified benefit, mentioned in the introduction, is one of the most salient examples of this near-completion of the process—although the bill establishing the new RUA scheme, which was supposed to be voted in 2020, had to be postponed due to the COVID-19 pandemic. It is interesting to note that, whether it is on the subject of pensions, unemployment, or assistance, the 'Macronists' have always clearly stated their ambition to complete this transformation of welfare into a so-called universal system. See, for instance, Aurélien Taché, 'En matière de protection sociale, on prône un système plus universel', interview by Manuel Jardinaud and Mathidle Goanec, *Mediapart*, March 28, 2018, https://www.mediapart.fr/journal/economie/280318/aurelien-tache-en-matiere-de-protection-sociale-prone-un-systeme-plus-universel?onglet=full.

[127] Benoît Hamon, *France Inter*, January 8, 2017.

wage relation and the right to work and unionize'.[128] This attempt to connect UBI with the values of the traditional socialist electorate, however, largely failed. In the end, it was the freedom of choice argument that essentially prevailed in the socialists' case for UBI.[129] And it is, in fact, hard to overlook the appeal of such an idea. At the same time, however, it is just as hard not to wonder how much of this freedom of choice UBI would actually offer. Besides, could not one suggest that something would be lost on the way? For even if UBI was, say, to drastically reduce unemployment by increasing (chosen) part-time work, it would nonetheless complete the historical shift from a collective to an individual conception of the right to work. A shift that was intellectually initiated with the idea of a negative income tax and confirmed with the introduction of the RMI.

For the Left, introducing the RMI had nonetheless been a way—admittedly 'for want of changing the rules of the economic system'[130]—to partially rescue the model of occupational universalism.[131] Its implementation certainly played an important role in the shift from economic interventionism to a politics of fiscal redistribution that Peter Sloman has recently described, in the British context, as the emergence of a 'transfer state'.[132] And yet, it may be overly critical to argue, with Donald Sassoon, that 'the

[128] Thomas Piketty, *Capital and Ideology*, trans. Arthur Goldhammer (Cambridge, MA: Belknap Press of Harvard University Press, 2020), 1002–1003.

[129] Among other issues such as 'extreme poverty', the 'return to work', or 'non-take up', the socialist presidents of départements, for example, listed the 'autonomy of the life plan' as an objective of the experimentation they wished to implement. See Marc-Antoine Sabaté, 'Comment le revenu universel est devenu de gauche', *AOC*, May 23, 2018, https://aoc.media/analyse/2018/05/22/revenu-universel-devenu-de-gauche/.

[130] Paugam, *La société française et ses pauvres*, 265

[131] This was, in particular, the argument held by Castel. See Robert Castel et al., 'Débat sur le revenu inconditionnel', *Revue du MAUSS Semestrielle*, no. 7 (1996): 175–176.

[132] See Peter Sloman, *Transfer State: The Idea of a Guaranteed Income and the Politics of Redistribution in Modern Britain* (Oxford: Oxford University Press, 2019). As we have seen, the RMI especially materialized the lasting political choice to alleviate poverty and reduce unemployment by supplementing low incomes rather than by raising wages and funding public services. This particular choice is, indeed, perhaps the most important aspect of the new world of welfare, in France as elsewhere, and certainly one the main feature of the current—and seemingly inescapable—path dependency of welfare reform. It is, for instance, manifest in Emmanuel Macron's decision to respond to the Gilet Jaunes's purchasing power expectations by raising not the minimum wage but rather the *Prime d'Activité*, a cash transfer for low-wage workers: see Marc-Antoine Sabaté, 'Revenu de base inconditionnel: quel instrument pour quelle justice fiscale? Réflexions à partir du cas des «Gilets Jaunes» en France', *Éthique Publique* 21, no. 2 (Winter 2019).

idea that a necessary condition for a just society was that it should provide a job for all those willing and able to work was relegated to utopia'.[133] Indeed, the conception of the right to work rather evolved during the 1980s—it was not anymore understood as mere openness of the market (as it was in 1789), nor as the state's duty to provide public employment to the unemployed (1848), nor to maintain the macro-economic conditions of full-employment (1945), but as a collective duty to assist the excluded in their individual effort towards reintegration. If UBI has only become justifiable in the wake of the problematization of exclusion (and the failure to tackle it), it is, then, ultimately because the new social question 'was framed as a problem of lack of support rather than of lack of work'.[134] One might argue that the republican ethos surrounding the implementation of the RMI somewhat preserved the collective nature of social rights. But it is not easy to see exactly how the mere guarantee of an individual freedom of choice—what Van Parijs appealingly pictured as 'the real freedom to live as unconventionally as one might fancy'—would enable not only individual, but collective autonomy.[135]

[133] Donald Sassoon, *One Hundred Years of Socialism*, 559.
[134] Palier, 'The Dualizations of the French Welfare System', 83.
[135] Van Parijs, *Real Freedom for All.*

CHAPTER 8

From 'Second Cheque Strategy' to 'Basic Income': Why Did André Gorz Change His Mind?

Walter Van Trier

One of the most unexpected events in the recent history of basic income is the publication in 1997 of *Misères du présent, Richesse du possible* by André Gorz, the French social critic and essayist.[1] After criticizing the idea of a universal and unconditional basic income for the previous fifteen years, Gorz changed his mind. Even if an unconditional income guarantee or so-called basic income could not be achieved immediately, he wrote, 'we must begin to conceptualize it and prepare the way for it as of now'.[2] To understand such a change of mind, this chapter will explore Gorz's evolving attitudes to universal basic income (UBI).

[1] André Gorz, *Misères du présent, Richesse du possible* (Paris: Galilée, 1997). An English translation was published in as *Reclaiming Work: Beyond the Wage-Based Society* (Cambridge: Polity Press, 1999). In this chapter, all translations are mine from the original French version.
[2] Gorz, *Misères*, 91.

W. Van Trier (✉)
Ghent University, Ghent, Belgium
e-mail: Walter.VanTrier@UGent.be

P. Sloman et al. (eds.), *Universal Basic Income in Historical Perspective*, https://doi.org/10.1007/978-3-030-75706-9_8

André Gorz was born in Vienna in 1923 as Gerhardt Hirsch, son of a Jewish father and a Catholic mother. Having already changed the family name to Horst in 1930 out of fear of growing anti-Semitism, the family moved to Switzerland shortly after Nazi Germany annexed Austria. Gerhardt Horst graduated in 1945 with a degree in chemical engineering, moved to Paris in 1949, and acquired French nationality in 1954; in France, his name was 'officialised' as Gérard Horst. After a long and painful illness of Gorz's wife, the couple committed suicide on September 23, 2007.

In several respects, the Swiss episode had an important, if not determining, influence on the later life of Gérard Horst. He met Doreen Keir, an English au-pair working in Lausanne, whom he married in 1949 and to whom most of his books were dedicated. He started a career as journalist, writing articles in the journal of the Swiss co-operative movement. And, probably most importantly, his interest in literature and philosophy brought him in contact with the writings of Jean-Paul Sartre, whom he met in person in Geneva in 1946. 'Without Sartre', Gorz would later say,

> I would probably not have found the instruments to think and to surpass what my family and history had done to me. From the moment I discovered *L'Être et le Néant*, I had the feeling that what Sartre said about the ontological condition of man corresponded to my experience.[3]

After moving to Paris in 1949, Gérard Horst became part of Sartre's and De Beauvoir's inner circle. In 1958 he joined the editorial board of *Les Temps Modernes* and became its political director in 1961, succeeding Maurice Merleau-Ponty after his death.

In the following decades, Gérard Horst's public life would develop along two separate tracks under two different names. As Michel Bosquet—a translation of his German name—he resumed his journalistic career in 1951, writing first for *Paris-Presse* and then as editor of the economics section of *L'Express*, a paper founded by Jean-Jacques Servan-Schreiber in support of the politics of Pierre Mendès France. Objecting to a change in editorial policy, he left *L'Express* in 1964 to participate in founding *Le Nouvel Observateur*, which became a highly influential leftist weekly. At the same time, under the name of André Gorz—a name referring to the little village where his father's old army binoculars were produced—he

[3] André Gorz, *Ecologica* (Paris: Galilée, 2008), 11.

started writing on ethics and philosophy. *Le traître*, a remarkable autobiographical book, was published in 1958 with a forty-page introduction by Sartre. His second book, *La morale de l'histoire* (1959), attempted to renew Marx's theory of alienation. After 1961, all of his following books—such as *Stratégie ouvrière et néo-capitalisme* (1964), *Le socialisme difficile* (1968), *Réforme et révolution* (1969), and *Critique de la division du travail* (1973)—focussed on socio-economic analysis and political topics. The only exception was *Fondements pour une Morale* (1977), a book reflecting on the moral implications of Sartre's *L'Être et le Néant*, which was based on a 1500-page manuscript originally written between 1945 and 1954.

Only in 1977, when the essay collection *Ecologie et Liberté* appeared in the bookshops, did the wider public learn that the two names on the title page—André Gorz and Michel Bosquet—referred to one and the same person. An introductory note explained that until then it was difficult to reconcile Bosquet's journalistic work on economic matters with Gorz's philosophical and political writings, the former not allowing for fundamental analysis, the latter being difficult to translate in a journalistic style. However (the introduction went on) on matters of ecology the two had come to merge. By this point, André Gorz had become an influential left-wing voice, not only in France but across continental Europe.[4]

Gorz's 1983 Reform Programme

In 1983, the year he retired, Gorz published *Les Chemins du Paradis: L'Agonie du Capital*.[5] Its analysis echoed the message contained in *Adieu au prolétariat: Au-delà du socialisme*, published three years earlier, which had concluded that 'the stage of full development of productive forces' was nearly reached and 'that the principal task was no longer maximizing production or full employment, but a different organization of the economy in which a full income ceases to be conditional on full-time work or, if one wants, where the satisfaction of needs is guaranteed to all in exchange

[4] For full biographical information and a critical review of Gorz's intellectual development, see Willy Gianinnazi, *André Gorz, une vie* (Paris: La Découverte, 2016) and Françoise Gollain, André Gorz, *Une philosophie de l'émancipation* (Paris: L'Harmattan, 2018). About his relation to Sartre, see also: Finn Bowring, *André Gorz and the Sartrean Legacy* (London: Palgrave, 2000).

[5] André Gorz, *Les Chemins du Paradis, L'agonie du Capital* (Paris: Galilée, 1983). An English version was published as *Paths to Paradise: On the Liberation from* Work (London: Pluto Press, 1985).

for a quantity of work, occupying only a limited fraction of one's life'.[6] In *Les Chemins du Paradis*, Gorz elaborated on the programme for societal reform which was needed to reach this goal.

Written at a time when most European nations were experiencing high and persistent unemployment, many read *Les Chemins du Paradis* primarily as an attempt to formulate an alternative to traditional full employment policies. This reading was based on the fact that Gorz's proposal rested on a diagnosis very similar to the one at the root of many traditional employment policies: that technologically induced productivity improvements would lead to a situation in which producing the same amount of goods would demand progressively less and less working time. Yet this interpretation of Gorz's book is too restrictive, since his reform proposal differed from conventional Keynesian and supply-side policies in at least two fundamental respects.

Contrary to the conventional view which deplores unemployment because of 'produce foregone', to use a phrase of Nobel Prize-winning economist Bob Solow, Gorz's starting point is the ethical claim that the main goal of social development is the full flourishing of the individual. This implies, he argues, that everyone needs room in their life for activities which have nothing to do with economic rationality and are undertaken neither for utilitarian motives nor for economic gain.[7] From this perspective, the development of the productive forces is, of course, a blessing. A diminishing volume of socially necessary work implies that economic activity need no longer crowd out other activities, allowing individuals to spend more time engaging in meaningful and personally rewarding activities outside the economic sphere.

A second—and perhaps more important—difference with other proposals to fight unemployment was Gorz's view that the 'micro-electronic revolution' (as it was still called then) caused irreversible changes and required a fundamentally new approach. 'We arrive', Gorz wrote,

> at the precise point announced by the first visionaries of post-capitalism when they saw a different social order beyond the bourgeois society and industrial capitalism: one where the efficiency of the machine would destroy work, the logic of capital and of market exchanges, so as to make appear the

[6] André Gorz, *Adieu au prolétariat, Au-delà du socialism* (Paris: Galilée, 1980), 177.

[7] André Gorz, 'La Plus Grande Liberté Possible (entretien avec Peter Glotz et Tilman Fichter)', *Les Temps Modernes* 42, no. 483 (1986): 85.

> 'available time' as the measure of the 'real richness'. The micro-electronic revolution brings us to all this; but the inertia of our mental categories hides them for us: we go on miserably to expect that the future will bring us back the past, that a new upward economic cycle will guarantee us full employment, that capitalism will rise from its agony and that automation will bring more work than it destroys.[8]

In other words, for Gorz, the prospect of steadily rising productivity transformed the utopian goal of a society characterized by 'multi-activity' and 'auto-valorisation of time' into a real possibility. To reach this goal, Gorz argued, one needed a political programme which combined the *reduction* of working time with its *redistribution*. Such a policy would reduce the burden of socially necessary labour and spread it over more members of society as well as providing everyone with the right and the possibility of temporarily breaking-out of the wage-labour relationship.[9] Another essential ingredient was a '*social income*'. In practice, Gorz's reform programme would amount to a system in which everyone was expected to provide a minimum number of hours of paid work in the course of his or her lifetime. How this volume of labour was distributed over the life cycle was up to each individual to decide. In exchange, each person would receive a regular, fixed, and life-long income supplement.

In the French public debate, this third feature became known as 'the second cheque', a term originally coined by the sociologist Guy Aznar. In the preface of one of Aznar's books, Gorz reminded the readers that he and Aznar had travelled 'shoulder to shoulder' at least since 1970, when both men had been amongst the founders of the ecological action group *Les Amis de la Terre*.[10] This made it difficult to distinguish between each other's thought, he added. For instance, like Gorz, Aznar advocated a policy of working time reduction primarily to allow citizens to flourish and develop in realms outside the economic sphere and not as a solution to unemployment. Since Aznar presented his 'second cheque' as a compensation for the loss of income due to working time reduction, especially amongst the low paid, it is not surprising that many commentators interpreted Gorz's social income as something similar.

[8] Gorz, *Chemins*, 14.

[9] André Gorz, 'The New Agenda', *New Left Review*, 184 (November/December 1990): 44–45.

[10] André Gorz, 'Preface', *Travailler moins pour travailler tous*, ed. Guy Aznar (Paris: Syros, 1993), 9.

Yet, for Gorz, the meaning of the social income was quite different. It symbolized the potential released by the radical novelty of the productive forces in the post-industrial era, and in particular their huge productivity gains. For him it was nothing less than the start of a project for a new civilization, recognizing 'available time' as 'the measure of real richness', allowing citizens to exercise the new freedoms and providing opportunities for paid work and social integration by it opened up by the reduction and redistribution of work.

Why Does 'Work' Provide a 'Ticket to Citizenship'?

Like most of Gorz's books, *Les Chemins du Paradis* caused much public debate. One controversial point was the exact meaning of the 'second cheque', or what Gorz himself called the 'social income'. Some, like Ulrich Beck or, John Keane, and John Owen, wondered why the payment was limited only to those in employment and asked Gorz why he did not make the payment universal.[11] Others focussed on passages which suggested that the 'social income' would be distributed to all—for instance, the statement that it was intended 'to cover the needs of the citizen and no longer of the worker'—and interpreted it to mean a universal and unconditional basic income.[12]

This latter reading, however, is clearly wrong. In writings and interviews after the publication of *Les Chemins du Paradis*, Gorz emphasized again and again that his intention was to uncouple 'income and work time, and not income and work itself'. It would be wrong, he stressed, to conceive of the social income as 'a new entitlement granted by the State'. The only difference with a conventional payment for work done was that the amount of work to be performed could be freely distributed over the lifetime, whereas the income stream from the 'social income' was a regular and consistent one.[13] 'The income paid during the interruptions to or intermissions in work', Gorz argued, 'must be seen as the deferred or anticipated payment of your share of the socially produced wealth: as an

[11] Ulrich Beck, *The Brave New World of Work* (Cambridge: Polity Press, 2000); John Keane and John Owen, *After Full Employment* (London: Hutchinson, 1986).

[12] Gorz, *Chemins*, 90–91.

[13] André Gorz, 'Qui ne travaille pas mangera quand même', *Futuribles* 101 (Juillet/Août 1986): 70.

income you have earned and which is owed to you, not granted to you, by society for the basic amount of work you are committed to do'.[14]

Given that he considered its potential for limiting the realm of 'work' and extending the realm of autonomy as the most significant promise of rising productivity due to technological advancement, why did Gorz want to make the social income conditional on being employed?

After publishing *Les Chemins du Paradis*, Gorz frequently elaborated on what made him object to making income guarantees universal and unconditional. His first objection related to questions of quid pro quo or distributive justice: an unconditional basic income would transform 'work' into something optional. Since a certain amount of work was necessary for society, this was unacceptable: no one should be excused from doing his or her part. Moreover, a basic income would absolve society from concerning itself with the equitable distribution of necessary work. A second objection was that by itself a basic income would neither create a public space in which non-economic activities could flourish nor help those denied access to work in the economic domain. Hence, for Gorz, a basic income risked turning the economic sphere into the exclusive domain of profit fanatics and efficiency maniacs, while marginalizing the unemployed (and other benefit claimants) even more.

Of fundamental importance to understanding Gorz's critique of basic income is his particular view of the relationship between citizenship and employment. Referring explicitly to Durkheim, Gorz conceived of full citizenship in a modern and complex society as requiring two modes of integration. Citizenship requires that one belongs to a *primary community*, based on solidarity and necessary for mediating between private and social life, but it also requires that one has a place in the *functioning of the social system*, a system so complex that it escapes the comprehension of its agents and requires their specialization in function of the demands of an impersonal whole. It is by this second mode of integration, participating in the production of the social whole, that one acquires rights and duties. 'Today', Gorz argued, '"work" refers to this functionally specialized activity, rewarded because of its usefulness for the social system'.[15] That is why

[14] André Gorz, 'On the Difference between Society and Community, and Why Basic Income Cannot by Itself Confer Full Membership of Either', in Philippe Van Parijs, ed., *Arguing for Basic Income* (London: Verso Books, 1992), 178–184, at 184.

[15] André Gorz, 'Revenu minimum et citoyenneté. Droit au travail vs. droit au revenue', *Futuribles* 184 (Février 1994): 57.

Gorz conceived of employment as the ticket to citizenship and argued that the right to work should be considered a political right.

It is important to note that, according to Gorz, neither of these modes of integration should be subordinate to the other. Neglecting their autonomy or blurring the boundaries between them would not only be wrong, but dangerous, he argued.[16] It is this claim that explains why Gorz considered traditional full employment policies as well as implementing a basic income unacceptable.

Focussing on the creation of jobs in a period when technological advancement reduces the socially necessary working time for existing jobs, Gorz argued that traditional full employment policies could only reach their goal by transforming into jobs activities which had previously existed outside the economic domain. The result would be 'a civilisation in which personal and social relations become the concern of professionals ... [and] ... in which learned and programmed social behaviour speeds up the disappearance of spontaneous behaviour. (...) Nobody will experience ever again the need to help, for instance, a blind person to cross the road because there will be people paid to do so.'[17]

Whereas traditional employment policies risked subordinating every activity to the economic domain, Gorz argued that basic income proposals exhibited a different flaw. Its advocates replaced the right to work with the right to income, and so implicitly considered each and every activity as useful for the social system, blurring the difference between the two modes of integration. Gorz conceded that implementing a basic income at sufficiency level was potentially superior to conventional full employment policies, since it might enable the transition from a society of full employment to a society of full activity. However, he added, advocates of a high basic income were not only highly unrealistic but plainly wrong if they expected that once work was made really optional, it would cease to be the privileged mode of social integration and that activities in the private domain would be recognized as of equal social value:

> The unconditional income will be no more than a favour granted by the State. It places its beneficiaries in a relation of dependence without according them any power or any rights. In fact, the unconditional character of the

[16] Conrad Lodziak and Jeremy Tatman, 'A Dialogue with Gorz', in *André Gorz: A Critical Introduction* (London: Pluto Press, 1997), 118.

[17] Gorz, 'Revenu minimum', 56.

> payment means that society can easily do without the one who stays or prefers to stay at the margin. Belonging to a self-organised community, precious as it may be, does not protect against the feeling of exclusion or the marginality of the unemployed: they cannot experience themselves as citizens alike to the others. ... From the acceptance of duties towards society spring the duties of society towards me; from my recognition of the rights society holds on me, spring the rights I hold on society; there is no full citizenship outside this relationship.[18]

For Gorz, the conclusion was clear. Although the need and the urgency to guarantee everyone a sufficient income would grow as the volume of socially necessary labour contracted and paid work became intermittent, making income guarantees unconditional was not an option. In the modern and complex society of today, it was essential to accept the duty of carrying part of the burden of the socially necessary work to be performed in order to receive the rights of citizenship.

So Why Did Gorz Change His Mind? And When?

In the May/June 1996 issue of the *New Left Review*, Finn Bowring argued that Gorz's writings had been 'widely misrepresented and significantly misunderstood', especially but not solely by his British readers.[19] The idea of a universal and unconditional income guarantee was a case in point. Those asserting that Gorz would have toyed with—let alone advocated—the idea in *Les Chemins du Paradis* were mistaken, Bowring wrote: in fact, 'Gorz has always been a critic of ... a basic universal income'.[20] Yet, a little less than a year later, in his book *Misères du présent, Richesse du possible*, Gorz announced his change of mind on precisely this point. What made André Gorz change his mind? Why did he lift his objections against a universal and unconditional basic income?

Throughout his life Gorz's thought was shaped by an unrelenting dialogue with academics, politicians, trade union leaders, or representatives of other social movements. For instance, discussions with Herbert Marcuse inspired his cultural critique of capitalism; a dialogue with Ivan Illich led him to adopt the distinction between 'autonomy' and 'heteronomy'; conversations with Jürgen Habermas showed up in the rephrasing of some of

[18] Gorz, 'Revenu minimum', 57–60.

[19] Finn Bowring, 'Misreading Gorz', *New Left Review* 217 (May/June 1996): 102–22.

[20] Bowring, 'Misreading', 112–13.

his analyses in terms of 'system' and 'life world'. Equally important, however, was his experience of social movements. In the 1970s, for instance, when the IG-Metall union led the struggle for working time reduction in Germany, Gorz discussed the union's proposals with its representatives. In the 1980s and 1990s, Gorz was in constant dialogue with the ecological movement (for which he was an important '*maître à penser*') and was a regular contributor to debates within the French movement of the unemployed. It is, therefore, likely that his change of mind about basic income was influenced by controversies and debates he was involved in prior to 1996.

One of these controversies concerned the so-called *Revenu Minimum d'Insertion* (RMI), introduced in 1988 by the Rocard government.[21] This reform introduced a form of social protection characterized by an almost universal, but conditional, right to a minimum income and help with social and professional integration. As well as being conditional on age and residency on French soil, a core element of the reform was a contract with the local social service administration, specifying which actions the claimant would undertake to 'insert' himself or herself in society. Given that this form of activation could be interpreted as an application of the idea of a 'second cheque', Gorz's involvement in the debate was unavoidable, even to the point of being considered as 'a beacon'—'*un auteur-phare*'—on these questions.[22]

In the spring of 1995, confronted with the precarious situation of a large part of the working population as well as with reports questioning the effectiveness of the RMI in dealing with the resulting situations of poverty, core members of the *Mouvement pour l'Anti-Utilitarisme dans les Sciences Sociales* and of the collectif *Transversales* organized a meeting of concerned academics, intellectuals, and activists. The result of the meeting was a collective article, '*Appel à débattre sur les moyens de résorber le chômage*', published on June 28, 1995, in *Le Monde*.[23] It was signed by thirty-

[21]The debate around the introduction of the RMI is discussed in the contribution of Marc-Antoine Sabaté in this volume. For a review of the history of the RMI and an extensive evaluation of its effects, see Michèle Lelièvre and Emmanuelle Nauze-Fichet, *RMI, l'Etat des Lieux. 1988–2008* (Paris: La Découverte, 2008).

[22]AECEP, 'Histoire et perspective de l'AECEP', in Guy Aznar, Alain Caillé, Jean-Louis Lavalle, Jacques Robin, Roger Sue, *Vers une économie plurielle. Un travail, une activité, un revenue pour tous* (Paris: Syros, 1997), 159.

[23]The article is reproduced in *Recherches* 7 (1996): 89–92. The issue is completely devoted to a critical discussion of unconditional basic income guarantees. It contains articles by

five well-known intellectuals, ranging from the 'degrowth'-advocating economist Serge Latouche via a well-respected social policy specialist, Chantal Euzéby, to the former Socialist deputy Jean-Michel Belorgey, who had been closely associated with the Rocard government and the RMI.

Calling for an urgent public debate on the need for a really innovative social and economic policy, the article identified three major goals: facilitating the social distribution of regular jobs by reducing working time, recognizing the importance of developing the social economy, and affirming that in our societies no one should live below a certain level of necessary material resources. The collective admitted that important differences still existed among its members, in particular with respect to how (un) conditional the benefit system ought to be. Nevertheless, they agreed that, in the long run, the analysis implied going beyond the existing *Revenu Minimum d'Insertion* and that, in the short run, the precarious situation necessitated relaxing conditions around the RMI in order to make it available 'for each person whose resources did not reach the guaranteed minimum level, even if his or her actions in pursuit of "re-insertion" would in all likelihood be unsuccessful'.[24]

Although some influential left-wing intellectuals, like Dominique Méda, Robert Castel, or Pierre Rosanvallon, did not sign the proposal, the organizers later noted that, being the first public statement underwritten by advocates as well as opponents of unconditional income guarantees, its importance could not be overestimated—certainly not, they added, if one takes into account 'what it takes to overcome amongst intellectuals what Freud called "the narcissism of the small difference"'.[25] But a real surprise to many was that amongst those who did sign was André Gorz. Reflecting on the debate that led to the final version of the '*Appel*', the organizers recalled that Gorz, who in the past had been quite hostile to the idea of making the RMI unconditional—an idea put forward in the draft version written by Alain Caillé—came to the meeting in Paris to explain why he had changed his mind: 'given the depth of the crisis, he considered it now

Robert Castel and Dominique Méda, explaining their objections to it. For an overview of the recent French debate on the right to a guaranteed income, see also: Laurent Geffroy, Garantir le revenue: Histoire et actualité d'une utopie concrete (Paris: La Découverte, 2002) and Timothée Duverger, *L'invention du revenue de base: La fabrique d'une utopie démocratique* (Lormont: Le Bord de L'Eau, 2018).

[24] *Recherches* 7 (1996): 91.

[25] AECEP, 'Histoire', 159.

necessary to implement an unconditional income guarantee at a sufficiently high level'.[26]

A contribution to a book casting Gorz as 'a thinker for the XXIst century' by Philippe Van Parijs—the most prominent academic advocate of universal basic income—confirms that Gorz's change of heart occurred more or less around the time of writing the collective article for *Le Monde*. Though Van Parijs had written a hostile review of *Les Chemins du Paradis* (in which he compared Gorz's proposal to forced labour—'not a road to paradise, but a dead-end street with the purgatory as its terminus'), this triggered a life-long and increasingly friendly dialogue between the two men.[27] In his contribution, Van Parijs refers to two letters by Gorz written on January 19, 1997, and October 15, 1997, respectively.[28] In the first letter, Gorz wrote that he had accepted the case for a strictly unconditional basic income, 'a social income at sufficiency level', some six months before; in the second letter he announced that he had finally decided to become a member of BIEN—then the Basic Income European Network, now the Basic Income Earth Network.

Significantly, however, Gorz emphasized that his change of mind was for reasons different from those spelled out in Van Parijs's philosophical writings. Instead, Gorz referred to what he saw as fundamental changes in the socio-economic structure. These changes are discussed at length in *Misères du présent, Richesse du possible* and I will come back to them below. For now, the important point to note is that these letters, apart from confirming the timing, also make clear that lifting the objections to the unconditionality clause was not a mere pragmatic reaction to the precarious situation in France, as suggested by how the organizers of the Paris meeting told the story of writing the '*Appel*'. It was the result of a fundamental rethinking of his conceptual framework.

In this respect, an interesting name on the list of signatories to the '*Appel*' is that of Antonio Negri, the Italian philosopher and co-author

[26] Ibid. After his retirement, Gorz and his wife led a rather secluded life, welcoming many friends and acquaintances in their house in Vosnon, but only very rarely attending meetings somewhere else. Hence, that he travelled to Paris for the first time in ten years is quite significant for the importance he attached to explaining his changed view about unconditional income guarantees.

[27] Philippe Van Parijs, 'De la nature du paradis et du moyen d'y parvenir', *La Revue Nouvelle* 80, no. 7 (1984): 69–74.

[28] Philippe Van Parijs, 'De la sphère autonome à l'allocation universelle', in *André Gorz: un penseur pour le XXIe siècle*, ed. Christophe Fourel (Paris: La Découverte, 2009), 161–78.

(with Michael Hardt) of a book, *Empire*, that became one of the icons of the anti-globalist movement. Amongst Marxists and Marx commentators, Antonio Negri is well known for his controversial reading of the famous fragment on machines and automation in Marx's *Grundrisse*.[29] In this fragment, Marx seems to suggest that technological developments are likely to lead to labour time being disconnected from the value of goods produced, and science or creativity becoming the most important factor in the production process. Negri popularized the term 'general intellect' to refer to this 'new' productive force. André Gorz, who referred to the same fragment in several of his books, had been reading Marx's *Grundrisse* since 1959 at the suggestion of the French labour sociologist Jean-Marie Vincent. It was also Vincent who introduced Gorz to the writings of the Italian 'operaismo' movement, of which Negri was (with Mario Tronti and Ranieri Panzieri) one of the intellectual leaders.[30] In the 1960s, Gorz introduced the ideas of this movement to France through articles in *Les Temps Modernes*.

In 1990, Antonio Negri and Jean-Marie Vincent founded (with Denis Berger) *Futur Antérieur*, a journal focussing on the impact of immaterial labour and the damaging effects of neo-liberal policies on the Welfare State. The journal functioned as an intellectual meeting place and provided the first building blocks of a research programme that would be further developed by academics connected to *Multitudes*, a journal started in 1998 on the initiative of Yann Moulier Boutang. At its core was the idea of a 'new great transformation' or a third phase in capitalism. In this new phase, called 'Cognitive Capitalism', production was considered to be in essence immaterial, and communication, knowledge, emotions, feelings, and imagination the most important productive forces.[31] The impact of these theories is clearly visible in *Misères du présent, Richesse du possible* and even more so in Gorz's next and last book, *L'Immatériel*.[32] Indeed, in

[29] K. Marx, *Grundrisse der Kritik der politischen Ökonomie (Rohentwurf) 1857–1857*, (Frankfurt/Wien: Europaïsche Verlaganstalt/Europa Verlag).

[30] Gorz, *Ecologica*, 10.

[31] For an introduction to the literature on 'cognitive capitalism', see among others: Christian Azaïs, Antonella Corsani and Patrick Dieuaide, eds., *Vers un capitalism cognitive: Entre mutation du travail et territoires* (Paris: L'Harmattan, 2001); Carlo Vercellone, ed., *Sommes-nous sortis du capitalisme industriel?* (Paris: La Dispute, 2003); Yann Moulier Boutang, *Le Capitalism Cognitive: La Nouvelle Grande Transformation* (Paris: Editions Amsterdam, 2007).

[32] André Gorz, *L'Immatériel. Conaissance, valeur et capital* (Paris: Galilée, 2003).

several interviews, he acknowledged that writing *Misères du présent, Richesse du possible* was partly the result of a critical dialogue with proponents of the Cognitive Capitalism thesis.[33]

Did Gorz Really Change His Mind?

In *Misères du présent, Richesse du possible*, Gorz gives four reasons justifying why he abandoned the conditionality clause, a crucial element of the position he had defended since 1983.[34] Each of these reasons relates to different aspects of Post-Fordism or Cognitive Capitalism.

First, an important characteristic of present-day production processes, Gorz argues, is that intelligence and creativity are now the most important forces of production and that the volume of goods produced is less and less related to the time necessary to produce it. If it is 'impossible to measure the working hours of self-employed or of craftworkers or the producers of intangible services', then it makes no sense to relate the 'social income' to a particular quantity of socially necessary labour.[35]

Second, for Gorz, to justify making an income guarantee conditional on performing equivalent work, two conditions have to be met: it needs to be work in the public sphere benefitting everyone, and it must have payment as its aim without payment corrupting its meaning. Meeting these conditions is less and less possible, he argues. Hence, income guarantees need to be universal and unconditional if they are intended to promote voluntary, artistic, cultural, family, and mutual-aid activities. Only then can one preserve the nature of activities having their full meaning only when done for their own sake.

Third, in recent decades modern progressive enterprises extended the employment contract to include continuing education and training, considering it as an integral part of working time and paying for it accordingly.

[33] See, for instance, *Liberation*, September 25, 1997, or Françoise Golain, *Une critique du travail. Entre écologie et socialisme* (Paris: La Découverte, 2000), 224–230. For critical appraisals of Gorz's writings by the early inspirers of the cognitive capitalism theories, see amongst others: Jean-Marie Vincent, 'Paradoxes autour du travail', *Futur Antérieur* 10 (1992) and Toni Negri, 'Recension. Misères du présent, Richesse du possible de André Gorz', *Futur Antérieur* 43 (April 1998). For an overall assessment, see Françoise Gollain, 'L'apport d'André Gorz au débat sur le capitalism cognitive', *Revue du Mauss* 35 (2010): 541–58.

[34] Gorz, *Misères*, 140–50.

[35] Gorz, *Misères*, 140.

However, Gorz points out, this approach subordinated both the *right* to education and training, and the *nature* of that training, to the company's interests. By contrast, an unconditional income guarantee would allow individuals to develop their capacities as they wished. This autonomy is intrinsically valuable on a variety of levels: moral (autonomy of value-judgement), political (autonomy of decision-making regarding the common good), cultural (invention of lifestyles, consumption models and arts of living), and existential (the capacity to take care of oneself rather than leave it to experts and authorities to decide what is good for us).

Fourth, Gorz argues that the system of wealth distribution prefigured by unconditional income guarantees is the one most compatible with the emerging economy in which labour is less and less central to the production process. 'The economy tends to a situation in which the amounts to be levied and redistributed to cover individual and collective needs exceed the amounts distributed by and for production', Gorz claims.[36] Therefore, in order not to impede the further development of the productive forces or to cause grave inequalities a new approach to distribution is needed.[37]

Whether this elaborate justification for lifting the conditionality clause is convincing is open to debate, not least because the reform package proposed in 1997 differed only marginally from that of 1983. Right up until his latest writings, Gorz still maintained that the strategy suggested in *Les Chemins du Paradis* was the right one and continued to uphold the triple objective of making wage-labour disappear, keeping the economic domain within appropriate limits, and building a society which would give citizens the opportunity to flourish and gain control over time. Likewise, Gorz qualified his support for basic income in *Misères du présent, Richesse du possible* by insisting that it should be at 'sufficiency level', and severely criticized proposals by known advocates of basic income, such as Claus Offe and Yoland Bresson. And, finally, at several instances Gorz sustained his analysis with references to writings from the 1960s and 1970s, including some of his own writings from that period. Policies proposed in 1997 were presented as 'pursuing goals similar to those embodied in "revolutionary reforms" which some of us proposed in the early 1960s'.[38]

All this provided room to doubt whether Gorz really changed his mind and whether his advocacy of unconditional income guarantees was really

[36] Gorz, *Misères*, 146.
[37] Gorz, *Misères*, 139–40.
[38] Gorz, *Misères*, 131.

unconditional.[39] At the very least, one could wonder why he had only concluded as late as 1997 that the strategy proposed in 1983 was not compatible with social, economic, and technological developments, when at least some of these developments had been discernible decades previously—for instance, in C. Wright Mills's 1951 book *White Collar*.

However, illustrating very well that Gorz really did change his mind is the important change in the role income guarantees play in restricting the domain of economic rationality and safeguarding the domain of autonomous activities.

As mentioned above, in *Les Chemins du Paradis* Gorz insisted that the social income should be conditional on employment for two reasons: to ensure that the socially necessary work was done, and to maintain the distinction between two essentially different modes of integration. In *Misères du présent, Richesse du possible*, Gorz takes the opposite position. Lifting the conditionality clause is justified by the goal of safeguarding the domain of autonomous activities.

> For only if [the income guarantee] is unconditional will it be possible to protect the unconditional nature of those activities which are only fully meaningful when done for their own sake. ... I see this as the only way to preserve the voluntary sector and to protect it from socialisation and economicisation—while at the same time making them accessible to all.[40]

Gorz returned to this theme in his last book, *L'Immatériel*. Echoing a distinction he had made frequently since 1983 between left-wing and right-wing versions of basic income, and rejecting both of them, Gorz now distinguished between two conceptions of '*le revenu d'existence*' (as basic income is sometimes called in France). Sometimes they are present in the writings of the same author, Gorz notes, but it is important to note the difference between them.

[39] Guy Aznar—Gorz's fellow-traveller for many years and who also signed the '*Appel*'—wrote that he deplored Gorz's change of mind and still believed firmly in the objections against unconditional income guarantees as formulated in the writings of those he referred to as 'Gorz I'. See Guy Aznar, *La fin des années de chômage. La stratégie des emplois pluriel*, (Paris: Syros, 1999). Despite his enormous respect for his work, Robert Castel conceived of Gorz's latest writings as 'a skid' in his trajectory' and based on analyses that were both sociologically wrong and politically dangerous. See Robert Castel, 'André Gorz et le travail: une interpretation critique', in *Sortir du capitalism. Le scenario Gorz*, eds. Alain Caillé and Christian Fourel (Lormont: Le Bord de l'Eau, 2013), 43–56.

[40] Gorz, *Misères*, 143–44.

Some conceive of basic income as a payment necessitated by the fact that time expended outside of 'work' has become a decisive contribution to labour productivity, but Gorz warns that this conception of UBI contained a formidable trap. If one believes that the process of production profits from the skills and knowledge people develop in their daily lives, then every human activity can be conceived of as contributing to the production of human capital. Yet justifying basic income in this way legitimizes the notion that every aspect of our lives is a form of 'work':

> If a basic income compensates the invisible work as a productive source of visible work, this compensation authorizes the requirement that invisible work makes visible work as productive as possible. This means that one stays within the confines of economic value and productivism. One acknowledges that capital has the right to require that the development of human capacities should be undertaken in view of the advantage firms could get from it.[41]

The other conception of basic income, by contrast, aims at protecting life from being infected by the 'commodity imaginary' and, hence, at preventing it being transformed into 'work'. However, Gorz argues, basic income can only take on this meaning—as an attack against 'work-as-a-value'—if it neither requires nor remunerates anything. Its role is to restrain the domain of value-creation in the economic sense and to allow the expansion of activities which create nothing that can be bought, sold, or exchanged for anything else. Basic income must liberate the individual from the constraints of economic value-creation and facilitate the full development of human faculties beyond what is functionally useful for production.

Gorz's embrace of basic income, then, meant abandoning his pre-1997 view that 'work' should never be conceived of as 'optional' and that jobs were essential 'tickets to citizenship'. Indeed, commenting in 1999 on his change of mind, Gorz acknowledged that it meant accepting a notion of citizenship no longer linked to 'paid work': 'the right to have rights' was the phrase he used, implicitly invoking the work of Hannah Arendt and linking the unconditional income guarantee to the politics of human rights. Gorz's new conception of citizenship even included 'the right to refuse "undignified work": in particular those jobs or quasi-jobs which

[41] Gorz, *Immatériel*, 30.

merely pay half the minimum wage and are presented as a favour that society gives to the unemployed'.[42]

Even if one can quarrel about whether it is 'status' (employment) or 'desert' (producing socially necessary goods) that grounds citizenship rights in Gorz's earlier writings, it is clear that his 1997 book signals a remarkable shift.

What Is New About 'Work' in 'Cognitive Capitalism'?

Remarkably, *Misères du présent, Richesse du possible* does not provide a clear and explicit answer to the question of what had made Gorz's old conception of citizenship obsolete. The case for lifting the conditionality clause rests almost completely on arguments pointing out that Post-Fordist or Cognitive Capitalist conditions cause conditional income guarantees to have perverse effects or call for unconditional income guarantees to harvest the new opportunities provided by these conditions. No explicit argument for why this necessitates rejecting his old conception of citizenship is given. Why do Post-Fordist or Cognitive Capitalist conditions imply that 'neither the right to an income, nor full citizenship, nor everyone's sense of identity and self-fulfilment' can continue to 'depend upon being employed'?[43]

As explained above, Gorz's original conception of citizenship rested on a kind of Durkheimian social contract theory in which paid work played a foundational role:

> The essential aspect of the obligation to be employed in exchange of the guarantee of a full income is that this obligation is the basis of a corresponding right: obliging individuals to produce by their labour the income they are guaranteed, society takes on the obligation to guarantee them the possibility of employment and gives them the right to demand this. Being obliged by society is the foundation of the rights they have on society; the right of being provided full citizenship, of being individuals just like the others, taking on their part, lighter and lighter as time goes on, of the burden of necessities and liberating them, at the same time, to be incomparable

[42] André Gorz, 'Miseria del presente, ricchezza del possibile (Intervista di Patrick Dieuaide, Pierre Péronnet et Carlo Vercellone)', in Andre Fumagalli and Maurizio Lazzarato, eds., *Tute Bianche. Disoccupazione di massa e reddito di cittadinanza* (Roma: DeriveApprodi, 1999), 132.

[43] Gorz, *Misères*, 90–91.

> persons who, for the rest of their time, deploy their multiple capacities, if they desire to do so.[44]

Equally important was that 'work'—that is, paid work or what in French he called '*le travail-emploi*' (work-as-a-social-status), distinguishing it from '*travail-valeur*' (work-as-a-value) or '*travail-marchandise*' (work-as-a-commodity)—should be kept within its own proper boundaries. In his 1988 book *Métamorphoses du travail, Quête du sens*, Gorz warned against extending the domain of what was properly called 'work in the economic sense' by blurring the difference with other activities. When we talk about 'housework' or 'the work of an artist' or 'working on one's self', he argued, the meaning of the word is totally different when it refers to 'work' in a 'salaried society' or a 'labouring society'.[45]

In *Misères du présent, Richesse du possible*, Gorz returns to this theme and distinguishes between two different meanings of 'work'. On the one hand, 'work' refers to a necessary activity, carried out in the modern period according to norms defined by society and at the demand of society. On the other hand, more fundamentally and beyond its social determination, there is what Gorz calls 'work that you do'. Both dimensions have important, though different, effects. The latter provides you with mastery of self and of the surrounding world necessary for the development of human capacities, whereas the former makes you feel capable of doing what

[44] André Gorz, *Métamorphoses du travail, quête de sens* (Paris: Galilée, 1988), 216. Many commentators interpreted Gorz's emphasis on 'work' as based on its importance for social integration and social cohesion—a view expressed by many advocates of activation policies. Yet, Gorz did not share this view. Never, he wrote in *Misères du présent, Richesse du possible*, has 'work as a value' so shamelessly been exalted as in times when it could no longer fulfil its function as a source of 'social ties', 'social cohesion', 'integration', or 'socialization', ascribed to it by Marie Jahoda in her famous study of the unemployed in Marienthal. See Gorz, *Misères*, 98.

[45] In French, Gorz uses '*société salariale*' (borrowed from the economist Michel Aglietta) and '*société du travail*' (borrowed from the philosopher Hannah Arendt). In *Reclaiming Work*, these terms are translated as 'wage-based society'. This is quite misleading, because 'wage' has a quite different connotation from 'salary', especially in the French context. In Aglietta's work, the salaried society refers to a complex configuration of labour market institutions, providing stability of employment and elaborate social protection. Moreover, publications in English about Aglietta's theories do translate the term as 'salaried society'. In the second case, 'labouring society' is the original term used in Hannah Arendt's *The Human Condition*. Not only does it seem a bit strange to re-translate the French term back into English using a term different from the original one, but also, and more to the point, for Arendt the distinction between 'labour' and 'work' is fundamental.

society needs, which in return gives you recognition, socializes you, and by its demands confers rights on you. Drawing people out of their private solitude, it is an aspect of citizenship.[46]

It is clear that these two distinctions do not match. In the 1988 case, the distinction is between two types of 'work', belonging to two different 'spheres' or 'domains', say 'system' versus 'life world' to use Habermas's terminology. This interpretation is impossible for the 1997 analysis. The 'work that you do' does not map on a particular domain. It refers to the activities you deploy when performing 'the work that you are given to do under specific social conditions'.

This shift from a distinction based on domains of 'work' to a distinction based on dimensions of 'work' helps explain why Gorz changed his view on the relationship between employment and citizenship. Whereas changes in the socially determined conditions under which necessary activities are performed do not necessarily affect activities outside the domain of work in the economic sense of the word, this is hardly the case for 'work that you do'. Moreover, although Gorz still seems to connect citizenship with socially necessary activities—'work that you are given to do under specific social conditions'—it is difficult to see 'mastery of self and of the surrounding world necessary for the development of human capacities' as totally alien to the emancipatory capacity of 'work'.

A close reading of the diagnostic part of *Misères du présent, Richesse du possible* illustrates why Gorz's confrontation with the writings of the Cognitive Capitalism theorists may have triggered this change in his conception of 'work'. Firstly, Gorz believed that the nature of labour relations had undergone a transformation. Using Herbert Simon's terminology (1951), one could describe this change as a movement from a society of 'employment contracts' to a society of 'sales contracts', that is, a society predominantly characterized by short-term contracts, career interruptions, high mobility, and individualized reward systems. This shift was complemented by a similarly individualizing second shift in the organization of the production process. Here, Gorz referred to modern management strategies which replaced hierarchical organizational structures with self-organizing networks, using quality circles, high-performance work systems, teamwork, and their likes.[47]

[46] Gorz, *Misères*, 139.
[47] Gorz, *Misères*, 51–64.

A third shift was described by Gorz—using Marxist terminology—as a move from a labour market selling or buying 'abstract labour' (i.e., 'labour that is measurable, quantifiable and detachable from the person who "provides" it') to one selling and buying 'concrete labour'. In lay terms, people are no longer hired because of what they do, but because of who they are. 'In the post-Fordist enterprise, technical knowledge and professional skills are only of value when combined with a particular state of mind, an unlimited openness to adjustment, change, and the unforeseen.'[48] Characteristics like 'personality', 'looks', or 'creativity'—those elements which human capital literature tends to refer to as 'soft skills' or 'people skills'—become crucial productive resources and integral parts of labour power. When workers are encouraged to actively cultivate, care for, and develop these characteristics, it is in the service of an organization whose rights one should never contest. This 'sale of self', Gorz says, is the accepted lot of all those creative individuals with a real, but limited and very much dominated, control over their work, like the jobbing producers of ideas, fantasies, and messages, journalists, artists, or copy-writers—'all who give wholly of their persons in the service of activities which are gratifying in themselves, but by which they become the venal and eager instruments of an alien role in which they sell themselves'.[49]

This triple shift brought about by Post-Fordism and Cognitive Capitalism affected deeply what, according to Gorz, constituted during the industrialist period the emancipatory capacity of 'work'.

> In a 'salaried' or 'labouring' society, labour services are commodified. This means that they have a price and are regulated by universal rights. They have the status of *general labour* qualifying the worker as a *general social individual*, capable of performing a socially determined task and making oneself generally useful to the social system. The wage pays for services rendered, not for the person providing the service. Indeed, the functional utility of labour efforts resides precisely in its being impersonal, answering to an impersonal demand of the social system. It gives 'work' a public status, certified by an employment contract. That is why it confers economic citizenship and protects in principle as well against arbitrary decisions by employers as against a labour market functioning without any restrictions whatsoever. Yet, it is important to note that being commodified is not a completely

[48] Gorz, *Misères*, 95.

[49] Gorz, *Misères*, 75. See also André Gorz, 'La personne devient une entreprise. Note sur le travail de production de soi', *Recherches* 18 (2001): 61–66.

> negative characteristic. Indeed, it is also what makes waged-labour emancipatory as compared to housework or slavery.[50]

The move towards market-mediated relations eroded the collective regulation at the core of a 'salaried' or 'labouring society' and was bound to result in more precariousness and anxiety. Employment would no longer provide a firm basis for constructing a long-term life plan and developing a sense of belonging. Moreover, given the prospect of much harsher competition in the labour market, the socialization through jobs was liable to become anti-social—giving way to 'me-first' and '*sauve qui peut*' behaviour and attitudes.

The shift in Gorz's social and economic analysis, then, reflected his belief that it was necessary to come to terms with the ways in which Post-Fordism and Cognitive Capitalism were changing the nature and significance of work. Where Post-Fordism and Cognitive Capitalism prevailed, fewer and fewer jobs retained the social characteristics necessary to serve as devices for emancipation and, hence, tickets to citizenship.

Conclusion

When *Misères du présent, Richesse du possible* was published, most commentators focussed on Gorz's arguments justifying unconditional and universal income guarantees. Much less attention has been given to the fact that his new analysis not merely made 'work' optional, but implied a changed conception of citizenship. As this chapter shows, Gorz's embrace of basic income was intimately linked to his assessment of how 'work' changed as a result of the transition to a new phase in capitalism, called 'Cognitive Capitalism'. Without this, it is difficult to see why Gorz would change his mind about the conditionality clause for anything other than purely pragmatic reasons.

Gorz's *Misères du présent, Richesse du possible* deserves a place apart in the basic income literature in two respects. Many basic income advocates make their case by referring to developments in the labour market. They point, amongst other things, at the precariousness of jobs (Guy Standing), at the disappearance of work (Jeremy Rifkin), or at the growing number of 'bullshit jobs' (David Graeber), but none of these arguments quite reflect Gorz's position. In so far as Gorz believed in 'the end of work', this

[50] André Gorz, 'Revenu minimum', 59.

was not because socially necessary work no longer existed, but because in his view under present Cognitive Capitalism 'work' no longer constituted a basis for citizenship.

However, the latter claim also implies a specific position at a deeper level. Advocacy of basic income generally relies on two sorts of arguments: principled and pragmatic. The foregoing makes clear that Gorz's argument is not really a pragmatic one. But what about the principled case?

In present-day literature, the principled case for unconditional basic income relies predominantly on a so-called real libertarian or left liberal theory of justice, of which Philippe Van Parijs is the most prominent representative.[51] In this view, based on the fundamental idea of self-ownership, unconditional basic income is an instrument of freedom, allowing us to reach a society in which all members are (equally) as free as possible. Questions about economic sustainability or political achievability are considered important, but lexicographically dominated by its ethical justifiability. Gorz, on the other hand, reasoned quite differently. Even if Gorz's aim of reaching a society of autonomous and flourishing individuals resembles in many respects that of principled basic income advocates, in his story basic income does not play the role of a device allowing a particular, immutable principle of justice to be realized. Rather, it expresses the nature of the basic structural adjustment needed to allow the potential inherent in the ongoing historical developments to be released: '*It has heuristic value: it reflects the most basic and advanced meaning of present developments*'.[52]

For many, André Gorz was 'an unforgettable inspirer and uncompromising questioner', as Philippe Van Parijs once called him—a characterization which he much appreciated.[53] It is fitting, then, that Gorz's analysis left advocates of basic income with a deep question. Ten years before changing his mind, elaborating on the emancipatory character of work, he wrote: 'If I am relieved of any social obligation and, more precisely, of the obligation to earn my living by working, even as little as it may be, I cease to exist as a social individual as capable as anyone else. … I am a supernumerary of the human species. … It is not the guarantee of a social

[51] The most compelling argument for this view is Philippe Van Parijs, *Real Freedom for All* (Oxford: Clarendon Press, 1995). See also: Philippe Van Parijs and Yannick Vanderborght, *Basic Income: A Radical Proposal for a Free Society and Sane Economy* (Cambridge, MA: Harvard University Press, 2017).

[52] Gorz, *Misères*, 91.

[53] Van Parijs, 'De la sphère', 162.

minimum that will change this one bit. … Whatever the importance of the guaranteed minimum, it does not change the fact that society does not expects anything from me, and, hence, denies me an existence as a social individual in general.'[54] So, after conceding in *Misères du présent, Richesse du possible* that 'work' in the emancipatory sense is really dead, being only central to our 'work imaginary' as something akin to phantom pain, and that '*the aim must be to disconnect from "work" the right to have rights*', Gorz leaves us with the question: What *does* constitute citizenship under conditions of Cognitive Capitalism? And in what sense, if any, can the instalment of an unconditional income guarantee be conceived as a right?[55]

[54] Gorz, *Métamorphoses*, 254–5.
[55] Gorz, *Misères*, 90–91, 98.

PART III

Global Perspectives

CHAPTER 9

Basic Needs and the Discovery of Global Poverty

Samuel Moyn

The development of universal basic income schemes fit both chronologically and substantively with an epoch-making revolution in theories and practices of global development. In the 1960s, 'global poverty' was perceived for the first time as a phenomenon that divided north and south. In the 1970s, approaches to development centred around basic needs—rather than overall growth or other ends like the mitigation of inequality at national or global scales—were pioneered. From that time to our own, they have made remediation of the worst immiseration the main priority in development in the agendas of international institutions and the non-governmental sector.

As with universal basic income proposals in their origins and the present, there is every reason to worry that attacks on global poverty play multiple functions beyond their honourable official goal. The invention of basic needs was not solely a moral breakthrough to welcome, since it worked in tandem with calls for equality associated with the global south's 'New International Economic Order' (NIEO) proposals calling for more

S. Moyn (✉)
Yale University, New Haven, CT, USA
e-mail: samuel.moyn@yale.edu

P. Sloman et al. (eds.), *Universal Basic Income in Historical Perspective*, https://doi.org/10.1007/978-3-030-75706-9_9

equalization of states—calls that were marginalized in the process.[1] In what follows, the stress falls on the way that the problem of 'basic needs' of fellow humans around the world emerged in competition with the global south's own call for structural justice, in the era before and after the NIEO's programmatic declaration in the United Nations on May 1, 1974. In fact, the cause of addressing global poverty arose on the grave of demanding global fairness.

International development on a global scale had always been a minor affair compared to the projects that the elites of each postcolonial state shouldered to launch growth and build modernity in their country. In the tradition of colonial development schemes, the United States committed to bringing a better way of life to the world in Harry Truman's storied Point 4 programme in 1949, the West European countries did the same as their imperial designs were slowly displaced, and the United Nations and other international organizations formed their own units and projects.

The funding for such ventures always remained minimal. Americans were notoriously stingy relative to their wealth—not meeting the United Nations expectation for foreign assistance, though it never approached even 1 per cent of national income. A persistent track record of Europeans doing proportionately better began rapidly with their economic recovery after World War II and decolonization, yet all told the amounts never exceeded a tiny percentage of northern spending. And with Americans in the lead, these amounts were often linked to security imperatives.[2]

Despite the fact that the United Nations had dubbed the 1960s the 'development decade', there was a widespread sense that something had gone awry. When the World Bank commissioned former Canadian Prime Minister Lester Pearson in 1968 to ratify business as usual, a large number of critics of his commission took the opportunity to cry foul. The poor countries were not catching up, and in the face of this 'widening gap' it

[1] On the New International Economic Order, see Adom Getachew, *Worldmaking after Empire: The Rise and Fall of Self-Determination* (Princeton, NJ: Princeton University Press, 2019), chap. 5; Samuel Moyn, *Not Enough: Human Rights in an Unequal World* (Cambridge, MA: Harvard University Press, 2018), chap. 5.

[2] The historiography of development is now staggeringly large, yet it mostly stops in the early 1970s. For one overview, see Joseph M. Hodge, 'Writing the History of Development', *Humanity* 6, no. 3 (Winter 2015): 429–63 and 7, no. 1 (Spring 2016): 125–74.

was also plain that the strides they were making still left their own poor behind.[3]

Even in cases where national growth did occur, in the 1970s it suddenly became troubling how unevenly distributed it was. For development economist Mahbub ul Haq, the verdict on all this was grim, even as the UN made the 1970s the 'second development decade' to try again. Born in 1934 in Punjab, Haq had done his training in England and the United States before serving his Pakistani government in the 1960s and then moving to the World Bank in 1970 to direct policy planning.

In Pakistan, Haq's own views had been orthodox: start national growth, through a combination of state planning and free market policies, and tolerate massive inequality, on the theory that the results would (someday) reach the masses. The conditions for a future welfare state might only come about by exacerbating division in the short term. The trouble was that it was generally agreed by the 1970s that what little initial growth by such strategies—especially when they took the form of substituting for Western imports to develop indigenous industry providing cheap versions of foreign products—worsened not merely national but international inequality and did not look like they would ever improve the lot of the poor.

In fact, not only were the poor nations falling ever further behind, but the poor within them often fared worse too. The main results were to entrench the power and wealth of tiny elites, and Haq became notorious for denouncing the handful of twenty-two families that had come to control Pakistani commerce in all sectors. In a piece that became well known in part because Indira Gandhi was found to have plagiarized it in a policy speech, Haq concluded: 'The very institutions we created for providing faster growth and capital accumulation frustrated later on all our attempts for better distribution and greater social justice'. Disarmingly, from his new Washington, DC outpost Haq concluded it was time for a major rethink.[4]

[3] For responses to the Pearson report, see Barbara Ward et al., eds., *The Widening Gap: Development in the 1970s* (New York, NY: Columbia University Press, 1971). See also the much-noticed Edgar Owens and Robert Shaw, *Development Reconsidered: Bridging the Gap between Government and People* (Lexington, MA: D. C. & Co., 1972).

[4] Mahbub ul Haq, *The Strategy of Economic Planning: A Case Study of Pakistan* (Karachi: Oxford University Press, 1963); Mahbub ul Haq, 'System Is to Blame for the 22 Wealthy Families', *Times* (London), March 22, 1973; Peter Hazelhurst, 'The Funny Coincidence of

Like his university friend and later Nobel Prize winner, the Indian economist Amartya Sen (who popularized and refined many of his friend's ideas), Haq spoke from within a mainstream development economics that he shifted profoundly. He did so from the cynical perspective that it was not worth dreaming about a welfare world that was never going to come to pass. Poverty alleviation suddenly emerged as a prime imperative precisely on the ruins of false expectations.[5] There was not only no relatively quick fix (as the NIEO seemed to demand) for countries struggling to grow rapidly only to see themselves fall ever further behind, but also no distant millennium in which a fundamentally unequal would ever correct itself. 'The pursuit of elusive present-day Western standards', Haq decided, 'cannot be reached even over the course of the next century'. Acceptance of global inequality was the beginning of wisdom. 'The gap will continue to widen and the rich nations will continue to become richer.' It was 'hopeless' to expect the reversal of that trend. A mere two years before the NIEO achieved unprecedented visibility in 1974 for a protest against expanding global inequality, Haq concluded that global sufficiency was the best available hope.[6]

Sometimes celebrated for mastering the obvious if heartrending fact that individuals suffer now, Haq was in fact making a momentous ethical choice between material equality and basic provision. The new goal was to give up on international disparity in order to help the world's poor now. Development for the sake of basic needs directed attention to immediate personal suffering rather than indefinite collective liberation. 'The objective of development must be viewed as a selective attack on the worst forms of poverty', Haq insisted in 1971, the scales having fallen from his eyes. 'We were taught to take care of our GNP [gross national product], as this will take care of poverty. Let us reverse this and take care of poverty, … worry[ing] about the *content* of GNP even more than its rate of increase.'[7]

Mrs Gandhi and a Pakistani Economist', *Times* (London), April 12, 1972; Mahbub ul Haq, 'Mrs Gandhi's Speech', *Times* (London), April 26, 1972.

[5] For older roots, see Sheyda Jahanbani, *'The Poverty of the World': Discovering the Poor at Home and Abroad, 1935–1973* (Oxford University Press, forthcoming).

[6] Mahbub ul Haq, 'Employment in the 1970's: A New Perspective'," *International Development Review* 4 (1971), rpt. in *The Poverty Curtain: Choices for the Third World* (New York, NY: Columbia University Press, 1976), 35.

[7] Mahbub ul Haq, 'The Third World Crisis', *Washington Post*, April 30, 1972, rpt. 'Crisis in Development Strategies', *World Development* 1, no. 7 (July 1973): 29, as well as in *The Poverty Curtain*, 40.

Haq spoke of basic needs from the start but he was initially vague about what precisely a direct antipoverty agenda implied. He flirted as much with recommending that Third World states strive for a minimum income as with identifying a list of fundamental necessities in order to aim to ensure their provision. Indeed, when Haq later initiated plans for the now famous 'Human Development Index' after moving to the United Nations Development Programme in the 1980s, it was for him a way of simplifying outcomes to supplant the mantra of gross national product with a measurement of equal clarity rather than a refractory set of heterogeneous needs and rights to fulfil. In his own mind, the abandonment of international inequality as a problem did not entail a total loss of interest in national inequality. But it was usually appended as an afterthought to the fulfilment of sufficient minima when it came to food, health, and services. 'Development goals', he explained in a classic 1972 address, 'should be expressed in terms of the progressive reduction and eventual elimination of malnutrition, disease, illiteracy, squalor, unemployment, and inequalities'.[8]

There was nothing conceptually new about 'basic needs' in 1971–72. In Western intellectual history, some set or other of fundamental needs was long since a commonplace way of gesturing towards the content of a minimally adequate life.[9] And the 'human needs of labor' had therefore been debated in the origins of welfare states, most notably in English reformer Seebohm Rowntree's early twentieth-century agitation to attend to the poor in industrial cities. Needs had been central to socialist traditions (especially Karl Marx's own thought) too.

For all their familiarity, however, the concept played the signal role in global development thinking of displacing national growth as the index of development and reaching individuals with their needs directly. Pundits in the 1970s often traced the roots of the needs approach to the psychologist Abraham Maslow (who propounded an abstract hierarchy of human needs in 1943) or to the Indian economist and state planner Pitambar Pant (who had joined the growth consensus in his home country but called early for baking in strategies to afford minimum provision). On the brink of their

[8] Haq, 'Crisis', 30, in *Poverty Curtain*, 43, as well as chap. 4 and 74–75 on international efforts. On the prominence of GNP, see Dirk Philipsen, *The Little Big Number: How GDP Came to Rule the World and What to Do About It* (Princeton, NJ: Princeton University Press, 2015).

[9] Dana Simmons, *Vital Minimum: Need, Science, and Politics in Modern France* (Chicago, IL: Chicago University Press, 2015).

fame, there was nothing intellectually revolutionary about 'basic needs'. What mattered was the service that concept could play in becoming the mantra that led the field away from its prior doctrines—and for its sternest critics, opposing and palliating the global south's demands for worldwide equality.[10]

In part this was because, certainly at first, little more was involved than a gesture towards what the national and international development had so spectacularly missed. Were basic needs 'concept or slogan, synthesis or smokescreen?' asked Reginald Herbold Green, an American development economist close to ecumenical Protestant discussions and adviser to African countries before becoming a founder of a University of Sussex development institute. 'It is amazing how two such innocent, five-letter words could mean so many different things to so many different people', even Haq acknowledged.[11]

The remarkable fact was that, for all its ambiguity, basic needs ricocheted across the intergovernmental and intellectual space, albeit in slightly different versions. The other premier site of basic needs visions, even as the Bank moved to canonize its own, was the International Labour Organization (ILO). It announced basic needs within its 'World Employment Program', which had begun in the 1960s as a rubric for the organization to reinvent itself for a postcolonial world. With most of its aims—a humanized workplace and even a right to strike—achieved in the developed countries for which it had been devised after World War I as a reformist answer to the Soviet Union, the ILO now moved on in search of a new mission. Its first move had been to intervene in reform under late imperial rule, to push through the abolition of forced labour and to begin to approximate northern labour standards. In a postcolonial world, it was forced to shoulder a different and more complex task of participating not

[10] Seebohm Rowntree, *The Human Needs of Labour* (London: Longmans, Green, 1937). See, for example, Agnes Heller, *The Theory of Need in Marx* (New York, NY: St Martin's Press, 1976); Michael Ignatieff, *The Needs of Strangers* (New York, NY: Viking, 1984). On Pant, see A. Vaidyanathan, C. R. Rao, T. N. Srinivasan and J. N. Bhagwati, 'Pitambar Pant: An Appreciation', *Economic and Political Weekly*, April 28, 1973, and 'Pitambar Pant', in *Poverty and Income Distribution in India*, eds. T.N. Srinivasan and P.K. Bardhan (Calcutta: Statistical Publishing Society, 1974).

[11] R.H. Green, 'Basic Human Needs: Concept or Slogan, Synthesis or Smokescreen?', *Institute for Development Studies Bulletin* 9, no. 4 (1978): 7–11; Mahbub ul Haq, 'Foreword', in Paul Streeten et al., *First Things First: Meeting Basic Human Needs in the Developing Countries* (Oxford, 1981), ix.

in the northern welfare state project but in the southern development one.[12]

The ILO's turn to basic needs occurred out of the recognition that it made little sense to adapt a strategy devised for northern industrial conflicts without recognizing the entirely different organization of labour and production in the global south. In the several years leading up to its World Employment Conference in 1976, therefore, the ILO broadened out, officially to place employment in its proper setting, but in reality to offer a full-scale development approach of its own. The conference was the most visible moment during the years of 1975–77 when 'basic needs' took the United Nations system (of which the ILO is loosely a part) by storm. Haq was a massive influence in these years, and Sen consulted for the World Employment Programme during the formulation of the report.

For the ILO, devising conditions for full or at least fuller employment remained essential, but in a setting in which food, shelter, and clothing, along with essential public services, were basic needs that development must achieve first and soon. Employment was a means to these ends, not merely an end in its own right. Much vagueness in the ILO's vision remained, though it called for beneficiary participation in the strategy to avoid the risk of top-down imposition. And while it held out the prospect of flexibility, the ILO anticipated the Bank's policies in arguing that the genius of 'basic needs' was setting an absolute minimum of essential goods and services that would have the virtues of universal application and easy measurement. 'Basic needs can be relative as well as absolute', the conference declaration explained. 'In the present situation, however, it is both legitimate and prudent to concentrate first on meeting basic needs in the absolute sense'. The wretched of the earth had simply waited too long for help to reach them.[13]

[12] For the move from late empire to the 1960s, see Daniel Roger Maul, *Human Rights, Development and Decolonization: The International Labour Organization, 1940–70* (New York, NY: Palgrave Macmillan, 2012), chap. 7 or Sandrine Kott, 'The Forced Labor Issue between Human and Social Rights, 1947–1957', *Humanity* 3, no. 3 (Winter 2012): 321–35.

[13] See Tripartite World Conference on Employment, Income Distribution and Social Progress and the International Division of Labour, *Employment, Growth, and Basic Needs: A One-World Problem* (Geneva: International Labour Office, 1976), 33. For various assignments of credit for the ILO "breakthrough", see Thomas G. Weiss et al., eds., *UN Voices: The Struggle for Development and Social Justice* (Bloomington, IN: Indiana University Press, 2005), 239–45.

What the World Bank began to flirt with, and the ILO propounded, various non-governmental groups ratified in the same period, in what contemporary observers considered a nearly celestial convergence of normally competing agendas. English economist and influential public educator about north-south issues Barbara Ward, shortly after becoming a baroness, chaired a session in Cocoyoc, Mexico, in fall 1974 that led to a widely publicized declaration insisting that 'human beings have basic needs: food, shelter, clothing, health, and education' and that 'any process of growth that does not lead to their fulfillment—or even worse, disrupts them—is a travesty of the idea of development'. Perhaps most interestingly, the Argentine geologist Amílcar Herrera led a team funded by the Fundación Bariloche that proposed that the wealthy end their 'overconsumption' in order to fulfil the basic needs of the global poor. Announced in the same year of 1976, his report was alone in the explosion of basic needs discourse to connect the wildfire search for 'agreed floors' to remedy poverty with 'an essentially egalitarian income distribution' as a distant goal. But like all the other proposals, it was primarily directed, in an era of many neo-Malthusian fears of overpopulation, at challenging the premise that statist growth could suffice for humanity.[14]

Despite the swift proliferation of basic needs rhetoric in these years across the spectrum of intergovernmental and non-governmental discussion, the World Bank became most closely associated with them in its reboot after the former US secretary of defense Robert McNamara during the Vietnam War became the institution's president in 1968. Despite McNamara's proximity to Great Society visions in the Democratic Party before his appointment, it took Haq's influence after 1970 to bring home to McNamara the importance of a direct attack on poverty. Its activity transformed under McNamara's direction thanks to more generous

[14] 'Declaration of Cocoyoc', *International Organization* 29, no. 3 (Summer 1975): 896; Amílcar Herrera, *Catastrophe or New Society?: A Latin American World Model* (Ottawa: International Development Research Center, 1976), esp. 103. The Bariloche ideas were especially associated with the United Nations Institute for Training and Research (UNITAR) and the Argentine turned Ivy League economist Graciela Chichilnisky. See the survey in D.P. Ghai, 'What Is a Basic Needs Approach All About?', in Ghai et al., *The Basic Needs Approach to Development: Some Issues Regarding Concepts and Methodology* (Geneva: International Labour Office, 1977) and more recently in Gilbert Rist, *The History of Development: From Western Origins to Global Faith*, 3rd ed. (London: Zed Books, 2008), 162–69; for Chichilnisky, see her 'Development Patterns and the International Order', *Journal of International Affairs* 31, no. 1 (Fall-Winter 1977): 275–304 and Sybille Duhautois' forthcoming dissertation on UNITAR and futurism.

lending. The institution's outlays that went directly towards poverty remediation around the world rose by a factor of six (from 5 to 30 per cent of its overall programmes) over the course of the next decade. All the same, at first the Bank moved only slightly to a position known at the time as 'redistribution with growth' before moving in the mid-1970s to assert ownership of the basic needs paradigm.[15]

In McNamara's evolving thinking over the crucial first decade of his stewardship of the Bank, he was far more apt to refer to 'absolute poverty' as the global scourge. The notion that there was some itemized schedule of necessities to which the Bank's lending should be partly targeted emerged slowly and never fully ousted the imperative of continued growth. Indeed, the crisis years of 1972–74 during which growth targets were often missed due to widespread drought and high oil prices caused McNamara considerable consternation, in part because the worst off suffered most. And he was not above worrying moralistically about the need for global 'equity' as the activism that culminated in the NIEO was making worldwide structural justice fodder for headlines.

All McNamara meant, however, was that inequality was unacceptable to the extent that the poorest were not benefited by it to some extent, or were actually made worse off. He was perfectly frank to the Bank governing board on this point in September 1977. 'For developing nations to make closing the gap [between them and wealthy nations] their primary development objective is simply a prescription for needless frustration.' As Haq had argued, abandonment of chimerical global equality allowed achievable goals. 'Unlike "closing the gap", reducing poverty is a realistic objective, indeed an indispensable one', McNamara explained. Uncoincidentally, it was in this same address that basic needs most clearly entered McNamara's rhetoric. 'The attack on absolute poverty—basic human needs and their satisfaction—cannot be forgotten, cannot be forever delayed, and cannot be finally denied by any global society that hopes tranquilly to endure.'[16]

Part of McNamara's own reasoning was candidly preventive: a world with escalating disparity in income and wealth that did not at least provide

[15] See the internal history Devesh Kapur et al., *The World Bank: Its First Half Century*, vol. 1, *History* (Washington, DC: Brookings Institution Press, 1997), chaps. 5–6 and Patrick Allan Sharma, *Robert McNamara's Other War: The World Bank and International Development* (Philadelphia, PA: University of Pennsylvania Press, 2017), chap. 3, esp. 67.

[16] Robert S. McNamara, *The McNamara Years at the World Bank: Major Policy Addresses, 1968–81* (Baltimore, MD: Johns Hopkins University Press, 1981), 277, 445–46, 472.

a floor of protection for the indigent was one ripe for disorder. After his humbling failures directing the Vietnam War, he was, after all, an old hand at grappling with discontent once it escalated into the impossible form of open insurrection. 'Too little, too late is history's most universal epitaph for political regimes which have lost their mandates', he now sagely observed. In stages from 1970, McNamara's move to a more and more explicit antipoverty agenda for the Bank reflected the insight that 'policies whose effect is to favor the rich at the expense of the poor are not only manifestly unjust, but in the end self-defeating'. But there was also much heartfelt rhetoric about the moral necessity of providing a sufficient minimum. It did not require a radical transformation in lifestyles in developed countries, he assured his Washington audiences repeatedly. It did require them to take seriously their age-old religious injunctions. 'The rich and powerful have a moral obligation to assist the poor and the weak.'[17]

Not only did McNamara in these decisive years come nowhere near the Bariloche radicalism that conditioned basic needs fulfilment for the worst off on decreasing consumption for the privileged (though he did constantly if somewhat half-heartedly call for more foreign aid beyond the fraction of 1 per cent of national income then canonized as obligatory). More importantly, the World Bank was widely seen as defining basic needs downwards even as it acted to be their premier standard-bearer in international affairs. Ultimately, for all the talk of a plurality of basic needs that did justice to the many-sidedness of human fulfilment, the Bank's true contribution was to monetize a basic minimum measurement to test whether continuing growth benefitted the most glaringly poor. Even as it was doing so, the main legacy of McNamara's Bank was to abet rise of Third World debt that spelled the doom of the NIEO advocacy for global equity and prepared the way for structural adjustment programmes later.[18]

The sheer radicalism with which the development community turned on national growth strategies spoke in large part to new ethical proprieties of wealthy observers of a world their prior schemes did not seem to have served well (unless, after Vietnam, it was clear they had made things worse). And while a few in the debate preserved a concern for equality within developing nations as the whole purpose of shifting antipoverty

[17] Ibid., 177, 165, 240.

[18] Rob Konkel, 'The Monetization of Global Poverty: The Concept of Poverty in World Bank History, 1944–90', *Journal of Global History* 9, no. 2 (July 2014): 276–300; Sharma, *McNamara's Other War*, chaps. 7 and 8.

strategies, the main effect of the departure was to narrow the optic to sufficiency. Under the reign of 'basic needs', development focused on short-term sufficiency targets within nations, so as to displace short-term national growth strategies that postponed both sufficiency and equality alike. Meanwhile, the embrace of the concern with basic provision within the nations of the global south almost never went along with a comparable stress on international distributive equality.

It was Amartya Sen who provides the most interesting case of the significance of the move to basic needs. The evidence shows clearly, after all, the adjustment of his central priorities in 1973–76, when he embraced the positions that have made him an icon in an age of sufficient distribution. Born in East Bengal (now Bangladesh) in 1933, and schooled in Rabindranath Tagore's educational ambiance at Santiniketan commune in West Bengal, Sen's earliest interests after taking his economics degree as a stellar undergraduate and graduate student at the University of Cambridge lay in the new theory of 'social choice'. Nonetheless, thanks to the influence of some of his Indian and English economics mentors, such as Marxist Maurice Dobb, Sen devoted his dissertation and first book to quasi-socialist development economics, offering his own theory of how to achieve growth and national launch. As late as 1972, he conceptualized the problems of needs and poverty within a larger framework of material inequality. Only after 1973, closing a period of writing about national inequality as he passed through various American and English universities, did Sen turn his attention to poverty and deprivation.[19]

Hired by the ILO as a consultant in the early 1970s as part of its World Employment Programme, Sen was on the ground floor of the basic needs movement. But he theorized it in a very different way. With memories of the Bengal famine of 1943 he had witnessed as a boy brought back by the world food crisis of these years, and especially the loss of a million men, women, and children to starvation in his now Bangladeshi home province, Sen called for more precision in theorizing poverty while stressing the conditions for and prevention of the worst deprivation that occurred in famine. For Sen, though hired as part of the ILO's broader programme, these events focused the mind on shorter-term visions, especially on how

[19] Amartya Sen, *Choice of Techniques: An Aspect of the Theory of Planned Economic Development* (Oxford: Blackwell, 1960); Amartya Sen, *On Economic Inequality* (Oxford: Clarendon Press, 1973), chap. 4; Timothy Shenk, *Maurice Dobb: Political Economist* (New York, NY: Springer, 2013), 172–74, 180.

vesting entitlements to provision in individuals would likely lead them to seek the sufficiency necessary to survive even disastrous harvests and other events that implicated an 'irreducible core of absolute deprivation'. Not attention to the extent of food or the growth of population but rather 'guaranteed minimum values of exchange owing to the social security system' would do most to avert famine and penury.[20]

Sen's focus on subsistence in famine and the straits of poverty generally was not only hived off from his continuing thinking about national inequality. Before the world food crisis, he had insisted on their interrelationship but now emphasized that 'inequality … is … a *distinct* issue from poverty'. Sen also negated any interest in international inequality. His sole mention of that concern through the age of the NIEO's rise and fall was to remark that 'in some discussions one is concerned not with the prevalence of poverty in a country in the form of the suffering of the *poor*, but with the relative opulence of the nation *as a whole*'. But he bypassed those discussions, except to share in Harvard University economist Richard Cooper's remark that it 'falls uncritically into the practice of … anthropomorphizing nations … as though they are individuals and extrapolating to them on the basis of average per capita income the various ethical arguments that have been developed to apply to individuals'. With collective ethics peripheral, including inequality among nations, vesting entitlements to basic needs in persons is what would now matter.[21]

Like repeated outbreaks of global famine, fears of 'limits to growth' on an overpopulated planet that pervaded the decade were clearly an important reason for the coming of basic needs in the 1970s, and the understandable imperative to ensure that ordinary people did not get lost in the crisis of prior statist growth programmes. But the NIEO was the

[20] Amartya Sen, *Poverty and Famines: An Essay on Entitlement and Deprivation* (Oxford: Clarendon Press, 1981), 7, 13n. For his first introduction of an entitlement approach, see Amartya Sen, 'Famines as Failures of Exchange Entitlements', *Economic and Political Weekly* 11, no. 31/33 (August 1976): 1273–80. For his other ILO study, see Amartya Sen, *Employment, Technology, and Development* (Oxford: Clarendon Press, 1975).

[21] Sen, *Poverty and Famines*, 10, and 14–17 on the analytical distinction between poverty (or sufficiency generally) and inequality; Richard Cooper cited in Amartya Sen, 'Ethical Issues in Income Distribution: National and International', in *The World Economic Order: Past and Prospects*, eds. Sven Grassman and Erik Lundberg (London: Macmillan, 1981), 477. For his earlier consolidation of poverty and inequality, besides *On Economic Inequality*, see Amartya Sen, 'Poverty, Inequality, and Unemployment: Some Conceptual Issues in Measurement', *Economic and Political Weekly* 8, no. 31/33 (August 1973): 1457–64, rpt. in augmented form in Srinivasan and Bardhan, eds., *Poverty and Income Distribution in India*.

historically unique factor, not ongoing poverty and death, outrageous though they certainly were. The sudden revulsion at the fact that that postcolonial visions of distribution lacked basic provision for individuals arguably said as much or more about the horrified as about the horror. As one insightful observer put it, the spiking anxiety about the global poor in World Bank and other circles mostly followed from '*their* past neglect of what a number of Third World governments and many development economists [there] have for a long time taken to be a major area of concern'.[22]

As a vision of minimum provision, basic needs turned away from national inequality on the brink of its explosion as a wrong apart from poverty, or international equality as a good that states might reasonably pursue. In case anyone was confused, immediately after the NIEO burst on the scene, the Aspen Institute convened a series of groups to propose 'a new international economic order *to meet human needs*'. 'Nations are not people', its report concluded, sounding a common theme about where the global south went wrong. 'Alongside the "gap" between the average citizens of poor and rich societies, equally significant "gaps" were becoming obvious *within* countries. ... It is high time that the world community come together to set agreed floors under individual human needs.' By the late 1970s, in turn, it was routine to attack basic needs as a transparent rationale for bypassing the NIEO demands and locking in servicing the poor as the fundamental task in the global south, each country doing so on its own in informally dependent and unchanging relationship to former colonial masters.[23]

Meeting in Belgrade in summer 1978, the foreign ministers of the Non-Aligned Movement (an alliance of mostly southern states), voiced a near-universal suspicion of sudden interest in the basic needs of individuals. Not that minimum provision for all was unimportant, but it needed to be viewed 'as one of the many priority objectives for national policy, and not as a substitute for authentic development'. And 'at the international level', even more important, 'this strategy should not obscure the urgent need for fundamental change in the world economic order'. Even in the United Nations Human Rights Commission, Indian delegate Vijaya Lakshmi

[22] Deepak Lal, 'Distribution and Development: A Review Article', *World Development* 4, no. 9 (1976): 727.

[23] *The Planetary Bargain: Proposals for a New International Economic Order to Meet Human Needs* (New York, NY: Aspen Institute for Humanistic Studies, 1975), 16–17.

Pandit (Jawaharlal Nehru's sister) insisted that 'equity and social justice were primary requisites for the implementation of economic, social, and cultural rights everywhere' and consequently worried that 'the basic needs strategy has been used as an excuse to imply that the only problem of developing countries is [providing] a minimum necessary for subsistence'. 'Poverty cannot be eradicated by isolating it from the system', Pakistani intellectual Altaf Gauhar added bitterly, 'any more than disease can be cured by suppressing the symptoms. And this is what is wrong with the "Basic Needs" approach'.[24]

To be sure, there was no reason a concern for using some of their surplus to address grinding poverty and starvation could not fit in the NIEO agenda of the postcolonial states. In expert fora such as one convened by UNESCO in 1978, the precise relationship of basic needs, human rights, and the NIEO was the subject of an outpouring of earnest discussion. What held true in theory did not necessarily follow in practice, however, especially since basic needs had never been applied to accelerating northern consumption alongside southern poverty. Prominent theorist Johan Galtung insisted that, given 'the way the BN approach has been launched, and applied predominately *only* to the Third World, the Third World has every reason to regard it as a ploy for side-tracking the world economic issue raised by the NIEO'. More than this, it was not implausible for the new states to fear that basic needs were going to be one more means of eroding their hard-won sovereignty. 'In the light of past history, the First World's disavowal of interventionist intentions does not carry conviction, nor does its protestation that the BN approach will not have any unintended consequences', Galtung summarized.[25]

True, some treated basic needs as a valuable supplement to the NIEO, none more interestingly than Haq, the figure most responsible for the

[24] Declaration of the Conference of Ministers for Foreign Affairs, Belgrade, July 25–30, 1978, in *The Collected Documents of the Non-Aligned Movement, 1961–1982* (Baghdad, 1982), 321; Commission on Human Rights, Summary Record of the 1489th Meeting, February 21, 1979, UN Doc. E/CN.4/A/SR.1489, para. 29 for the first citation and Alston, 'Human Rights and Basic Needs', 26–27 for the second; Altaf Gauhar, 'What Is Wrong with Basic Needs?' *Third World Quarterly* 4, no. 3 (July 1982): xxii.

[25] UNESCO, Expert Meeting on Human Rights, Basic Needs, and the Establishment of a New International Economic Order, Paris, June 19–23, 1978, UN Doc. SS.78/Conf.630/12; Johan Galtung, 'The New International Economic Order and the Basic Needs Approach', *Alternatives* 4 (1978–79): 462–63.

coming of 'basic needs' to development economics after declaring the dream of global equality a fantasy. How Haq's engagement with the NIEO in the mid-1970s squared with his insistence earlier and before expert audiences that the whole rationale for a turn to basic needs was that the south would never catch up to the north never did emerge with much clarity. Unlike Sen, however, Haq agreed with popular rhetoric of the time that 'the search for a new economic order is a natural second stage in the liberation of the developing countries'. 'It is my own conviction', he added resentfully in Sweden in November 1974, mere weeks before the NIEO declaration, 'that the developed countries simply do not care ... what happens in the Third World'. In response to the bromide that 'the Third World has to reconcile itself' to the existing international order, Haq responded that 'the Third World *is* the future international order'. And in the mid-1970s Haq's arguments for the redistribution, if not directly of income and wealth, then of 'future growth opportunities', was occasionally noticed in the global north.[26]

Haq understood something like the NIEO to be the international equivalent of the coming of the national welfare state, achieved once again through strategic pressure from below. 'On the national level', Haq explained in 1975, 'a turning point was reached in the 1930s, when the New Deal elevated the working classes to partners in development and accepted them as an essential part of the consuming society. On the international level, we still have not arrived at that philosophic breakthrough when the development of the poor nations is considered an essential element. ... [Yet] we may be nearing that philosophical bridge.' This time around, pressure from below was provided by dissident states as the functional equivalent of trade unions: entities that represented individuals, who could not exert sufficient power on their own for change. And by the end of the decade Haq wrote sensitively of how the stampede of development experts and donor nations, not to mention the United States government, to care for global poverty was understandably leading to alarm in the global south about distraction from a fuller-fledged agenda. It had

[26] Mahbub ul Haq, 'Inequities of the Old Economic Order', Overseas Development Council Development Paper No. 22 (1976), rpt. in Charles K. Wilber, ed., *The Political Economy of Development and Underdevelopment*, 2nd ed. (New York: Random House, 1979), 184; Mahbub ul Haq, 'Development and Independence', *Development Dialogue* 1 (1974): 7; Stephen S. Rosenfeld, 'On Inequality Among Nations', *Washington Post*, October 22, 1976.

gone so far by 1980 as to put at risk the compatibility of concerns for international and intranational distribution, global equality, and basic needs. That basic needs were so diversionary, Haq affirmed, was predictably causing the global south to 'throw out the baby with the bathwater'.[27]

Positioning himself as an impassioned Third World intellectual, Haq in the end sought a uniquely balanced and conciliatory position, adopting an ethical rage at global inequality but without ignoring national distribution and governance. He participated in the founding of the Third World Forum, an association of global southern intellectuals, and chaired its task force on thinking through a new international economic order. Somewhat subversively, Haq went so far as to observe that the risk of rebellion within states of which McNamara warned as a rationale for more generosity applied globally too and for the sake of equality not just sufficiency. But as the NIEO waned, Haq increasingly concluded that 'the real task of development lay back home' and indeed that 'no degree of international agitation can ever obscure that fact; no amount of international resource transfers can ever substitute for national decisions on fundamental reforms'. He added:

> The intellectuals from the third world face a cruel dilemma here. If they stress the issue of reform of national orders ahead of the international order, they run the risk of providing a convenient excuse to the rich nations to postpone serious discussions on the reform of the present world order as well as of losing the support of their own national governments. Yet what can possibly be gained by greater equality of opportunity internationally if it is denied to the vast majority within the national orders?

Paul Streeten, Haq's fellow World Bank economist, agreed that the overriding necessity was to explain that basic needs by no means interfered with the NIEO. In fact, putting them together saved each from its own worst pathologies, basic needs from 'degenerating into a global charity program' and the NIEO from serving postcolonial elites alone. For all their promise, however, such rhetorically conciliatory attempts to make basic needs get along with some version of the NIEO were not representative.[28]

[27] Mahbub ul Haq, 'Towards a New Planetary Bargain', remarks in Richard N. Gardner, ed., *New Structures for Economic Interdependence* (Rensselaerville: Institute on Man and Science, 1975), 20; Mahbub ul Haq, 'Basic Needs and the New International Economic Order', in Khadija Haq, ed., *Dialogue for a New Order* (New York, NY: Pergamon, 1980), 235–36.

[28] Haq, *Poverty Curtain*, 149, 184–85; Third World Forum, *Proposals for a New International Economic Order* (Mexico City: Third World Forum, 1975); Mahbub ul Haq, 'The Third World Forum: Intellectual Self-Reliance', *International Development Review* 1

There was not even much subterfuge about it: basic needs were often openly advertised as a means to seek the weak point of the NIEO nations, delegitimizing their ethical claims by stigmatizing their holdover 'British socialism' and political misrule, as American Daniel Patrick Moynihan did in a widely read *Commentary* article and then as United Nations ambassador. And others observed that basic needs was more marketable a program for the rich facing a hierarchical world. As one analyst observed, 'For some bilateral donors, a B[asic] H[uman] N[eeds] approach is perceived to be more clearly humanitarian and is perhaps more likely to be supported by a domestic constituency that does not generally view foreign assistance as a major priority'.[29]

Can global antipoverty be meaningfully analogized to universal basic income schemes? It can, and not just on chronological grounds. Both are causes stressing the moral importance of what I have called sufficient provision, as opposed to egalitarian distribution, of the good things in life. Universal basic income schemes do more aggregation and monetization in order to reach a single figure, compared to basic needs arguments that

(1975): 8–11; Streeten, 'Basic Needs: Premises and Promises', 143. For rueful conclusions that postcolonial states were on their own, Mahbub ul Haq, 'Beyond the Slogan of South-South Cooperation', *World Development* 8, no. 10 (October 1980): 743–51 and, for similar conclusions about the need for the south not to wait around for the north to change, see the influential Eliot Janeway lectures at Princeton by Jamaican economist W. Arthur Lewis, *The Evolution of the International Economic Order* (Princeton, NJ: Princeton University Press, 1978). For conciliatory positions see also R.H. Green and Hans W. Singer, 'Toward a Rational and Equitable New International Economic Order: A Case for Negotiated Structural Changes', *World Development* 3, no. 6 (June 1975): 427–44 and Paul Streeten, 'The Dynamics of the New Poor Power', in G.K. Helleiner, *A World Divided: The Less Developed Countries in the International Economy* (Cambridge: Cambridge University Press, 1976). This was a permanent concern of Streeten's; see Paul Streeten, 'Basic Needs and the New International Economic Order', in *Perspectives on Economic Development: Essays in the Honour of W. Arthur Lewis*, eds. T. E. Barker, et al. (Lanham, MD: University Press of America, 1982), and Paul Streeten, 'Approaches to a New International Economic Order', *World Development* 10, no. 1 (1982): 1–17. And Haq still defended the NIEO agenda into the 1980s, for example in the University of Texas colloquy with Walt Rostow recorded in Roger D. Hansen, ed., *The 'Global Negotiation' and Beyond: Toward North-South Accommodation in the 1980s* (Austin: Lyndon B. Johnson School of Public Affairs, 1981), esp. 53–56.

[29] See Daniel J. Sargent, *A Superpower Transformed: The Remaking of American Foreign Policy in the 1970s* (Oxford: Oxford University Press, 2016), chap. 6, esp. 178–79; Danny M. Leipziger, 'The Basic Human Needs Approach and North-South Relations', in Edwin P. Reubens, ed., *The Challenge of the New International Economic Order* (Boulder: Westview Press, 1981), 260.

insisted that the different needs of human beings were plural and not fulfilled simply by providing what they cost. (As I have studied elsewhere, it was precisely for this reason that some advocates of basic needs and human rights were in such close dialogue in the 1970s and 1980s, without always coming to terms about their relationship.[30])

Notwithstanding this difference, theories and practices of basic needs in global development have been compatible with neglect of inequality—even with its expansion. And as many have argued, this may be the most serious failing of universal basic income schemes too. Both work on floors, leaving other projects to obliterate ceilings on hierarchy. Ignoring matters of unequal income, wealth, and power, fulfilling basic income and needs may entrench rather than undermine our worst hierarchies, locally and globally.

[30] Moyn, *Not Enough*, chap. 6.

CHAPTER 10

Jobs or Income Guarantees? The Politics of Universal Basic Income and Cash Transfers in Southern Africa

E. Fouksman

What is the universal basic income debate like in the global South? In many ways, basic income in the developing world has been having a surge of attention and advocacy in parallel to the resurgence of interest in the policy in the global North over the last decade.[1] In the global South, this wave of interest and activism has been broader in scope than UBI alone. Rather, basic income has been a part of evolving conversations around universal social protection (as both a universal human right and an aim of social and development policy) and cash transfers (as a more efficient alternative to and benchmark for other development interventions, as well as a

[1] Karl Widerquist, 'Basic Income's Third Wave', *Open Democracy*, October 18, 2017, https://www.opendemocracy.net/beyondslavery/karl-widerquist/basic-income-s-third-wave.

E. Fouksman (✉)
King's College London, London, UK

University of the Witwatersrand, Johannesburg, South Africa

University of Oxford, Oxford, UK
e-mail: liz.fouksman@kcl.ac.uk

P. Sloman et al. (eds.), *Universal Basic Income in Historical Perspective*, https://doi.org/10.1007/978-3-030-75706-9_10

way to achieve universal social protection). Much like universal basic income, cash transfers give cash to individuals on a regular basis. Unlike universal basic income, cash transfers can be (though need not be) conditional on certain behaviour (such as vaccination or school attendance), targeted to certain populations (such as children), and are usually time-bound rather than ongoing. Over the past two decades, cash transfers have become the favourite intervention of many international development organizations, and the focus of poverty alleviation strategies of many middle-income countries. Cash transfers have been implemented by the national governments of countries as varied as Mexico, Brazil, and South Africa, researched by intergovernmental organizations such as the World Bank, and fund-raised for and piloted by development NGOs such as GiveDirectly. Covid-19 expanded this interest further, with many countries using cash as a way to cushion the economic hardship caused by the pandemic.[2]

The popularity of cash transfer programmes speaks to a deep-seated disillusionment with the austerity policies of structural adjustment imposed by the IMF in the global South in the 1980s and 1990s. Structural adjustment emerged out of the confluence of the global debt crisis and the rise of neoliberal economic hegemony in the early 1980s. Countries had to adhere to the conditions of the programmes in order to receive further international loans and aid to service their debts. These conditions varied between countries, but largely focused on reducing fiscal deficits, privatization of state assets and trade liberalization. With the IMF's focus on macroeconomic stability and growth as the key solutions to poverty, as well as an insistence on limiting government spending, the programmes limited social and welfare investment, furthering both economic insecurity and inequality across the global South.[3] By the late 1990s and early 2000s,

[2] M. Garcia and C. Moore, *The Cash Dividend: The Rise of Cash Transfer Programs in Sub-Saharan Africa* (Washington, DC: World Bank, 2012); The World Bank, 'Should We Just Give Cash?', October 22, 2015, http://www.worldbank.org/en/news/feature/2015/10/20/should-we-just-give-cash; U. Gentilini, M. Almenfi, I. Orton, P. Dale, *Social Protection and Jobs Responses to COVID-19: A Real-Time Review of Country Measures*, (Washington, DC: World Bank, 2020); Ariel Fiszbein and Norbert R Schady, *Conditional Cash Transfers: Reducing Present and Future Poverty*, World Bank Policy Research Report (Washington, DC: World Bank, 2009).

[3] Doris A. Oberdabernig, 'The Effects of Structural Adjustment Programs on Poverty and Income Distribution', *Seminar in International Economics, Vienna* 4 (2010); Timon Forster, Alexander E. Kentikelenis, Bernhard Reinsberg, Thomas H. Stubbs, and Lawrence P. King,

even proponents of the programmes began to acknowledge that state institutions and spending on welfare and public goods had a role to play in providing economic security and reducing inequality.[4]

Yet at the same time, cash transfers address the continuing preoccupations of mainstream international development practice with government transparency, decentralization, and economic growth.[5] Giving money directly to the poor also sits well with the ongoing salience of participatory approaches to development, which argue that the poor themselves know best what they need to escape poverty.[6] Cash transfers have thus become the key mechanism of a widespread interest in social protection among bodies such as the United Nations, the World Bank, and the International Labour Organization.[7] And because their impacts are easy to measure against a control (and because running basic income experiments has a long history since the 1970s), cash transfers fit exceptionally well into the current empirical turn of development economics, which has increasingly focused on randomized control trials to test the efficacy of development programmes.[8] This itself has been part of a broader evidence-based turn in social policy. Researchers have thus amassed a large body of quantitative evidence on the impact of cash transfers, making them appealing to both development professionals and proponents of income guarantees.[9]

All of this has led to a high level of enthusiasm and optimism amongst scholars of social protection in the global South. Some have termed the flowering of cash transfer programmes 'the development revolution from

'How Structural Adjustment Programs Affect Inequality: A Disaggregated Analysis of IMF Conditionality, 1980–2014', *Social Science Research*, 80 (2019): 83–113.

[4] Alfredo Saad-Filho, 'Growth, Poverty and Inequality: From Washington Consensus to Inclusive Growth', *UN/DESA Working Papers*, ST/ESA/2010/DWP (New York, 2010), http://www.un.org/esa/desa/papers/2010/wp100_2010.pdf.

[5] Richard Ballard, 'Geographies of Development II: Cash Transfers and the Reinvention of Development for the Poor', *Progress in Human Geography* 37, no. 6 (2013): 811–21.

[6] R. Chambers, 'Putting the Last First', in *The Living Economy: A New Economics in the Making*, ed. P. Ekins (London: Routledge, 1986).

[7] International Labour Office, *Social Security for All: Building Social Protection Floors and Comprehensive Social Security Systems. The Strategy of the International Labour Organization*, 2012; International Labour Office and World Bank, 'Joint Statement by World Bank Group President Jim Yong Kim and ILO Director General Guy Ryder', 2015.

[8] A. V. Banerjee and E. Duflo, *Poor Economics: A Radical Rethinking of the Way to Fight Global Poverty* (New York, NY: PublicAffairs, 2011).

[9] Francesca Bastagli et al., *Cash Transfers: What Does the Evidence Say?* (London: Overseas Development Institute, 2016).

the global South', or 'a new politics of distribution'.[10] Many such scholars see all varieties of cash transfers, including universal basic income experiments, as closely related. Take for instance Joseph Hanlon, Armando Barrientos, and David Hulme, who in their book *Just Give Money to the Poor* (2010) use a basic income pilot in Namibia, pension grants in South Africa, and conditional, means-tested child benefits in Brazil as examples of the same phenomenon of 'giving money to the poor'.[11] In some ways this optimism has been justified: at roughly the same time as the international development community has become infatuated with cash transfers, several countries in the global South—including India, Brazil, Namibia, and South Africa—have held serious national conversations around instituting universal basic income as national policy. Yet none of these countries have actually implemented a UBI, and several have chosen limited and means-tested cash transfer policies as an *alternative* to basic income.

This chapter will use the recent history of UBI in the global South, and in particular in South Africa and Namibia, to make the case that delineating between different ways of 'just giving money to the poor' is crucial to understanding the politics of UBI. I argue that the tendency to group together a wide array of proposed and implemented forms of income transfers is not only conceptually misleading, but can be dangerous for advocates of universal basic income. In particular, I contend that the critical difference between various cash transfer policies lies in their targeting—in delineating who should and should not benefit from the cash. In many countries that have implemented cash transfers, the beneficiaries are explicitly those who are *physically unable to work*, in particular children and the elderly, making cash transfers not so different from traditional welfare schemes in the global North—and very different indeed from a true UBI.

I will argue here that this widespread emphasis on aiding those physically unable to participate in labour markets is a key and purposeful political choice in the design of social protection policies. This chapter makes the case that such a delineation of beneficiaries is linked to longstanding

[10] Joseph Hanlon, Armando Barrientos, and David Hulme, *Just Give Money to the Poor: The Development Revolution from the Global South* (Sterling, VA: Kumarian Press, 2010); James Ferguson, *Give a Man a Fish: Reflections on the New Politics of Distribution* (Durham, NC: Duke University Press, 2015).

[11] Hanlon, Barrientos, and Hulme, *Just Give Money to the Poor*. The Bolsa Familia cash transfer program in Brazil is both means tested (as are old age grants in South Africa), and includes behavioural conditionalities around sending children to school and getting vaccinations.

distinctions between the deserving and undeserving poor, to a widely held insistence that work remains the key mechanism of resource distribution, and ultimately to the fact that no country in the global South (and beyond) has yet adapted a full-fledged universal guaranteed income. In particular, the chapter uses the history of basic income campaigns and cash transfers in Namibia and South Africa to explore the links between political, social, and cultural blocks around universality. I draw both on this history and on my own ongoing qualitative research in the two countries to unravel the way people understand money and deservingness and transform these understandings into political agendas. In particular, I argue that three ideological factors have played key roles in the politics of UBI in southern Africa: cost, productivism, and political framing. I look at the ways in which spurious estimates of the cost of the policy have been successfully deployed as a tool to justify a rejection that is in fact predicated on a productivist insistence that jobs—not grants—are ideologically and morally the right focus of social and economic public policy. Yet I also make the case that part of what has made this rejection possible is that UBI has frequently been framed in developmental and welfare terms by its proponents in southern Africa, rather than as a radical form of distributory justice. Reframing the policy in terms of wealth and racial inequality, postcolonial reparations, or rightful shares of natural resource wealth could thus open up future possibilities for a more durable new 'politics of distribution' (Ferguson 2015).

Fertile Ground: A Note on Context

Why look to Namibia and South Africa to understand the recent history of UBI politics? The two countries have socio-economic and historical dynamics that should in theory make them ideal sites for a politics supporting radical redistributory measures. They both have a history of settler colonialism, followed by neo-colonial apartheid regimes based on the racially justified exploitation and dispossession of the majority of the population by a white minority. (Indeed, Namibia was itself a colony of the South African apartheid regime.) Both achieved independence in the 1990s and have become functioning democracies, in which the party of the liberation struggle now holds political power. Both of these liberation parties have a political history of radical left and socialist leanings before independence, but neither has enacted radical redistributory systems after independence. Rather, both governments have expanded on their inherited welfare systems aimed at those physically unable to participate in the labour force. In Namibia, this is a system of social grants for the elderly, orphans, and the disabled. In South Africa, this is a more expansive system that now additionally gives grants to the caretakers of *all* children under the age of eighteen. All of these grants are means-tested, apart from Namibia's pension grant.

Despite these forms of social protection, Namibia and South Africa are now some of the most unequal countries in the world.[12] Both have extremely high rates of unemployment: Namibia's stood at 33 per cent in 2018, and South Africa's at 29 per cent in 2019, and once 'discouraged jobseekers' (those that are not actively looking for work) are included the unemployment rate in South Africa was at 39 per cent. Unemployment has only worsened during the Covid-19 pandemic. Despite strong labour unions, South Africa has a liberalized labour market and a high level of outsourcing and contract workers. Despite this, South Africa is the site of quite a high level of automation, particularly in the agriculture and service sectors: as a telling example, tickets in South Africa's cinemas are usually sold by a machine, not a human. And both South Africa and Namibia are rich in natural resources, in particular in mineral wealth.

The Promise of Basic Income in Namibia and South Africa

Such histories and present realities make South Africa and Namibia seem ripe for radical redistribution. And in fact, both South Africa and Namibia have considered implementing UBI as national policy. South Africa seriously considered the policy in the late 1990s and early 2000s.[13] A coalition of trade unions (including COSATU, one of South Africa's most politically important unions), church groups, academics, and NGOs pushed for the policy within the context of debates around social policy, welfare, unemployment, and poverty alleviation at the time, and presented it to a variety of government committees and departments tasked with such

[12] World Bank, 'GINI Index (World Bank Estimate)', 2018, http://data.worldbank.org/indicator/SI.POV.GINI/.

[13] For a more detailed history of basic income grant debates in South Africa beyond the scope of this chapter, see Franco Barchiesi, 'South African Debates on the Basic Income Grant: Wage Labour and the Post-Apartheid Social Policy', *Journal of Southern African Studies* 33, no. 3 (2007): 561–75, https://doi.org/10.1080/03057070701475575.

questions. The coalition pitched the proposal as an effective way to deal with South Africa's ongoing high rates of poverty, and the trade unions saw basic income as a way to ease the distributive burden on their members—particularly workers who had to spend their salaries supporting unemployed dependents.[14] COSATU also saw UBI as a way of supporting 'employability and opportunities for self-employment'.[15]

These efforts led to serious consideration of and even support for UBI in the South African government. Most promisingly, the government-appointed Committee of Inquiry into a Comprehensive System of Social Security for South Africa (known as the Taylor Committee, after its chair) supported a basic income grant. In its 2002 report, the Committee proposed a universal basic income grant of ZAR100 (around US $10 at the time), recouped and funded by progressive taxation.[16] However, the Committee was also careful to seek political consensus by proposing that the UBI be rolled out gradually, alongside government work programmes.[17]

Like South Africa, Namibia also had its basic income moment. In Namibia, a small basic income was proposed by the government's tax commission (NAMTAX) in 2002, to be financed by progressive income and luxury goods taxation. A coalition formed around the idea, largely spearheaded by leadership within the Evangelical Lutheran Church (which

[14] J. Seekings, 'Basic Income Activism in South Africa, 1997–2019', in *Political Activism and Basic Income Guarantee*, eds. R. Caputo and L. Liu (Cham, Switzerland: Palgrave Macmillan, 2020); Guy Standing and Michael Samson, *A Basic Income Grant for South Africa* (Cape Town, South Africa: University of Cape Town Press, 2003).

[15] Barchiesi, 'South African Debates on the Basic Income Grant'.

[16] An important aside about cost, universality, and taxation: while a UBI is disbursed universally, almost all UBI funding proposals suggest that it be funded through some sort of redistributory tax scheme. This in effect would mean that *net contributors* to the scheme would be the rich (who would via taxes return their basic income to state coffers, and then contribute to funding the UBI for others), and *net beneficiaries*, would be those with lower incomes. This is a critical point, as it underscores both that with an appropriate tax code, a UBI is redistributory and in its net effect targeted at the poor, and that basic income's net cost (after all taxes and transfers are accounted for) is far less than its gross cost (see footnote 21 for more details on gross vs. net cost). For more details on funding and universality, see E. Fouksman, 'Why Basic Income Costs Far Less Than You Think', *The Conversation*, August 14, 2018; Karl Widerquist, 'The Cost of Basic Income: Back-of-the-Envelope Calculations', *Basic Income Studies* 12, no. 2 (2017).

[17] Barchiesi, 'South African Debates on the Basic Income Grant'; Taylor Committee, *Transforming the Present—Protecting the Future. Report of the Committee of Inquiry into a Comprehensive System of Social Security for South Africa* (Pretoria: Government Printer, 2002).

holds wide influence in Namibia) and consisting of NGOs, other church groups, academics, and trade unions (including NUNWU, Namibia's largest trade union federation). The BIG (Basic Income Grant) Coalition focused its efforts on convincing the Namibian government that UBI was 'both an efficient and an affordable tool to fight poverty'.[18] The trade unions saw a basic income as a useful 'fall-back position for the retrenched workers', while emphasizing that the private sector must simultaneously keep creating 'decent jobs'.[19] Like its counterpart in South Africa, the coalition framed UBI as an effective form of welfare provision and poverty eradication, and trade unions viewed the policy as an augmentation to job creation—a path to economic participation and a form of social protection and unemployment insurance for their members.

The key achievement of the Namibian coalition was the implementation of a two-year basic income pilot in the village of Otjivero in 2008 and 2009. The pilot gave every resident NAM$100 (then about US $10) per month, funded by donors (largely German church groups). The results of the pilot were extremely positive: poverty, malnutrition, and crime dropped dramatically; economic engagement and school attendance rose; and alcohol consumption and 'sin spending' did not increase.[20] Otjivero community members enthusiastically took ownership of the project via a local committee and through outreach tours to other parts of the country.

Turning Away from Universality

However, both the South African and the Namibian state ultimately refused to implement a UBI. In Namibia the IMF advised the Namibian government in 2005 that the policy was unaffordable—based on incorrect figures that calculated the gross rather than the net cost, and forewent a

[18] Herbert Jauch, 'The Rise and Fall of the Basic Income Grant Campaign: Lessons from Namibia', *Global Labour Journal* 6, no. 3 (2015): 341.

[19] Peter Naholo, 'Speech of Mr. P. Naholo (Acting General Secretary NUNW)', in *The Basic Income Grant in Namibia Resource Book*, eds. Claudia Haarmann and Dirk Haarmann (Windhoek: Desk for Social Development (DfSD), Evangelical Lutheran Church in the Republic of Namibia (ELCRN), 2005), 8.

[20] Claudia Haarmann et al., *Making the Difference! The BIG in Namibia: Basic Income Grant Assessment Report, April 2009* (Windhoek: Basic Income Grant Coalition, 2009); Claudia Haarmann and Dirk Haarmann, 'Piloting Basic Income in Namibia—Critical Reflections on the Process and Possible Lessons', in *Pathways to a Basic Income: 14th Congress of the Basic Income Earth Network (BIEN)* (Munich, 2012), https://doi.org/https://basicincome.org/bien/pdf/munich2012/haarmann.pdf.

tax analysis of the policy.[21] Though the BIG Coalition vocally pointed out the basic arithmetical errors made by the IMF, and eventually got the IMF to admit that its calculations were flawed, the IMF delegation refused to formally withdraw its recommendations or rework its report. The Namibian government initially vacillated between accepting the IMF's rhetoric of unaffordability and backing a UBI. Between 2007 and 2010 Namibia saw live political debate and some cautious political support of UBI, but in 2010 President Pohamba dismissed the idea, and reiterated his objections in 2014 in a parliamentary debate. His reasoning was based on both a misunderstanding of universality (he questioned why the rich should get a payment, ignoring the fact that the rich would return their basic income through the tax system, and then contribute to the scheme via increased taxation) and a productivist logic which emphasized deservingness via hard work. Pohamba stated in parliament that people 'who do nothing' should not receive money and that the grant would make people lazy.[22] Trade unions followed the president's lead, leaving the BIG Coalition in 2010 (though with much internal contestation).[23]

Hopes were reignited in 2014 with the election of President Geingob, a long-time BIG Coalition supporter who had contributed financially to the Otjivero pilot. Geingob generated further excitement by appointing Bishop Kameeta, a key leader of the coalition, as head of the Ministry of Poverty Eradication and Social Welfare. Yet Geingob's presidency has failed to substantiate these hopes. In 2016 he released the Harambee

[21] In other words, the IMF made the common mistake of calculating the cost of basic income by simply multiplying the size of the grant by the population of the country. This is the *gross cost*, and it fails to account for the fact that the tax system would 'claw-back' the basic income from those that do not need it—thus a proportion of the population would simply receive the UBI and then return it via taxes, without any actual cost to the state. The real or ***net cost*** must take into account both transfers ***and*** taxes, and thus accounts for the difference between net contributors to and net beneficiaries of UBI. It is inevitably a small fraction of the gross cost (depending on the accompanying tax scheme). For more on the difference between gross and net cost estimates, and the importance of focusing on net cost, see table 1 and figure 1 on page 79 of Thomas Straubhaar, 'On the Economics of a Universal Basic Income', *Intereconomics* 52, no. 2 (2017), and Scott Santens, 'The Cost of Universal Basic Income is the Net Transfer Amount, Not the Gross Price Tag', *Medium*, July 10, 2017, https://medium.com/basic-income/the-cost-of-universal-basic-income-is-the-net-transfer-amount-not-the-gross-price-tag-acb8aa5eab73.

[22] Haarmann and Haarmann, 'Piloting Basic Income in Namibia—Critical Reflections on the Process and Possible Lessons', 8; Jauch, 'The Rise and Fall of the Basic Income Grant Campaign: Lessons from Namibia', 345.

[23] Jauch, 'The Rise and Fall of the Basic Income Grant Campaign'.

Prosperity Plan, which only mentioned basic income in order to explicitly state that it was *not* part of the plan, and focussed instead on creating food banks and infrastructure-oriented youth work programmes.[24] Nor does Namibia's Fifth National Development Plan (2017–2022) mention basic income, though it does speak about streamlining and expanding social protection—alongside encouraging the work ethic.[25] In the spring of 2018 the Ministry of Poverty Eradication and Social Welfare released both a Strategic Plan and a Blueprint. The Strategic Plan only mentions 'a revised BIG' in passing in a table, but never revisits or expands on the reference (or even explains what the acronym stands for).[26] The Blueprint mentions the Otjivero pilot and the benefits of basic income, but does not mention implementing the policy.[27] It does discuss expanding Namibia's current social grant system to include 'the unemployed and the poor and vulnerable persons' not currently covered by grants.[28] However, this is mentioned briefly, and lacks any details on implementation. It is also buried between the objectives of promoting better access to existing grants (implying that Namibia's existing targeted system will stay in place); 'graduating' people from social assistance to 'productive and sustainable activities' (indicating an ongoing focus on job creation rather than redistribution); and establishing a system of food banks (signalling that the poor are not to be trusted to spend cash on the right basic goods). The latest Harambee Prosperity Plan II, meant to run from 2021–2025, mentions a *Conditional* Basic Income Grant, which could in 2022 replace food banks and food parcels, but would only be available to the very poorest. This is also mentioned briefly, without details on targeting or implementation. Indeed, President Geingob has in 2021 stated that he is not convinced by a universal basic income, once again referencing reservations around cost and universality. Thus, while a UBI is certainly still possible in

[24] Republic of Namibia, *Harambee Prosperity Plan, 2016/17–2019/20: Namibian Government's Action Plan towards Prosperity for All* (Windhoek: Republic of Namibia, 2016), 39–40.

[25] Republic of Namibia, *Namibia's Fifth National Development Plan* (Windhoek: Republic of Namibia, 2017), 54.

[26] Ministry of Poverty Eradication and Social Welfare, *Strategic Plan 2017/2018–2021/2022* (Windhoek: Republic of Namibia, 2018), 14.

[27] Ministry of Poverty Eradication and Social Welfare, *Blueprint on Wealth Redistribution and Poverty Eradication* (Windhoek: Republic of Namibia, 2018), 37.

[28] Ibid., 44.

Namibia, does not seem very likely in the near future—nor does it seem to be a favoured policy of the executive branch.

In South Africa, the turn away from UBI happened earlier. Though the Taylor Committee recommended a basic income as South Africa's poverty alleviation policy, by 2003 it was clear that the government and the African National Congress more broadly were set against the policy. The Treasury and the Minister of Finance insisted that a basic income would be unaffordable and financially unsustainable. But such claims were spurious: a number of concrete and highly feasible costing proposals had been put forward by trade unions and by the basic income coalition.[29] In examining the state's rhetoric around UBI at the time, the true point of disagreement emerges: a preference for job creation over redistribution as the main approach to poverty alleviation.

President Mbeki declared in his 2003 State of the Nation Address that the government should 'reduce the number of people dependent on social welfare, increasing the numbers that rely for their livelihood on normal participation in the economy'. That same year a government spokesperson insisted that the best form of social inclusion of the poor was 'the opportunity, the dignity and the rewards of work'.[30] Having rejected a universal grant, the South African state went on instead both to experiment with public work programmes, and to expand its existing, targeted social grant system. It used reforms such as gradually raising the upper age limit for the child support grant (from age seven to eighteen) and increasing the income threshold for those eligible for grants to expand the number of beneficiaries. Nearly a third of the South Africa population currently receive a grant from the state. Yet the government has insisted on keeping eligibility limited to children, the elderly, and the disabled: those who physically cannot work.

[29] Standing and Samson, *A Basic Income Grant for South Africa*. One such proposal was put forward by trade unions in 1999, which proposed that a universal grant would be recouped from anyone with an income above ZAR3000 (US $300) via taxes, and incomes above ZAR5000 (US $500) would pay an additional 'solidarity tax' to fund the policy (as described by Barchiesi, 'South African Debates on the Basic Income Grant').

[30] Quoted in Barchiesi, 'South African Debates on the Basic Income Grant', 574.

Basic Income for What—And Whom?

There are a number of shared themes across these two histories, themes that tie into the history of cash grants in the global South more broadly. In both Namibia and South Africa, UBI was advocated and debated as an effective social policy for poverty alleviation, or an efficient way to structure the tax-benefits system. Redistribution, if mentioned at all, was largely a necessary means by which to achieve poverty reduction in these campaigns. In his chapter in this volume, Peter Sloman has outlined three varieties of political meanings that justify and conceptualize basic income. These are views of basic income as a share of national or communal assets (such as land or mineral wealth); as a share or distribution of the productive output or productive capacity of society; and as a social security system that ensures basic sustenance. While the first two framings have in the past been used by socialists or radical liberals, the final framing fits more neatly with 'redistributive market liberalism', which uses wealth or income transfers to augment the market.[31] It is a technocratic vision of UBI as a useful means to reach the goal of welfare. It is this framing and understanding of basic income that has been dominant in the history of the political narratives and campaigns in South Africa and Namibia—and, indeed, in the broader promotion of targeted cash transfers by international development organizations across the global South. In both South Africa and Namibia, UBI was campaigned for as the best form of social security provision and welfare—*not* as a way of promoting a just distribution of commonly held resources or righting the historical wrongs of settler colonialism and apartheid. I would argue that the lack of conversation about reparative justice and redistribution was a missed opportunity—and perhaps a key weakness—for both of the campaigns.

In framing basic income as an effective poverty alleviation policy, the campaigns made themselves open to a counter argument that insisted that job creation—not a guaranteed income—should be the state's solution to poverty. Indeed, not only the rebuttal of basic income by the South African and Namibian states, but even the focus of many of the key advocates of UBI themselves was oriented around work and job creation. As noted earlier, trade union activists in particular framed UBI as a way both to

[31] J. Kay, 'Staking a Moral Claim', *New Statesman*, October 11, 1996, 18–20, cited in Peter Sloman, 'Universal Basic Income in British Politics, 1918–2018: From a "Vagabond's Wage" to a Global Debate', *Journal of Social Policy* 47, no. 3 (2018): 627, https://doi.org/10.1017/S0047279417000800.

augment job creation (by supporting entrepreneurial risk taking) and to aid their already employed members (by easing their distributive obligations towards unemployed dependants). This made the UBI campaign vulnerable to a debate over who is deserving of income—with the default answer being the *working* or *entrepreneurial* poor. Indeed, the campaigns themselves promulgated these assumptions by highlighting the potential for UBI to increase economic participation and economic growth (alongside poverty alleviation). It then became easy for UBI sceptics in the government to argue that work and employment should remain the key mechanism of income distribution and poverty alleviation, and thus the focus of state provision. This rhetoric remains central in South Africa and Namibia today. President Geingob made work programmes a central part of his welfare proposal upon taking office, and one of the first actions of South Africa's current president Cyril Ramaphosa upon taking office was convening a job summit (the latest of many), re-emphasizing in his opening speech that job creation should be the key plank of a fight against poverty.[32]

This focus on jobs and job creation as the key lever of poverty alleviation is not only found among political elites. It also echoes the findings of my own qualitative research with the long-term unemployed poor. This ongoing qualitative research project focuses on the long-term unemployed or precariously employed Namibian and South African poor. Between 2016 and 2019 I conducted over ninety open-ended interviews with the help of local interpreters over three sites: inner-city Johannesburg and the villages of Otjivero and Spitzkoppe in Namibia. Most of my interlocutors are in their twenties and thirties, and are South African or Namibian nationals. Many of them I spoke with multiple times, exploring their views on social grant expansion, the role of the state in welfare provision, and work and working.[33]

This research has shown a deeply ingrained preference for job provision by the state rather than an untargeted grant for the unemployed. While grants to those physically unable to work—in particular children and the elderly—were lauded by the people I spoke with, many worried that more

[32] Republic of Namibia, *Harambee Prosperity Plan, 2016/17–2019/20*; Cyril Ramaphosa, 'Opening of Jobs Summit', *The Presidency of South Africa*, October 8, 2018, https://www.gov.za/speeches/president-cyril-ramaphosa-jobs-summit-4-oct-2018-0000.

[33] For a more detailed analysis of this research, see E. Fouksman, 'The Moral Economy of Work: Demanding Jobs and Deserving Money in South Africa', *Economy and Society* 49, no. 2 (April 2020): 287–311.

widely guaranteeing an income would encourage laziness. Many spoke about 'just sitting' or 'lying on the bed', and argued that financial pressure was necessary to encourage activeness and economic participation. (Interestingly, very few admitted that *they* would just sit or become lazy if they received a grant, but most were sure that other members of their community would.) Some even worried about economic collapse brought about through indiscriminate social grants.

Another common theme was misspending. Many of my informants told me that money that one received in return for labour would be better spent than money received as a government grant, which was more likely to be spent on alcohol and gambling. Such worries are contradicted by extensive research showing that 'sin spending' does not increase with cash transfers.[34] It is also contradicted by my informants themselves, who were quick to add that *they* themselves would not be lazy or misspend a government grant—but continued to worry that other community members would.

Most surprisingly, even many former UBI recipients in Otjivero, the site of Namibia's basic income experiment, stated a preference for the state provision of jobs over direct transfers. They did not share concerns about laziness or misuse of UBI, and unlike my interlocutors elsewhere, they were emphatic that UBI was a good policy and that they would like to see it reinstated in their village. Nevertheless, more residents of Otjivero that I spoke with stated a preference for job creation by the state over a cash grant. They brought up a variety of social and psychological reasons for this, including viewing work as good for the body and for physical health, and a way to alleviate boredom.[35] What is shared across my interlocutors is not only a normative fixation on job creation, but also a view of cash grants from the state as benevolence meant to alleviate poverty and suffering that should go only to the deserving: those that would spend the money properly, and would not degenerate into laziness. Like South African and Namibian policymakers, my informants view work as

[34] See for instance Johannes Haushofer and Jeremy Shapiro, 'The Short-Term Impact of Unconditional Cash Transfers to the Poor: Experimental Evidence from Kenya', *The Quarterly Journal of Economics* 131, no. 4 (2016): 1973–2042.

[35] For more details, see E. Fouksman, 'Defending the Wage: Visions of Work and Distribution in Namibia', forthcoming in *Beyond the Wage: Ordinary Work in Diverse Economies*, eds. William Monteith, Dora-Olivia Vicol, and Philippa Williams (Bristol: Bristol University Press).

paramount, and cash transfers as welfare provision meant only for those who cannot work through no fault of their own.

A Political Resurgence?

Some scholars of social protection have read this history of UBI and cash transfers in southern Africa in a positive light. In *Just Give Money to the Poor*, Hanlon, Barrientos, and Hulme frame the rise of cash grants as an intellectual and policy *revolution* that is emerging out of the global South. They point to both the basic income pilot in Namibia and the social grant system in South Africa as examples of this same revolution, and seem to suggest that giving cash to those physically unable to work (children, the elderly, the disabled) is not only revolutionary but is just a step away from the universal basic income.[36] Yet this interpretation obscures the fact that the South African social grant system is an expansion of the apartheid welfare system, itself modelled on European welfare schemes. It also elides the fact that the Namibian pilot was meant to function as an advocacy tool in the political struggle to universalize Namibia's already existing social grant system (which is a more limited form of what South Africa has). As such, the two examples are in fact of strikingly different policies, one squarely in the old tradition of welfare for those physically and bodily excluded from the labour force, the other an advertisement for a universal and unconditional income guarantee.

The anthropologist James Ferguson has also framed the expansion of cash grants in southern Africa as a possible stepping-stone towards something like a universal basic income. In *Give a Man a Fish* (2015), Ferguson makes the case that the expansive nature of social grants in southern Africa could be a piecemeal move towards universality.[37] He argues that South Africans see these grants not as charity or a gift, but rather as a *right*, or as a rightful share. He points out that grant recipients grumble as they stand in line to receive their grants, a posture better fitting of expectation than gratitude. He also makes the case that a similar sense of expectation can be seen among progressive writers and the bureaucrats charged with grant administration: the latter for instance are willing to forgo enforcing the means test for the grants. Altogether, Ferguson argues that a new politics

[36] Hanlon, Barrientos, and Hulme, *Just Give Money to the Poor*.

[37] Ferguson, *Give a Man a Fish*.

of distribution is emerging in southern Africa, one where distributive labour and distributive claims lie at the crux of political demands.

And indeed, new campaigns for UBI in South Africa have been slowly emerging over the past five years, once more spearheaded by civil society organizations such as the Black Sash, amongst others. Yet these emergent campaigns were not making claims for a universal redistribution of wealth or income. Indeed, often they avoided the UBI label altogether, calling instead for an expansion of the current grant system to include, for instance, grants for the unemployed on the basis on the right to economic security, rather than distributive justice. The COVID-19 crisis in both South Africa and Namibia engendered a widening of the social grants scheme (for the first time including the able-bodied unemployed), though these new emergency grants have thus far been short-term. It has also rallied civil society for another push towards a basic income in South Africa, particularly with the emergence of the C-19 People's Coalition #paythegrants campaign, which has expanded from a focus on emergency cash transfers during COVID to a broader basic income campaign, supported by a coalition of other civil society organisations. Yet while both the Department of Social Development and the Presidency have repeatedly mentioned the possibility of a future basic income grant in South Africa, the Treasury has continued to resist the idea by echoing the same rhetoric of fiscal responsibility and the preference for job creation.

Once again, I would argue that the framing of these campaigns is crucial—and it is thus important to avoid the workfarist, productivist logic which became the stumbling block for the basic income campaigns of the early 2000s. My own research, as well as several other empirical studies, shows that the South African poor do *not* seem to see social grants as a universal, unconditional right. While they do expect to keep receiving the grants, they view them as 'rightful' only for those who are excluded from performing labour (children, the elderly, the disabled). For instance, Hochfeld and Plagerson (2011) have found that a number of mothers receiving the child support grant express gratitude towards the state, and some even speak of the grant as a gift rather than a right.[38]

[38] E. Fouksman, 'The Moral Economy of Work'; H. Dawson and E. Fouksman, 'Labour, Laziness and Distribution: Work Imaginaries among the South African Unemployed', *Africa* 90, no. 2 (2020); Tessa Hochfeld and Sophie Plagerson, *The Social Construction of the Cash Transfer Mother in Soweto, South Africa: The Emergence of Social Stigma?* (Brighton: Institute of Development Studies/Centre for Social Protection, 2011).

In short, eliding the differences between social grants that are meant to aid those who cannot physically perform labour, and a rights-based argument for universal distribution of resources, can mask the crucial differences between the two. Likewise, a poverty alleviation or economic security argument for UBI has fundamentally different implications than a rightful or justice-based distributory one. These differences in framing could once again prove crucial in the success or failure of the political campaigns around UBI in the global South.

In many ways it is an auspicious moment for the resurgence of UBI politics in southern Africa. UBI has returned to the political agenda of rich countries, as the editors note in their introduction to this volume, and new experiments are being planned and run in both the global North and the global South, including a long-term UBI trial in Kenya run by GiveDirectly, a western NGO. The COVID-19 pandemic also furthered debates about basic income, with a number of governments, such as the USA, sending money unconditionally to large segments of the population. Yet I would argue that this moment too holds dangers for distributory politics. Because cash transfers and social protection across the global South are being framed in technocratic, developmentalist terms, this resurgent interest holds the danger of depoliticizing rights-based claim making, reshaping it into debates about poverty alleviation and aid effectiveness.[39] And both advocates and governments used the language of crisis in advocating for basic income or cash in response to COVID-19, rather than ongoing justice-based claims. Indeed, as noted above, while the South African state has shown some interest in a basic income in response to the most recent round of civil society campaigns, it has also repeatedly insisted on employment or public work schemes as the best approach to dealing with COVID-19's economic effects.[40]

[39] E. Fouksman and E. Klein, 'Radical Transformation or Technological Intervention? Two Paths for Universal Basic Income', *World Development* 122 (October 2019), https://doi.org/10.1016/j.worlddev.2019.06.013.

[40] See for instance South Africa's 2020 Presidential Employment Stimulus, which aimed to create or support 800,000 (largely short term) jobs in 2020–21.

A Future Politics of Distribution

However, while a distributory politics of UBI might not *yet* have come into being in southern Africa, my fieldwork in Johannesburg points to the potential for such a politics—requiring, once again, a shift in framing. Towards the end of my interviews, I would propose the idea of distributing southern Africa's mining profits directly to citizens on a monthly basis. What if the profits from selling the natural resources found in the ground were simply divided up, and all South Africans or Namibians got an equal share or dividend of these profits every month? Nearly everyone I asked about this was strongly in favour of the idea—including the very same people who earlier in our conversation were resistant to UBI or even to extending the current social grant system to include the unemployed. Even those who were concerned about laziness and the misspending of social grants would insist that such a 'universal natural resource dividend' was a good idea. When I tried to unpick what it was that changed their minds, many of the people I spoke with insisted that a social grant and a dividend of mining wealth are quite different things. The first is a form of aid from the state, the second something that intuitively should belong to all members of a nation. Several of my interlocutors told me that while it mattered if money *from the state* was misspent on alcohol, or led to laziness, a share of mining wealth is rightfully owned by the people who receive it—and they can thus spend it however they want. This clearly demonstrates that the way something like a basic income is framed and understood matters enormously for political and grassroots support. Indeed, this is not simply the case in southern Africa—one can see this in places like Alaska, a politically conservative US state which nevertheless overwhelmingly supports its own universal natural resource dividend.[41]

The fact that the long-term unemployed poor in southern Africa view social grants and resource dividends as quite different policies points to a potential future politics of distribution. This new politics could perhaps be more durable than that of the early 2000s in southern Africa. This would not be a politics oriented merely towards poverty alleviation, or towards supporting the deserving working poor through gaps in employment or

[41] Matthew Berman, 'Resource Rents, Universal Basic Income, and Poverty among Alaska's Indigenous Peoples', *World Development* 106 (2018): 161–72, https://doi.org/10.1016/j.worlddev.2018.01.014; Karl Widerquist and Michael Howard, *Alaska's Permanent Fund Dividend: Examining Its Suitability as a Model* (New York: Palgrave Macmillan, 2012).

shielding them from their distributory obligations to support others. Nor would it be a utilitarian politics of efficient social protection and effective altruism, which is currently the discourse around cash transfers and cash transfer trials in the international development community. This could be exactly what Ferguson has argued for—a politics of rightful shares. Yet this rights-based political framing of UBI is currently nascent in the global South. The political and popular conversation around economic and social rights on southern Africa has largely focused on labour rights (reflected in debates around minimum wages and working conditions); the right to economic security (but via social grants or employment schemes, not a redistribution of wealth); rights to public goods and services (such as the right to free higher education, or free water and electricity, all the focal points of popular protest movements in South Africa); and rights to capital via either existing Black Economic Empowerment programmes (whose goal is to open South Africa's corporate sector to non-whites), or calls for the redistribution of land and the nationalization of natural resources (which are demands of the populist left in South Africa, discussed more below).[42] Demands for access to a direct share of national wealth are still largely missing, and both more intellectual and political work has to happen for such demands to fully come into being.

Thinking of UBI as a universal natural resource dividend is useful in shifting the debate away from poverty alleviation, but also has its limits. After all, many countries have limited natural resources. And there is a strong justice-based argument for new forms of wealth distribution that go beyond only natural resources to redistribute all wealth, within and between countries. One such case is based on the historical nature of wealth. James Ferguson builds on Kropotkin to make a normative argument for universal forms of distribution, such as UBI, based on the right to a share of all national wealth generated with past effort. As Thomas Pogge has argued, if the well-off of the present are not to be held responsible for the sins of their ancestors, why should they also be able to benefit from their past wealth accumulation? This point can also be made globally:

[42] H. Dawson, 'Youth Politics: Waiting and Envy in a South African Informal Settlement', *Journal of Southern African Studies* 40, no. 4 (2014): 861–82; Karl von Holdt et al., 'The Smoke That Calls: Insurgent Citizenship, Collective Violence and the Struggle for a Place in the New South Africa. Eight Case Studies of Community Protest and Xenophobic Violence' (Johannesburg: Centre for the Study of Violence and Reconciliation, 2011); Roger Tangri and Roger Southall 'The Politics of Black Economic Empowerment in South Africa', *Journal of Southern African Studies* 34, no. 3 (2008): 699–716.

as Ayelet Shachar points out, one form of this benefit is simply being born in a wealthier country. On this basis both Shachar and Pogge propose forms of global redistribution.[43]

Such justice-based arguments are compelling, particularly because they shift the conversation at least partly away from poverty alleviation to rights-based distributory demands. However, these arguments can be difficult to translate into persuasive grassroots campaigns, particularly in the face of broadly held moral logics linking deservingness with work and productivism.[44] Another justice-based argument that I believe might be easier to deploy in grassroots campaigns is the case for UBI as reparations. As Elise Klein and I argue in forthcoming work, reparations for the dispossession and suffering (both past and ongoing in the present) created through slavery, colonialism, and settler colonialism could be a compelling—and, from a justice perspective, perhaps necessary—way to make the case for redistributing past wealth accumulation on a global scale.[45] Placing UBI within a reparations way of thinking would link it to the ongoing ramifications of social and historical injustices. It would also do the work of acknowledging specific histories of expropriation, racism, and colonialism, while at the same time still universally redistributing from those who have largely benefited from this history (the rich) to those who have been its victims (the poor), thus underscoring the intersection of class, race, and history with global capitalism.[46] It would offer recognition—as important as redistribution—of such injustice.[47] Indeed, the Movement for Black Lives in the United States has adopted a reparations argument for universal basic income, which (due to the intersection of race and class in the USA) would be especially beneficial to the black community. The

[43] Ferguson, *Give a Man a Fish*; Thomas Pogge, *World Poverty and Human Rights: Cosmopolitan Responsibilities and Reforms*, 2nd ed. (Malden, MA: Polity Press, 2008); Ayelet Shachar, *The Birthright Lottery: Citizenship and Global Inequality* (Cambridge, MA: Harvard University Press, 2009).

[44] Fouksman, 'The Moral Economy of Work'.

[45] E. Klein and E. Fouksman, 'Reparations as a Rightful Share: From Universalism to Redress in Distributive Justice', *Development and Change* (forthcoming).

[46] Satnam Virdee, 'Racialized Capitalism: An Account of Its Contested Origins and Consolidation', *The Sociological Review* 67, no. 1 (2019): 3–27.

[47] R. L. Brooks, *Atonement and Forgiveness: A New Model for Black Reparations* (Berkeley, CA: University of California Press, 2004).

Movement has also made the case for an additional dividend—which it calls a 'U+BI'—to be paid out to people of colour.[48]

The critical issue here is not the precise framing of UBI (be it as a natural resource dividend, a rightful share of past generations' wealth creation, or reparations for slavery or colonialism). Rather it is the shift to claiming UBI as a *right*—and a right not to economic security, but rather to a share of collective wealth. It is this shift that would allow the UBI movement to link to demands already being made by radical left movements in South Africa and Namibia, and widen their demands to include broader views of wealth and distributory justice. For instance, the left-wing Economic Freedom Fighters (EFF) party in South Africa has focused its redistributory demands on the national ownership of mines and on land redistribution. While land is undoubtedly symbolically important in southern Africa, it is also a rather old-fashioned notion of wealth. Framing UBI as a right and as a form of reparations could shift the EFF's redistributory demands from land to *wealth* in a broader sense. Most importantly, one cannot counter-propose job creation as an alternative policy to a reparatory or rights-based call for UBI. This could then move the conversation around livelihood and resource distribution beyond a focus on work, engendering a more durable politics around the demand for a UBI in southern Africa, and in the global South more broadly.

[48] Dorian T. Warren, 'Universal Basic Income and Black Communities in the United States', 2015, https://drive.google.com/file/d/0BzQSUaxtfgvIWmRMVEhCdS1nR1hYV2RpelB4TkJVbUtSZXo4/view (accessed 10 Dec. 2020); *The Movement for Black Lives, A Vision for Black Lives: Policy Demands for Black Power, Freedom, & Justice* (Movement for Black Lives, 2016).

CHAPTER 11

From Freedom to Finance: How Development Conditions and Paradigms Frame the Basic Income Debate

Louise Haagh

Introduction

This chapter explores how basic income discourse has been shaped by developments within capitalism. My main aim here is not a comprehensive review of capitalist variety or economic thinkers, but to set out a basic framework to explore the ideational difference that capitalist context makes, with reference to three related aspects of arguments about basic income: their *orientation* (e.g. towards society or the market); their level of *abstraction* from general cooperative problems and other institutions in society; and in the same context the significance or otherwise of a global spike in interest in basic income in reshaping those trends. I argue that one important driver behind discourse dynamics is the way the origin of and subsequent debate about the idea have been developmentally

L. Haagh (✉)
University of York, York, UK
e-mail: louise.haagh@york.ac.uk

P. Sloman et al. (eds.), *Universal Basic Income in Historical Perspective*, https://doi.org/10.1007/978-3-030-75706-9_11

dis-embedded historically, with roots in crisis-ridden Anglo-American capitalist development.

This trajectory helps explain how basic income advocacy has been framed in reaction to capitalist crises and peaks of inequality, as well as by the influence of neutralist ideations of the role of the state. To illustrate the importance of the form of capitalist emergence for ideas about basic income, I will primarily focus on and compare the Anglo-liberal and Nordic contextually rooted arguments, respectively. Highlighting pitfalls that conceptual abstraction poses, I argue that the narration of a unitary tradition of radicalism has also entailed divorcing the case for basic income from conditions of formal economic development.

Relatedly, in the contemporary context, the focus of basic income advocacy has moved from freedom to finance without escaping the contradictions within narrative abstraction linked with the dis-embedding of governance from real political problems. I argue that the discursive transition in focus from ideal conditions to real finance constraints coincides with and feeds on a parallel progressive informalization of economic governance on a global scale. In conditions of real dis-embedding of economic governance from institutions rooted in society, the established tendency towards abstraction moves basic income discourse from different forms of systemic utopia to real forms of present illusion, as once again moral urgency stands at odds with real development trends.

The chapter is organized as follows. The first section provides analytical context, in terms of the argument and approach, critically appraising the narrative construction of a tradition of radicalism through the lens of political economy. The second and third sections then consider the re-emergence of the case for basic income in the late nineteenth and early twentieth centuries in different utopian and pragmatic forms, to show how contextual difference matters, comparing US and Nordic thinkers. Finally, the fourth and fifth sections focus on the contemporary period, first comparing arguments for basic income in the USA and Denmark at the apogee of embedded liberalism in the 1960s and 1970s, and then evaluating the impacts on the narrative of the gradual embedding of neo-liberalism till the 2010s. Last, I conclude.

Basic Income in Capitalist Contexts

A Political Economy Approach to Ideation

If basic income *advocates* have sought unity within a constructed tradition, may this also explain why basic income *debate* is so polemical? With social democrats being charged with blocking progressive ideas and many progressives charging BI proponents with intransigence and anti-solidarity views, a more detached perspective is needed that can reveal undercurrents that move more superficial polemics.[1] As a way towards illuminating discursive dynamics, I propose that a political economy approach to ideation (PEI) offers a way to elaborate the dynamics of discursive dis-embeddedness in terms of a comparative focus on political development as welfare capacity. In this I build on two interpretative approaches, as follows. Institutionalist political economy (IPE) compares institutions and how they function.[2] Ideational institutionalism (II) on the other hand tries to explain how ideas intercede in changing institutions through ideational justification, whilst also showing how institutional barriers are hard to break down and ideas are reshaped in real contexts.[3] PEI draws on and extends both fields by highlighting underlying drivers of institutions as an incidental factor in shaping the relationship between the formalization of cooperation in society and the level and form of discursive abstraction, deriving from this a critical perspective on basic income narrative ascendency.

One way to consider the context of the basic income proposition in different societies is to acknowledge the way that the shape of the social state reflects alternative levels of formalization of human activities and social relations. Human IPE accordingly builds on the idea that core challenges of governing society are pre-political, shaped by realities of human economy in the form of conditions of human development and social

[1] See, for instance, Philippe Van Parijs, 'Basic Income and Social Democracy', *Social Europe* blog, April 11, 2016, at https://www.socialeurope.eu/44878, and Jon Cruddas and Tom Kibasi, 'A Universal Basic Mistake', *Prospect*, June 16, 2016.

[2] Ha-Joon Chang, 'Breaking the mould', *Cambridge Journal of Economics*, 26, no. 5 (September 2003): 539–59.

[3] See Colin Hay, 'The "Crisis" of Keynesianism', in *The Rise of Neoliberalism and Institutional Analysis*, eds. John L. Campbell and Ove K. Pedersen, (Princeton, NJ: Princeton University Press, 2001), 193–218, at 226–7; Peter Kjær and Ove K. Pedersen, 'Translating Liberalization' in *The Rise of Neoliberalism and Institutional Analysis*, eds. John L. Campbell and Ove K. Pedersen, 219–48.

interdependence.[4] More embedded governance then refers to greater formal development of inclusive institutions of governance both in and outside production. Consequently, the social state and welfare capacity—comprising relatedly publicly organized income, employment standards and services—develop through the social embedding of the formalization of economic cooperation and fiscal capacity.[5] More specifically, in human IPE, the notion of hybrid property—comprising institutions that align individual and social interest in shared risk—is extended to consider mechanisms that protect human development processes through systems of institutions and policies.[6] Hybridity thus represents higher levels of formalization of economic life, through education equality and occupational inclusion, as premised on higher levels of resource sharing and transparency in the form this sharing takes. A prevailing and more equal social wage is a product of equality in human development as constructed through core institutions that align the human trajectory with the standard of social opportunities. Ultimately, hybridity thus understood is a condition for the flourishing of social and economic rights, and basic income is no exception. As a relevant example, Ugo Columbino has shown that tax-neutral and sustainable financing of basic income is most plausible today in societies with high levels of formal female inclusion.[7] Here I will discuss how levels of hybridity shape what political actors and scholars can take for granted.

The intractable character of obstacles to cooperation entailed in more dis-embedded forms of capitalism is one contextual reason why—I claim—ideations of justice that labour on these conditions or on ideas about

[4] Louise Haagh, *The Case for Universal Basic Income* (Cambridge: Polity, 2019); Louise Haagh, 'Welfare-As-Freedom, The Human Economy and Varieties of Capitalist State', in *Economic Policies for a Post-Neoliberal World*, eds. Malcolm Sawyer and Philip Arestis (London: Palgrave, forthcoming).

[5] Louise Haagh, 'Alternative Social States and the Basic Income Debate', *Basic Income Studies*, 10, no. 1 (June 2015): 45–81; Louise Haagh, 'Public Ownership within Varieties of Capitalism', *International Journal of Public Policy*, 15, nos. 1–2 (2019), 153–86.

[6] Ha-Joon Chang, 'Institutions and Economic Development: Theory, Policy and History', *Journal of Institutional Economics*, 7, no. 4 (2011): 473–98; Ugo Pagano, 'Property Rights, Asset Specificity and the Division of Labour under Alternative Capitalist Relations', *Cambridge Journal of Economics*, 15, no. 3 (September 1991): 315–42. Louise Haagh, 'Democracy, Public Finance, and Property Rights in Economic Stability', *Polity*, 44, no. 4 (October 2012): 542–87.

[7] Ugo Columbino, 'Evaluating Alternative Basic Income Mechanisms', *Statistics Norway Discussion Paper* 578 (Bergen: Statistics Norway, 2009).

them—even when divergent in terms of levels or forms of distribution—are also similar in unacknowledged respects. Put simply, where the formal development of governance of society is more dis-embedded—from real constraints of human economy that beg cooperative solutions for stable governance—ideations of justice and economy are more likely to favour mono-institutional solutions, as quick redistributive measures appear relatedly more apparent and morally urgent. An example is where a form of basic income is positioned as central to distribution and justice (centralism) in conditions where the formalization of production is weak or failing. On this account, debates about alternative governing options that take Anglo-American economic development as their reference point may not be as internally variant as they may seem. In conditions where more reformist solutions to problems of governing society are (or are viewed as) intractable, claims to 'radicalism' are not necessarily or typically as transformative in terms of democratization of society or the human condition as they purport to be. This perhaps can only truly be appreciated by looking at Anglo-liberal debates from 'the outside'. The two means of adopting that sort of analytical distance used here are theoretical and comparative, respectively: theoretical in taking human economy embeddedness of governance as an external reference, and comparative by noting that Nordic capitalism is—according to this external standard—more embedded. Programmes that might look very different when comparing levels or forms of distribution—neo-liberalism, radical liberalism and libertarianism—may similarly abstract from realities of governing. To be clear, I do not mean to contest the significant differences between and within neo-liberalism, radical liberalism and libertarianism, but rather point to unacknowledged similarities that are shaped by the contextual rooting of these traditions in Anglo-liberal conditions of modernity and subsequent capitalist development.

To further elaborate, Carles Boix has identified two distinct routes to the consolidation of political democracy in the modern period, one in which elites are domesticated through economic reforms that disperse the allocation of money and property in society, and another where mobile elites tolerate democracy, with the consequence—and condition, I argue—that inequality in property remains unresolved.[8] Extrapolating this distinction as relevant to the Nordic-Anglo-liberal contrast, I argue that in the latter case, states both have had, and continue to have, less autonomy in

[8] Carles Boix, *Democracy and Redistribution* (Cambridge: Cambridge University Press: 2003).

terms of infrastructural power; and in turn they rely on ultimately thin and less stable, and more punitive and redistributive, instruments of governing.

In this case, both persistent or structural inequality and conjunctural peaks of inequality and capitalist crises can be linked with deeper *crises in governance*. Historically, crises in governance typically involve crises of incorporation, in the case of the displacement of rural and later urban labour, whilst as welfare expansion proceeds in the course of globalization, more visible manifestations of new incorporation crises are linked with crises in public finance and services. In Anglo-liberal modernity, inequality and discursive abstraction became bedfellows under conditions of successive crises in governance. The more abstract form of Anglo-liberal (orthodox) economics and liberal egalitarian theory reinforces the tendency to draw out a basic income's centrality in the expansion of freedom. This tendency towards centralism is in turn more likely to be reasserted in the form of crisis discourse in periods and contexts of more dis-embedded liberalism, thereby reinforcing the association of illusion and crisis.

Basic Income Narration and Radicalism: Discursive and Real

The fact basic income as an idea has never been realized is a contributing factor to the illusory tenor of the narrative and to the way construction of a global tradition proceeds through reinvention of the idea of radicalism in new contexts. Reference to basic income as 'radical' can be confusing and misleading, not least as in basic income advocacy, an equivocation of both egalitarian and market radicalism is often made. In this respect, it is useful to realize that claims of radicalism often involve a degree of abstraction in one or two senses, relative or substantive, the first being from *existing* conditions that *discursively* are sought to be altered in a 'radical' way. Radical claim-making thus often leads to singular or absolute statements about the necessity of particular or simple rather than complex reforms. A second form of abstraction and discursive radicalism is from general *real* constraints, such as the need to govern social life inclusively, that act on society's level of stability, as examined above in terms of dis-embeddedness from real cooperative problems in society.

A relevant hypothesis is that the language of radicalism in the first sense may feed on dis-embeddedness of governance in the second 'real' sense, in which case the claim of radicalism may be out of proportion to the level of real social change and transformation actually envisaged and/or possible. Discursive and real radicalism, respectively, invoke and involve simplified governance, which is why the two are often mutually constitutive in some way.

One reason why extensive marketization projects tend to be linked with inegalitarian social conditions, and to reproduce them along with more market-ideational notions of freedom, is that elites' position and mobility tend to be tied to the minimization of horizontal institutions of collective risk and accountability. In turn, social reformers may also come to believe that political routes to social reform are intractable.

Hence, in another twist, in more embedded conditions of governance, discursively radical proposals are likely to take embedded governance for granted and become egalitarian-utopian projects, whereas in dis-embedded conditions, discursive radicalism and reformism are likely to be more market-utopian in some way. In inegalitarian societies, elites are more likely to regard reformist projects as 'radical'. Hence, social groups or advocates of an idea may be charged with being 'radical', even when being in fact reformist, in so far as reformism threatens real or/and ideational structural change enacted by elites against society.

To distinguish utopian from substantively radical claims, we can refer to utopian positions in general as those which contest the status quo. Pragmatic positions are those which can be associated with necessities of incremental policy change or in general immediate governance imperatives. In this context, a substantively radical proposition such as to dis-embed governance from society can come in the guise of pragmatism—which is a trick neo-liberal movements have played very well in the context of the 1970s and 1980s and beyond.

At the same time, under certain conditions, utopian egalitarian ideals can marry with real radicalism in terms of acceptance of the dis-embedding of governance of society through the market. The contemporary period of penetrative globalization generates complex dynamics of this kind partly because of the speed of change acting on society. Specifically, in a context in which the extension of globalization is based on market supremacy, discursive radicalism is hypothetically more likely to be domesticated in the terms of a positive language of market embedding, in varying degree and effect.

Construction of a tradition of basic income radicalism is shaped by (without necessarily acknowledging) these contextual influences. For libertarian advocates, basic equality in resources becomes the source of support of transactional freedom as an egalitarian standard, whereas for neo-liberals, minimum (automatically means-tested) guarantees perform the same role. For radical liberals, 'pre-distribution' of income and services is a trade-off for more spontaneous organization of work. As distinct from the above, for socialists or social democrats, more unconditional income security progresses with wider social-egalitarian conditions. How these different meanings evolve in basic income narration is closely tied to social and increasingly global conditions, yet without this necessarily being fully explicated. In so far as basic income advocates have sought unity under conditions of progressive global dis-embedding of governance, the contextual divergence of their meanings is washed out to present a united front.

Basic Income Radicalism in Historical Construction

Leading basic income scholars and advocates refer to Thomas Paine as the first modern radical, customarily, and trace the tradition of basic income radicalism to Paine[9] and Spence.[10] From the perspective of a political economy of ideation, however, one potential problem with placing Paine as originator of a radical tradition is that it involves transporting a justification relating to natural inheritance and mankind which was rooted in circumstances of extension and concentration of private property in eighteenth-century Britain. The lack of BI reform subsequently is then traced to the outcome rather than the essence of that failure—for example, the object of 'radical' discourse becomes the lack of *compensation*, rather than the absence of or prospects for a more deeply reformist alternative path of cooperative development. A number of rhetorically supportive binary conflicts are set down as connected with BI advocacy per se (e.g. labourism vs. socialism, today's efforts vs. past efforts, inheritance vs. cooperation and basic income vs. social democracy). Narrating radicalism in this case is then also a form of prediction.

Arguably, both Paine's and Spence's reference to common heritage was not as much a general philosophy, as the legacy has been claimed, as it was a reaction to immediate loss in favour of consolidating the possessions of rural elites. When the registrations of new landholdings that emerged from the enclosure movements of the nineteenth century in Britain were finally published in 1872, it was revealed that 0.6 per cent of the

[9] Guy Standing, *Basic Income* (London: Penguin: 2017), 12, 26.

[10] Philippe Van Parijs and Yannick Vanderborght, *Basic Income: A Radical Proposal for a Free Society and a Sane Economy* (Cambridge, MA: Harvard University Press: 2017), 71.

population owned 98.5 per cent of the land.[11] This stands in sharp contrast to land reform in Nordic states, where reform of status and property went together in the pre-industrial period. By the end of the 1800s, in Denmark, about 80 per cent of agrarian cultivation was in the hands of small-scale cooperatives.[12] National resource ownership continued to be protected.[13]

In this context, Paine's 'radicalism' may owe more than commonly surmised to how he was portrayed by authorities. Paine's linkage of theological arguments with secular concerns was thought extremely radical for his time.[14] Meanwhile, Paine himself underscored the moderate nature of his proposal, specifically how he did not contest inequality as such, but destitution as its by-product. He sought to fix destitution, not inequality. 'I care not how affluent some may be, provided that none be miserable in consequence of it.'[15] At the same time, Paine's liberal reformism had reference to economic conditions that were not yet modern. His ideas predated the emergence of an industrial society and conflicts in labour relations that were to be associated with later egalitarian (anti-capitalist) discourse.

Different notions of freedom and justice were born from alternative capitalist conditions with lasting effect. In the USA, the role of the Republican North in opposing and in effect abolishing slavery belies the way 'freedom' came to be interpreted in terms of free rights to individual contract,[16] which in turn legitimized heavy-handed state repression of labour acting collectively.[17] The point here is how the polemical focus of basic income narrative has roots in its construction around Anglo-liberal history and scholarly thought, in which an opposition between collective and individual power is materialized through extensive privatization of property and governance.

[11] Simon Fairlie, 'A Short History of the Enclosure in Britain', *The Land* 7 (Summer 2009), 27.

[12] Ingrid Henriksen, 'Agriculture in Denmark, 1870–1939', paper given at the 14th International Economic History Association (IEHA) Congress, Helsinki, August 21–25, 2006, 17.

[13] Andreas R. Sanders, Pål T. Sandvik, and Espen Storli, 'Dealing with Globalisation', *Business History* 58, no. 8 (November 2016): 1210–35.

[14] Gregory Claeys, *Thomas Paine: Social and Political Thought* (London: Routledge, 1989), 213–14.

[15] Harry T. Dickinson, *The Political Works of Tomas Spence* (Newcastle upon Tyne: Averom, 1982).

[16] Eric Foner, *Free Soil, Free Labor, Free Men*, (Oxford: Oxford University Press, 1995).

[17] Robin Archer, *Why is There No Labor Party in the United States?* (Princeton, NJ: Princeton University Press, 2007).

Basic Income at the Apogee of Emergent Capitalist Crises

The Gilded Age and the Single-Tax of Henry George

Core tenets of the contemporary basic income proposal were consolidated in the course of later capitalist development, the idea of a flat tax, and of basic income as a simplifier, being cases in point. For Henry George, the progressive US economist writing in the late nineteenth century, the single-tax proposal was intended to simplify and purify politics in order to vindicate the ideal of equality of liberty under the American republic, as against the infection of public rights by private commercial corruption in the Gilded Age of emergent American capitalism. On this basis, George's thought reinvented classical economists' view of market efficacy and public neutrality in a new form in terms of contributing to public justice.

Through George the idea of an inheritance in natural resources from which the bulk of common resources should be extracted in rent became more of a general philosophy (referred to as Georgism). George's thinking about accruing rent from land for public expense has been influential in subsequent reasoning for basic income as a form of systemic justice.[18]

Giving the example of Ireland, George argued that poverty could only be explained by systems which prevented initiative by the fear that any reward for exertion would simply be extracted in the form of rent.[19]

His idealization by contrast of the US settler economy can be gauged from his depiction of the equality he saw in that stage of market expansion. 'Who should crouch where all were freemen; who oppress where all were peers?'[20] On this basis he seemed to see global capitalist expansion in positive terms.

> Go into one of the new communities where Anglo-Saxon vigor is just beginning the race of progress, where the machinery of production and exchange is yet rude and inefficient; where the increment of wealth is not yet great enough to enable any class to live in ease and luxury, where the best house is but a cabin of logs or a cloth of shanty, and the richest man is forced to daily work; and though you will find an absence of wealth and all its con-

[18] As represented in Philip Bess, 'Henry George's Land Value Tax', *American Affairs* 2, no. 1 (Spring 2018): 56–75.

[19] Henry George, *Progress and Poverty* (New York: Appleton and Company, 1881), 113.

[20] Ibid., 5.

> comitants, you will find no beggars. There is no luxury, but there is no destitution.[21]

It is plain from this that George equated capitalism and modern development itself with the Anglo-liberal form and specifically global expansion and labour migration. George was not against capital or labour movement, but rather the monopolization of natural resources for purposes of rent.[22] Crucially, George did not seek to break with the market or competition *as such*. In fact, he saw the tendency to concentration in development as inevitable. The formation of large cities and the enlargement of agricultural production were not to be arrested. The idea of equal distribution in property he thought impossible.[23] George hoped that with the abolition of all taxation except on land values and the positive effects on wealth creation and distribution he expected from it, America 'would then approach the ideal of Jeffersonian democracy, the promised land of Herbert Spencer, the abolition of government!'[24]

George did not conceive that state policy could ever effect as thorough (and, in particular, as cleanly generated) a form of equality and fairness as that which would arise from 'the play of individual action'.[25]

At the same time, George saw himself as a reformist. As he put it:

> The ideal of socialism is grand and noble; and it is, I am convinced possible of realization, but such a state of society can't be manufactured—it must grow.[26]

This incremental approach, however, equated to a simple one in terms of policy for two key reasons relating to George's view of the economy and government respectively. First, he thought concentration within the private organization of production was inevitable, and necessary *for raising efficiency*.

[21] Ibid., 6–7.
[22] Ibid., 317–21.
[23] Ibid., 294.
[24] Ibid., 365.
[25] Ibid., 287.
[26] Ibid., 288–9.

> That concentration is the order of development there can be no mistaking. ... All the currents of the time run to concentration. To successfully resist it we must throttle steam and discharge electricity from human service.[27]

Second, government could not be trusted with the economy. Returning to a 'tribal state' would involve 'anarchy and perhaps barbarism'. 'Instead of an intelligent award of duties and earnings, we should have a Roman distribution of Sicilian Corn, and the demagogue would soon become the Imperator.'[28]

On this basis, George attacked the notion of 'a graduated tax on incomes'.[29] Whilst he admitted that the intended end was good, being the 'prevention of immense concentration of wealth', he disparaged the means as 'the employment of a large number of officials clothed with inquisitorial powers'.

We can see then how George's progressive thinking turned into a thesis against government interference in the economy in light of the nature of the problems he worked on. Whilst George's proposals for a single tax have been linked with providing a foundation for a citizens' dividend, it is not entirely clear that this is what George had in mind.

In terms of how the tax proceeds would be used, it could be deduced that he meant the preservation of income in the form of untaxed individual earnings from production, as one part would be distributed in wages between individual producers, 'according to the part each had taken in the work of production'.[30] The other part—public benefits—referred to what today we would call public infrastructure and services: public construction of roads, railroads, message by telegraph, heat, light, public baths, universities, research, and so on.[31]

The characteristics of the tax system which would effect these outcomes had four features which would amount to a justification for a single tax—'to abolish all taxation save that upon land values'—namely that the tax should be (i) as light as possible on production, (ii) easily and cheaply collected, (iii) fixed at a level (certain) and (iv) flat.[32]

[27] Ibid., 294.
[28] Ibid., 288.
[29] Ibid.
[30] Ibid., 395.
[31] Ibid., 409.
[32] Ibid., 365, 367.

George's thought can be described as an accommodation to stark inequality in a way that created a gulf between his reformist ideals and their feasibility in political reality. George's ideas would not take hold in Anglo-liberal practice, which may be a reason why they have remained part of an Anglo-liberal-led discourse of ideal radicalism of left and right alike.

On examination, many of the practical features of the system George indicated can be associated with economies in which government plays a strong role in (i) regulation and leading production, and (ii) abating and directing competition through planning. In the early twentieth century, Nordic states effectively regulated land and in general natural resources ownership to ensure private possession was limited, and public control remained central.[33] The USA with more limited and compensatory forms of welfare came to rely far more on contributions from the better off than Nordic states did: precisely the reverse of the ideal relation between low and uniform tax and social equality that George envisaged and hoped for.[34]

Social Libertarianism Against Social Democracy: Hohlenberg

A social libertarian argument for radical pre-distribution—in terms of nationalization of the economy to favour economic equality with limited government—put forward in Denmark in the 1930s, provides a relevant comparator to Georgism, as well as to the 1930s New Deal, reflecting two different contexts of crises. Birnbaum and Christensen's translation of Johannes Hohlenberg's writings has brought his thinking to a wider audience.[35] Like Cunliffe and Erreygers, they emphasize the 'continuity in the arguments presented for and against basic income throughout the history of this idea "irrespective of their different contexts"'.[36]

Whilst recognizing the importance of continuities, here, as noted, I want to emphasize the extent to which these are constructed and punctuated by contextually grounded differences in reasoning about basic income

[33] Sanders et al., 'Dealing with Globalisation'.

[34] Haagh, 'Alternative Social States and the Basic Income Debate'; Haagh, 'Public Ownership within Varieties of Capitalism'.

[35] John Cunliffe and Guido Erreygers, 'Basic Income? Basic Capital!', *Journal of Political Philosophy*, 11 no. 1 (March 2003): 89–110.

[36] Johannes Hohlenberg, Simon Birnbaum, and Erik Christensen, 'Anthroposophical Reflections on Basic Income', *Basic Income Studies*, 2, no. 2 (December 2007): 2.

and its role in society. Birnbaum and Christensen note two aspects of Hohlenberg's personal and social context I want to accentuate, the first being Hohlenberg's personal interest in Danish existentialist philosophy and his trajectory in advancing alternative education, and the second being the 1930s context which prompted a debate about income assistance and employment in otherwise very different countries.[37]

With respect to the second condition, it must be recognized how Hohlenberg rallied against the social state and employment-based solidarity systems whilst also taking both for granted in specific ways that reflected the context of his time. In the 1930s, Danish labour market policy involved significant expansion of existing social protection systems, for example, extension of the 1907 unemployment insurance system administered by unions, and disability and social pensions.[38]

According to Furåker et al., in terms of conditionality, decommodification was highest in Denmark in income protection policy among the Nordic states at this time, with state policy being both more liberal and passive compared with Sweden.[39] A key reason is that social protection institutions were already relatively well established and socially embedded. Public subsidy of the UI funds consolidated in 1921 was reinforced in 1932. The way the Danish approach was marked by the ability to rely on existing institutions of social protection has even led some to argue that the unemployment problem in Denmark has been exaggerated, as numbers were enlarged by the rapid rise in registration that followed expansion of the existing UI system.[40]

On this basis, arguably, the Danish tradition of advocacy for basic income, being socially libertarian, compared with the later emergence of movements in other Nordic states, stems in part from the more socially liberal tradition of income support, and its more autonomous governance, as well as the fact that this approach was relatively effective. Workers and employers successfully relied on the UI system as a soft cushion during

[37] Ibid., 3.

[38] Walter Galenson, *The Danish System of Labor Relations: A Study in Industrial Peace* (Cambridge, MA: Harvard University Press, 1969).

[39] Bengt Furåker, Leif Johansson, and Jens Lind, 'Unemployment and Labour Market Policies in the Scandinavian Countries', *Acta Sociologica* 33, no. 2 (January 1990): 153–7.

[40] Niels-Henrik Topp, 'Unemployment and Economic Policy in Denmark in the 1930s', *Scandinavian Economic History Review* 56, no. 1 (March 2008): 71–90, at 76.

adjustment, as indicated in the finding that '50 to 75 per cent of the unemployed returned to their old firm'.[41]

The way Hohlenberg could take economic security for granted is reflected in his thinking. Hohlenberg had less faith in competition than George, and was also involved in forming alternative rural banking institutions which still exist today. Similarly, his critique of labour unions was different to George's, in that he focussed on the unions' *conformity*, as distinct from George's concern about their combative tactics against much greater odds.

By 1937, when employment in Denmark was on the up, Hohlenberg criticized compliant workers against a background of production for the war economy, in 'He Who Does Not Work Shall Not Eat'. Here Hohlenberg separated, rhetorically at least, the people who could and could not create their own occupation:

> It is possible to view the current potential of liberation from material work as a gift of fate. ... There will always be more than enough people willing to go back to the treadmill because, not being able to maintain their personality in the empty space of freedom, they need a fixed and authorised framework for their lives.[42]

The way Hohlenberg here pits his social existentialism against social democracy or labour personality arguably presents an irreconcilable proposition, and makes perhaps the first appearance of a massive contradiction in continental European advocacy for basic income based on mockery of the systems that would enable a basic income to come into being—at least at the time. Summing up, George's and Hohlenberg's positions on social inheritance were both remarkably different and similar.

The different thinking of George and Hohlenberg clearly reflected the circumstances of material and institutional order they faced. A point of comparison between George and Hohlenberg is that they were both radical utopians in their time, and yet their views were so differently accented by their context that the social heritage argument for which they are both known meant something almost completely different in practice.

[41] Ibid., 78.

[42] Hohlenberg, Birnbaum, and Christensen, 'Anthroposophical Reflections', 13–15.

Finance Crises and the Systematization of Income Support

Social Capitalism Before and After the 1930s

If Hohlenberg and George wrote in different epochs of capitalism, both reacted to the shape of formation of modern systems of state and economy from a position of social utopia and opposition. Comparing two other thinkers who represent US and Nordic capitalism, Friedman and Myrdal, both writing in the 1930s in positions of government, renders a different, but equally interesting, pairing. Through her research at the Hoover archives, Jennifer Burns has uncovered what she describes as an uncanny resemblance of ideas and meeting of minds between Gunnar Myrdal, the Swedish social democrat and social economist, and Milton Friedman, the neo-classical economist, faced with the problem of mass unemployment in the 1930s. The two men were even in touch with one another towards the end of the 1930s about the merits of more systematic approaches to income assistance.[43]

At the same time, the different contexts of capitalism and crisis in the USA and Sweden prior to the 1930s coloured the character of state responses, systemic thinking about those responses, and also the views of dominant technocratic thinkers like Friedman and Myrdal. Even though the US unemployment problem was far greater—prompting the New Deal—the response to the Great Depression was not structural on the scale seen in Nordic states, especially Sweden. Türegün argues that despite larger amounts of federal spending, the New Deal had less positive effect compared with Sweden's more fiscally moderate spend given the 'fragmented structure of US federalism'.[44] However, arguably, it is hard to separate the negative effects of this fragmentation from the contribution and effect of fragmentation in economic interest representation, as I discuss below.

The USA and UK represented both a more socially disorganized and repressive form of capitalism before the Depression, even though social spending, if not the social state, was more advanced in the UK. A key

[43] Jennifer Burns, 'A View From The Hoover Archives: Milton Friedman On A Guaranteed Annual Income', Hoover Institution, 2019, available online at https://Soundcloud.Com/Hoover-Institution/A-View-From-The-Hoover-Archives-Milton-Friedman-On-A-Guaranteed-Annual-Income.

[44] Adnan Türegün, 'Revisiting Sweden's Response to the Great Depression of the 1930s', *Scandinavian Economic History Review* 65, no. 2 (May 2017): 127–48, at 130.

indicator of social organization of capitalism and the social state—being organized skill development in risk-sharing institutions—was distinctly absent in the Anglo-liberal cases, in which the notional apprenticeship system in the UK of the 1920s has been characterized as essentially exploitative, with raw capitalism reasserting itself during the roaring twenties in both the UK and USA.[45] As Fig. 11.1 shows, the UK and USA saw a sharp fall in union membership, whereas it soared in the Nordic states at that time. Unionization rates picked up again in the context of the Depression, but then tailed off (in the USA already by the 1940s, and in Britain by the 1950s), and flattened completely in both countries between 1950 and 1960, a period of continued massive expansion in density in Nordic states.

Scholars seeking to explain the failure to form a welfare state or a labour party in the USA highlight workers' inability to unite for welfare schemes nationally and state repressions in favour of capital interests as key factors in reinforcing a dispersed form of radicalism.[46] A similar argument about arrested social reform can be made for Britain, however, especially compared with Nordic states, considering the UK's lack of genuine supra-sectoral national wage coordination and limited provision for training.[47]

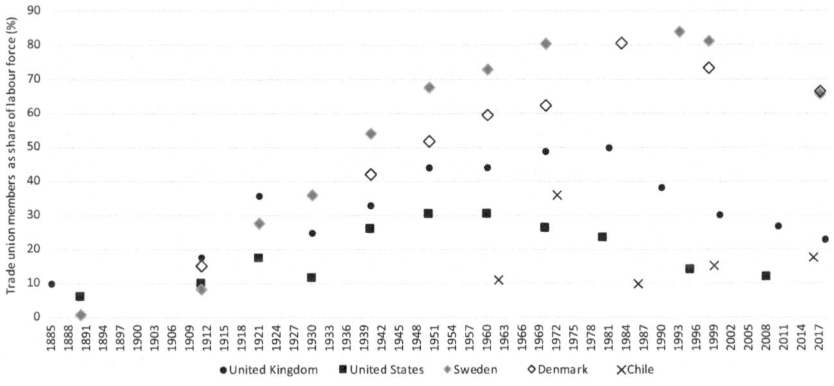

Fig. 11.1 Trade union density rates in five OECD countries

[45] Kathleen Thelen, *How Institutions Evolve* (New York: Cambridge University Press, 2004).

[46] Theda Skocpol, *Protecting Soldiers and Mothers* (London: Belknap Press, 1995).

[47] Colin Crouch, *Industrial Relations and European State Traditions* (Oxford: Oxford University Press, 1994); David Finegold and David Soskice, 'The Failure of Training in Britain', *Oxford Review of Economic Policy* 4, no. 3 (October 1988): 21–53.

Whilst Robin Archer has identified state repression as a key factor in impeding the formation of an effective labour politics in the USA in the nineteenth century—reinforcing instead an orthodox Marxist, doctrinaire, and ultimately fragmenting, combative tradition in defence of particular trades—others have suggested that a lack of skilled labour and an influx of low-skilled immigrant labour set the course of American capitalism on a labour-displacing path during the Gilded Age.[48] A bread-and-butter crafts-based unionism emerged in its wake, under the leadership of a powerful personality, Samuel Gompers, from the formation of the AFL in 1886 till Gompers' death in 1924.

The fact that the US labour movement became decidedly anti-communist (even, on some accounts, an instigator of McCarthyian public outings of communist influencers) and yet continued to face legal subordination (for instance, the 1947 Taft Hartley Act required union leaders to denounce communism whilst also limiting their rights) is evidence of the overall trajectory and status of legal disempowerment of American unions.[49] In a characteristic example, in 1905 the Supreme Court in the case of *Lochner v. New York* declared unconstitutional a legal intervention to limit working hours on the grounds that it violated the principle that individuals have 'liberty of contract' as derived from the Fourteenth Amendment to the Constitution.[50] It is on the basis of state legal repression that we can make sense of US unions' opposition to state protection systems such as national health insurance and redistribution in the early twentieth century in terms of being a defensive resignation to the reality that such systems were not likely to favour labour autonomy.[51] In the USA, an unemployment insurance scheme as such did not come into effect till the 1930s and, though this coincided with labour mobilization and rising unionization, new protective labour legislation remained subject to political reversal.

Early formation of social state measures in Nordic states made the foundation for a completely different course. It is significant that social funding

[48] Archer, *Why is There No Labor Party in the United States?*, 198–9; Thelen, *How Institutions Evolve*, 184–5.

[49] Jennifer Luff, 'Labor Anticommunism in the United States of America and the United Kingdom, 1920–49', *Journal of Contemporary History* 53, no. 1 (January 2018): 127–30.

[50] 'Labor in America – The Trade Unions' Role', University of Groningen online archive, http://www.let.rug.nl/usa/outlines/economy-1991/labor-in-america-the-trade-unions-role/index.php.

[51] Luff, 'Labor Anticommunism', 117.

capacity—albeit very small across the capitalist North—was already three times higher in Denmark, and more than twice as high in Sweden compared with the USA in 1880. Denmark's level was twice that of Germany and France at this stage. By 1930, Denmark was spending nearly six times the US level, and Sweden more than four times the US level.

By 1960, US spending was relatively higher, at about two-thirds of the Danish, British and Swedish (which were at roughly similar levels). The US New Deal spending rise was from this perspective an important but from the outset by design a temporary commitment, whereas in Denmark and Sweden institution-extension or -building was involved. This accords with later trends which see Anglo-liberal countries spend significantly in crises on a temporary basis. The USA was financing relief rather than funding welfare.

The social foundations behind different approaches to unemployment in Nordic states and the USA in particular promoted different ways of understanding the role of income guarantees, as respectively temporary and programmatic, or systemic and permanent.

When comparing the thinking of Myrdal and Friedman, it is important to note the different context of Swedish compared with Danish social reform. For example, the basis for what Rokkan calls a 'resource democracy'—based in broad alliances between workers and owner-farmers—already existed before the Depression in Denmark. By contrast, Sweden required state involvement to formalize the same coalition in the 1930s.[52]

Sweden's approach to unemployment during the 1930s was to use public works to foster social integration and state capacity to organize the labour market and provide stable housing for families. In 1934, the Social Democrat-led government began centralizing labour exchanges under a Social Board, and in 1939 it set up a tripartite Labour Market Board which took over the administration of the labour exchanges.[53]

It has been argued that more widespread poverty in Sweden generated the basis for this more concerted and planned state response in the 1930s and after.[54] State repression of unions in the nineteenth century was greater in Sweden, which is said to have contributed to Swedish unions'

[52] Stein Rokkan, 'The Growth and Structuring of Mass Politics', in *Nordic Democracy: Ideas, Issues, and Institutions in Politics, Economy, Education, Social and Cultural Affairs of Denmark, Finland, Iceland, Norway, and Sweden*, ed. Erik Allardt et al. (Copenhagen: Det Danske Selskab, 1981): 53–79, at 70–72.

[53] Türegün, 2017, p. 133.

[54] Giovanni A. Cornia, *Child Poverty and Deprivation in the Industrialized Countries, 1945–1995* (Oxford: Clarendon Press, 1997), 285.

radicalism.[55] Housing conditions were worse than in the rest of Europe, which prompted the term 'people's home' as a metaphor for the aim of Sweden's reform programme.[56]

The developmentalist versus relief orientation of social programmes in Sweden and the USA, respectively, is the issue when judging the thin agreement on the need to systematize income support between Myrdal and Friedman. Despite an emphasis on employment in the US New Deal programmes, the focus was on employment relief, which was means-tested as a rule. This created a third status category, neither stigmatized assisted poor (primarily women—who were intentionally deprioritized in public works) nor the upright contributory male breadwinner enrolled in social insurance.[57]

Different attitudes to the role of men and women also have to be underscored as informing of (and being generated by) the distinct evolution of capitalist institutions. Some even argue that this was a decisive factor in the post-war Swedish welfare system, for example, the choice to rely on incorporating women (albeit mainly in public employment) rather than depend on mass migratory labour, when faced with labour shortages in the 1950s.[58] In this comparative light, the US work relief effort of the 1930s could not be more different.

Friedman, Myrdal and Government Reform

When examining Friedman's views on welfare and income support, it is important to understand how his later more doctrinaire views were coloured by his political experience in government. Whilst Friedman would later be linked with a distinct Chicago School of economics, he did not start out his career as a theoretical economist. As Robert Murphy usefully clarifies, the Austrian and Chicago Schools—the latter of which Friedman championed in the 1960s—differed in terms of the latter's focus

[55] Ole Hasselbalch, *The Roots: The History of Nordic Labour Law* (Stockholm: Stockholm Institute for Scandinavian Law, 2009).

[56] Yvonne Hirdman and Michel Vale, 'Utopia in the Home', *International Journal of Political Economy* 22, no. 2 (July 1992): 5–99, at 27.

[57] Chad A. Goldberg, 'Contesting the Status of Relief Workers during the New Deal: The Workers Alliance of America and the Works Progress Administration', *Social Science History*, 29 no. 3 (October 2005): 337–71, at 341.

[58] Sven Steinmo, *The Evolution of Modern States: Sweden, Japan, and the United States* (Cambridge: Cambridge University Press, 2010).

on policy experimentation, as distinct from the Austrian School's focus on the a priori primacy of human action.[59]

Jennifer Burns argues that Friedman's experience in the 1930s of attempting to collect data for the national survey to catalogue the extent of unemployment, poverty, and need in the aftermath of the Depression gave birth to the thinking behind the Negative Income Tax (NIT—being the proposal to means-test income support through the tax allowance automatically, thereby rendering subsistence security apparently unconditional).[60] This experience made Friedman understand the loopholes which existed in reaching people effectively. In his 1939 paper, Friedman discussed the need to find 'an objective method for determining a minimum standard of living'.[61] His experience as a tax advisor to the Treasury would also have influenced his view of the automaticity of means-testing within the NIT.

At the same time, it is important to acknowledge how in his position as a government official, Friedman was a witness to the practical contradictions of the 1930s relief effort. During the New Deal, Roosevelt upheld notions of pay for skilled work, and 'prevailing wages' for different places, that could never be sustained in peace time, and were widely attacked later, including by Friedman, in the same breath as defending a form of basic subsistence security and the flat tax, restated as the Negative Income Tax, which he would compare to the British system of 'personal allowances'.[62] The point here is that Friedman's thinking, despite his 'real' experience in government, could not escape the contradictions of US capitalism. It speaks to the irrationality of the hierarchical mode of capitalism and the fiction of the market in it, that after forty years, Anglo-liberal states have neither been able to shed social spending nor make it anti-paternalist as Friedman envisaged. It can then be argued that the Depression with its post-war aftermath contributed to making things *seem* similar—for example, the formation of welfare states—that were never comparable. In the USA, and arguably eventually Britain, the Depression

[59] Robert P. Murphy, 'Mises Daily Articles', Mises Institute, May 26, 2020, available online at https://Mises.Org/Library/Chicago-School-Versus-Austrian-School.

[60] Burns, 'A View From The Hoover Archives'.

[61] Ibid.

[62] Goldberg, 'Contesting the Status of Relief Workers'; Milton Friedman, *Capitalism and Freedom* (Chicago, IL: University of Chicago Press, 1962), 137–44, 174, 184; Milton Friedman and Rose Friedman, *Free to Choose: A Personal Statement* (San Diego, CA: Harvest, 1980), 120–21.

and the Second World War arrested a seminal suppression of society that, as the 1920s had witnessed, worked through labour relations, and the entanglement of the state in social programmes came to be viewed as an aberration that had to be shed.

The key points to note about Friedman and Myrdal are that neither actually defended a universal basic income, and the points on which they agreed were very thin and motivated by crisis conditions.

Firstly, whilst Myrdal was supportive of an income guarantee, he was unhappy with Friedman's focus on food in determining a minimum standard. Myrdal—according to Burns—was not happy to stop at income or indeed the cost of food, wanting to include wider needs, for example, housing and other services. Relatedly, and secondly, he questioned the assumption behind the alleged scientific standard, namely the centrality of individual choice. He clarified that he worked 'on the basis of another political ideology. I would prefer quite another kind of assumption'. Friedman had argued that 'in a democracy … [choices] of individuals are "the fixed standard"'.

Thirdly, it is clear that Friedman was unhappy about the scale of public programmes in the 1930s as representing any sort of policy direction—and he did not agree with universal income or welfare coverage. Friedman was generally a critic of the New Deal programmes, specifically in so far as they subsidized wages or prices and created 'monopoly'.[63] His indulgence of poverty relief schemes was thus backed up by market neutralism on broad political grounds.[64] In his 1962 NIT proposal, Friedman referred to individuals as 'consumer units', the same term incidentally that he had used in discussing the 'permanent income' in 1957 in *A Theory of the Consumption Function*.[65]

Whilst Myrdal supported unconditional cash payments in the 1930s—for example, pensions and child allowances—his main interest was in finding ways to support families, and reward child-rearing. Cash payments for working-age adults would contribute to family expenses, and in this sense the logic was means-testing. According to Olsson, Alva and Gunnar Myrdal's 1934 book *Crisis in the Population Question* was the inspiration for proposals from the 'non-socialist' parties for the introduction of cash

[63] Friedman, *Capitalism and Freedom*, 122–4, 189.

[64] In the 1962 book, Friedman makes frequent reference to the 1930s in defending the cost efficiency of the NIT scheme: Friedman, *Capitalism and Freedom*, 193–4).

[65] Ibid., 193.

benefits for families with children in 1935.[66] Whilst the Social Democrats supported unconditionality, it is not clear that they supported universality of the payments initially. Rather, this emerged in trade with other parties.[67] This is quite important because it shows both the need for and the difficulty of finding broad political support for universal and unconditional schemes. Nordic resourcist democracy and related proportional representation systems might have been the key. Notably, farmers' push for proportional representation in all Nordic countries has been argued to be the basis for the formation of the red-green alliance.[68]

The central point is that Myrdal's approach to cash payments was pragmatic and tied to wider egalitarian reformist goals, and in this he would diverge increasingly from Friedman's approach to economics and policy. The way their views were different relates to how they were contextually grounded. Their areas of agreement on unconditional cash payments were decidedly *thin* and *temporary.*

Basic Income and the Welfare State

Income Guarantees and 1960s Liberalism in America and Britain

In the contemporary period from the 1960s and 1970s until today, basic income advocacy has taken on its modern shape in two broad stages: one which engaged the fact of mature welfare states, followed by a new stage of debate under conditions of neo-liberal globalization.

The 1960s saw the re-emergence of a case for basic income on grounds of pre-distribution and shared inheritance, framed in response to fears of automation on both sides of the Atlantic. In the American context, Friedman's market-liberal case which couched the argument for NIT as supporting principles of economic and individual liberty—already mentioned—is better known, yet it is not the only one. Within US debates, there was also a progressive liberal case which—in tandem with the prominence of a social liberalism in the 1960s that spoke to a revival of American

[66] Sven Olsson, 'Sweden', in *Growth to Limits: The Western European Welfare States since World War II*, ed. Peter Flora (New York, NY: De Gruyter, 1986), 1–116, at 81.

[67] Ibid.

[68] Türegün, 'Revisiting Sweden's Response', 128, 135–6.

democracy—portrayed basic income as a response to structural crises in American capitalism.

This approach was well exemplified in a 1964 signed declaration involving US academics and representatives from sections of the labour movement and business calling for UBI as a measure against deep crisis in the US economy and for 'a new kind of society', co-signed by Myrdal.[69] The letter sounded out the terms of a radical modern American revolution, with invigoration of government action and redistributive measures at the forefront.

Among the recommendations were the following.

- 'Public works involving an expenditure, on a matching basis, of $2 billion or more a year in Federal funds.'
- 'A major revision of the tax structure aimed at redistributing income as well as apportioning the costs of the transition period equitably.'
- 'Government licensing to regulate the speed and direction of cybernation to ease hardship.'
- The letter called for provision for 'every individual and every family with an adequate income as a matter of right'.

Equally as important, however, as the demand for a form of basic income was the diagnosis of the situation which demanded it. According to the letter,

> The continuance of the income-through-jobs link as the only major mechanism for distributing effective demand—for granting the right to consume—now acts as the main brake on the almost unlimited capacity of a cybernated productive system.

This call for government action and notionally a UBI as a form of employment compensation indicates a very different approach to Friedman's, which was premised on a continued central role of the market in labour. On the other hand, both sets of positions suggest the centrality of the Anglo-American context as a backdrop for neutralist arguments as concerns, respectively, the labour market and automation.

[69] 'Guaranteed Income Asked For All', *New York Times*, March 23, 1964, https://www.nytimes.com/1964/03/23/archives/guaranteed-income-asked-for-all-employed-or-not.html. Myrdal was noted as reluctant to sign the letter because he only partially agreed with it.

Within Britain, in the same period, the implications of Keynes's theories in terms of the role of the state in the economy also became the subject of heated debate amongst progressive economists of a more radical liberal bent. In his 1964 book, *Efficiency, Equality and the Ownership of Property*, for instance, James Meade opposed the extent of the role of state intervention in economic governance envisaged by Keynes. Meade defined 'the welfare state' as 'the taxation of the incomes of the rich to subsidize directly or indirectly the incomes of the poor'.[70] He distinguished this 'welfare state' from the Trade Union and Minimum Wage principles. The point to make here is two-fold: firstly, how Meade's frame of reference was the Anglo-liberal economy and, secondly, how he thought about equality and inequality in terms of income distribution, and, in that context, how he saw market processes as rational and inevitable.[71]

Having considered the forces working on distribution (inherited income, earnings power, demography, and luck[72]) Meade thought he might solve the problem of avoiding disincentivizing the talented by suggesting that the state should tax wealth and inheritance rather than income, which in turn would encourage redistribution through bequests in 'small parcels' over an individual's life-time.[73]

However, there is a problem in the logic of the argument, for surely anyone motivated primarily to accumulate property would not fail to notice that escaping tax on immediate income was a merely borrowed freedom. Viewed this way, Meade's scheme can be seen as a massive incentive to immediate consumption *over* the incentives to save and accumulate!

The basic assumptions behind Meade's 1964 proposals for a just economy were essentially restrictive, both by separating the market (efficiency) and the problem of equality, and by his quite simple views on both; for example, efficiency would emerge from inherent talent in the labour market, and equality would come about through wealth-tax-based redistribution. Monetary policies dominated his policy arsenal.[74] Like American liberals in the 1960s, Meade also foresaw automation potentially eliminat-

[70] James Meade, *Efficiency, Equality and the Ownership of Property* (London: Allen and Unwin, 1964), 39.

[71] On the early formation of Meade's contribution, see Peter Sloman, *Transfer State: The Idea of a Guaranteed Income and the Politics of Redistribution in Modern Britain* (Oxford: Oxford University Press, 2019), 48–50.

[72] Meade, *Efficiency, Equality and the Ownership of Property*, 44–52.

[73] Ibid., 55.

[74] Ibid., 72–3.

ing employment, and so felt redistribution was urgent 'if automation reduces markedly the importance in productive processes of men relative to that of machines'.[75] It is noteworthy how the contemporary idea that basic income is a radical alternative to social insurance and social democracy—represented in Van Parijs's 'resolutely non-welfarist approach'—has a striking similarity to Meade's presentation of the case in terms of what came to be known as 'pre-distribution'.[76]

'Revolt from the Centre': 1970s Thinking on Basic Income in Northern Europe

The period when the UBI proposal first emerged as a serious policy proposal, in the 1970s, is perhaps the time when regional differences in approach are most evident, given the different turns in welfare state development that were consolidated during the 1960s and 1970s in Europe and America.

In 1975, taxation in Denmark was only 37 per cent of GDP, scarcely higher than Britain's 34 per cent. By 2000, Denmark's rate had increased to 47 per cent, whereas Britain's had fallen to just under 33 per cent, and Germany fell somewhere in between. These ratios have since remained roughly similar, whilst the US rate of around 25 per cent has stayed fairly stable. As the Nordic welfare state expanded, income support became more generous, less conditional, and more comprehensive.

Although it is not my main focus here, we can note how a tradition of market-liberal thought historically was more influential in continental European countries like Germany, Austria, and Belgium (as compared with Nordic states). This includes the greater influence of ordo-liberal, market-rational ideations of society along with the Austrian School's emphasis on subsidiarity, whereas by contrast Nordic liberalism was always more prone to (and some say gave birth to) Keynesian ideas.[77] The welfare state context of the mid-continental countries was also different to the Nordic. It was not supported in the same degree by nation-wide solidaristic unionism and wage bargaining as in Nordic states,[78] a movement which

[75] Ibid., 75.

[76] Philippe Van Parijs, *Real Freedom for All: What (If Anything) Can Justify Capitalism?* (Oxford: Oxford University Press, 1995), 255, and also 21, 27, 34–41.

[77] Ola H. Grytten, 'Why was the great depression not so great in the Nordic countries?', *The Journal of European Economic History* 37, no. 2–3 (September 2008): 369–403.

[78] Crouch, *Industrial Relations*; Eric S. Einhorn, E.S. and John Logue, *Modern Welfare States: Politics and Policies in Social Democratic Scandinavia* (Westport: Praeger Publishers,

never fully recovered in numbers after Fascism in countries like Germany and Austria, and arguably also which did not enjoy the combination of state subsidy and autonomous governance of the Danish systems. The spectre of labour market dualism, which was influential in both Offe's and (later) Van Parijs's[79] writings, was thought to be intractable.

Offe and Wiesenthal refer to the fragmented form of worker interest representation in Germany and its inherent internal contradictions and tendency to opportunism.[80] Offe elaborates the idea of the 'over-burdened state' in terms of responsibility for inherently unresolvable contradictions in the modern welfare state.[81] As Wilson notes about Offe's position, he was 'too influenced by the view that [full] employment cannot be restored to see [a state guarantee of employment] as a credible option'.[82] Rather it could be predicted that 'labour markets will continue to exhibit a declining absorption potential'.[83] Through these steps, Offe transitions towards the 'end-of-work' thesis, this being both reality and an opportunity, perhaps even a desirable social state: in the end, the idea of organizing society around work is the problem.

Whilst this view is not the same as the inheritance argument, or the inevitability of work-displacing innovation, the sociological 'end-of-work' thesis, which presents the end of work as an opportunity for societal freedom, also entails a bleak view of the active state and a positive view of dispersed agency.

Whilst this perspective has become increasingly influential in basic income advocacy, it was not (yet) the position of Danish writers on basic income during the late 1970s. The backdrop for Danish writing in the late 1970s was the long-term expansion of the welfare state, culminating in its recent crisis, which was manifested in rising global debt and domestic unemployment. Published in 1978, Niels Meyer et al.'s book *Revolt from the Centre* diagnosed the problem of Danish society as economic surplus,

2003); and Kathleen Thelen, *Varieties of Liberalization* (Cambridge: Cambridge University Press, 2014), 8–11.

[79] Philippe Van Parijs, 'Basic Income and the Two Dilemmas of the Welfare State', *Political Quarterly* 67, no. 1 (January 1996): 63–66.

[80] Claus Offe and Helmut Wiesenthal, 'Two Logics of Collective Action: Theoretical Notes on Social Class and Organizational Form', *Political Power and Social Theory* 1 (1980): 67–115, at 102–4.

[81] Claus Offe, *Contradictions of the Welfare State*, (Cambridge, MA: MIT Press, 1984).

[82] Shaun Wilson, *The Struggle over Work: The 'End of Work' and Employment Alternatives for Post-Industrial Societies* (London: Routledge, 2012 [2004]), 52.

[83] Ibid., 53.

in the midst of a social and psychological deficit, citing foreign debt and high unemployment.[84] The point of note is that Meyer et al.'s response is distinct from the 'end-of-work' thesis, in a way that can be traced to a contextually grounded view of the feasibility of social reform even in the context of what is arguably a devastating critique of capitalism itself.

Meyer et al. argue that the economic and psychological problems they have identified are linked, propelled by a constant mindless increase in expectations driven by the focus and reliance on relentless growth (to service global debt, and domestic wants). The hierarchical character of competition is signposted. 'The driving force in economic development is competition between the superpowers and "super-companies" to monopolize opportunities afforded by technical progress.'[85] All of society's institutions are affected. For example, the health profession spends most of the system's available resources, and even its research capacity, on 'sustaining sick life'.[86]

The most important difference between the mid-continental writers and the Nordic argument as presented in Meyer et al. is that where the former adopt an essential fatalistic position, Meyer et al. reject the concept of necessity in economic development and envisage an active state and society in organizing and regulating work. The context is a recent past—the 1960s—of material opulence, which they see (as noted) as a backdrop to the protest movements, followed by the 1970s, which they recognize as a period of rising unemployment—in particular youth unemployment, which must be *actively met*.[87] Rather than viewing technology as inherently labour saving, they regard the form of capitalism as implicated: the capital class uses technology to gain control of the production process by ridding it of the labour problem.[88] The motivation to raise economic efficiency, they argue, 'made fashionable' a form of organization of production which entailed breaking up the work process within corporations so as to 'incite' a spirit of greater competitiveness within and between units, pitting workers and teams against each other.[89] Large-scale companies and

[84] Niels I. Meyer, K. Helveg Petersen, and Villy Sørensen, *Oprør fra Midten* (Copenhagen: Gyldendals Bogklub, 1978), 9.

[85] Ibid., 9 (author's translation).

[86] Ibid., 28–29.

[87] Ibid., 71, 81–82, 106.

[88] Ibid., 34–40.

[89] Ibid., 129.

production units are destructive for society. The implication is to undermine social cohesion.[90]

In short, Meyer et al. also present a critique of capitalism in this period, but, as distinct from the 'end-of-work' theorists, do not see employment-alienating and -rationing forms of development as inevitable. They recognize the form of work in society as a product of social organization. Their concern is the way narrow interests get in the way of societal interest and prevent the 'incomes policy', which they believe to be needed to deal with unemployment, social malaise and economic dysfunctions arising from the laissez-faire economy. Meyer et al. have faith that the state and an active society can still work in symbiosis.

They think competition for high wage growth per se is part of the waste economy (producing and wasting at a rapid rate) and a result of intractable inequalities across occupational boundaries, including within the public sector, and so propose *a society of socially organized local employment and equal wages.*

This reveals how Meyer et al.'s work—although deeply reformist—was consciously embedded in the institutional realities and practical public policy debates of the 1970s in Denmark, characterized by high growth of public sector employment in the preceding decades. In fact, although quite conflictual, it is arguably the case that Nordic societies adjusted rather better to the 1970s crises because they did in the end work macroeconomic solutions through institutional changes at a tripartite level.

In summary, three characteristic features of the more realistically embedded proposition for basic income and a right to work in Denmark in the 1970s represented in Meyer et al. are:

1. The way basic income features as a *small* embedded part of a broader analysis of the state and Danish economy and society (basic income is not mentioned till p. 117, and again on p. 131);
2. The way the right to basic income is combined with a right to work, which is arguably more prominent in the analysis, alongside other rights such as to housing and being in a community;
3. How—given the last—basic income is justified in relation to a wider view of sociality in human nature which justifies a strong role for development planning, albeit in a democratic setting.[91]

[90] Ibid.

[91] Ibid., 77.

Construction of a Basic Income Movement Under Neo-Liberal Expansion

Libertarianism of the Left

The 1970s and 1980s—discussed in the last section—can be described as the beginning of the development of a global narrative about basic income. At the same time, it is also a bridge towards a new synthesis between more established Anglo-liberal arguments, emphasizing heritage, and an improved marriage between security and market efficiency, on the one hand, and the influence of postmodernism and libertarianism, on the other hand.

This new synthesis is well represented in Van Parijs's work of the 1990s, but also in other texts, for example, Standing's rejection of the twentieth century of 'labour' in favour of a more self-organized life of occupation.[92] A more definitive break with the post-war dual labour market and welfare state enables a more optimistic futuristic vision, as exemplified in (at the same time) affirmation of the end of the age of stable social positions and optimism about the future of a liberal project in which human ingenuity wins out.[93] This is the beginning of a global cosmopolitan utopia with basic income at the centre, in which the deepening of insecurity and uncertainty *becomes* the basis for a case for UBI as an alternative vision in itself.

At the same time, this is also a period in which arguments for basic income become more ubiquitous and varied in ways that are beyond my scope. What I want to focus on is the overall adaptation of diverse narratives to the gradual expansion and embedding of global neo-liberalization. The latter can be exemplified by the ways in which the forces of established order begin to assimilate the case for basic income within a case for more radical market-affirming visions, not inconsistent with Friedman's, but in different ways more deep and global. Two relevant examples of narrative adaptations of this kind are the way the distrust in state bureaucratic solutions in Georgism is extended within right-libertarian discourse, and the

[92] Guy Standing, *Beyond the New Paternalism: Basic Security as Equality* (London: Verso, 2002).

[93] Robert van der Veen and Philippe Van Parijs, 'A Capitalist Road to Global Justice', *Basic Income Studies* 1, no. 1 (June 2006).

adjustment in the positions of the global financial institutions vis-à-vis the role of income support in relation to organized work and the labour market.

Libertarianism of the Right

The idea of simplicity and limiting government corruption in Henry George has continued to inspire radical economic thought in America. However, as the rise of a more embedded form of Anglo-liberal capitalism in the post-war period became contested by neo-liberal reaction, this was also reflected in the manner of the resuscitation of Georgism, which has involved more right-wing positions, for example, turned against public expenditure as such.

As Hemmel and Fleischer note about the right-libertarian Murray's support for basic income in the US today, the consequence is that the defence of basic income must be grounded in a restriction on other government expenses.[94] This is because 'redistribution through a UBI may be stickier than redistribution through other mechanisms, in which case a UBI may be most-worst rather than least-worst from a libertarian point of view. Murray himself anticipates this critique and proposes that a UBI be coupled with a constitutional amendment limiting future increases in cash-based or in-kind redistribution.'[95]

As another libertarian defence of George's land tax argues:

> If we are going to deal with welfarism, we need to stop *freeholder's benefit*—which is what site location value increments as a result of public expenditure amount to—this is nothing but a disguised form of social scrounging.[96]

Hemmel and Fleischer go on to argue that the modern labour market can be construed as the modern equivalent of land, in which case a basic income is justified as the alternative to jobs.[97]

Thus, between George's single-tax proposal and the libertarian case for basic income today occurs a significant change. In George's thought and

[94] Daniel Hemel and Miranda P. Fleischer, 'Atlas Nods: The Libertarian Case for Basic Income', *Wisconsin Law Review* 2017, no. 6 (November 2017), 1269.

[95] Ibid., citing Charles Murray, *In Our Hands: A Plan to Replace the Welfare State* (revised edition, Washington: The AEI Press, 2016).

[96] David J. Webb, 'Why Libertarians Should Support a Land Value Tax', Ludwig von Mises Center for Property and Freedom, September 27, 2012, available online at https://misesuk.org/2012/09/27/why-libertarians-should-support-a-land-value-tax/.

[97] Hemmel and Fleischer, 'Atlas Nods', 1213.

scheme, equality would arise in the cooperation among producers in the market. By contrast, the libertarian argument set out in Hemmel and Fleischer is a compensatory one.

Basic Income in Neo-Liberal Embedding

The adjustment of the basic income narrative to the embedding of an advanced stage of global neo-liberalism linked with financialization and the corresponding weakening of states can also be looked at through the prism of changes in thinking within global development institutions. Starting from the mid-1990s, basic income advocacy was adapted to new developments in global capitalism. First, advocacy became linked to a case for a better design of anti-poverty policy, specifically cash grants schemes erected to allow the poor to subsist within the recently marketized economies of Latin America.[98]

Whereas in principle the debate around Conditional Cash Transfers (CCTs) was linked to national redesign, the interests of global development institutions were in defining a wider blueprint for development governance. Here one can speak about two narrative transitions in which basic income played an important role, the first represented in the growing interest in UBI among development funders, and the second a link made within that context to the global restructuring of the state. Illustrating the first transition is a re-adaptation of neo-classical thinking within development institutions. In the 1980s and 1990s, when CCTs were first introduced, the neo-classical doctrine of the leisure-work trade-off (LWTO), which essentially implies that individuals will only work under induced necessity and insecurity, was central within debates about designs, as exemplified in the work of Ravallion, an influential World Bank economist.[99]

[98] Guy Standing, 'How Cash Transfers Promote the Case for Basic Income', *Basic Income Studies* 3, no 1 (July 2008): 1–30; Eduardo Suplicy, *Renda da Cidadania*, (São Paulo: Cortez Editora, 2002); Rubén Lo Vuolo, *Citizens' Income and Welfare Regimes in Latin America: From Cash Transfers to Rights* (Basingstoke: Palgrave Macmillan, 2013); Louise Haagh, 'Basic Income, Occupational Freedom and Anti-Poverty Policy', *Basic Income Studies* 2, no. 1 (June 2007).

[99] Martin Ravallion, 'Targeted Transfers in Poor Countries', Social Protection Discussion Paper Series no. 0314 (Washington: The World Bank, 2003), 11. For a discussion, see Louise Haagh, 'Working-Life, Well-Being and Welfare Reform, World Development' 39 no. 3 (2011): 450–73.

In a major transformation in his and the World Bank's vision, away from the punitive design of CCTs by the 2010s, Ravallion now sees basic income playing a market-sustaining role, exemplified in reference to Van Parijs's 1992 case for a vision of 'Basic Income Capitalism', which combines free markets and the private ownership of the means of production with a basic income for all.[100] This is significant in the following way: the LWTO, as a guide for social policy, may be logical in conditions of real opportunities, but less so if opportunities are acknowledged to be scant.

The transition in Ravallion's thinking can then be said to reflect a recognition of the precarity of work as more than a transitional phenomenon linked to the neo-liberal phase of 'adjustment', including its inevitability. This suggests that the end of the project of full (by implication stable) employment—whether state- or market-promoted—is now accepted by neo-liberals and global agencies as inevitable.

A second transition concerns the relationship between this gradual acceptance among development institutions of employment precarity, and the construction of the relation of basic income and state governance away from a planned approach to development. Quoting Van Parijs's left libertarian case for Basic Income Capitalism, Ravallion argues that basic income 'has a strong appeal in allowing guaranteed protection from poverty, while retaining the economic advantages of an open and competitive market economy'.[101] Arguably, Ravallion's take here is fairly general, but it is noteworthy that basic income is invoked in an argument *against* mainstream critics of inequality—and, moreover, one that portrays labour informality as a positive way of contesting protections within the formal sector.[102] Ravallion's emphasis on absolute rather than relative poverty, and counterposing of UBI with 'right to work' policies, also signals an acceptance of employment uncertainty as a new organizing principle of work going forward.[103] A UBI would allow the pursuit of reductions in global inequality to occur through the competition mechanism by enabling economic wage migration through the *movement of people*. Free migration

[100] Philippe Van Parijs, 'Basic Income Capitalism', *Ethics* 102, no. 3 (April 1992): 465–84.

[101] Martin Ravallion, 'Inequality and Globalisation', *Society for the Study of Economic Inequality*, ECINEQ WP 2017-435 (2017): 20.

[102] Ibid.; Branko Milanovic, *Global Inequality: A New Approach for the Age of Globalization* (Cambridge, MA: Harvard University Press, 2016).

[103] Martin Ravallion, 'Guaranteed Employment or Guaranteed Income?', Center for Global Development Working Paper 482, July 26, 2018, available online at https://www.cgdev.org/publication/guaranteed-employment-or-guaranteed-income, 20–21.

becomes a standard of economic freedom and even security, as 'the ability to move freely across borders … [is] an important source of insurance' for people.[104] Interestingly, this reflects in some way George's idealization of the early settler economy, but goes well beyond George's positive view of migration which, after all, was more geographically confined and temporally finite, as George recognized.

As in Ravallion's work, the IMF's endorsement in the same year of UBI for developing countries such as India is framed in terms of India's lack of state capacity. Conversely, UBI is not recommended for rich countries that have the administrative apparatus to means and behaviour test, in which the state is able to push labour market compulsion.[105]

Significantly, the IMF acknowledges that there is little evidence that the 'trust' in the entrepreneurial logic implied in the theory of 'optimal taxation', a dogma behind neo-liberal restructuring, has been repaid in the form of higher productive investments. In short, the theory that undergirded the global institutions' push for structural adjustment was wrong.

Against this seemingly innocuous recognition of the *massive principled* failure of neo-liberalism, the IMF concludes that it is time to consider reintroducing higher tax rates on top earnings. More progressive taxation is then envisaged as part of a new redistributive pact, of which a UBI is also part, at least in some developing countries.

There is also an adjustment in the classic scholarly defence of UBI in the 2010s which meets with greater political opportunity and realism. In a 2016 blog, Van Parijs summarizes many of the arguments of Van Parijs and Vanderborght (2017), which represents an adaptation of the case for basic income that accommodates the idea of a gradual transition to UBI within the contemporary welfare state, albeit without abandoning classic positions on neutrality.[106] Representing a strategic accommodation to the new reality of greater public debate about UBI as a policy instrument, the level of the basic income appears not to be above subsistence (i.e. other assistance benefits will be needed).

[104] Ravallion, 'Inequality and Globalisation', 20.

[105] International Monetary Fund, *Fiscal Monitor*, October 2017; Ravallion, 'Guaranteed Employment or Guaranteed Income?'

[106] Van Parijs and Vanderborght, *Basic Income*, 99. A basic income entails a scheme of redistributive as distinct from cooperative justice (103) and is not intended 'to equalize outcomes or achievements. Rather, it aims to make less unequal, and distribute more fairly, real freedom, possibilities, and opportunities' (107).

On the other hand, the construction of a binary opposition between the case for basic income and social democracy, and invoking neutrality, suggests that Van Parijs' position is still ultimately a substantively radical (market system-shifting) position. This is also indicated in Van Parijs's mention of an embedding of UBI in the welfare state potentially involving a move to 'individualized' and 'simplified' earnings-related contributions. Whether endorsed by Van Parijs or not, the invocation of his work by the global development institutions in favour of a redistributive pact from rich to poor, premised on support for an expanded global competition economy, shows how becoming popular also involves risks of usurpation. In the globalization of basic income, arguably it is Friedman's technocratic vision that has won out. This is also indicated in Burns' placing of President Trump's emergency cash payments as (unconsciously) in the same tradition.[107]

In the same period, a realistic adaptation of the argument for BI has also occurred in Nordic (as in other) states, as BI discourse has moved towards immediately tax-neutral funding calculations. Whilst Meyer sees the BI proposal in a new context as allocating merely 'a cheap parking space for the poor', party political proposals (such as the first endorsement of BI by a political party in Denmark, The Alternative Party) are more hopeful; but they are also framed around a transition away from state subsidy of unemployment insurance, the system administered by unions since 1907.[108] In the context of fairly conservative, labour-incentive-orientated, experiments in lifting conditions on income assistance in Nordic states, Meyer's critique now sits at the margins.[109]

In all, what in the reports of global institutions and experiments in partial forms of basic income can seem subtle points of tinkering may be part of a wider transition in global financialized capitalism. Financialization extracts profits from risk and hence feeds on the destruction of hybrid property, embracing in the end states' regulatory and fiscal powers—the

[107] Jennifer Burns, 'The Efficiency of Cash Payments is a Conservative Principle', *The Hill*, April 20, 2020.

[108] Niels Meyer, 'The Danish UBI from 1978 and its Relation to Present UBIs', paper presented at Nordic Conference on Basic Income, Copenhagen, September 22–23, 2016; Louise Haagh, 'The Developmental Social Contract and Basic Income in Denmark', *Social Policy and Society* 18, no. 2 (April 2019): 301–17.

[109] Louise Haagh, 'The Philosophy and Economics of Basic Income Revisited', in *The Palgrave International Handbook of Basic Income*, ed. Malcolm Torry (London: Palgrave Macmillan, 2019): 253–99.

very capacities on which basic income depends. Many mainstream economists accept that austerity measures implemented after the 2008 crisis were opportunistic, an extension of the neo-liberal project to cut down the size of states.[110] On the other hand, it is evident that states—like Britain—with already looser regulation would have found it hard to impose the costs of the crisis on finance itself in any case. As Prunkert put it, even before the crisis 'participating governments [had] lost the privilege to encapsulate their market'.[111]

In this context, established defenders of BI may in the end cede control of the narrative as concomitantly states and society have lost sovereignty. Relatedly, the IMF's case that the rich ought to redistribute to the poor may not translate into a plausible case that they *will*. Ultimately, then, an underlying tension within basic income narratives within and outside of Europe today is the way the rise of a moral case for basic income is contradicted by weaker public capacity.

The two narrative transitions described represent a culmination of the movement from an ideal to a real form of illusion, in the context of the reaction to a relatively more embedded capitalism in the 1970s, and the shift to a dis-embedded global development model over the course of time.

Conclusion

A characteristic trait of basic income advocacy is how it has been linked historically with real or imagined crises in development, and the construction of basic income as a compensatory or restorative response. The case for basic income as a form of pre-distribution, which is often dated to Meade's writings of the 1960s, is not new in that context. As briefly discussed, Henry George's ideas about rendering a just distribution from taxing land continued the theme of corruption of riches which was never settled in the era of enclosure, whilst later Anglo-liberal writers, including Friedman, also aimed for a politically purified economy. By contrast,

[110] Enrico Bracci, Christopher Humphrey, Jodie Moll, and Lleana Steccolini, 'Public Sector Accounting, Accountability and Austerity: More than Balancing the Books?', *Accounting, Auditing & Accountability Journal* 28, no. 6 (August 2015): 878–908, at 880–1.

[111] Jenny Preunkert, 'Financialization of Government Debt? European Government Debt Management Approaches, 1980–2007', *Competition & Change* 21, no. 1 (February 2017): 27–44.

although different in many ways, the writings of Hohlenberg and Myrdal, one utopian and the other pragmatic, took embedded forms of social equality as a fact or a goal, in both cases with a basis in previous democratisations.

The postmodern and post-libertarian narratives of the 1970s and 1980s represented a new watershed moment in the developmental narration of basic income advocacy. Danish writing in this period was again counterfactual, in the sense that a wider range of shared institutions were comprised in the prospective achievement of both greater equality of income and social standing, reflecting the wider social embedding of Nordic economies at the time.

Over the course of the 1990s and 2000s, basic income narratives have become increasingly concerned with the finance of poverty and development, a process which started in the Global South and then moved Northward as the insecurity endemic in neo-liberal globalization has broken up systems of economic stability.

Through different capitalist epochs, the context of capitalism has shaped views about the meaning of freedom, justice and equality and the role and centrality of basic income in relation to them. The tendency to place basic income at the centre of systemic solutions has tended to be more prominent under conditions of dis-embedded development, and the recent period has proved to be no exception. The way the discussion about basic income has moved from freedom to finance in the period of global embedding of neo-liberalism has paralleled a growing visibility of the case for basic income and apparent unity of advocacy that are not necessarily stable.

Arguments for freedom that seemed more plausible under embedded liberalism have given way to concerns about how to finance basic income against the grain of defunded states, rendering a direct connection between finance for basic income and attainment of individual freedom in society even less plausible.

CHAPTER 12

Philippe Van Parijs on the History of Basic Income: An Interview

Daniel Zamora Vargas and Philippe Van Parijs

Daniel Zamora Vargas (DZV): The first question I want to ask you is how did you first come up with the idea of Basic Income (*allocation universelle*)? When did you formulate it?

Philippe Van Parijs (PVP): I have told this story so many times that I wonder if it corresponds to what actually happened. As far as I can remember, it happened in December 1982, when I was living in the centre of Louvain-la-Neuve with my family. There were two questions that were an important starting point. The first was how we could find an answer to the problem of unemployment without resorting to the solution that was being proposed by the Right and the Left: a growth of production and consumption that would outpace the increase in productivity. Given the ecological limits to growth, I wondered if there was not a way to find something else.

D. Zamora Vargas (✉)
Institut de sociologie, Université Libre de Bruxelles, Brussels, Belgium
e-mail: daniel.zamora.vargas@ulb.ac.be

P. Van Parijs
Université Catholique de Louvain, Louvain-la-Neuve, Belgium
e-mail: philippe.vanparijs@uclouvain.be

P. Sloman et al. (eds.), *Universal Basic Income in Historical Perspective*, https://doi.org/10.1007/978-3-030-75706-9_12

I was aware of a proposal made by the economist Philippe Defeyt and the progressive Jesuit Gérard Fourez, in a small paper that was never published, for allowing the unemployed to keep their benefits if they started out as self-employed. Of course, that proposal immediately raised the problem of creating unfair competition for those who were already self-employed. But pushing the idea further, I wondered what would happen if the principle was extended? What if the unemployed could also keep their benefits while becoming employees? And what if we extended it to those who were already employed or self-employed, etc.? That was the first path.

My second line of approach came out of more theoretical reflections on capitalism and the possible alternatives to state socialism. This goes back to the semester I spent in Bielefeld, in the spring of 1977, when I began working on a book whose initial title was *What (if anything) is intrinsically wrong with Capitalism?* It was during my post-doc stay there—after my doctorate in Louvain and before my doctorate at Oxford, both focussed on the epistemology of the social sciences—that I began reading, from the first to the last line, the original edition of the first volume of *Das Kapital.* I still have my notes which summarize, in German, section by section, the famous volume. Starting inevitably from Marx and going through Schumpeter and others to reflect critically on capitalism, I was trying to specify precisely what was problematic about capitalism. The idea was to propose an alternative to capitalism as we know it, in a context where we were now aware that socialist regimes had not been fantastically successful. Both from the point of view of efficiency and from the point of view of equality, not to mention human rights, socialism seemed to be a disaster. It was the quest for a utopia that could provide an alternative to both the neo-liberal and the paleo-socialist utopias that constituted the second path, very different from the first but converging with it, that led me to the idea of a basic income—and to see it as much more than an improvement to our welfare system.

DZV: In 1977–1978 you spent a year in California at Berkeley, where you deepened your knowledge of economics. What exactly did you study? Did you also discover the neoliberal authors there?

PVP: No. I remember, for example, taking part in a very technical seminar on *Disequilibrium Economics.* I also read Samuelson's textbook in its entirety. I had already read Gérard Debreu's *Theory of Value*,[1] which is the classical formulation of the so-called Arrow-Debreu theory of general equilibrium. In a way, I was getting immersed in the neoclassical

[1] Gérard Debreu, *The Theory of Value: An Axiomatic Analysis of Economic Equilibrium* (New Haven, CT: Yale University Press, 1959).

approach—but neoclassical does not mean neoliberal. It would be superficial, for example, to call the Keynesian Samuelson neoliberal.

As far as neoliberalism is concerned, I discovered it less in the United States than in Oxford, where I returned in 1978, after my stays in Bielefeld and Berkeley. It was on the advice of Jonathan Barnes—a professor of Greek philosophy and a convinced libertarian, my co-supervisor at Oxford for one term—that I discovered Robert Nozick. I found it an extremely stimulating challenge. For me, as for the Marxist G.A. Cohen, Nozick proposed a version of neoliberalism that was more radical and therefore more stimulating than those of Gary Becker or Milton Friedman, whose approach remained very instrumental. For Becker and Friedman, it was a matter of managing relations between individuals in such a way as to achieve the social optimum, whereas in Nozick there was something much deeper.

I've always had—starting in my adolescent rebellions—this libertarian impulse, which I didn't think was very present on the left. For Nozick, what matters is allowing each and everyone to live as he or she wishes, including by realizing, with willing others, collective utopias. Of course, the naivety of such an approach is that it focusses on a purely formal freedom. Part of my theoretical project has been to make room for the appeal of the libertarian approach but at the same time to say 'Look, if you take freedom seriously, it has to be real freedom and freedom for all'. This is obviously a far cry from an approach that seeks to manage interactions between individuals through incentives (or nudging) to achieve an economic optimum.

Nevertheless, whether in its extreme form *à la* Nozick or in its softer, more instrumental forms, *à la* Friedman, there were perhaps things to be taken from neoliberalism. In 1983, at the suggestion of Albert Carton of the CSC (*Confédération des syndicats chrétiens*—the Belgian Christian Trade Union), a team was formed to prepare an issue of *La Revue Nouvelle* (published in March 1984) on 'Neoliberalisms' in the plural.[2] The idea was that the label 'neoliberalism' covered extremely different things, ranging from caricatures to things to be taken really seriously.

DZV: So at the time of your stay in Oxford, you hadn't yet discovered Friedman's negative tax or Stigler's 1946 paper on 'The Economics of Minimum Wage Legislation'?

[2] 'Néo-libéralismes', *La Revue Nouvelle*, no. 3 (March 1984).

PVP: No. I had read Milton Friedman at that time, but it was the monetarist facet of his work, especially his discussion of the Phillips curve: by questioning the sustainability of the trade-off between unemployment and inflation rates, he dealt a serious blow at least to the naive versions of the Keynesian approach to unemployment. Much more broadly, during my time at Oxford in 1978–1979, I wrote two long essays on inflation theories and on crisis theories under the guidance of Andrew Glyn, a Marxist-oriented economist, a truly fantastic man and extremely generous with his time. This gave me a good understanding of the theories of stagflation, underconsumption crises, profit-squeeze, etc., and it gave me a lot of insight into the theories of inflation and crisis theories. My goal was to do political philosophy, but I felt that I had to have a good education in the epistemology of the social sciences—the domain of my first two books (*Evolutionary Explanation in the Social Sciences* and *Le modèle économique et ses rivaux*[3]), one of which is my Oxford thesis—and in political economy.

DZV: And during your stay in both Oxford and Manchester you never read anything about Juliet Rhys-Williams' proposal?[4] The UK is one of the rare countries where this debate began as early as the interwar period.

PVP: I returned from Oxford to Belgium in January 1980. It was at the end of 1982 that the idea of a basic income came to me, and it was during 1983—notably during a semester spent in the Economics Department of the University of Manchester—that I gradually discovered that I was not the first to have had this idea. The first text I discovered, thanks to a friend who had heard me present the idea, was a 1979 working paper from Aston University in Birmingham by someone called Stephen Cook.[5] I immediately tried to make contact, but was told that he had passed away, and his text did not contain the slightest reference to Rhys-Williams or anyone else. I don't know how I discovered Rhys-Williams' book, but it must have been in 1983 or 1984.

DZV: And what about Rawls? He would go on to play an important role…

[3] Philippe Van Parijs, *Evolutionary Explanation in the Social Sciences. An Emerging Paradigm* (Totowa, NJ: Rowman & Littlefield Publishers, 1981); Philippe Van Parijs, *Le modèle économique et ses rivaux. Introduction à la pratique de l'épistémologie des sciences sociales* (Paris: Droz, 1990).

[4] Juliet Rhys Williams, *Something to Look Forward To* (London: MacDonald and Co., 1943).

[5] Stephen L. Cook, *Can a Social Wage Solve Unemployment?* (Working Paper no. 165. Birmingham: University of Aston Management Centre, 1979).

PVP: I had bought Rawls's book at the beginning of my first stay in Oxford, in autumn 1974: the paperback edition had just come out. But, as mentioned, I devoted the following years to philosophy of science and economics, and it was only after my return to Belgium in 1980 that I read *A Theory of Justice*. Although I found Nozick's provocative prose and [John] Roemer's mathematicized Marxism intellectually more exciting, I soon realized that it was in Rawls that I (and many others with me) could find the deepest, most systematic, and ultimately most plausible reflection on how best to reconcile the importance we give to equality, freedom, and efficiency in an explicit conception of social justice. One of my books—*Sauver la solidarité*[6]—was dedicated to him as 'an indispensable ally for elaborating the Left of our time'.

But before returning to Belgium, shortly after my return from Berkeley to Oxford in 1978, I had another very important encounter—with G.A. Cohen, then at University College London. It came during a seminar entitled 'Historical Materialism' which he taught jointly with Charles Taylor, then professor at Oxford. And I ended up presenting at the seminar, in the last session, a paper that would later be published in the *New Left Review* under the title 'From Contradiction to Catastrophe'.[7]

It was in this context that I discovered analytical Marxism, as masterfully illustrated by Cohen's first book, *Karl Marx's Theory of History: A Defence*.[8] I found it a very stimulating way of trying to make the critique of capitalism more rigorous. Slightly later, I discovered the work of John Roemer, which offered a rigorous and very stimulating reformulation of the core of Marxist economic analysis. Together with Cohen, Roemer, Jon Elster, Erik Olin Wright and Robert van der Veen, I participated in the first meeting of what was to become the 'September Group' in London in September 1981—a group that has since expanded and still meets annually four decades later.

DZV: So that's the theoretical corpus that brings you to Basic Income?

PVP: It was all of this that fed the ambitious project that evolved from *What (if anything) is intrinsically wrong with Capitalism?* to *Real Freedom*

[6] Philippe Van Parijs, *Sauver la Solidarité* (Paris: Cerf, 1995)

[7] Philippe Van Parijs, 'From Contradiction to Catastrophe', *New Left Review*, no. 115 (1979): 87–97.

[8] G. A. Cohen, *Karl Marx's Theory of History: A Defence* (Princeton, NJ: Princeton University Press, 1978).

for All: What (if anything) can justify capitalism?[9] I was trying to formulate a left-wing alternative to state socialism, either in its Soviet form (which proved counterproductive) or in its watered-down social-democratic form (which was not particularly exciting). I remember in particular the day Guy Spitaels, then Belgium's Deputy Prime Minister, came to Louvain-la-Neuve, in the early 1980s. I asked him: 'Your socialist movement in Belgium has abandoned the revolutionary path in favour of reform. So be it. But haven't you also abandoned socialism?' He replied roughly: 'What you have to do first is to make the walls of the house hold together. Afterwards we can discuss something else.' In the face of such resignation, I understood how for some people there could be something exciting and galvanizing in the idea of a neoliberal utopia. It offered an alternative that was not simply the defence of what already existed, or a set of sticking-plasters.

It was in the context of this quest that, in December 1982, I came up with a very simple idea that was going to occupy an unexpectedly central place in my subsequent thinking and action. It was then that I scribbled for the first time (on an electoral leaflet from the Socialist Party for the communal elections in Ottignies) the expression 'allocation universelle', and sketched a first draft of the idea in an internal note for my colleagues in the 'Economie et Société' Unit of the economics department of the University of Louvain (see Fig. 12.1). To my astonishment today, I used the expression 'negative tax' in it, but to designate something other than what had been proposed under that name by Friedman and others for over two decades. It was only months later, in the Economics Department of Manchester University, thanks to Richard Blundell—who lived on the same street as me during the semester I spent there and often gave me a lift to the university—that I made the connection with the vast theoretical and empirical literature on the negative income tax. He once said to me, 'Basically what you're proposing is the negative income tax', and he drew me the graph—I can still see it on the board in his office. Only then did I make the connection between the two, and then I read Friedman's proposal in *Capitalism and Freedom* (1962).

DZV: But when you wrote the first proposal, were you in Louvain?

PVP: Yes. I had become a tenured researcher at the Belgian National Fund for Scientific Research (FNRS), one of its first outside the fields of

[9] Philippe Van Parijs, *Real Freedom for All: What (if anything) can justify capitalism?* (Oxford: Oxford University Press, 1995).

L'ALLOCATION UNIVERSELLE

Aux membres d'ECOS.

La note qui suit n'a aucune ambition académique. Elle n'en entretient pas moins de multiples rapports avec bon nombre de discussions au sein d'ECOS, par exemple sur la question des inégalités ou de la réduction du temps de travail ou sur la question des issues capitaliste et socialiste à la crise.

Dans cette note, en effet, il s'agit de prospective politique et plus précisément de la question générale suivante. Pris de scepticisme à l'égard de la possibilité et/ou de l'efficacité du Grand Soir (c'est-à-dire de la collectivisation de l'ensemble des moyens de production comme remède aux maux fondamentaux dont souffre notre société), sommes-nous pour autant contraints de reconnaître que le meilleur des mondes possibles (ou du moins atteignables, même à long terme, à partir du nôtre) ressemble à s'y tromper à la société dans laquelle nous vivons ? Ou bien existe-t-il des mesures dont il n'est pas trop fou de croire à la fois qu'elles peuvent être acceptées par une majorité de la population et qu'elles peuvent (sans effets secondaires catastrophiques) modifier en profondeur le mode d'organisation économique de notre société de manière à extirper de celle-ci ce qui nous y semble le plus intolérable ? Et s'il en existe, quelles sont-elles ?

La note suggère une réponse possible à cette question. Elle en poursuit brièvement un certain nombre d'implications, tant pour mettre en relief la radicalité de l'impact bénéfique que l'on pourrait espérer de ce type de mesure, que pour explorer quelques-uns des problèmes que son application soulèverait. Ce que j'attends de vous, c'est que vous me "lucidifiez" sur cet impact et ces problèmes (entre autres en me renvoyant à la littérature pertinente sur tel ou tel point, qui doit être énorme mais que je ne connais pas du tout). D'avance merci (même si de la suggestion la discussion ne laisse rien subsister.)

p.v.p.
décembre 1982

Fig. 12.1 Covering note for paper on 'L'Allocation Universelle' by Philippe Van Parijs, December 1982. (Source: Philippe Van Parijs)

nuclear physics and medicine. It was a great status. From then on I never applied for a job again. Having become a FNRS doctoral fellow as soon as I finished my studies, I have never had a single day of unemployment in my entire life—an incredible privilege. When I returned from Oxford after almost six years abroad, the University had moved from Leuven to Louvain-la-Neuve and I joined a research centre called 'Economie et Société'. It included Jacques Gouverneur (who was doing Marxist economics), Jean-Philippe Peemans (who was doing development economics also from a Marxist perspective), Michel De Vroey (who specialized in the history of economic thought), Philippe Devillé (a macroeconomist), Isabelle Cassiers (who would later become our expert on alternatives to GDP), and finally Robert Leroy, the head of the unit, who covered labour economics and who would play a short-lived but crucial role in launching the first public debate on basic income. It was there, in a small internal seminar in January 1983, just before I left for Manchester, that my proposal was first discussed to see if it held up. And in this first version, it certainly did not. I assumed, for example, that a Basic Income costing on average more than 80 per cent of per capita GDP could be financed by an inheritance tax. After my return from Manchester in autumn 1983, everything followed on fairly quickly.

In the same spirit as the 'Neoliberalisms' group that I had coordinated with Albert Carton and which was finishing its work, I formed, with Philippe Defeyt and Paul-Marie Boulanger, a small group that undertook to discuss what was not yet called 'basic income' but 'allocation universelle' in preparation for a special issue of *La Revue Nouvelle*.[10] In the spring of 1984, perhaps on the occasion of one of the meetings of this group, Robert Leroy told me that the King Baudouin Foundation was organizing a competition for scenarios of the future of work. Leroy himself was a man of futuristic scenarios. He had published his own in a book entitled *Un scénario égalitaire*,[11] in which he proposed that wages should be set according to the irksomeness of the work. There were, however, in his proposal both normative and implementation problems that seemed insoluble to me. But it was nevertheless somewhat inspired by this that I then wrote (under the pseudonym 'Collectif Charles Fourier') a short text on basic income that was more polished than my earlier note. It was meant to be a thought-provoking text, without constituting a real proposal. It was

[10] 'L'allocation universelle', *La Revue Nouvelle*, no. 4 (1985).

[11] Robert Leroy, *Un scénario égalitaire*, (Louvain-La-Neuve: Ciaco, 1983).

this text, published in October 1984, which received the Foundation's 'Agora travail' prize, but which still today, when read without taking this context into account, causes misunderstandings. In the spirit of the competition, I wanted to encourage people to think 'out of the box'. The key phrase, which should have made the nature of the literary genre clear, was: 'Do it all. And then observe what happens. Ask yourself, in particular, what happens to work…'

The prize gave us the opportunity to bring together the few people in Europe interested in the idea whom I had gradually begun to spot, most of whom didn't know each other. For example, there were advocates of basic income that I had spotted in Denmark who were completely unaware that there had been proposals in the Netherlands, and in the Netherlands they had never heard of the French economist Yoland Bresson who founded the 'Association pour l'instauration du revenu d'existence' in 1985. So we brought them together in Louvain-la-Neuve in September 1986.[12] It was there that BIEN (Basic Income European Network) was founded, which later became the Basic Income Earth Network in Barcelona in 2004.

DZV: And how did BIEN go from this small group to the world organization that it is now? Did it happen very quickly?

PVP: No. For many years, the network only existed through the three newsletters per year that I sent by post from Louvain-la-Neuve to about a hundred contributors, and through the biennial 'congresses', which were first very modest, then became more and more extensive. As for many small international organizations, it was really the internet that was a gift from heaven!

DZV: Let's go back in time a bit. You mentioned the great importance of your economic readings and the great debates on unemployment and inflation. What about André Gorz?

PVP: Absolutely, you're right to talk about him. For me, the one of his books that really made a difference was *Farewell to the Working Class*, published in 1980. Of all the books I've read in my life, it's perhaps the one that had the most impact on me. The book reinforced in me the idea that there was a need to formulate a future for the Left that would stand out

[12] See in particular Anne G. Miller, ed., *Basic Income: Proceedings of the First International Conference on Basic Income*, Louvain-la-Neuve, Belgium, 4–6 September 1986 (Antwerp: Basic Income European Network, 1986).

strongly from both the hard and soft versions of socialism. I read it shortly after my return to Belgium from Oxford in 1980.

DZV: Gorz also had this idea that Keynesianism had served its purpose, that full employment was over ...

PVP: In other words, the Keynesian strategy in the long term seemed to me to be doomed. This is linked to Friedman's argument on the short- and long-term Phillips Curve: Keynesian measures were useful in the short term to revive demand, but in the long term, there was no real trade-off between inflation and unemployment. So something else was needed, something microeconomic rather than macroeconomic.

One strategy one might think of is the massive expansion of wage subsidies. Its foundation was later developed most systematically by Edmund Phelps in his *Rewarding Work* and it was partly implemented in the form of the Earned Income Tax Credit in the US and similar schemes elsewhere. But there is an alternative, more freedom-friendly and resisting the sacralization of paid work: the swelling of the 'autonomous sphere', as advocated by André Gorz.

DZV: That's really the aspect that struck you in the book?

PVP: Actually it's difficult, in retrospect, to remember what I specifically retained from it. I read a lot of other things from Gorz and we ended up meeting. What I remember is the feeling I had when I read it: the feeling that it expressed clearly, much better than I could have done, a whole series of problems that I perceived in a confused way. I immediately felt that he was putting his finger on something that I hadn't found at all in orthodox Marxist writings. It was much more enlightening to me than what I had found by spending a lot of time reading Ernest Mandel, for example, or Paul Mattick and Paul Sweezy. There was something refreshing about Gorz, something that was really very new to this Marxism, and it certainly made me more receptive to the idea of a basic income—as an instrument for the systematic promotion of the autonomous sphere—when it came to me shortly after reading *Farewell to the Working Class*. That didn't mean that at that time he would have supported that particular proposal, but it was within this more general framework that a leftist alternative was taking shape. Perhaps the books that mark us do in fact function as revelators of what we were already thinking in some way.

DZV: When did you start writing to him?

PVP: I think it was in 1984. At that time I was asked to comment on an article by Gorz for the Belgian magazine *Virages*.[13] And that's when I received an outraged response from him—he was probably not used to a more 'American' style of debate! I immediately apologized, and that's how we started our long correspondence.

DZV: I also wanted to ask you about your relationship with the return of the theme of poverty at that time. During the 1970s and 1980s, it was also the time when the idea emerged that we should help the poor as poor people and no longer as poorly housed, unemployed, or pensioners. What emerged was a more global vision of poverty and perhaps also a more monetary one. Is this something you had been following?

PVP: A little. It was undoubtedly, among other things, the time of the rise of ATD Fourth World ('Aide à Toute Détresse'), founded by Father Joseph Wresinski.[14] But I must say that in Belgium the Catholic Left was not so receptive to basic income. There are other countries, especially Ireland and Austria, where it was and still is to a large extent the Catholic Left that has been at the forefront of the defence of basic income. Their position is of course very far from the position of the Church of the sixteenth century, which was opposed to civil institutions assisting the poor. On the contrary, it is necessary that public authorities should deal with poverty, but they must do so in a way that respects the dignity of people. It is this idea of dignity that is central to the specifically Christian contribution to the public debate on basic income in several countries. In Belgium, the close link between the Catholic movement—in particular the MOC (Mouvement Ouvrier Chrétien—Christian Workers' Movement)—with the largest trade union in the country (the CSC), and thus also with the management of social security, may explain a more lasting scepticism.

DZV: If we leave the Belgian context, during the 1980s, it was mainly in the Netherlands and in England that there seems to have been a real public debate.

PVP: It was only in the Netherlands that there was a real beginning of public debate, mainly led by the food workers' union FNV Voedingsbond and the small left-wing Christian party PPR (Politieke Partij Radikalen). It

[13] André Gorz, 'Au delà de la société de travail', *Virages* 2 (1984): 8–12.

[14] See, for instance, Frédéric Viguier, 'Le rôle des associations de lutte contre la pauvreté dans la protection sociale française depuis 1945: le cas d'ATD Quart Monde', *Revue d'Histoire de la Protection Sociale* 6 (2013): 12–34.

happened in particular thanks to the young head of the party's research department, Bram van Ojik, who was to become much later, from 2012 to 2015, leader of Groenlinks (which in the meantime had absorbed the PPR). In Belgium there was the publication of the April 1985 issue of *La Revue Nouvelle* and the reactions it aroused, but that's almost all.

DZV: But in Europe, before the 1980s, there wasn't much.

PVP: There was a book published in Denmark in 1977, translated into English in 1978 under the title *Revolt from the Centre*,[15] which was co-authored by a philosopher, a politician and a physicist. It had been widely debated in Denmark, but hardly beyond. The only place where there was a broad debate, which lasted until 1985, was the Netherlands. I was a guest lecturer at the University of Amsterdam in the first semester of 1985 and I had a wonderful end to my stay. While I was there, there was a 'Werkgroep Basisinkomen PvdA' (the Dutch socialist party's working group on basic income) which published four issues of an ad hoc magazine advocating the adoption of the idea by the party, and a small group of precarious people called *Nederlandse Bond Tegen het Arbeidsethos* (Dutch Council Against the Work Ethic) was agitating against the 'work ethic'. In a Calvinist country, however, this was not going to be a great success!

There was also the report of the highly respected 'Wetenschappelijke Raad voor het Regeringsbeleid' (WRR—the Dutch Scientific Council for Government Policy) on the future of social security, which pleaded for the introduction of a 'gedeeltelijk basisinkomen' (partial basic income)—an income which would be truly universal but insufficient to replace social assistance for a person living alone. The Dutch government is required to respond to every WRR report. In his response, published a few months later, Christian Democrat Prime Minister Ruud Lubbers vigorously rejected the idea in the name of the principle at the heart of Dutch social security: the link between social protection and labour market participation. The WRR report came out in the last month I spent in Amsterdam. I still remember the headline in the weekly *De Groene Amsterdammer*: 'The triumphant return of Basic Income'. That was June 1985. The chairman of the commission that had written the WRR report, Nic Douben, was invited to the founding congress of BIEN in 1986, together with

[15] Niels I. Meyer, Kristen Helveg Petersen, and Villy Sørensen, *Revolt from the Centre* (London: Boyars, 1981). The book was originally published in Danish under the title 'Oprør fra Midten'.

Greetje Lubbi, the president of the union that was campaigning for the idea.

DZV: Do you think there is a reason why it appeared earlier in some countries than others? Was it related to internal political developments, or specific intellectual developments in these countries?

PVP: Yannick Vanderborght wrote his PhD thesis on this subject. He made a comparison between different countries, to see if there is a way to determine the factors that make it more likely that ideas similar to basic income will be debated and become politically feasible. For me it's still very difficult to say. There are certainly quite a few contingent elements, but the context can be more or less favourable. One of the factors that I think is important for the Netherlands is that there is a system that combines cash benefits, tax credits and other tax benefits in such a way that the state can be said to pay, explicitly or implicitly, a kind of income to almost the entire population. Since nearly everyone is already, in one way or another, a recipient of transfers, the barriers to financing and administrative possibilities are much lower than in other countries.

DZV: In particular, what do you think of the role that ATD Fourth World played in this debate? They helped to precipitate this discussion on poverty and the need to establish a 'vital minimum' independently of the classic social security system. It was in this context that, at the end of the 1970s, they favored the idea of a negative income tax and opened the debate leading to the introduction of the French RMI (Revenu Minimum d'Insertion).

PVP: ATD's interventions in France certainly contributed to the introduction of the RMI, on the initiative of Prime Minister Michel Rocard, in 1988. For the French Left, it should be kept in mind that the introduction of the RMI marked a kind of admission of defeat. Jaurès had hoped that one day social insurance would replace social assistance, whose survival in a tweaked form was at best tolerated alongside 'real' social security. Modernizing and amplifying social assistance through the RMI amounted to recognizing the vanity of this hope while at the same time constituting a major advance, which forced ATD, among others, to reflect on how to move forward: towards more selectivity or not.

I don't know if any ATD officials advocated a negative tax. In any case, it cannot be said that ATD was particularly favorable to the idea of a universal basic income: the idea of distributing the same income to the rich as to the poor undoubtedly seemed to be in tension with their focus on the poorest. More recently, however, at a hearing organized in Geneva in June

2017 by Philip Alston, the United Nations Special Rapporteur on Extreme Poverty, the representative of ATD Fourth World came out very strongly in favour of basic income.

DZV: It's interesting that you mention Alston, who now defends basic income as a strategy for fighting poverty. At what point did the allowance become a path considered in development policies?

PVP: Conditional Cash Transfers (CCT) are now part of the common discourse of international organizations: direct cash transfers to poor households with conditions such as health checks and schooling for children. But it is difficult to implement means tests in a largely informal economy without giving way to clientelism and corruption. For this reason, development economists such as Pranab Bardhan, Esther Duflo, and Abhijit Banerjee, among others, have taken up the defence of basic income with or without health and schooling requirements.

DZV: What do you think stimulated this growing interest, and the experiments around the world? After all, in developing countries, the question of full employment has never been thought about in the same way: the informality of work has always been dominant.

PVP: Basic income is relevant wherever economic security for all is a goal worth pursuing, not only in countries where attempts have been made to achieve this goal through access to paid employment for all. There is therefore no reason to consider it less relevant for less developed countries. The informal nature of the economy makes it much easier to administer fairly, though admittedly more difficult to finance fairly than a more targeted system.

Experiments to date have been carried out with external funding, for example with UNICEF in Andhra Pradesh and the NGO Give Directly in Kenya. However, in countries such as India, it is not out of the question to finance a basic income in a sustainable manner with internal resources, provided some state subsidies are phased out. The level would certainly be modest compared to what is possible in more developed countries, but it would be sufficient to reduce extreme poverty very significantly without having the perverse effect of deepening the poverty trap.

At the first BIEN congress outside Europe, in Cape Town in 2006, a South African colleague told me: 'Philippe, you are as arrogant as Karl Marx. He thought that socialism could only happen in industrialized countries, just as you think that basic income could only be established in developed countries. But just as it was in agrarian Russia that the socialist revolution took place, it is in a country like South Africa that the basic income will be introduced for the first time.' The future will tell if he was right.

Index[1]

[1] Note: Page numbers followed by 'n' refer to notes.

P. Sloman et al. (eds.), *Universal Basic Income in Historical Perspective*, https://doi.org/10.1007/978-3-030-75706-9

The manufacturer's authorised representative in the EU is Springer
Nature Customer Service Centre GmbH, Europaplatz 3, 69115 Heidelberg,
Germany. If you have any concerns regarding our products, please
contact ProductSafety@springernature.com

Printed and bound by CPI Group (UK) Ltd, Croydon, CR0 4YY
30/09/2026
02225698-0018